PENGUIN

ARKANA

ARKANA

IN THE ZONE

Transcendent Experience in Sports

Michael Murphy founded the Esalen Institute (with Richard Price) in 1962 and helped initiate Esalen's Russian American Exchange Program. He is also the author of *Golf in the Kingdom, Jacob Atabet, An End to Ordinary History, The Future of the Body,* and *The Life We Are Given* (with George Leonard). He lives in San Rafael, California.

Rhea A. White worked for four years at the Duke University Parapsychology Laboratory and is editor of the *Journal of the American Society for Psychical Research.* She has also been employed as a reference librarian since 1965. She is founder of the Exceptional Human Experience Network and edits and publishes the journal *Exceptional Human Experience.* Her most recent book is *Parapsychology: New Sources of Information.* She lives in Dix Hills, New York.

PENGUIN

ARKANA

MICHAEL MURPHY AND RHEA A. WHITE

P E N G U I N / A R K A N A

IN THE ZONE

TRANSCENDENT EXPERIENCE IN SPORTS

PENGUIN BOOKS
Published by the Penguin Group
Penguin Books USA Inc., 375 Hudson Street, New York, New York 10014, U.S.A.
Penguin Books Ltd, 27 Wrights Lane, London W8 5TZ, England
Penguin Books Australia Ltd, Ringwood, Victoria, Australia
Penguin Books Canada Ltd, 10 Alcorn Avenue, Toronto, Ontario, Canada M4V 3B2
Penguin Books (N.Z.) Ltd, 182–190 Wairau Road, Auckland 10, New Zealand

Penguin Books Ltd, Registered Offices:
Harmondsworth, Middlesex, England

The Psychic Side of Sports first published in the United States of America
by Addison-Wesley Publishing Company 1978
This revised edition with the title *In the Zone* published
in Penguin Books 1995

1 3 5 7 9 10 8 6 4 2

LIBRARY OF CONGRESS CATALOGING IN PUBLICATION DATA
Murphy, Michael, 1930 Sept. 3–
In the zone : transcendent experience in sports / Michael
Murphy and Rhea A. White.
p. cm.
Rev. ed. of: The psychic side of sports. c1978.
Includes bibliographical references and index.
ISBN 0 14 01.9492 4
1. Sports—Psychological aspects. 2. Mind and body. I. White,
Rhea A. II. Murphy, Michael, 1930 Sept. 3– Psychic side of sports.
III. Title.
GV706.4.M87   1995
796'.01—dc20   94-44134

Printed in the United States of America
Set in Sabon
Designed by Katy Riegel

For my brother, Dennis Murphy
M.M.

To the Energy that moves us all
R.A.W.

CONTENTS

Introduction   ix

1. THE SPIRITUAL UNDERGROUND IN SPORTS   1

2. MYSTICAL SENSATIONS   7
    Acute Well-Being   9
    Peace, Calm, Stillness   11
    Detachment   14
    Freedom   16
    Floating, Flying, Weightlessness   17
    Ecstasy   18
    Power, Control   20
    Being in the Present   22
    Instinctive Action and Surrender   24
    Mystery and Awe   27
    Feelings of Immortality   30
    Unity   31

3. ALTERED PERCEPTIONS   34

   Altered Perception of Size and Field   37
   Alterations in Time Perception   40
   Extrasensory Perception   48
   Out-of-Body Experiences   63
   Awareness of the "Other"   66

4. EXTRAORDINARY FEATS   74

   Exceptional Energy   75
   Energy Reaching Out: Psychokinesis   87
   The Invisible Barrier   98
   Mind Over Matter   99

5. SPORT AND MYSTICISM   103

   The Spiritually Evocative Elements of Sport   104
   The Perennial Philosophy   114
   Extraordinary Powers   136

6. MIND/BODY TRAINING   149

   Elements of a Mind/Body Training Program   150

7. EVOLUTIONARY POSSIBILITIES   167

Bibliography   181
Acknowledgments   285
Index   289

INTRODUCTION

Have you ever felt a special exaltation while playing a game or pursuing a physical adventure? Has sport ever lifted you beyond yourself in a way best described with religious language? If so, you are not alone. Since 1978, when an earlier version of this book was published, many studies of athletic "peak-experience" and "flow state" have been published in sport and psychology journals; talk about "the zone" has increased; and movies such as *Field of Dreams* have attracted worldwide audiences.

But in spite of this growing recognition, few people appreciate the great variety of experiences characterized by terms such as "play in the zone" or "peak performance." The stories in this book show that sport produces a range of metanormal* events that approaches the richness of experience evoked by religious practice. In the pages that follow, we identify more than twenty types of extraordinary athletic feats, exalted states of consciousness, and altered perceptions; and we believe that sport psychologists will eventually identify many more.

This study is informed by our lifelong interest in both sport and

---

* We use the word "metanormal," as well as the word "extraordinary," as technical terms to represent human functioning that in some respect radically surpasses that which is typical of most people living today.

human transformation. Michael Murphy helped organize Esalen Institute's archives on extraordinary functioning, which include some ten thousand studies of remarkable mind/body changes. He used the Esalen archives, as well as other sources, to write *The Future of the Body*, a comprehensive collection of evidence that humankind harbors immense untapped potentials. Working on that project, he came to believe that by gathering data from many fields—including medical science, religious studies, and sport—we can identify extraordinary versions of most, if not all, our basic attributes, among them sensorimotor, kinesthetic, communication, and cognitive abilities; sensations of pain and pleasure; vitality; volition; sense of self; love; and various bodily structures. Every human capacity, it seems, has a variety of metanormal expressions.

Rhea White has assembled possibly the largest collection of case reports dealing with metanormal functioning, some of which she has published in her journal *Exceptional Human Experience*. In developing her archive, she—like Murphy—was inspired by William James; by Frederic Myers, who pioneered the study of extraordinary capacities and was a founder of psychical research; and by Abraham Maslow, who explored peak-experience and self-transcendence. During the last one hundred years, these and other pioneering researchers have created a field of inquiry we like to think of as a kind of "natural history," in this case a natural history of extraordinary functioning. Rather than studying plant or animal specimens, this discipline identifies patterns of human development by comparing metanormal experiences from all walks of human life, including sport and physical adventure. The material in this book has a place, we believe, in this emerging field of study.

William James, whose *Varieties of Religious Experience* is often cited today, also wrote *The Energies of Men*, which was about energy reserves of the human organism. It is these "hidden human reserves," a phrase Russian sport psychologists have frequently used, that athletes often draw on. It is our contention that there are levels of energy (third and fourth and who knows how many more "winds") that only a few sport psychologists recognize. We want to highlight the existence of these energies, give them names, provide examples of them, and show how sport and adventure evoke them. Sport is valued today for such benefits as relaxation and entertainment. It can also show us how to tap our metanormal capacities.

The experiences we cite here represent only a preliminary effort. The more we read through the literature of sport and the more we talk to athletes and coaches, the more we realize that the range of extraordinary athletic states is greater than most people think. Sport evokes mind/body illuminations beyond those we have named. There are sporting "zones" beyond those commonly described by athletes, especially ones involving apparent psychic abilities and contact with the sacred. We now hope, as we did when an earlier version of this book was published, that someone working with people who are actively engaged in sport will gather firsthand examples of metanormal experiences to create a larger and more comprehensive collection.

We also hope that this book will contribute to efforts our readers might be making to extend their own athletic peak experiences to the rest of their life. Both of us are interested in long-term transformative practices, and we believe that sport has much to teach us about them. There are striking parallels between sport and religious discipline, for example, which we discuss in Chapters 5 and 6. As philosopher Klaus Meier wrote, play is liberating and revelatory, enabling humans to "luxuriate in the intense, fully-lived release, if not explosion, of [their] subjectivity." (1116: p. 38)*

Each of us has contributed to every chapter, but Murphy is the primary author of chapters 1, 5, 6, and 7 and White of 2, 3, 4, and the bibliography. In most chapters, we have added new case material. Sixty-two new experiences have been added to those that were included in the first edition.

And we have expanded the bibliography, from 538 to 1550 entries, with the emphasis on scholarly reports, making it one of the most comprehensive listings of articles, books, and dissertations related to metanormality in sports. In addition, 20 percent of the entries have been annotated, including some items in the bibliography of the first edition that we expect will be most useful to students of this field.

---

* The number in parentheses following a quotation or cited work refers to a book or article listed in the bibliography. If a page number is included, it refers to the reference cited.

IN THE ZONE

TRANSCENDENT EXPERIENCE IN SPORTS

1

THE SPIRITUAL
UNDERGROUND
IN SPORTS

For many years we have investigated extraordinary functioning in sport—moments of illumination, out-of-body experiences, altered perceptions of time and space, exceptional feats of strength and endurance, states of ecstasy. From personal interviews, books, magazines, letters, and dissertations, we have gathered thousands of these incidents from famous and not-so-famous athletes. These tales are part of a sports underground—stories that athletes sometimes tell each other but that rarely appear in the sports pages. It's no wonder; many such tales are surpassingly strange, and sportspeople often have trouble accepting them.

I (Murphy) awakened to this underground of metanormal experience after writing a semifictional tale about a golf pro named Shivas Irons. The book, *Golf in the Kingdom*, triggered responses I had not expected. In 1972, the year of its publication, many people wrote to me describing their own sublime or uncanny experiences in golf and other sports. Some related moments of surpassing joy or a serenity for which they could not rationally account. Others wanted to tell me about the unearthly beauty the game of golf had revealed; in the words of a woman correspondent, "All the fairways and greens and people on the course were filled with a holy light." Still others described self-surpassing abilities. A man wrote about an inspired round at his club that ended with a birdie on the long, uphill 5-par 18th hole. For the first time in his life, he reached the green in two shots, and as he walked up the long fairway, he felt as if he were walking *downhill*. Reading *Golf in the Kingdom* had prompted his letter. Ordinarily, he didn't share this kind of experience. My book had shown him that he wasn't alone in feeling that golf could evoke mysterious states of body and soul, including some sort of levitation! This letter, and others like it, alerted me to the fact that many people have illuminations in sport that they are reluctant to talk about.

Later that summer, a woman phoned to say that my book reminded her of a luminous moment she had while skydiving. She had been caught in a thermal upwind and had ridden her parachute for over an hour several thousand feet above the ground. During that ride in the sky, a ring of light had formed around her, and for a moment it had turned into dazzling figures—figures with human shapes made of nothing more substantial than light. She was a mother and a sensible woman, a practical earthbound type, she said, but her experience had made her believe in something like angels. Could I tell her what they might have been?

I was cautious when I answered. Had she ever had visions before?

She said that she hadn't. Her husband thought it was some kind of hallucination, but the experience had been too vivid for that. No, those figures had been utterly real.

I asked a few more questions, but could feel her backing away, responding to my caution with growing shyness about confiding in me. Finally she hung up without leaving her name or address. That conversation was a good lesson in talking to people about these things. Skepticism can distance you from someone who has had an experience as strange as hers. That's why most sports reporters miss this element in their stories. Athletes will seldom make fools of themselves for the press. To understand these uncanny moments you must approach them sympathetically.

As other stories of this kind came my way, I began to realize that there was a side to athletic experience more complex than conventional sports wisdom accounted for. There was something uncanny about hearing these things, a sense of déjà vu that I had felt while watching or participating in certain athletic events. It was as if something secretly familiar was pressing to be recognized, something I had always sensed but could render only fictionally when I wrote about it. As people began to tell me that *Golf in the Kingdom* encouraged them to accept these uncanny aspects of their experience, I decided to explore this domain systematically. Several correspondents claimed that by acknowledging these sometimes strange experiences they found more excitement and significance in sport. Games, they said, were more interesting than ever if you did not suppress these mysterious openings.

A year later, my efforts converged with Rhea White's. She had had a luminous and uncanny round of golf, and contacted me after reading *Golf in the Kingdom*. With eighteen years of experience in parapsychological research, she brought to our project a detailed familiarity with phenomena such as clairvoyance and psychokinesis and a personal interest in mysticism and altered states of consciousness. She is also a professional reference librarian, and her experience in literary research has enabled her to locate and sift through a huge amount of material. As of this writing, she has read through some six thousand books, articles, letters, and dissertations, looking for incidents such as the ones in this book.

In collecting these stories, we have decided to define sports in a broad sense. Thus we are including feats of adventure such as Lindbergh's flight across the Atlantic and Joshua Slocum's solo voyage around the world in the 1890s. Epic undertakings such as these provide some of our richest material, for spiritual experience seems to depend to some extent on the distance a person has come from his or her ordinary habits and on a willingness to give up set responses. Stepping into *terra incognita* by deed seems to trigger openings into the *terra incognita* of metanormal experience. Mountain climbing, distance running, long sea voyages in small boats, and other sports that require a prolonged sacrifice of safety or comfort provide us with more startling spiritual encounters than low-risk games like racquetball or tennis. But low-risk games can become theaters of the occult, too. Arthur Ashe (16) and other tennis players have talked about "the zone," a psychological space in which one's performance seems supernormal. There are times when the tamest games are as fierce and as trying as the ascent of a dangerous mountain.

The experiences we quote are primarily from adults who have spent years honing their athletic skills, but the extraordinary sport experience can occur in youth and even to those who aren't "natural" athletes. Edward Hoffman's collection of spiritual experiences in childhood contains the account of an eleven-year-old Little League baseball player who described himself as not "a very well coordinated hitter." In a game against his league's top team, he came to bat in the ninth inning with two outs, the bases loaded, and his team one run behind. He prayed, "with more intensity than I had thought possible," that he would not embarrass himself. Then: "I let the first pitch go by. Strike one. On the next pitch, something happened. As the pitcher began his regular windup, the illumination on the field seemed to become brighter, and everything became silent and luminous. Everything went into slow motion. I found myself observing—hearing—thinking—with absolute clarity and calm that I was going to slam the ball into right field, and everything would be all right. . . . The pitch came, and the ball floated in as big as a basketball. I hit it squarely and it flew just over the second baseman's mitt into right field. . . . The world went into real time and color. I ran to first, tumbled onto the grass, and laughed until I cried. The runners scored and the game was over." (912: pp. 102–103)

The many reports we have collected show us that sport has enormous power to sweep us beyond our ordinary sense of self, to evoke capacities that have generally been regarded as mystical, occult, or religious. This is not to say that athletes are yogis or mystics. Very few of us approach games with the lifelong dedication and conscious aspiration for enlightenment that the mystical path requires. It is simply to recognize that similarities exist between the two fields of activity, both in their methods and the states they evoke. The great seers of the contemplative traditions have explored the inner life more deeply than most of us, and they have opened up spiritual territories that we may or may not enter. But many athletes and adventurers have followed partway, however inadvertently, through the doorways of sport.

Yet we have found that athletes can be as shy about these things as our Victorian ancestors supposedly were about sex. Some athletes have even denied stories that they had told us on previous occasions. Experiences of dramatically altered consciousness can be traumatic. Most people have trouble accepting metanormal powers and states of mind if they have no context for them, no language or philosophy to support them. We hope that this book will help sportspeople accept their encounters with the sublime and uncanny. Chapters 2, 3, and 4 describe various kinds of extraordinary functioning, including mystical feelings and sensations, altered perceptions, and athletic feats that seem to defy scientific explanations. In the last three chapters, we examine some of the ways in which the timeless truths of our religious heritages, East and West, provide a framework for understanding such experiences.

But when claims are made for the mystical aspects of athletics, there is inevitably a response from the skeptics. Many athletes and coaches are wearied by the notion that sport is some kind of yoga. Marathon runner Frank Shorter, for example, said: "People [say that] running is supposed to produce some psychoelevating morphine derivative in the blood, or it's . . . some sort of religious experience. Maybe it is—but that shouldn't be the main reason you do it. It isn't a major reason for me, or even a minor one. I just like to go out and do it." (231: p. 37)

That attitude, that you should "just go out and do it," is a common one among athletes. There are several good reasons for it, among them a wisdom about talking the spiritual side of athletics to death and a refusal to build up false expectations about it. The athlete's silence about these matters is not unlike the Zen Buddhist attitude: If you experience illumination while chopping wood, keep chopping wood. If there is something in the act that invites the ecstasy, it doesn't need an extra hype or solemn benediction. And there is wisdom in letting people discover these experiences their own way, for too many expectations can dampen the spontaneity and release that are part of sport's glory. They can take the fun out of sports in the name of religion.

For *the mystical moment occurs as often as it does in sport in part because you don't have to have one.* You are simply there to have a good time or pursue a particularly delicious passion, when suddenly—it happens. Many coaches and athletes know this and therefore will not burden us with exhortations about the spiritual things they are doing.

Appreciating this, we come to our subject with some trepidation. By exploring these events in detail, will we raise false hopes that athletics is a special path to mystic insight? We will respond to part of that question at once by saying no, sport *does not* provide a guaranteed way to metanormal experience. It is not the same thing as religious discipline. Part of its glory is that it is not. Because both of us are avid fans—both as participants and as spectators—we don't want to ruin the fun we are having by loading sport with unnecessary baggage. Our aim instead is to enhance the understanding and enjoyment of sports by examining these phenomena. For there is some degree of blindness and fear about these things, an avoidance of the spirit in athletics. And this can be as destructive to enjoyment and adventure as inflated claims or solemn incantations. Much that appears to be tough-minded wisdom turns out to be nothing but timidity and ignorance about the awesome human potential that sport reveals.

2

MYSTICAL SENSATIONS

A winner's confidence can radiate like an aura and be a palpable threat to every competitor. Pitcher Gene Conley said, "I'll never forget Ted [Williams] coming to the plate. You talk about a guy putting you back on your heels on the mound. He dug in, and he looked so big up there and the bat looked so light in his hands, and he didn't swish it around, he snapped it back and forth, and he looked so darned anxious, as if he was saying, 'Okay, kid, let's see what you've got.' Confidence just oozed out of him. He took something away from you even before you threw a pitch." (213: p. 203)

The great defensive tackle of the Pittsburgh Steelers, Joe Greene, described the effort required for peak performance as "playing with every part of yourself [with] the will to get the job done." (1198: p. 31) When this is achieved, he wrote, it feels "beautiful. You are going all out. You are full of the desire to succeed. You are full of a feeling of power . . . of superior confidence. You reach a peak in every part of your being. You reach an emotional high, a physical high, all of them together. It's almost like being possessed. [But while] it *is* a kind of frenzy, of wild action. . . . you are never out of control. You have great awareness of everything that is happening around you and of your part in the whole." (1198: pp. 31–32)

An entire team can catch the fever of invincibility. In *Life on the Run*, Bill Bradley described a game the Knicks played against Milwaukee in which the New Yorkers trailed by 19 points with five minutes remaining in the fourth quarter. With fans heading home, Bradley wrote, "Suddenly, we 'caught fire.' Everything we shot went in and our defense held Milwaukee scoreless for five minutes. We won by three points, accomplishing what came to be known as 'a believer feat.' Those who saw it believed in our invincibility. I even think we did." (56: p. 92)

Theologian Michael Novak described this contagious confidence in his *Joy of Sports*: "When a collection of individuals first jells as a team, truly begins to react as a five-headed or eleven-headed unit rather than as an aggregate of five or eleven individuals, you can almost hear the click: a new kind of reality comes into existence at a new level of human development. A basketball team, for example, can click into and out of this reality many times during the same game; and each player, as well as the coach and the fans, can detect the difference. . . . For those who have participated on a team that has known the click of communality, the experience is unforgettable, like that of having attained, for a while at least, a higher level of existence: existence as it ought to be." (362: pp. 135–36)

Joe Greene told Oates that all eleven men on the defense playing with peak intensity is the ultimate sports experience. "You are surrounded with that frenzy. . . . Everybody is at the same intensity. It's a super, super feeling." (1198: p. 32) He added that his Steelers came closer to that level than any other team of their time, but there was only one occasion when every player was at peak at the same time—the 1974 playoff game at Oakland for the AFC championship. Oakland was the dominant team in the league then, but, according to Green, Pittsburgh "got into a state of mind as a team that it didn't matter what Oakland did, they were going down." (1198: p. 32) He added that the feeling during the game "beggars description. The game was on Oakland's home field, in front of their fans, but our intensity was at such a high level, it just didn't make any difference. . . . Oakland only got twenty-five yards running all day. They never had a chance." (1198: p. 32)

Beyond extraordinary teamwork, athletes report other kinds of metanormal experience. Their accounts support each other; men and women in very different sports tell similar stories. Their experiences range from surges of speed and power to moments of mystery and awe, from ecstasy to peace, from instinctive right action to intimations of immortality, from detachment and freedom to a sense of unity with all things, from a feeling of being "at home" to uncanny incidents when the body, as if weightless, tells the brain that it is floating or flying. The experiences reported in this chapter involve extraordinary feelings described by artists, mystics, and lovers, as well as by athletes. We present twelve different categories of these, but the number could be greatly expanded.

ACUTE WELL-BEING

Many sportspeople claim that a sense of well-being is a natural attribute of athletic excellence. Joe Namath touches on this feeling when he tells about throwing a touchdown pass: "It's pretty hard to describe how that feels, throwing a pass and seeing a man catch it and seeing him in the end zone and seeing the referee throw his arms in the air, signaling a touchdown, signaling that you've done just what you set out to do. It's an incredible feeling. It's like your whole body's bursting with happiness." (347: p. 84)

Racing car driver Dick Simon said that "there is something about the sensation you feel in a racing car at speed that is unlike anything else. It brings out all the good feelings in you." (254: p. 105) Psychiatrist Thaddeus Kostrubala began running to improve his physical fitness. After about two months, he reported: "I became aware of two things. The first was the feeling that I was not at all fatigued after an hour of this type of running-walking. Strangely, at the end of the session I had a sense of energy and a kind of pleasure. It wasn't connected to any achievement factor that I could see, for I would feel that way even if I had not fulfilled my own present expectations—such as running a mile. I did not understand this odd shift in feeling. It was a sense of well-being, a sense of energy. . . . I seemed to be more cheerful." (259: p. 66)

Another physician and runner, George Sheehan, wrote:

That first 30 minutes [of running] is for my body. During that half-hour, I take joy in my physical ability, the endurance and power of my running. I find it a time when I feel myself competent and in control of my body, when I can think about my problems and plan my day-to-day world. In many ways, that 30 minutes is all ego, all the self. It has to do with me, the individual.

What lies beyond this fitness of muscle? I can only answer for myself. The next 30 minutes is for my soul. In it, I come upon the third wind (unlike the second wind, which is physiological). And then I see myself not as an individual but as part of the universe. In it, I can happen upon anything I ever read or saw or experienced. Every fact and instinct and emotion is unlocked and made available to me through some mysterious operation in my brain. (448: p. 36)

Sometimes this sense of well-being is accompanied by the experience of coming home. For example, mountain climber Arlene Blum wrote that her first experience of climbing "on a glacier . . . was like coming home to a place of beauty, splendor, and peace —a place where I felt I belonged and to which I would return again and again." (625: p. 20)

This sense of homecoming in sport can be experienced as a return to childhood bliss. For example, physician/marathoner/mountain climber Robert Schaller recalls that in his earliest climbs he entered a new world and felt born anew. He "felt like a child running free through a candy store. The feel of the trail under my feet, the smell of the wilderness, watching the ever-changing cloud patterns . . . Everything suddenly had more meaning. I realized that life would go on no matter what I did. It gave me an anchor in life." (1318: pp. 69–70)

William Glasser, in *Positive Addiction*, presented personal accounts from meditators, runners, and craftsmen. He concluded that they had formed "positive addictions" to these pursuits, "a trancelike, transcendental mental state that accompanies the addictive exercise. *I believe now that it is this same state, the positive addiction . . . state of mind, that the exercisers reach indirectly and that the meditators are trying to reach directly.*" (173: pp. 46–47)

PEACE, CALM, STILLNESS

Most of us are caught in lifestyles that offer little opportunity for the renewal provided by deep quiet and stillness. But in areas where few people would expect to find it—in risk sports, in running, in the bruising melee of football—athletes sometimes find stillness and peace. This can be found in any stage of a sport. Sometimes it precedes—although it is integrally related to—actual participation. In Zen archery, achieving and maintaining a state of calm is the primary goal before, during, and after the act of releasing the arrow. Sollier and Gyorbiro wrote, "The purpose of Zen archery is not to hit the target, but rather the concentration achieved by the archer in order to create a style that expresses his perfect mental serenity. When the archer does hit the center of the target in such a state of mental calm, it is proof that his spiritual discipline is successful." (465: p. 23) Sometimes such calm is the end result of a sports activity. Eric Ryback, who at the age of eighteen hiked the entire length of the Pacific Crest Trail from Canada to Mexico, said that at the very end, when he saw his father running to meet him, "if I ever had a moment of complete peace on the trek, it was then." (419: p. 196)

This sense of stillness can occur while the athlete is fully engaged. Steve McKinney recalled how he felt when he broke the world downhill ski record: "I discovered the middle path of stillness within speed, calmness within fear, and I held it longer and quieter than ever before." (304: p. 77) Malcolm Smith, describing what it is like to ride motorcycles at speed, said "you feel a calmness through your body, even though you know intellectually that you're right on the brink of disaster." (424: p. 179)

The experience is just as likely to occur during individual competition or in a team sport. Billie Jean King, writing of the perfect shot, said, "I can almost feel it coming. It usually happens on one of those days when everything is just right, when the crowd is large and enthusiastic and my concentration is so perfect it almost seems as though I'm able to transport myself beyond the turmoil on the court to some place of total peace and calm." (251: p. 199)

We have assumed that the words *peace* and *calm* in these descriptions refer solely to the athlete's subjective awareness, not to measurable objective factors. But there is evidence that certain athletes are able to maintain a state of physiological quietude in the most trying circumstances. For example, the breathing and pulse rates of deaf stuntwoman Kitty O'Neil were monitored continuously while she was achieving a speed of 612 miles per hour, strapped onto a liquid fuel rocket, in an attempt to break the men's land speed record. The instruments revealed that her pulse and breathing rates did not exceed their resting rate. (247: p. 28)

Certain sports are more conducive than others to feelings of peace and calm. Stillness is almost inevitable in sports such as deep-sea diving, soaring, gliding, and mountain climbing, where silence is part of the environment. In a certain sense, going to the mountain heights or the ocean depths or flying alone high in the sky, in situations that stretch the athlete to the limit and strip away the comforts of everyday life, may create a silence like that which mystics reach through withdrawal and contemplation. These athletes, too, have withdrawn from the world; temporarily, at least, they too become ascetics, and the single-minded pursuit of their sport becomes a form of concentrated meditation. Mountain climber Richard M. Emerson described this mystical state: "After so much effort, to sit there—totally alone at 25,000 feet, surrounded by a still and motionless world of rock and ice and blueblack sky—was satisfying in a very special way. It was not the euphoria of altitude. It was the exhilaration of wilderness. Every feature of my surroundings gave evidence of violent force, yet all was calm and fixed—like a terrible battle scene suddenly frozen in a timeless tableau; the rock and ice polished by snow—blasting winds, the graceful sweep of flutings carved on the walls by avalanche, the grind and furor of the icefalls far below. But everything was silent and motionless." (215: p. 154)

Colette Richard, a blind woman, became a mountain climber and cave explorer. She described what it was like to be resting high on a mountain: "I sat there listening with my whole being, and with my whole strength contemplating that mountain that I so dearly love. . . . Was there anyone in the world, at that moment, as happy as I? For the silence was not emptiness. The silence was Life, making one with the Word. That region was filled with silence—that is to say, filled with life." (403: p. 158) Accompanying renowned speleologist Norbert Casteret, Richard spent a night alone deep in the earth, where she found "total silence." Later she observed, "Up in the heights the silence is white and luminous, a poetry of sunshine, glaciers, keen air and the scent of snow. . . . Underground it is a mineral stillness, immovable, a mysteriously living silence." (403: p. 158)

French skier and mountain guide Patrick Vallençant has specialized in skiing steep pitches of fifty to sixty degrees. In his book, *Ski Extrême* (published in French in 1979), he wrote: "At the beginning of any steep descent, concentration of incredible intensity fills me. . . . When I concentrate so, the world disappears. . . . There is man, and a slope of snow, in unison. . . . To ski a very steep slope is completely beautiful; it is pure, hard, vertical, luminous in a dimension that, by its nature, is foreign to us, yet I become a part of this cosmic dimension. . . . The skis cut through space and I perceive the steepness of the slope with extraordinary acuteness. It is a marvelous phenomenon and I gain a fullness far beyond what we normally comprehend. I see this with such intensity that I have made skiing the steeps the goal of my life." (1137: pp. 22, 24)

Vallençant's motivation for this is plain from the following quotation: "There is something better in us because of our feats in these mountains; we become more at peace with ourselves. . . . I have the impression, after a descent, of dropping all restraints— my heart is open and free, my head is clear . . . all the beauty of the world is within the mad rhythm of my blood." (1137: p. 25)

Howard Slusher, in *Man, Sport and Existence*, eloquently described the significance of such moments in the life of an athlete. He refers to the "spirit of the sport," and adds that it is associated with quiet: "In searching for the 'sounds' of sport one quickly hears the roar of the crowd, the crack of the bat and the thundering of racing feet. But if one listens a little harder and a little longer, one comes to hear silence. There is silence within the performer, in the tenseness of the crowd, in the fear of the hunter and in the beauty of the ski slopes.

"Man soon learns that silence is an integral part of life and that certainly it is prominent in sport. Silence is not simply the absence of sounds. Rather it is presence." (458: p. 168)

DETACHMENT

When he broke the four-minute mile, Roger Bannister "felt complete detachment." (30: p. 238) Dancer Jacques d'Amboise described the supreme moments when he felt in command, when he could do anything with his body. "When you're dancing like that, you seem to be removed. You can enjoy yourself doing it and watch yourself doing it at the same time." (535: p. 9)

Before a race, driver Jackie Stewart insisted on isolating himself from everyone, including his wife, bending all energies to induce a state of detachment. In his book *Faster*, he described how he prepared for a race:

The process is akin to a deflating ball. The point of it is to shape my mood, really to expel mood, all mood. Beginning the night before, I start to pace myself into an emotional neutrality, a flatness or isolation that is imperative for a good start. By the time I go to bed, I will have obliterated all contact with people around me, Helen included. Usually I'll be reading, lying there beyond anybody's reach, trying to cleanse my mind, empty it of all extraneous thoughts, all impingements, anything that might encroach. Around eleven or twelve, perhaps, I'll go off to sleep. I'll awaken at half past six or seven, stay in bed, pick up my reading, then probably doze off to reawaken around nine. Breakfast in my room, always in my room, and usually alone, and perhaps, too, I'll have a massage, if one's available. Then back to sleep, up at noon, dress, and leave for the track.

By now I'm fairly bouncy. After the calm of being alone, the ball has started to inflate again. I'll have thoughts of what I'm going to do on the first lap, where I'm going to pass if someone gets off ahead of me, but immediately I'll then become aware of having to change my mood, of the need to put aside all these thoughts lest I lock myself into a plan that might interfere with my driving. More than anything, I know I need to stay loose, so I force myself to deflate, consciously, concentrating on it. I don't want Helen around me, I don't want to be bugged by reporters or film people or magazine photographers, by people wanting my autograph or by anyone. I'm into it, I need to be alone.

By race time I should have no emotions inside me at all—no excitement or fear or nervousness, not even an awareness of the fatigue that's been brought on by pacing myself. I'm absolutely cold, ice-cold, totally within my shell. I'm drained of feeling, utterly calm even though I'm aware of the many things going on around me, the mechanics, people running about, the journalists and officials and everything else.

Stress, I think, enters into it but mainly in a positive way. It's what really lies behind the routine of deflation, the knowledge or discipline, call it what you will, of anticipating what my emotions can become and anticipating too the need to rechannel them, negotiate them, as it were, into a more favorable currency. (474: pp. 30–32)

In a description of soaring, flyer Richard Wolters wrote: "Things seem unreal . . . you're detached. People and their emotions are down there only because you know it. When you break with below, there is a whole new vista." (533: p. 18) In a study of parachute jumpers, Benjamin DeMott said, "Pressed for an account of his motives, the articulate jumper is likely to characterize the sport in terms suggesting that for him it amounts to a ritual of divestiture—a means of stripping off layers of institutional lies and myths that encrust the Individual. . . . Man diving is man alive; the ecstasy is that of non-connection—the exhilaration of sinking the world to nothingness, or at least to stillness, and thereby creating the self as All." (111: p. 110)

Charles Lindbergh noted during his famous cross-Atlantic flight: "How detached the intimate things around me seem from the great world down below. How strange is this combination of proximity and separation." It made him acutely aware of "the grandeur of the world outside. The nearness of death. The longness of life." (293: p. 228)

FREEDOM

David Hemery, who set a world record at the 1968 Olympics in the 400-meter hurdle, winning by a wider margin than anyone had in forty-four years, wrote of the event: "Only a couple of times in my life have I felt in such condition that my mind and body worked almost as one. This was one of those times. My limbs reacted as my mind was thinking: total control, which resulted in absolute freedom. Instead of forcing and working my legs, they responded with the speed and in the motions that were being asked of them." (200: p. 57)

Other athletes say the feeling of freedom is a constant factor in their sport. Scuba diver Jim Gott said: "Beneath the seas, the diver . . . flies, unburdened even by the law of gravity. His every movement has a feeling of freedom to it." (176: p. 199) Similar feelings are described by airplane pilots as reported in a book by the editors of *Flying Magazine*: "To fly over open country, to fly just for the sake of flying, is to know freedom. In flight, the world is open to you. Light is a message, a dialogue, in which the sun and clouds and the radiance of the land are all participants; at night, it is radiated in pinpoints of brilliance that mark autos, towns, isolated houses, and huge cities. Even in cloud, flight means the freedom from or the mastery of that which we normally fear, for flight in cloud can mean the mastery of intelligence over mystery. . . .

"The best joy is flight itself: to know you are up there, seeing from where you see, feeling the coolness of new breezes, making for yourself the choices of involvement or detachment, and knowing, above all, that for the moment you are a completely separate entity. . . . that is the closest this life will bring us to sporting with angels." (150: p. 229, 231)

Mountaineers, while exerting all their energy to remain attached to a vertical piece of earth, nonetheless value climbing in part because of the freedom from gravity it provides. Lionel Terray said that what he and his climbing companion, Pierre Lachenal, "loved about climbing was the sensation of escaping from the laws of gravity, of dancing on space, which comes with technical virtuosity. Like the pilot or the skier, a man then feels freed from the condition of a crawling bug and becomes a chamois, a squirrel, almost a bird." (487: p. 192)

FLOATING, FLYING, WEIGHTLESSNESS

One of the most pleasurable experiences sport can provide is the feeling of floating or weightlessness. It is built into the structure of some sports, such as skiing, parachuting, and flying. Steve McKinney said that when he broke the world record in speed skiing, it was like "riding a magic carpet of air, into which our will power was sensuously intertwined. It was this air carpet, about four to six inches in depth, that we found at speeds over 100 mph. We left the snow and actually flew through the speed trap." (304: p. 74) The feeling is also present in scuba diving. As Jacques Cousteau put it: "To halt and hang attached to nothing, with no lines or air pipe to the surface, was a dream. At night I had often had visions of flying by extending my arms as wings. Now I flew without wings." (94: p. 6)

In the sports just mentioned, one has the feeling of floating in part because one actually *is* floating. But sometimes on the ground there is a feeling of lightness, a floating sensation, even a sense of weightlessness. Long-distance runner Bill Emmerton, completely exhausted after six hundred miles of running, suddenly "had this light feeling, I felt as though I was going through space, treading on clouds." (279: p. 40) Marathon runner Ian Thompson observes: "I have only to think of putting on my running shoes and the kinesthetic pleasure of floating starts to come over me." (10: p. 61) Another runner, John Roemer, said, "I want to stick my arms out and float." (173: p. 110) William Glasser administered a questionnaire to runners and found repeated mentions of wanting to float or fly. In *Art of the Dance*, Isadora Duncan conceived a type of dancer who can "convert the body into a luminous fluidity, surrendering it to the inspiration of the soul. This . . . sort of dancer understands that the body, by force of the soul, can in fact be converted to a luminous fluid. The flesh becomes light and transparent, as shown through the X-ray—but with the difference that the human soul is lighter than these rays. When, in its divine power, it completely possesses the body, it converts that into a luminous moving cloud and thus can manifest itself in the whole of its divinity." (124: p. 51)

The experience of becoming lighter, of being weightless, or of rising in the air—bears a strong resemblance to mystical ecstasies in which the feeling of being outside oneself is a primary feature.

It is also experienced in some of the newer approaches to the study of consciousness. The editor of *Brain-Mind Bulletin*, Marilyn Ferguson, claimed that floating is a common experience of "participants in muscle-relaxation and alpha biofeedback training. It is a typical meditation phenomenon. Mystics frequently speak of enlarging, of loss of body sensations, bubbling up, or becoming airborne. Sensory-deprivation subjects may lie quietly in their isolation chambers, then suddenly feel as if they have risen several inches and are buoyant." (142: p. 68)

ECSTASY

In Pelé's first World Cup appearance in 1958, he believed that "he played that whole game in a kind of trance, as if the future was unfolding before his own disinterested eyes. His feeling is confirmed by newsreel footage of the Brazilian squad moments after the final whistle. As he twists and turns in his teammate's arms, Pelé's youthful face is gripped by an almost pained wonder. He looks like a child, caught in some unnamed, private ecstasy. Each time he looks at the camera, he turns away quickly." (48: p. 27)

Some may think that the experience of ecstasy attributed to athletes by writers and spectators is just a projection. But to the athletes themselves, these moments are utterly real. Quarterback Francis Tarkenton said that he played football for one reason: "I love it. Nothing in my life compares to the ecstasies I get from this game." (428: p. 94) Leuchs and Skalka say that while skiing, the athlete can experience "the magic moment when you are right on the mark, when everything falls into place and the only sensation you feel is the ecstasy of what you are doing. Skiier, skiing, skied are one." (281: p. 5) Mountain climber Lionel Terray said he climbed mountains because "the simplest climbs made me crazy with joy. The mountains were a sort of magic kingdom where by some spell I felt happiest." (487: p. 23)

Poet/writer Diane Ackerman seeks activities that put her on the edge. In an absorbing book about how she learned to fly, she tells why she chooses to put her life in jeopardy: "For a compulsively pensive person, to be fully alert but free of thought is a form of ecstasy. . . . Being ecstatic means being flung out of your usual self. When you're enraptured, your senses are upright and saluting. But there is also a state when perception doesn't work, consciousness vanishes like the gorgeous fever it is, and you feel free of all mind-body constraints, suddenly so free of them you don't perceive yourself as being free, but vigilant, a seeing eye without judgment, history, or emotion. It's that shudder out of time, the central moment in so many sports, that one often feels, and perhaps becomes addicted to, while doing something dangerous. . . . the fear of leaning into nothingness." (542: pp. 8–9)

Jesse Francis Lewis questioned fifty-three students regarding their ecstatic experiences and the contexts in which they occurred. He found that a common facet of the ecstatic experience was a surge of energy. He wrote: "with great regularity, ecstasy involved either activity or the impulse to activity. . . . This may appear as a sort of release of energy, in screaming, jumping, walking or running, or may be more quiet as in smiling or standing." (284: p. 43) Similar findings were reported in a classic survey made by Marghanita Laski, who studied the "triggers," or circumstances, leading up to the experience of ecstasy. She found that one was movement. In particular, she wrote, "the kinds of exercise or movement that seem to be relevant to ecstasy are two: regular rhythmical movement such as walking, jogging along on a horse, riding in a carriage, etc.; and swift movement, such as running, flying, galloping." (273: p. 198)

Almost all risk sports involve regularity or swiftness of motion, and these are sports in which euphoria and ecstasy are frequently experienced. Ian Jackson tells about his first experience of surfing: "I began an accelerating paddle rhythm. . . . If you've ever had a close brush with death . . . you know the feeling that shot through my body. It was a pure adrenaline flash. . . . As I pulled out over the shoulder of the wave, I balanced for a moment in ecstasy. Then my knees buckled and I toppled into the warm water, laughing uproariously. It was an instant addiction." (224: p. 17) A woman participant in Outward Bound said of her first rappel while rock climbing: "It must be like flying, it's so exhilarating, so euphoric. It's a giddying rush that's free of any effort on my part." (86: p. 33)

Not only are individual players or whole teams transported at peak moments, but this ecstasy can be shared by fans. Jim Naughton wrote that Michael Jordan's performances put his fans "in touch with something larger than themselves. . . . They rise when he rises . . . but what they feel most keenly is [his] joy." (1184: p. 134) He quoted Whittier College religion professor Joseph Price as saying: "There is a genuine sense of playfulness, a sense of wonder about the way [Jordan] plays the game, and his sense of joy transmits a feeling of ecstasy. . . . They can celebrate because he celebrates . . . he succeeds in doing that which all of us aspire to do." (1184: p. 155)

Rhythmic dancing has long been known to trigger ecstasy. Heinrich Zimmer, the eminent student of Indian culture, points out that "dancing is an ancient form of magic. The dancer becomes amplified into a being endowed with supra-normal powers. His personality is transformed. Like yoga, the dance induces trance, ecstasy, the experience of the divine, the realization of one's own secret nature, and, finally, merging into the divine essence." (537: p. 151) This ecstasy can be experienced by the audience as well as the dancers. Writing of her sister-in-law, Isadora Duncan, Margherita Duncan said, "When she danced the Blue Danube, her simple waltzing forward and back, like the oncoming and receding waves on the shore, had such an ecstasy of rhythm that audiences became frenzied with the contagion of it, and could not contain themselves, but rose from their seats, cheering, applauding, laughing and crying. . . . We felt as if we had received the blessing of God." (124: p. 23)

POWER, CONTROL

A sense of self-mastery and power is among the supreme rewards of sport. It can arise in almost any athletic activity, although in our collection of cases it appears to happen most when high risk is involved. University of Illinois psychotherapist Saul Rosenthal (160), through surveys of many athletes, has identified a powerful form of well-being that comes from risk in sports such as skiing and auto racing. Bullfighter El Cordobes has described many performances in which he "was hypnotized by his own success . . . unable to think of anything else but that splendid, drunken feeling of power each movement, each pass of the bull, gave him." (88: p. 305)

This intoxicating power is often felt above the earth. It is one aspect of the "break-off" phenomenon experienced by pilots at high altitudes. Richard Wolters said of being caught up by a thermal, which is the peak moment in soaring: "You'll stumble into it, but you'll know what it is . . . instantly. Then you'll become a believer! It'll push up right from the seat of your pants. Its strength will astonish you, and you will truly climb on wings. . . . This is the power; to use it is the skill. This is what the whole thing is about." (533: p. 62)

When this sense of power happens frequently enough so that it can be expected to recur and its coming can be counted on, it is transformed into a feeling of invincibility. Decathlon champion Bruce Jenner said that partway through the 1976 Olympics, "a strange feeling began to come over me. In four events so far, I'd set three personal bests and come within a couple hundredths of my electronic p.r. [personal record] in the hundred. I started to feel that there was nothing I couldn't do if I had to. It was a feeling of awesome power, except that I was in awe of myself, knocking off these p.r.'s just like that. I was rising above myself, doing things I had no right to be doing." (228: p. 77)

Often the sense of control in sport extends to one's equipment or surroundings. On good days drivers feel they can do anything with their cars. "They say they can attach a lawn mower to the car and mow the lawn." (254: p. 94) An experience of oneness and of being in effortless control is described by surfer Midget Farrelly: "Sometimes you reach a point of being so coordinated, so completely balanced, that you feel you can do anything—anything at all. At times like this I find I can run up to the front of the board and stand on the nose when pushing out through a broken wave; I can goof around, put myself in an impossible position and then pull out of it, simply because I feel happy. An extra bit of confidence like that can carry you through, and you can do things that are just about impossible." (141: p. 23)

Mountain climber Gaston Rebuffat and three companions reached the summit of the Matterhorn at 7:30 in the evening and were engulfed by an electrical storm. They had to descend in growing darkness over rocks slippery with snow. By eight it was very dark, so they had to make the dangerous and sheer descent from the recollection of holds revealed by lightning flashes. In these perilous circumstances the four men tapped the reserves of control and strength that they required to descend safely. Rebuffat recalled: "We moved quickly, though with the utmost caution. That sounds contradictory, but it is strictly true. What mysterious, secret force, apparently dormant in us, came to our aid? Side by side with the accumulation of difficulties and this danger that we so much disliked, we felt reserves of energy and skill, which every man carries within him and which reveal themselves only in great emergencies, coming to life deep within us. In spite of the clashing thunder, the blinding snow, the squalls of wind that jostled us, we experienced a solemn pleasure; the pleasure of maintaining our self-mastery and remaining calm and precise in spite of the perils." (1283: p. 208)

At its fullest, the feeling of being in control is a unifying experience involving the athlete's entire sense of self, the environment, and even his destiny. Champion race driver Mario Andretti insisted: "Only a race driver can know—can feel—the joys of motor racing. When a man is competing in a race car, when he is pushing himself and the machine to the very limit, when the tires are breaking free from the ground and he is controlling his destiny with his own two hands, then, man, he is living—in a way no other human can understand." (8: p. 5) Andretti's experience is corroborated by a study of racing car drivers which concludes that "Driving these speeds and performing a task which is quite obviously highly dangerous at the limits of one's ability and the limits of the car's capacity, gives rise to a particular exhilaration and feeling of successful control of objects and oneself." (264: pp. 193–94)

BEING IN THE PRESENT

Regardless of the sport, successful athletes say that when they are performing at their best they are immersed in the present moment, totally involved in whatever confronts them. John Brodie, former San Francisco 49er quarterback, has said that "a player's effectiveness is directly related to his ability to be right there, doing that thing, in the moment. All the preparation he may have put into the game—all the game plans, analysis of movies, etc.—is no good if he can't put it into action when game time comes. He can't be worrying about the past or the future or the crowd or some other extraneous event. He must be able to respond in the here and now." (343: p. 20)

When athletes are truly immersed in the present, they are totally unaware of distractions. Auto racer Jochen Rindt told Peter Manso that when driving, "you completely ignore everything and just concentrate. You forget about the whole world and you just . . . are part of the car and the track. . . . It's a very special feeling. You're completely out of this world. There is nothing like it." (308: p. 168)

Ben Hogan was one of golf's legendary concentrators. On one occasion, Clayton Heafner finished second in a big tournament, in which Hogan came from behind to defeat him, although Heafner was playing his best golf. All through the round Heafner had been aware of Hogan, and at the end consoled himself with the thought that it was not he who had lost the tournament but Hogan who had won it by "shooting the lights out." Later, in the locker room, Heafner bumped into Hogan, who looked up from a telegram he was reading and said, "Oh, hi, Clayt, how'd it go today?" (49: p. 53)

Football player Jack Snow said he concentrated "to the point of self-hypnosis. I pick out a spot in the end zone or behind the end zone and I tell myself I won't let anyone stop me from reaching it, and I don't. If a plane crashed in the stadium, I don't think I'd notice it until the play was over." (287: p. 49)

Golfer Arnold Palmer wrote that tournament play "involves a tautness of mind but not a tension of the body. It has various manifestations. One is the concentration on the shot at hand. The other is the heightened sense of presence and renewal that endures through an entire round or an entire tournament. There is something spiritual, almost spectral about the latter experience. You're involved in the action and vaguely aware of it, but your focus is not on the commotion but on the opportunity ahead. I'd liken it to a sense of reverie—not a dreamlike state but the somehow insulated state that a great musician achieves in a great performance. He's aware of where he is and what he's doing, but his mind is on the playing of his instrument with an internal sense of rightness— it is not merely mechanical, it is not only spiritual; it is something of both, on a different plane and a more remote one." (371: p. 141)

In these revelatory moments, we relinquish many self-made boundaries. This is experienced both physically and spiritually. Ron Widel says in the course of becoming the world's grand master frisbee champion and setting several world records, he recovered the spontaneous playful spirit he was taught to put aside when he became an adult. He discovered that his best performances occurred on days "you let yourself go. Your intuition and creativity surface. . . . The environment is moving and calls for timing, a sensing yourself as part of the process. . . . The further I have gone in controlling the intricacies of flying discs, the more my inner world has unfolded. You learn to control your time and space. The object has limitations that you do not. . . . You find more of yourself in losing yourself." (1519: p. 39) One of the first places we may have this experience is in sport. Religions teach that it is available at any and every moment. Widel noted that he has had similar highs in his work as a carpenter. At such times he became "part of the environment" and did not "separate myself from it with preconceptions, words, old ideas." (1519: p. 41) The key is to be in the moment, realizing it is moving, not static. To be is to move with the process of the universe as it unfolds in you and you in it.

INSTINCTIVE ACTION AND SURRENDER

Despite the many long years of instruction and practice that most athletes put in, they generally act spontaneously when they make outstanding plays. The conscious knowledge of correct and incorrect moves serves as kindling and logs to a fire, but in the white heat of the event they are burnt into nonexistence, as the reality of the flames takes over—flames originating in a source beyond conscious know-how, melding athlete, experience, and play into a single event. This is not to belittle deliberate training, for without wood there can be no flame. Perhaps we can speak of two stages, conscious and unconscious, neither of which could operate without the other. Because we can talk about it, think about it, read about it, the conscious aspect is familiar to all of us; to some, it is the only reality. We must, however, give equal recognition to the lesser known, spontaneous aspect—the state that can be recalled only after the play has been made, when the athlete talks about being "unconscious," "out of my mind," "in the zone," playing "over my head." He doesn't know how he made the play. "It was instinct."

Robert Deindorfer has described something he calls "Positive

Fishing," attributing the degree of success to the flow level attained by the angler. (715: p. 21) He cites a man named Henderson, who told him: "I get myself in sort of a groove. . . . Sometimes I get so wound up that I almost forget it's me catching the fish." (715: p. 28) Another angler told him, "When I'm fishing happy I fish better than I should. Things go better." (715: p. 31) A highly successful British match fisherman, Ade Scott, who is known for catching many fish at a time, also feels himself to be a different person: "Sometimes it isn't me whipping those fish off the water. I don't know who it is, but it isn't really me." (715: p. 32) This resembles Herrigel's instruction in regard to Zen archery. *You* do not let go the bow string, *it* just happens. Deindorfer noted that the wilderness environment in which anglers fish is profoundly conducive to this state. (715: pp. 38–39)

He wrote that absorbed concentration is a key requirement: "No mere mechanical skill . . . no great combination of rod, reel, line, and fly will produce over a period of time unless the participant manages to develop a soundproof, weatherproof, failure-proof attention span." Ade Scott, known as the "Bleak Machine," because he caught more of the fish known as bleak than anyone else, stated: "I wouldn't hear a gun if they shot it off right alongside me." (715: p. 145)

Masters of the martial arts are generally more conscious of such spontaneity than their Western counterparts. E. J. Harrison, who made firsthand observations of renowned fighters around the world, described a demonstration given by Matsuura, a high-ranking instructor at the Kodokan School of Judo: "Sitting on his knees with his back to me and his hands together, he made his mind blank of any conscious thought. The idea was that I was to remain behind him for as long a time as I desired. Then with all the speed and power I could muster I was to grab him by the throat and pull him over backwards. I sweated it out for maybe two or three minutes without making a move. Then I put all the power and speed I could into the effort. My next step was to get up from my back where I landed in front of him. His explanation was that the action was not conscious, but rather sprang from the seat of reflex control, the tanden, or second brain. These things are not taught in the Judo College." (394: p. 409)

One does not consciously have to plan how to act; instead, one lets the appropriate responses happen of themselves. This open secret at the heart of sports has been described by philosopher Michael Novak: "This is one of the great inner secrets of sports. There is a certain point of unity within the self, and between the self and its world, a certain complicity and magnetic mating, a certain harmony, that conscious mind and will cannot direct. Perhaps analysis and the separate mastery of each element are required before the instincts are ready to assume command, but only at first. Command by instinct is swifter, subtler, deeper, more accurate, more in touch with reality than command by conscious mind. The discovery takes one's breath away." (362: p. 164)

A famous explication of the importance of instinct in sport is German philosopher Eugen Herrigel's description of his efforts to learn Zen archery. The Zen master who taught him insisted that "the shot will only go smoothly when it takes the archer himself by surprise. . . . You mustn't open the right hand on purpose." (203: p. 48) Former heavyweight champion Ingemar Johansson found something similar in boxing. He insisted there was something about his right hand—the hand that delivered the knockout punch—that was strange. He told a *Life* reporter that it worked independently of his conscious mind and was so fast even he couldn't see it. "Without my telling it to, the right goes, and when it hits, there is this good feeling. . . . Something just right has been done." (232: p. 43)

Many athletes recognize the importance of not acting deliberately during their peak moments. They seem to know that conscious thought must be held in abeyance. Catfish Hunter, in describing the perfect game he pitched against the Minnesota Twins in 1968, said, "I wasn't worried about a perfect game going into the ninth. It was like a dream. I was going on like I was in a daze. I never thought about it the whole time. If I'd thought about it I wouldn't have thrown a perfect game—I know I wouldn't." (220: p. 37) At the 1956 Olympics, Olga Fikotova (later, Connolly), a Czech medical student, won the women's discus throw after only a year in the sport. When she made her winning throw, which set a new Olympic and Czech record, she was lost to the world: "From a weird distance I heard the judge say, 'You may begin,' but I did not see him. I saw nobody. Once in the ring, I firmly pushed my toes against its steel rim, then stepped back a hair in caution against fouling. Everything around me faded from perception; all sounds bleached into space. I did not consciously move—it seemed the ring itself spun my toes into the rehearsed footwork. A tornado of unconstrainable energy whirled me around, and jetted the discus through the air in a flat, low, bullet like fashion, lacking all the fancifulness of elegantly curved flight. My head snapped back in the release, but I remained balanced and did not foul. Somewhere inside I realized that my throw had exhausted all I had to offer: my energy, my dreams, months of fanatic work, my devotion to my people, they all flew ripping across the stadium." (90: p. 130)

Sometimes the unconscious, instinctive action in sport is perceived as coming from a greater power beyond oneself. Utah State University basketball star Wayne Estes, who in his senior year ranked just above Princeton's Bill Bradley and just below leading scorer Rick Barry of the University of Miami, scored 48 points in his final game. In a radio interview following the game he said "I was just putting the ball up. . . . Somebody else was putting it in for me." (252: pp. 25–26) In the 1953 World Series, George Shuba pinch-hit a home run. Blinded by the sun, he could barely see the ball, but he hit it out—the second player ever to pinch-hit a homer in a series. However, said Shuba, ". . . it wasn't me. There was something else guiding the bat. I couldn't see the ball, and you can think what you want, but another hand was guiding my bat." (241: p. 238)

The necessity for remaining open and empty, and the need for surrender, also figure prominently in the religions of the world. The purpose of surrender, of letting go, in both religion and sport, is not to diminish one's self but to achieve a level of functioning otherwise impossible. The feeling of a greater self taking over, so graphically described by athletes, has its Western counterpart in St. Paul's ". . . not I live, but Christ liveth in me." According to the *Tao Te Ching*: "When once you are free from all seeming, from all craving and lusting, then will you move of your own impulse, without so much as knowing that you move."

MYSTERY AND AWE

For many people, a sense of the numinous is experienced on athletic fields. In interviews with twenty athletes, physical education professor Kenneth Ravizza (396) found that eighteen had experienced awe and wonder during peak moments in sport. Maurice Herzog, in describing the successful ascent of Annapurna, said that as he and Pierre Lachenal approached the summit: "I felt as though I were plunging into something new and quite abnormal. I had the strangest and most vivid impressions, such as I had never before known in the mountains. There was something unnatural in the way I saw Lachenal and everything around us . . . all sense of exertion was gone, as though there were no longer any gravity. This diaphanous landscape, this quintessence of purity—these were not the mountains I knew: they were the mountains of my dreams." (205: p. 132)

A surfer, after riding his biggest wave, said: "Afterward I just sat there. I didn't want to talk about it. It happened so quickly. I didn't realize the magnitude of it until I was sitting on the beach." (396: p. 118) At these times, athletes feel they are treading on sacred ground—or even that the divine has invaded their lives. Basketball player Patsy Neal wrote:

> There are moments of glory that go beyond the human expectation, beyond the physical and emotional ability of the individual. Something unexplainable takes over and breathes life into the known life. One stands on the threshold of miracles that one cannot create voluntarily. . . . Call it a state of grace, or an act of faith . . . or an act of God. It is there, and the impossible becomes possible. . . . The athlete goes beyond herself; she transcends the natural. She touches a piece of heaven and becomes the recipient of power from an unknown source.
>
> The power goes beyond that which can be defined as physical or mental. The performance almost becomes a holy place—where a spiritual awakening seems to take place. The individual becomes swept up in the action around her —she almost floats through the performance, drawing on forces she has never previously been aware of. (350: pp. 166–67)

George Plimpton related a conversation he had with tennis player Sidney Wood on what it is like to be charged-up during a match: "He described the effect as 'total vision' . . . in which the feeling of omnipotence is overwhelming. 'You simply become more than yourself,' Wood said. 'When it happens, there are physical manifestations as well. The hair stands on end and starts to get all prickly.' " (385: pp. 59–60) Dick Schaap wrote a book centered on the moment at the Mexico Olympics when Bob Beamon broke the world record in the long jump by nearly two feet. After the footage had been determined, and Beamon had donned his warm-up pants: "Suddenly, the enormity of what he had done sank in, and Beamon fell to his knees, leaned his head against the Tartan running track, almost as if he were kissing the ground, then clasped his head in his hands. Waves of nausea rolled over him, and his heart pounded as it had never pounded before, and he could see stars in front of his eyes. 'Tell me I am not dreaming,' he mumbled. 'It's not possible. I can't believe it. Tell me I am not dreaming.' " (427: p. 97)

This fear, which sometimes can border on terror, may be due in part to the fact that "the athlete many times finds that things go beyond what he understands, and what he knows should happen logically." (350: p. 166) The German theologian Rudolf Otto described the human encounter with the awesome aspect of the sacred—with "that which is alien to us, uncomprehended and unexplained . . . that which is quite beyond the sphere of the usual, the intelligible, and the familiar, which therefore falls quite outside the limits of the 'canny' and is contrasted with it, filling the mind with blank wonder and astonishment" (366: p. 26) and a "consciousness of the absolute superiority or supremacy of a power other than myself." (366: p. 21) Thus the athlete knows that being in perfect control of the football, or the puck, or the bat may be a matter more of grace than of will, and that one can only "do it" by letting it happen, by letting something else take over. And it is the awareness of and closeness to that "something else" that can lead to terror. Otto calls it "the emotion of a creature, submerged and overwhelmed by its own nothingness in contrast to that which is supreme above all creatures." (366: p. 10) George Leonard described something very similar that occurs in sport: "Pressing us up against the limits of physical exertion and mental acuity, leading us up to the edge of the precipice separating life from death, sports may open the door to infinite realms of perception and being. Having no tradition of mystical experience, no adequate mode of discourse on the subject, no preparatory rites, the athlete might refuse to enter. But the athletic experience is a powerful one, and it may thrust the athlete, in spite of fear and resistance, past the point of no return, into a place of awe and terror." (279: pp. 39–40)

FEELINGS OF IMMORTALITY

It is not uncommon for athletes to experience a sense of immortality. Charles Tekeyan believed that this feeling is solely a matter of continued excellence in the flesh. He wrote, "An athlete at his peak feels invincible and immortal. . . ." (485: p. 2) The sense of physical immortality, however, is only one form of immortality found in sports. Another is the sense of continuity with ages past. Long-distance runner Bill Emmerton once saw himself in the chain of life stretching over many generations. According to George Leonard:

> Once, while making the run from John 'o Groat's to Lands End in Britain, he ran steadily for thirty-five hours with only the briefest of necessary stops. After some thirty-two hours of that run, between two and three a.m., he found himself in a fog on the Cornwall moors, totally alone, miles from anyone. Emmerton, Australian-born-and-bred, knew that he had ancestors in that region of England.
>
> "I was completely, utterly exhausted," he told me. "I'd just put six hundred miles behind me, fifty miles, day in and day out, through all kinds of weather conditions—six inches of snow, the fierce winds from the North Sea, the pelting rain, the hailstorms. Then, all of a sudden, I had this light feeling, I felt as though I was going through space, treading on clouds. I didn't know what it was, but I heard a voice saying, 'We're here to help you.' I reached out my arm and someone was there to help me. I could feel spirits, the spirits of my ancestors they said they were, and they gathered around me, coming so close I felt I could touch them. I've never revealed this to anyone before—never. But they were right there. And I was talking to them. I just started talking. It was this warm feeling, almost like an orgasm. And I was saying, 'Thank you. Thank you for taking care of me.' " (279: pp. 40–44)

Some sports more than others seem to draw back a curtain that screens out intimations of immortality, revealing a reality that has been there, unguessed, all the time. This occurs with some frequency in mountaineering and is exemplified by Frank Smythe's experiences in the Himalayas: "There is something about the Himalayas not possessed by the Alps, something unseen and unknown, a charm that pervades every hour spent among them, a mystery intriguing and disturbing. Confronted by them, a man loses his grasp of ordinary things, perceiving himself as immortal, an entity capable of outdistancing all change, all decay, all life, all death." (464: pp. 136–37)

Thus in sport as elsewhere there are various ways in which a sense of immortality arises—through a sense of one's invincible bodily strength, or in the awareness of being a link in a never-ending chain of being, or as part of a spiritual essence that cannot die.

UNITY

Many levels of unity are experienced in sports: a union of mind and body; a sense of oneness with one's teammates; a feeling of unity with the cosmos. An experience of inner unity is the apex of the sports experience for many athletes. Boxer Randy Neumann said of running to exhaustion: "It's an amazing sensation to feel your mind and body become a single force against . . . gravity. This is also the sensation experienced in a rare fight when you pull your whole being together and pit it against an opponent." (353: p. 91)

Patsy Neal describes the oneness that can be experienced in a moment of competition: "There seems to be a power present that allows the individual to 'walk on water,' or to create miracles in those precious moments of pure ecstasy. He runs and jumps and lives through the pure play process, which is composed of joy and pleasure and exuberance and laughter; even the pain seems completely tolerable in these few precious and rare moments of being, and of knowing that one is just that . . . a oneness and a wholeness." (350: p. 90)

Sometimes the sense of identity extends to teammates and even opponents. The latter is especially noticeable in the martial arts. A teaching manual states that when judo is practiced properly, "There will be no curtain to separate you from your opponent. You will become one with him. You and your opponent will no longer be two bodies separated physically from each other but a single entity, physically, mentally, and spiritually inseparable. Therefore the motion of your opponent may be considered your motion. And you can lure him to any posture you like and effectively apply a large force on him. You can throw him as easily as you can yourself." (508: p. 33)

Athletes also feel a sense of unity with their equipment. Jimmy Clark, one of the greatest auto racers of all time, once observed: "I don't drive a car, really. The car happens to be under me and I'm controlling it, but it's as much a part of me as I am of it." (289: p. 171) Similarly, Donald Bond, who made a study of flyers, found that they "commonly speak of the plane as if it were an extension of their own bodies." (51: p. 26)

Sometimes athletes feel at one with their environment. Theologian Matthew Fox said, "In the ecstasies of sport, we experience again our communion with nature: our bodies and whole selves are once again immersed in our origins—water, sky, earth and, because excellence is demanded of us, fire. Consider the surfer's union with the waves, the sea, the sky and wind." (153: p. 7)

In the ultimate experience of oneness, there is no longer any separation between the athlete and the universe itself. The founder of aikido, Morehei Uyeshiba, wrote: "The secret of Aikido is to harmonize ourselves with the movement of the universe and bring ourselves into accord with the universe itself. He who has gained the secret of Aikido has the universe in himself and can say, 'I am the universe. I am never defeated, however fast the enemy may attack. . . . When an enemy tries to fight with him, the universe itself, he has to break the harmony of the universe. Hence at the moment he has the mind to fight with me, he is already defeated.'" (501: p. 177)

Writer and adventurer Yukio Mishima wrote of flying an F104 at speeds of over one thousand miles per hour: "If this stillness was the ultimate end of action—of movement—then the sky about me, the clouds far below, the sea gleaming between the clouds, even the setting sun, might well be events, things, within myself. At this distance from the earth, intellectual adventure and physical adventure could join without the slightest difficulty. This was the point that I had always been striving towards." (327: pp. 1–2)

Explorer Richard Byrd, alone for months in the Arctic, living in primitive conditions at subzero temperatures, one evening knew unity with the universe:

> The day was dying, the night being born—but with great peace. Here were the imponderable processes and forces of the cosmos, harmonious and soundless. Harmony, that was it! That was what came out of the silence—a gentle rhythm, the strain of a perfect chord, the music of the spheres, perhaps.
>
> It was enough to catch that rhythm, momentarily to be part of it. In that instant I could feel no doubt of man's oneness with the universe. The conviction came that that rhythm was too orderly, too harmonious, too perfect to be a product of blind chance—that, therefore, there must be purpose in the whole and not an accidental offshoot. It was a feeling that transcended reason; that went to the heart of man's despair and found it groundless. The universe was a cosmos, not a chaos; man was as rightfully a part of that cosmos as were the day and night. (72: p. 85)

3

ALTERED PERCEPTIONS

In this chapter, we report on several kinds of altered perception that occur in sport. They range from subtle heightenings of alertness to extrasensory perceptions and the apprehension of disembodied entities. Like the feelings and sensations we described in the preceding chapter, some of these occur quite often, while others are strange and infrequent. Taken together, they resemble the range of altered perceptions reported by yogis, Zen masters, and other contemplatives.

Shifts in alertness are experienced by many athletes. These may involve a sharpening of vision or hearing, or a keener sense of interior (kinesthetic) sensations, or indeed of the whole person. Such fresh awareness can occur in the midst of vigorous action. For example, pro football's Mike Reid wrote music and played concert piano at the same time he was playing defense for the Cincinnati Bengals. He reported, "Mentally I'm more alert. I do my best work at the piano after a game." (399: p. 51) Aerobics research suggests that Reid's charged-up body could not return to his normal nonathletic state until several hours after he played a game. So his alert state at the piano comes as no surprise.

Former quarterback John Brodie once said, "Often in the heat and excitement of a game, a player's perception and coordination will improve dramatically. At times, and with increasing frequency now, I experience a kind of clarity that I've never seen adequately described in a football story." (343: p. 19)

Kathy Switzer, one of the first women to run in the Boston Marathon, said that after she took up running she discovered that "while I was running I found myself being able to think clearly. . . . I thought about my writing, my schoolwork—everything came so clear to me." (140: p. 100) She also discovered that it made her more sensuous. "When I'm training, I'm more physically sensitive to food, to weather, to touch . . . everything. . . . I also become more mentally sensitive to social problems, the ills of the world and so on. When I'm not in training, I'm more lethargic and apathetic.

"Everything I see and feel is more extreme when I'm in training. If I'm happy, I'm happier. If I'm sad, I'm sadder. If I'm emotional, I'm more emotional. I once ran thirty-one miles and after that there was nothing in the world I thought I couldn't do." (140: p. 97) Descriptions like this have been given by many joggers and runners. In fact, the clarity that Kathy Switzer describes is one of the reasons for the great popularity of the sport. This phenomenon has been confirmed by systematic research. Dorothy V. Harris, Director of the Center for Women and Sport at Pennsylvania State University, found mental alertness and clarity associated with all sports. In a systematic study she found that after vigorous exertion most people are "more alert, they can think more clearly, and are more effective mentally." (191: p. 53)

As a result of this heightened sensitivity, sport participants often report more vivid perceptions. Not only do their minds *feel* clear, but they actually *perceive* things more fully and vividly. Everything looks and feels fresh and new, as if encountered for the first time. Valentin Mankin, twice an Olympic yacht-racing champion, when asked what he focused on during a race, replied: "I try to feel the yacht with my body and watch the sea and the air with my eyes. To me every air current has a color of its own. I try to feel every wave with my feet. Like on horseback, I hold on with the tips of my toes. At the Mexico City Olympics, where I made my best showing, I saw all the air currents and made almost no mistakes. On the other hand, when I am in poor shape, the air becomes invisible." (367: p. 63)

Adam Smith tells of a diver who was skeptical about peak experiences in sport: "Then one day, in just 30 feet of water, something happened, and he said that suddenly he felt absolutely at one with the ocean, and he could *hear grains of sand on the bottom,* and he spent almost an hour listening to the grains of sand, and his life has been changed ever since." (460: p. 37) Athletes have exceptionally vivid memories of these moments of heightened sensory involvement. Pitcher Whitey Ford wrote, "You know the way Jack Nicklaus can remember every shot he took in a golf tournament? Well, I think I could tell you just about every pitch I threw in those 3,170 innings. And Mickey [Mantle] could tell you just about every pitch that was thrown to him. . . . Most guys have this total recall about the things they saw or did in ball games." (152: p. 174)

In a letter to Rhea White, a horsewoman described two rides that made her feel "god-like" because they took her "beyond the limitations of the human body—jumping fences so high and solid you can't see over or through them." On one occasion, she wrote: "Before we even took off, I knew and I'm sure the horse did too that this was special. Every step took a long time. The fences were just at the right place. . . . The horse jumped like a stag and I was in ecstasy." She notes that the special quality was not simply subjective because total strangers came up to her afterward to say they had never seen anything like it. She wrote that "for those few moments what we did was sublime."

The obvious explanation for the vividness of her memory is that it involved an outstanding event in her athletic career. It is to be expected that hitting a timely home run, or winning one's first major tournament, or running one's first marathon would be memorable. But what about the claims of Mickey Mantle and Jack Nicklaus that they remembered the major portion of *all* the events in which they participated? It appears that their experiences were memorable because of the unusual state they were in, a state of mind that apparently contributed to their outstanding performances. Could it be that some superstars are in this exceptional frame of mind much of the time? Does their exceptional mental state determine both the quality of their performance and the vividness of their recollection of it?

ALTERED PERCEPTION OF SIZE AND FIELD

Changes in spatial perception seem to happen when athletes are in an altered state of consciousness in which they perceive more details than usual. Stan Musial told Roger Kahn that he didn't guess what a pitch would be, he *knew*. Musial added, "I can always tell . . . as long as I'm concentrating." He went on to tell Kahn:

"I pick the ball up right away," he said. "Know what I mean? I see it as soon as it leaves the pitcher's hand. That's when I got to concentrate real hard. If I do, I can tell what the pitch is going to be."

"When can you tell?"

"When it's about halfway to home plate. . . . I can tell by the speed. . . . Every pitcher has a set of speeds. I mean, the curve goes one speed and the slider goes at something else. Well, if I concentrate real good, I can pick up the speed of the ball about the first 30 feet it travels. I know the pitcher and I know his speeds. When I concentrate, halfway in I know what the pitch is gonna be, how the ball is gonna move when it gets up to home plate."

Musial mentally sorts the deliveries of some 80 or 90 pitchers. Allowing four pitches to each, this means that in any given season he has classified something over 320 distinct deliveries. Then, through his great coordination and eyesight, he applies the knowledge during the three-fifths of a second it takes a typical pitch to reach him from the mound. The frequent result, professor, is what we in the trade call a clean blow. (242: pp. 15–16)

Perhaps, as Musial felt, concentration was the crucial thing, but there may have been other factors involved. For, as parapsychologists have noted, when conscious attention is centered on one thing, more subtle perceptual abilities come into play. We suggest that Musial's hitting ability may not have been due simply to heightened visual acuity but rather some intuitive factor.

Under special conditions, objects appear to be larger than they are in reality. For instance, in the 1955 U.S. Open Golf Championship, dark horse Jack Fleck came from behind to defeat Ben Hogan. In looking back on the final round, he said the turning point was the fifth hole, "after I had made four pars. I can't exactly describe it, but as I looked at the putt, the hole looked as big as a wash tub. I suddenly became convinced I couldn't miss. All I tried to do was keep the sensation by not questioning it." (359: p. 23) Other players report similar experiences; baseball players talk about how large the ball is when they're at bat, and basketball players see the hoop getting bigger and bigger.

Robert Deindorfer wrote: "At that ultimate point when the angler is totally captivated by the sensation, so hooked himself that realities around him fade, strange things can happen." He described "enlarged awareness," as in the case of angler Jim Beebe, who scanned the heavy waters of Minnesota's Lake of the Woods and described three fish his companions could not glimpse. He caught all three. Deindorfer added: "The eminent old English angler A. H. Chaytor once claimed that he frequently found he could practically call his shots with salmon. In his flow-induced vision the fish appeared closer, more detailed, almost bigger than life." (715: p. 34) At such times, Chaytor could often call correctly on which side of the jaw he would hook a salmon.

Some athletes can perceive an entire field, including all the players. Newspaperman Chris Lydon wrote of Bobby Orr: "He sees all the action on the ice and knows where everyone is going to be moments before they get there. He thinks of passes that occur to nobody else. Like Bob Cousy in his early days with the [basketball] Celtics, he hits open men who didn't realize they were open and weren't ready to receive a pass." (114: p. 62) Soccer's Pelé had a similar gift: "Intuitively, at any instant, he seemed to know the position of all the other players on the field, and to sense just what each man was going to do next." (352: p. 205) Former New York Giant Lawrence Taylor wrote that linebackers and receivers generally have this widened vision. "You get a visual on the field without having to go over everything in detail. It's like when you cut this way, you see everything in a flash, you get a picture of where everybody is, and when the ball comes you're able to stay concentrated on it—because the toughest part of being a pass catcher is mental, not physical. It's staying absolutely concentrated in traffic when your back is to the guy who wants to turn you into spare ribs. It's like that for defensive players, too. You get this speed flash on a pass play, so you automatically know that a ball is going to a certain place and what impact there's going to be afterward.

. . . Another way of thinking about this kind of 'seeing' is to imagine a dark room—you enter it blind but you somehow know if someone else is in the room." (1443: p. 35)

The startling difference between the widened perception developed by athletes and "normal" perception is described by Paul Martha of the Pittsburgh Steelers. "I always knew that a free safety is supposed to watch the quarterback and the receiver, too, but it was always difficult for me. . . . Then all of a sudden, midway through the 1967 season, I realized I was following the quarterback all the way—and the receiver, too. It just happened. It was like I had stepped into an entirely new dimension." (538: p. 161)

Although the ability to be aware of the entire field and all the players on it is partly a matter of alertness and concentration, peripheral vision also plays a role. Bob Cousy was noted for this ability. According to John Devaney, "As Cousy drove toward the foul line, his astonishing wide-angle vision would allow him to see Oftring and Kaftan on either side of him. If an opponent moved toward Cousy, zip went a pass to whoever was free, and *justlikethat* Holy Cross had scored again." (113: p. 91) Cousy himself said that he had "unusual peripheral vision. I can see more than most people out of the corners of my eyes. I don't have to turn my head to find out what's going on at either side. It sometimes appears that I'm throwing the ball without looking. I'm looking all right but out of the corners of my eyes." Joe Marcus reported that Pelé had "about twenty-five percent better peripheral vision than other athletes." (310: p. 31)

In studying brain surgery patients, California Institute of Technology scientist Dr. Colwyn Trevarthon discovered a second sight system that controls peripheral vision. Trevarthon hypothesized that this system evolved from the primitive type of visual awareness belonging to birds, reptiles, and other forms of animal life, which allows an automatic response to action in the surrounding environment. Thus, if there is unexpected movement in that space, Trevarthon explained, it "registers first through this second, more primitive system before the classical visual system becomes aware of it." (438: p. 14) Perhaps those athletes who have exceptional peripheral vision are not natively any better endowed than those who do not seem to have it. The difference may lie in the fact that they have discovered a way to allow the more primitive system to function.

Sometimes perception is altered in other unusual ways, as in the case of Hall of Fame pitcher Allie Reynolds, who told Robert Deindorfer that when he faced an especially difficult batter at a key moment, the strike zone would light up like a pinball machine. He said, "I see, I actually seem to see, a lot of little points of light, inside, outside, waist high, down around the knees, somewhere there in the strike zone. Each light represents the exact spot where I've thrown a ball to get that batter out some time before." (715: p. 166)

ALTERATIONS IN TIME PERCEPTION

During peak moments in sport, the athlete's sense of time is sometimes altered. Often it is perceived as moving more swiftly, as in the case of a chess player who said, "Time passes a hundred times faster. In this sense it resembles the dream state." (161: p. 36) Or it can be compressed into a centered moment in which there is neither before nor after. In an article on outstanding experiences in sport, Jo Ann Houts observed, "The sense of time is disoriented. A single play may seem like forever or an inning may seem like only a second. There is no conscious sense of past time or future time. The moment-to-moment passage of time is all that is relevant; in-the-moment perception is all that the player possesses." (218: p. 71)

The extraordinary moment in sport is filled with immense possibility. This is illustrated in a graphic description by football player Gary Shaw, who called it "the moment on a football field that for me soars above all others." (447: p. 234)

My life-long friend, Dee Wilson, and I frequently spent our late summer afternoons running pass patterns and playing touch football. Some days I would be quarterback and Dee the receiver, and on others it was vice versa. One September day we were playing two other friends on the otherwise empty field of a high school stadium. We were in good shape and had been playing for almost two hours. But now all of us were tired and it was getting dark, so we agreed the next play would be our last. Dee and I had been working on one pass pattern for a couple of days, and though it had been unsuccessful that afternoon, we had decided to try it again on this final play. What followed was an experience I'd never had before.

At the end of this pattern, Dee was to be about thirty yards downfield angling for the corner of the end zone. But as I dropped back and pointed my eyes toward his full strides into late afternoon, I began to feel some inexplicable postponement of time. My mind was quick and clear, yet all physical movement fell into a lingering genus of departure. With a sudden calmness, I could see the whole field and the three small figures elegantly brushing its top. As I watched their grace, I could feel the empty stands and their suspension of a lost past. This changeless spell brought an acute sense of temporariness and the feeling of inevitability fading with the dusk. Yet just as acute was the sense that this present intimately belonged to both past and future. This time and our movements were one. As I released the ball with the giving length and completeness of my arm, I could see the beginning of its easy soft arc. And it somehow seemed perfectly coordinated with the stadium, the ground, early evening and the four of us. As the ball was coming down some thirty long yards into the distance, two figures in ballet stretched into the air to meet it. In one easy motion of symmetry, Dee took the pass. . . . Then . . . he turned to me and grinned. I knew we had connected. (447: p. 234)

This slow-motion experience can be important to the outcome of a performance. According to racing car driver Jackie Stewart:

Some days you go out in a race car and everything happens in a big rush. You don't seem to have time to change gears or brake and the corners are all coming up too quickly. You're not synchronized. And thus the most important thing is to synchronize yourself with the elements that you're competing against, the motor car and the track. Your mind must take these elements and completely digest them so as to bring the whole vision into slow motion. For instance, as you arrive at the Masta you're doing a hundred and ninety-five mph. The corner can be taken at a hundred and seventy-three mph. At a hundred and ninety-five mph you should still have a very clear vision, almost in slow motion, of going through that corner—so that you have time to brake, time to line the car up, time to recognize the amount of drift, and then you've hit the apex, given it a bit of a tweak, hit the exit and are out at a hundred and seventy-three mph. Now, the good driver will do this in a calculated way such that as he gets out the other side he'll say, "Whew, I did that well." It wasn't a case of coming out and trying to catch the car and regain control. The driver who's fighting it, who doesn't have a mental picture in advance, will arrive at the corner to find that it's all happening very quickly. He's too heavy on the brake, the car is sliding too much, it's a big, deep breath in and a hope that I get around. Now this man doesn't have it. (308: pp. 180–181)

Runner Steve Williams said, "If you do a 100 right . . . that 10 seconds seems like 60. . . . Time switches to slow motion." (333: p. 34) Williams said he felt he could even control time to some extent. He recalled a race when he fell behind. Hating to lose, he said, "At my own decision, I froze those people where they were. My next recollection was being in front and through the tape." (333: p. 34)

In the most intense moments of a football game, John Brodie wrote, "Time seems to slow way down, in an uncanny way, as if everyone were moving in slow motion. It seems as if I had all the time in the world to watch the receivers run their patterns, and yet I know the defensive line is coming at me just as fast as ever. I know perfectly well how hard and fast those guys are coming and yet the whole thing seems like a movie or a dance in slow motion." (343: pp. 19–20)

The experience of time slowing down has also been noticed by spectators, implying that there may be an objective aspect to this experience. Veteran ballet reporter Herbert Saal said of the skill of Mikhail Baryshnikov: "The most exquisitely chilling weapon in the arsenal of this complete dancer was his *ballon*, his ability to ascend in the air and stay there, defying gravity, especially in the double *tour en l'air*, in which the male dancer revolves two full terms before landing. The Stuttgart Ballet's Richard Cragun can turn three times in a blur of motion. But Baryshnikov did it in slow motion. And it was unbelievable. He blasted off with the hesitation and majesty of a space-ship. He turned—once, twice—and every thread on his costume was plainly visible as he soared high above the audience like an astronaut looking back at earth." (420: p. 84)

If slowed perception is a feature of exceptional performance in sports, then most athletes would naturally want to induce it. Many golfers have recognized the importance of slow motion and have deliberately tried to swing more slowly in the interest of achieving *more power*. Bobby Jones is said to have felt it was not possible to swing a golf club too slowly. (237) This advice is given by many golfers. Dick Aultman reports that during the start of his down-swing, Jack Nicklaus's hands move more slowly than during the last part of his backswing. Aultman cites a British scientist, Dr. David Williams, who has concluded "that, all things being equal, the more leisurely the hands and arms start down, the greater the clubhead speed at impact." (19: p. 30)

Several golfers carry this advice a step further and advocate slowing the pace throughout an entire round. Larry Dennis wrote, "[Tom] Weiskopf credits last summer's [1973] streak of five vic-tories and a bunch of near misses to a decelerated pace on the golf course." (112: p. 81) And some golfers get ready for a tournament by moving slowly even when they are off the course. Cary Mid-dlecoff told a story about fellow golf pro George Knudsen who held the lead going into the final round of a tournament. Knudsen was driving Middlecoff and another pro, Fred Hawkins, to the golf course at the rate of about 16 miles per hour. When urged by his impatient passengers to hurry up, Knudsen "just looked . . . through those dark glasses and said, 'Man, this is my way to cool it. I started thinking this way last night.' " (175: p. 88) Knudsen shot a 65 that day and won the tournament.

Robert Deindorfer noted that in fishing, the rhythm an angler uses is very important. "Unless he develops the ability to slow him-self down to the proper leisurely beat, the flow conducive to the whole procedure won't be sufficient to lift confidence, concentra-tion, feedback, and other components to the levels required." (715: p. 69) Ideally, he wrote, relaxation should begin before one leaves home to go fishing.

A classic study of time distortion was made by Cooper and Erickson in 1954. (93) Working with fourteen subjects, they used hypnosis to slow down the subjects' perception of the passage of time. Under these conditions the subjects were able to accomplish more work than usual. For example, a college student who was gifted in designing clothes took ten seconds to fashion a dress while in a state of hypnotic time distortion. Later she said that to her the session seemed to last an hour. (Ordinarily, designing a dress took her several hours.)

It has been suggested that altered time perceptions as well as altered states of consciousness, such as hypnagogic imagery and creative reverie, are associated with various brainwave patterns. (Pioneer studies have been reported in this area by Barbara Brown [65] and Elmer and Alyce Green [181]). Keith Floyd speculated that time perception is related to brainwaves and that this may explain some superior athletic feats: "Having seen that time (and/or motion) goes slower the slower the brainwave rhythm, it would not be at all surprising to discover that those with superior skills —great athletes, for example—may merely be blessed with basal brainwave firing significantly slower than that of the general population." (148: p. 50)

The Backward Glance and Life Review

Among altered time perceptions in sport are brief and long-range glimpses of the past, déjà vu, and life review. Transatlantic sailor Robert Manry was awed by "the ocean's . . . enormous breadth and depth, by the ghostly presence of all the famous and infamous ships and men and women it has carried through the centuries." (307: p. 67) Los Angeles doctor Steve Seymour said, "I can blink my eyes and look out at a javelin thrower and see tens of thousands of warriors marching across the field and I can hear the voices of antiquity." (253: p. 40)

At other times, athletes experience déjà vu—the feeling that "you've been here before"—probably the most common altered state of consciousness. The Mets' Lenny Dykstra reported having a déjà vu experience in a 1986 playoff game against the Houston Astros. He wrote: "When Smith let it go, it was weird. It was like we were in a play and everyone played their part. It was like we had rehearsed it. He threw it. It was a forkball that didn't fork. I swung. It was like I had done it before and I was swinging just because it was my cue. 'OK, Lenny . . . swing.' So I swung." It was a home run. (751: p. 3)

Bob Brier, a Ph.D. in philosophy, a parapsychologist, and distance runner, described these experiences playing basketball in college:

We were playing at home and I was dribbling the ball in the left corner, near the out-of-bounds line. Suddenly I had the feeling I had been in this situation before. By *situation* I mean the crowd, my position with the ball, the man guarding me, etc. Now I had played on this court many times and realized that I had probably been in *similar* situations, but this had that special déjà vu feeling. . . . I had the feeling that I was going to take a turn-around jump shot and it was going to go in. Almost automatically and in a bit of a daze I took the shot and it went in. (This was not a shot that I normally took as I was the center and tended to stay close to the basket.) I didn't think much of the event till our next game, which was away. In the first half of the game I had the feeling again when I was in the left corner with the ball. Again I took the turn-around jumper and it went in. . . .

In all I had the feeling six times during my senior year. The third time I had it I knew I couldn't have been in that spot before because I had never played on that court. Still I had the feeling, took the turn-around jumper, and it went in. . . .

The last time I had the feeling it was at a crazy time to take the shot. I was guarded closely by a man at least four inches taller than I. Still I went up, arching the ball much higher than I normally would to clear his hands, and it went right in. My overall field goal percentage for that year was 43%, so the 100% on the six shots was considerably higher than my average. (60)

In *Sacred Summits*, mountain climber Peter Boardman described a déjà vu experience he had while climbing Mount Kangchenjunga. The experience occurred during Boardman's turn to lead while climbing the West Ridge. He wrote:

The involvement of my hands and the integration of moves that the rock demanded, *drew my mind away* from abstract thoughts. I brushed snow from holds and eased my weight from foot to foot, and *drew levitation* from the joy of the movement. I was in the shadow, and sunlight streaming from the ridge *drew me upwards,* gasping with excitement and straining against the invisible reins of thin air. . . . Light moving air touched my face and *drew my eyes to the south.* This was the point on the West Ridge which Joe Brown and George Band had reached twenty-four years before, and until now no one had been there since that expedition. . . . I was grateful to be alone for a few moments on the other side of the mountain. It was as if my insides, that had been hard, now thawed, and I felt released from the tension of the Ramp. The calm of the afternoon, the warm sun and the rough golden gneiss of the ridge *seemed to tell me that I had been there before.* The blue shapes were disturbingly familiar and were shimmering and *richly humming, like a memory.* (627a: pp. 157–58) [Italics added]

When they reached the top an hour and a half later, Boardman wrote: "We straightened up and looked around, our smiles expanding from deep inside us. . . . For a few moments I could hardly speak. For long seconds I felt overwhelmed by the happiness of pure carefree and uninterpreted emptiness." (627a: p. 158)

This is the luminous moment of mountain climbing, of any act of going beyond limits—of reaching a demanding summit outside oneself that matches an inner space in which there is pure mindlessness, the absence of abstract thinking. Boardman observed: "We had been on summits before. We had dreamed of them, for their lure endures forever and there is no escape, for summits match dreams." (627a: p. 158) The next day, he wrote, he "pondered the inevitable questions that accompany a mountaineering success. Had the mystical experience of reaching the West Ridge been no more than the result of a combination of lack of oxygen, food and water, and perhaps an excess of negative ions in the air? . . . Mountains do not reveal truth, I decided, but they encourage something to grow inside—something I was not yet able to explain fully. Our adventure had ended, and I tried to sense the birth of a new direction. . . . I was feeling ecstatic, yet did not hope to sustain this ecstasy through my life. I wanted to measure my life through contrasts, and to do that I had to return to the other life." (627a: pp. 164–65)

During special moments in sports, some athletes have seen their lives flash before them. This life review is also common at moments near death, as Raymond Moody (331) and others have shown. In his book *The Perfect Game*, Tom Seaver wrote that after his first victory in the 1969 World Series, when Rod Gaspar scored the winning run, "As Rod Gaspar's front foot stretched out and touched home plate, in the fraction of a second before I leaped out of the dugout to welcome him, my whole baseball life flashed in front of me, the perfect game I'd pitched when I was twelve years old, the grandslam home run I'd hit for the Alaska Goldpanners, the first game I'd won as a member of the New York Mets, the imperfect game I'd pitched against the Chicago Cubs, one after another, every minor miracle building toward that one magic day. I never realized before that a man's whole life could be encompassed in a single play." (440: p. 71)

Time Stopping

There are moments in sport when time seems to be arrested, only to proceed on its way as before, but not quite, leaving behind an exhilaration similar to the sense of shock experienced when the heart stops beating for a moment. Players and spectators alike refer to moments when time stops or even, as some put it, the world stops. For example, Julius Erving has said that a great dunk shot is "a time suspension." (373: p. 52) That is what Jimmy Breslin felt when watching Erving: "There were these moments when Doctor J. exploded, going up so high and his body bending and swaying so spectacularly, that he made you forget the world for an instant." (59: p. 301)

It has been observed that "there is a common experience in Tai Chi of seemingly falling through a hole in time. Awareness of the passage of time completely stops, and only when you catch yourself, after five or ten minutes, or five or ten seconds, is there the realization that for that period of time the world *stopped*." (216: pp. 180, 182) Roger Bannister's experience during his record-breaking race had this quality: "I felt that the moment of a lifetime had come. There was no pain, only a great unity of movement and aim. The world seemed to stand still, or did not exist. The only reality was the next two hundred yards of track under my feet. The tape meant finality—extinction perhaps." (30: pp. 213–14)

The sense of time stopping often occurs when one has no choice but to move forward. Gaston Rebuffat recalled an incident on one of his climbs of the Matterhorn in which he had reached a place from which he could not descend, and therefore had to climb upward. But he was on a straight rock surface that required pitons, which he did not have. Because the only holds available were tiny, he had to hoist himself up in one motion. But to do so, he wrote, one must be in "that certain uplifted mental and physical condition." (1283: p. 205) On this occasion, he was in such a state. "I was completely absorbed in my climbing. I coordinated my strictly precise movements, which seemed almost to perform themselves." (1283: p. 205)

EXTRASENSORY PERCEPTION

A "sixth sense" is attributed to certain athletes by their teammates, coaches, and opponents. This intuitive capacity is probably a composite of several sensory modalities and abilities such as timing, knowledge of the opponents' style of play, muscle memory, and subliminal perception. A number of athletes have gained reputations for this uncanny ability. Middle linebacker Ray Nitschke nominates former Cleveland Browns fullback Jim Brown as the smartest runner he ever played against. He said Brown "had a sixth sense that told him how the defense would react. Then he'd react accordingly. He was an artist—a brilliant football player who could not only beat you physically but mentally." (361: pp. 125–26)

Certain remarks that Lou Brock made about his base stealing suggest that his skill was more a matter of empathy and intuition than speed and muscle. When asked if it was a matter of surprise, Brock replied:

Not likely. How much surprise do you think I can generate when I get on first base nowadays? Maybe about as much as the sun when it rises in the East. What's really surprising is if I don't make any move at all, right? Actually, the only thing the pitcher doesn't know about me is the precise moment I'm going to go, and he knows that too, damn near.

You can surprise a rookie, maybe, but most of the time what you're doing is fishing in a very clear pool, where you can see the fish you're after and you lead him gently and patiently to the bait, and when he takes it, you yank.

You just gotta know when that is, which is the part that gets to be intuitive after a while. There's no place for it in the textbook. It's a little like knowing what an intimate friend is going to say a split-second before he said it. So you try to make that pitcher your very close buddy, by empathizing with all his moves and all his thoughts. You know at one point he has to commit himself, and then he can't go back on it. I have to too, but he has to first, and that makes a big difference. (62: p. 183)

Brock's emphasis on such mental factors as empathy and intuition and his de-emphasis of qualities such as speed and surprise raises the possibility that there may be something more involved, something not generally recognized—not only in base stealing, but in many aspects of sports. In addition to "luck," or coincidence, and picking up on subliminal sensory cues, there may be an element of extrasensory perception, or ESP, in sports. This includes the ability to obtain information about the contents of someone's mind (this form of ESP is known as telepathy), and the ability to obtain information directly from events themselves (clairvoyance). There is also ESP of the future, or precognition.

It is almost impossible to isolate ESP in the form of telepathy or clairvoyance in the sport situation, even if it is occurring, because almost all sports take place in settings where the players are within sensory range of one another; so sensory cues cannot be ruled out. In certain plays that are unusual, although some form of ESP may have occurred, it is more likely that the needed information was available through subtle sensory cues. For instance, Walt Frazier, former basketball star of the New York Knicks, praises fellow Knick Bill Bradley's passing skills, which, combined with Frazier's own ability to get the ball in the basket, led to some great plays. Frazier (1970) said that "as a game goes on, some defensive men get tired and careless. If I notice my man is watching the ball and taking his attention away from me for an instant, he's a pigeon. All of a sudden I just streak to the basket, going backdoor, and Bill hits me almost every time. Sometimes he has passed the ball before I've taken the first step. It's like telepathy. We look each other in the eye and he knows the mischief I'm thinking about." (158: pp. 162–63)

In his autobiography Bill Russell observed that something magical happened in certain games. It would usually start with three or four of the top players serving as catalysts. Then "the feeling would spread to the other guys, and we'd all levitate. . . . At that special level all sorts of odd things happened . . . It was almost as if we were playing in slow motion. . . . I could almost sense how the next play would develop and where the next shot would be taken. . . . My premonitions would be consistently correct, and I always felt then that I not only knew all the Celtics by heart but also all the opposing players, and that they all knew me. . . . These were the moments when I had chills pulsing up and down my spine." (1320: pp. 156–57)

Although something extraordinary seemed to be happening during the incidents we have described in this section, all of them occurred within a matrix of sensory factors that prevents us from saying that ESP occurred. There are other incidents, however, in which it seems more likely that telepathy or clairvoyance was involved. Flyer Jackie Cochran reports that on one occasion when her friend and fellow pilot Amelia Earhart was visiting her, they tried to see if Cochran could deliberately exercise her psychic ability.

The first night there, we heard that a passenger plane had disappeared en route from Los Angeles to Salt Lake City and Amelia asked me to try to locate it. We sat together for about two hours during which I gave names of various mountain peaks and the locations of roads and transmission lines and even of a pile of telephone poles up in the mountains near Salt Lake City. I also gave the location of the plane. Neither of us knew that area so Amelia called Paul Mantz in Los Angeles and asked him to verify names and locations on an air map and call us back. He called back with complete verification. Amelia, thoroughly excited by that time, dashed back to Los Angeles by car through the night and took off for Salt Lake in her plane at daybreak. She searched the area for three days and verified all my descriptions but found no wreckage of the transport and gave up. Next spring, when the snow on the mountain had melted, the wreckage of that plane was found within two miles of where, on the night it went down, I said it was.

A few weeks later, Amelia called me from Los Angeles with the news that a transport airliner en route to Los Angeles had gone down somewhere on the last leg of the flight. Would I try to give her the location? Within an hour, I called her back, told her exactly where the plane was, which way it was pointing down the mountainside and the condition of the occupants as between the dead, the injured and the safe. The plane was located promptly just where I said it would be; all my information proved correct. (82: pp. 88–89)

Before Amelia Earhart made her ill-fated flight, Cochran had several disturbing hunches about it. She mistrusted the navigator's ability, and supplied her friend with a bright-colored kite in case she was forced down, as well as fishhooks, lines, and a knife with blades for many uses. When Earhart made a preliminary solo flight, Cochran told her husband that one of the plane's engines had caught fire, but that it was being put out with little damage. The fire was reported later by the news media. Then the report came that Earhart's plane was missing.

With all this ability and preliminary work with Amelia, why didn't I locate her when she went down? The answer is that I did, or at least I think I did, but can never prove it one way or the other. . . . I told . . . where Amelia had gone down . . . but that Amelia was alive and the plane was floating in a certain area. I named a boat called the *Itasca* which I had never heard of at the time, as a boat that was nearby, and I also named another Japanese fishing vessel in that area, the name of which I now forget. . . . Navy planes and ships in abundance combed that area but found no trace. I followed the course of her drifting for two days. It was always in the area being well-combed. On the third day I went to the cathedral and lit candles for Amelia's soul, which I then knew had taken off on its own long flight. I was frustrated and emotionally overcome. If my strange ability was worth anything it should have saved Amelia. Only [my husband's] urging . . . ever prompted me to try my hand at this sort of thing again and he hasn't urged me for several years for he knows it upsets me. (82: p. 91)

It is likely that some sports motions such as solitary running and swimming may be conducive to ESP impressions. For example, marathoner Joan Benoit thinks she felt the passing of her Bowdoin coach, Frank Sabasteanski. He had been ill from cancer, but she felt he was "one of those people for whom you somehow expect a miracle." Benoit was doing a training run and described how she "suddenly felt hollow. I kept going, even though I had to battle for every step, thinking maybe the heavy traffic was getting me down." Shortly after she finished her run, she was notified by phone that her revered coach had died. She wrote: "It sounds spooky, but I must have felt his passing during my run. I wouldn't believe that story unless it happened to me; I'm no spirit medium, but I was close to the coach and maybe he did visit me while I was on the road." (597: p. 163)

John Fairfax, who rowed across the Atlantic, took his bearings from the planet Venus, and regarded her as his guiding "star." Near the end of the voyage he was approaching the Hogsty Reefs, and recorded this in his log:

I hope I am on course. Haven't seen any land, but it must be near. Feeling a bit wary about the Hogsty Reefs. Got a sixth sense for this sort of thing, and now something tells me I'm heading straight for them. It would be very bad luck indeed to have come so far only to pile up onto a flipping reef. . . . Come, Venus; you ought at least to come out— let me have a peep at your lovely body. No chance. I just can't get a sight, not even a single position line. Well, let's trust luck.

June 26   157th day

Near dawn and—ye gods! Saw her!—just as she was rising through a hole in the clouds. Horizon unbelievably black and low. How she managed to get through for me to see her I'll never know; but see her I did, for about two minutes, and all during that time she blinked and flashed at me like mad. Planets don't twinkle, so I knew right away there was something wrong somewhere and she was trying to warn me. Stopped rowing at once. Hit by a squall immediately after, and for two hours it was as if the sea and sky had gone mad. Lightning, thunder, rain, and the wind northeast, gusting up to Force 6 and 7. Magnificent spectacle of raw, naked fury! I felt, as never before, as if I were part of it and, deliriously happy, cursed and sang throughout it all, at the top of my voice, while *Brittania*, frightened out of her wits, screamed bloody rape. I felt full of energy suddenly, and the strength and power of the gods burned like lava in my veins. And I positively itched to grab the oars and row, row, row. But I didn't. My beloved had warned me not to and I heeded her, which probably saved my life. (139: pp. 191, 192)

This case is a good example of what Dr. Louisa E. Rhine called the "dramatic form" of ESP. (401) In such cases the percipient, instead of seeing a photographic representation of what is happening at a distance or is about to happen, sees the event dramatized in a meaningful way. In this case Venus was seen to "twinkle," thus dramatizing to Fairfax the fact that something was amiss. If he had not stopped rowing, he probably would have crashed on the Hogsty Reefs. These examples show how ESP might occur in sport. But we can never rule out coincidence, luck, and faint sensory cues, although in the Cochran and Fairfax cases it seems unlikely.

Mary Decker, who fell in the 3000 Meter race at the 1984 Olympics, was asked by an interviewer if she had visualized the race beforehand. She replied that she had seen the race and even dreamed of it for months before it took place. However, she added, "I never saw myself finishing the race." (1239: p. 67)

When drag racer Mickey Thompson, the holder of several speed records, was asked if he believed in premonitions, he replied: "When you live very close to death it doesn't take long to become devoutly superstitious about, or respectful of, the sense of odds and of the hunches that seem to help you to survive. You learn to listen to every whisper of guidance that comes out of nowhere. . . . When Athol Graham crashed I *knew* how, when and where it would happen. I tried desperately to warn him but he wouldn't hear me. I sent my son, Danny, far out of the danger zone. Then I set up my movie camera and filmed the tragedy just where I knew it would take place." (1457: p. 159)

Another sport situation in which ESP *may or may not* be involved is the "called play," in which the athlete predicts what he or she is going to do and then successfully does it. One of the best-known called plays in history was the home run hit by Babe Ruth against Charley Root of the Chicago Cubs in the 1932 World Series. In his autobiography, Ruth said he and his wife were heckled and spat upon prior to the game. He wrote:

I was so hopping mad by the time we got to our suite upstairs that I told Claire I'd fix them, somehow.

"I'll belt one where it hurts them the most," I said, without knowing just what I'd do—or how.

I guess it was while I was angry that the idea of "calling my shot" came to me. It wasn't exactly a new idea with me. I had hit a few home runs after promising to hit them, and in most of those cases I had been able to pick the very spot.

For instance, back in my early days with the Yanks, when we still played at the Polo Grounds, I teed off on one late in a tight ball game. The ball went up into the lower right field stands and hit a tall iron girder down the middle of which ran a white foul line.

I started to trot toward first base, but Billy Evans, umpiring behind the plate, called me back by yelling "Foul!"

I came back and walked up to him. "What was wrong with that?" I asked him, waving my arms and throwing my cap down to indicate to the fans that I was madder than I really was.

"It was an inch to the foul side of the line," Billy said.

"Okay," I said, stepping back into the batting box, "watch this one. It will be an inch fair."

I hit the next pitch almost exactly as I hit the first one. It went on a line into the stands and hit the same upright girder. I looked around at Billy.

"It was an inch fair," Billy said. "Go ahead."

There was a funny one in 1928, too. The Yanks were playing an exhibition game in Fort Wayne, Ind., and one of the first fans to show up at the ball park was the father of Ford Frick. He thought Ford might be traveling with us, but Ford had made other arrangements. So I fixed old man Frick up with a seat in a box behind the Yankee dugout. Even got him a cushion, for he was in his 70's then and mighty brittle-looking.

Fort Wayne gave us a lot of trouble that day. At the end of eight innings we were still tied up, and as I walked toward the plate I took a look at Mr. Frick. He looked very tired.

"I'll end it for you, Pappy," I called to him, "so you can trot home and get your nap." In the distance a long train of open cars was passing.

"See those cars, Pappy?" I yelled above the noise. "Watch."

I hit one over the right-field fence and into one of the cars which may still be traveling, for all I know. . . .

Some of these memories came back to me as I made up my mind to do something about the Cubs, and Cub fans in general, in that hotel suite in Chicago in 1932.

The Yanks and Cubs were two of the sorest ball clubs ever seen when they took the field for the third game, with George Pipgras pitching for us and Charley Root throwing for them. . . . While Root was getting ready to throw his first pitch, I pointed to the bleachers which rise out of deep center field.

Root threw one right across the gut of the plate and I let it go. But before the umpire could call it a strike—which it was—I raised my right hand, stuck out one finger and yelled, "Strike one!"

The razzing was stepped up a notch.

Root got set and threw again—another hard one through the middle. And once again I stepped back and held up my right hand and bawled, "Strike two!" It was.

You should have heard those fans then. As for the Cub players they came out on the steps of their dugout and really let me have it.

I guess the smart thing for Charley to have done on his third pitch would have been to waste one.

But he didn't, and for that I've sometimes thanked God.

While he was making up his mind to pitch to me I stepped back again and pointed my finger at those bleachers, which only caused the mob to howl that much more at me.

Root threw me a fast ball. If I had let it go, it would have been called a strike. But this was *it*. I swung from the ground with everything I had and as I hit the ball every muscle in my system, every sense I had, told me that I had never hit a better one, that as long as I lived nothing would ever feel as good as this.

I didn't have to look. But I did. That ball just went on and on and on and hit far up in the center-field bleachers in exactly the same spot I had pointed to.

To me, it was the funniest, proudest moment I had ever had in baseball. I jogged down toward first base, rounded it, looked back at the Cub bench and suddenly got convulsed with laughter. (418: pp. 191–94)

So goes Babe Ruth's version of the famous home run, many years after the event. Reviewing a number of Ruthian biographies, Roger Angell said, "The consensus of his biographers (. . . except for Mr. Sobol, who calls the whole thing an invention of Ted Husing's) is that Ruth did not point to the bleachers beforehand, but that he did hold up his fingers to count off the first two strikes and then held up one more, making his intentions unmistakable. Then he hit the homer, the longest, everyone agrees, ever struck at Wrigley Field." (12: p. 7) In other words, Ruth took two called strikes and then did predict he would hit a home run, even though the consensus of what occurred is not exactly as he recalled it in his memoirs.

A number of shots have been predicted in golf, including some amazing ones by Walter Hagen, who liked to bet on his ability to call them. In his autobiography, Hagen described an occasion when Horton Smith, the leader in the clubhouse, came out to watch and good-naturedly taunt him. Hagen said:

I figured for a moment. "I have a good chance to tie you," I told him. "I merely have to make the last three holes in six shots." I raised my voice for the gallery to hear. "Horton," I said, "I can make a 3, a 2 and a 1 to tie you."

I hit a long tee shot—long for me at least—and away we went up the hill, followed by the whole gallery. I hit my second shot to a plateau and found my ball about six feet from the hole. I gave it a quick glance, knocked it in and turned to the gallery. "Well, there is my 3. Now for a 2."

I hit a five-iron on the seventeenth about twenty feet from the hole. I could scarcely see the hole, for it was getting quite dark. I looked over the green, gave the ball a rap and to my surprise it holed.

"There you are," I said casually. "Now for a hole in one!"

I ran to the eighteenth tee, pulled out my two-iron, then had to wait while gallery fans were chased off the fairway. The hole was approximately 190 yards. Now about all I could see in the distance was the club house. I aimed for that hoot in the grill. I hit the ball well and a very loud cheer went up. I thought I had made it. Instead I had hit the flag gently and stopped about six inches away. The 2 gave me a second place. (187: p. 203–04)

Golfer Joe Ezar is said to have predicted an entire round. The president of Fiat Motor Company told him he would give him five thousand lire if he shot a 66, or ten thousand lire for a round of 65. Instead, Ezar asked how about a 64. For a 64 he was promised forty thousand lire. Ezar then wrote on a scorecard what he would shoot on each hole to get a 64, ending with a birdie on 18. His playing partner, British golfing great and three-time winner of the British Open Henry Cotton, told him he was crazy. Ezar retired to the bar where he put in a good night, waking the next day protesting he was too hung over to play. His caddie, who had a bet on the day's round, put him in a cold shower and got him to the first tee. Cotton advised him to drop the whole thing. He considered it an impossible feat, tantamount to asking for eighteen miracles in a row. But Ezar scored as predicted for the first eight holes. He then got a 4 instead of the predicted 3 on the ninth, but countered by a 3 in place of a predicted 4 on the 10th. On each of the remaining eight holes he again scored as predicted, ending with a 64. Cotton said, "You could call that round the biggest fluke of all time. . . . He had all the luck in the world, chipping in and holing impossible putts, but the figures came out just as Joe had predicted." (119: p. 67)

Canadian Olympic figure skater Kim Alletson dreamed in advance about the way she would qualify for the Olympics by her show in the Canadian Championships. About three days before she skated, she got a message in a dream that she "placed a low fifth in figures but somehow everything worked out all right and I pulled up to second and made the Olympic team." At the actual event, when she placed fifth in figures she wasn't very concerned because, as she wrote, "I knew already how everything would end up. And it did!" (1206: p. 128) Hale Irwin, the improbable winner of his third U.S. Open Golf tournament at age forty-five—the oldest ever to win that prestigious event—dreamed he would win it two weeks earlier. This is corroborated by his wife, with whom he shared the premonition. (1524: p. 6)

Johnny Bench recalled a World Series fifth game with both teams tied. He claimed that from the third inning he had the feeling he was going to hit a home run. When he led off the bottom of the ninth, he told one of the other players on his way to the on-deck circle, "not," he added, "in some crazy Little-League fantasy, but matter-of-fact" (p. 106). He hit a home run. (593: p. 106)

British trout fisherman Hugh Falkus described one of the mystical aspects of his sport that other anglers have noted. His concentration at times became "so intense that he often . . . *knows* he is going to catch a fish before it happens. According to him, these experiences customarily unfold after quiet periods when nothing has stirred. There is a sudden tingling of the senses, a lift in the spirit, a vague feeling that he will now hook a fish." Robert Deindorfer noted that although Falkus considered coincidence as the explanation, "he feels these eerie moments have occurred too often and for too many years for that. He feels it is triggered by a concentration so total that it stretches instincts and perceptions beyond the frontiers of everyday experience." (715: p. 156)

Wayne Gretzky, who suggested he be called "The Grateful One," wrote: "I don't get many premonitions, but when I do, I believe in them. When you've been as lucky as me your whole life, you pay attention to stuff like that." (860: pp. 61–62) In 1981, when he had had forty-five goals in thirty-eight games, the possibility of fifty goals in less than fifty games was very close. One night, Gretzky recalled, while driving to a home game with Philadelphia with winger Pat Hughes, "I suddenly got the strangest feeling. 'Geez, Pat, I feel weird,' I said. 'I might get a couple tonight.' " "That night," as he described it, "turned out to be one of the greatest of my life. It was almost eerie the way things happened." (860: p. 62) For example, he took a rebound off the back boards and shot it wide. The puck bounced off the goalie's leg for his first goal. He soon had three more. After cooling off in the last ten minutes of the game, he slapped home the fifth goal of the night and the fifty in thirty-nine games, with three seconds to go. He had the record.

Joe Namath predicted that the Jets would beat Baltimore in the 1968 Super Bowl. One of his teammates, Randy Rasmussen, said: "At the time I thought, jeez, Joe, just keep your mouth shut. But before I knew it I'd reexamined what was going on—everybody had—and we realized we all felt the same way. We'd seen the films, we *knew* we could win. Joe just said it, was all. And the thing is, the papers played it up like he was wisecracking. But he was serious as can be." (486: p. 82)

This is a good example of self-fulfilling prophecy in sport. Namath's prediction, based on his own confidence, fired the confidence of his teammates, and this put them in the supercharged state that enabled them to win. It can also happen that one player can fuel the confidence of a teammate, thereby causing a prophecy to be fulfilled. This may have happened in the 1990 NBA finals between the Pistons and the Blazers. Curtis Bunn reported that Piston Bill Lambeer had a premonition that Vinnie Johnson would win the game for Detroit. He told Johnson so at half-time, when Johnson was feeling a little down. He kept telling Johnson he was going to make big plays and score the winning shot. Johnson went out and scored 15 of his 16 points in the last period, including the winning fourteen-footer with seven tenths of a second left. The Pistons had been down by 7 in the final 2:07, but they scored the last 9 points, 7 of them by Johnson. (656: 159)

All these examples could be instances of fierce conviction and self-fulfilling prophecy. But what about true precognition? What happens when there are no sensory cues, when there is no self-fulfilling prophecy? Do some athletes have the ability to predict events before they happen? Racing car driver A. J. Foyt has had more than one hunch that proved to be correct. Bill Libby wrote that "going to Riverside to race stock cars the day after his thirtieth birthday in January, 1965, A. J. Foyt had a premonition of impending danger. He recalls, 'Usually I like to run there, but that one time I just didn't want to go. Before I left the airport, I called Lucy and told her where I'd parked the car and where to find the keys. That's something I'd never done before.'" (286: p. 133) During the race he went over a thirty-five-foot embankment in the worst accident of his long career.

Foyt also had a premonition involving the 1967 Indianapolis 500 when he predicted that Andy Granatelli's jet car, driven by Parnelli Jones, would not complete the race. He said, "I knew dead certain inside me that the jet car was going to break." (286: p. 86) In practice the new turbocar had awed all the other racers. Bill Libby wrote, "Few realized that the car had problems, but Foyt guessed it. He figured the gearbox would go. He said it before anyone else said it, before the car had qualified. . . . 'It won't last half the race,' he said. . . . 'It will take time to develop it. Its time may come, but it's my time now. I feel like I'm gonna win this race.'" (286: p. 160) Foyt did win the race, and the turbocar failed to finish because of mechanical troubles.

One of the most dramatic examples of what may be precognition in sport happened in the case of Wayne Estes, who was the second-leading college basketball scorer in 1965. Early in his last game, against Denver, Estes asked the coach to remove him from the game because he had lost his touch: In fact, he had no feeling in his hands. The coach refused, telling him the baskets would start to drop if he kept shooting. He was right. At halftime Estes had scored 24 points. But his hands still felt numb. He scored another 24 in the second half, and set a new single-game scoring record for Utah State's Nelson Fieldhouse. When a trainer pricked Estes' finger with a pin after the game, Estes did not react normally: the strange numbness was attributed to his being keyed up, but it was suggested he have a thorough examination if it didn't go away in a few days.

On the way home from the game, Estes and some friends passed a car accident and stopped to see if they could be of assistance. An ambulance had already arrived, however, and there was nothing they could do. Walking back to the car, "a sagging wire from a bent telephone pole was swaying overhead, its lowest point almost six and a half feet from the ground. His friends passed under it. Estes' forehead brushed the live wire. Several thousand watts of electricity shot through his body, killing him. 'Wayne's hands started to smoke, and he fell to the ground,' John Vasey, one of Estes' companions, said later." (252: p. 26) Could it be that the numbness and tingling in his hands that Estes experienced during the game was a symbolic precognition of the manner in which he was to meet his death a few hours later? In fact, two months before his death, Estes had bought a $10,000 life insurance policy—but only after asking "whether the triple-indemnity clause for accidental death applied to death by electrocution." (252: p. 26)

Perhaps the most common way an athlete foresees the future is in a dream. This is also true of precognitive experiences in the general population. (400) In his autobiography, Sugar Ray Robinson describes a nightmare he had the night before he fought Jimmy Doyle for the welterweight championship: "In the dream, Jimmy Doyle was in the ring with me. I hit him a few good punches and he was on his back, his blank eyes staring up at me, and I was staring down at him, not knowing what to do, and the referee was moving in to count to ten and Doyle still wasn't moving a muscle and in the crowd I could hear people yelling, 'He's dead, he's dead,' and I didn't know what to do. Then I woke up." (410: p. 140) In another account of the fight, he said: "I got up the next day and I called the fight off. I called the commission and everybody and I said I'm not fighting. They said, Ray, it's just a dream. I said, no, I've had premonitions before, and I'm just not going to do it. They called in all the priests, Catholic priests, and Protestant, got them to talk to me and everything, and I said all right. They talked me into going through with the fight. I went through with the fight, like I had said, knocked him out. He died right there in the ring. Boy, what a feeling I had. I felt like it was premeditated and I knew about it and still went ahead and did it. But it happened. . . . I've had other experiences like that. . . . I get . . . premonitions. If I get one now, I won't do it." (198: pp. 278–79)

A. J. Foyt, who had the premonitory experiences involving the 1967 Indianapolis 500 already described, also had a precognitive dream about that race. The race had been called partway through because of rain. Parnelli Jones, driving the turbocar, was leading by twelve seconds. Bill Libby wrote: "That night Foyt slept fitfully. He was disturbed. He had a sort of vision in which he was leading on the last lap when a smashup took place in front of him and he had to brake to beat it." (286: p. 162) When the race resumed, Jones in the turbocar led all the way until the 197th lap, when the jet car lost its power with only ten miles to go. Foyt drove on, well out in front with two laps left. Nothing, save an accident or mechanical failure could keep him from winning. Libby wrote: "He came through the next-to-last lap and into the last lap and around and into the last turn. All the while his mind was working hard and he thought about an accident and he slowed sharply.

" 'It was as though I had a premonition,' Foyt said later. 'I had dreamed about it, and then I came around the last corner and there it was! If I hadn't already slowed down, there is no way I could have gotten through it.' " (286: p. 163) Thus prepared by his vision or dream, he won his third Indianapolis 500.

Sometimes relatives, coaches, or other persons have precognitive experiences involving athletes they are close to. Miler John Walker said of his grandmother: "Sometimes it is almost as if we were one person. . . . She's so psychic you wouldn't believe it. She doesn't talk in terms of 'me' and 'you' when we're communicating—we are jointly 'us' to her." (509: p. 9) At the Montreal Olympics, after Walker had failed to win the 800 meters run, but a day before he was to win the 1500 meters, he received the following letter from his grandmother: "Don't worry about the 800 meters—I see us on the victory dais later in the Games. I hear the crowd cheering us. I see us running the lap of honor. We will triumph, we will win the 1500 meters gold medal." (509: p. 9)

Willie Shoemaker tells of a dream Ralph Lowe, owner of the horse Shoemaker was to ride in the 1957 Kentucky Derby, had about "his rider standing up and misjudging the finish in the 1957 Kentucky Derby." (452: p. 58) Lowe told Shoemaker the dream the Friday night before the race. Shoemaker assured him it would not happen. But it did. Runner Jim Ryun fell in the Munich Olympics, where he finished last. His wife reported that she dreamed about the fiasco in advance. "I had a dream that night before the race, and in my dream, Jim fell down. I didn't warn him because

I thought it would upset him. I've often wondered if I should have . . . if it would have made a difference." (376: p. 265)

In reviewing these cases, it appears that when the usual sensory channels are blocked, athletes sometimes use a more subtle sense or even ESP. It is possible that blockage of sensory abilities triggers psi capacities. Bob Banner (29) described a group that deliberately used physical exercises, especially basketball skills, to develop psychic abilities. They observed that in order to activate "extraphysical powers," they first had to master physical skills; then, at key moments, something else occasionally took over.

Physicist Joseph H. Rush introduced the term *psi enhancement* for a complementary relationship between normal sensori-motor functioning and the operation of some form of psi. He suggested that psi enhancement might be present in sport, providing that "extra edge of precise muscular control in a fast game." (415: p. 42) He hypothesized that psi enhancement tends to operate when the usual sensori-motor skills are frustrated or blocked, which seems to be the case in some of the preceding examples. The fact that athletes use the term *sixth sense,* a synonym for ESP, lends credence to this possibility.

OUT-OF-BODY EXPERIENCES

As noted in Chapter 2, athletes describe moments of feeling detached from the swirl of events or in which they seemed to be "floating" or "flying." In other, more extreme accounts, athletes say they were literally out of their bodies. Parapsychologists have established that some people can both "see" events happening at a distance as if they were actually there and "see" their own bodies as if from a point outside themselves. Even if this feeling is illusory, it remains a vivid experience. Moreover, objective information about the world outside is sometimes obtained in this state. For overviews of out-of-body experiences (OBEs), see Blackmore (621), Gabbard and Twemlow (820), Irwin (938), Mitchell (1143), and Rogo (1309). The latter describes methods of inducing OBEs that are very similar to those used in sports, such as relaxation, dietary control, breathing, yoga, visualization, and guided imagery.

A rock climber doing a solo climb recalled that "About 15 or

20 feet above the ground, I slipped and fell. . . . Objectively, the height wasn't great, but I think that I was very frightened of the coming pain or death, and for a moment abandoned the idea of living. As I fell, I seemed to be about 5 or 10 feet out from the rock face, looking at my body falling (in contact with the face). I vaguely recollect wondering if I could investigate this odd sensation by moving around to the other side of my body to look at it. Once I hit the ground, I was immediately preoccupied with my pain." (180: p. 25)

British geologist Robert Crookall made a lifelong study of out-of-body experiences. He published hundreds of cases, among them the following experience of Robert Kyle Beggs:

From my present perspective of more than twenty years I look back with awe upon the moment in July, 1929, when I drowned.

It was one of those grey, windy, rainy days. . . . Mildred Johnson, an excellent swimmer, and I had gone out a little way to ride the breakers, when I became aware of the murderous undertow. I was just about to call to Mildred that I was going back to shore when, over the sound of the waves, I heard a faint cry for help.

As I rode a high wave I saw a small boy desperately clinging to a piece of board. I shouted to Mildred to get help. . . . I managed to boost the frightened youngster up onto the small piece of board.

Suddenly a mountainous wave broke over me. I went down, down, down into the quiet depths. I was so tired that I did not care. I felt peace settle over me. Well, I thought, I had tried, and I was so very tired. It seemed then that a wonderful transition occurred. *I was no longer in the water but rather I was high above the water looking down upon it. The sky, that had been so grey and lowering, was iridescent with indescribable beauty. There was music that I seemed to feel rather than hear. Waves of ecstatic and delicate color vibrated around me and lulled me to a sense of peace beyond comprehension.*

In the water beneath me, a boat came into view, with two men and a girl in it. The girl was Mildred. Then I saw a blob of something floating in the water. A wave tossed it and rolled it over. *I found myself looking into my own distorted face. What a relief, I thought, that that ungainly thing was no longer needed by me.* Then men lifted the form into the boat, and—my vision faded.

The next thing I knew, it was dark and I was lying in the beach cold and sick and sore. Men were working over me. I was told later that they worked over me for more than two hours. I was given credit for saving a youngster's life. (99: pp. 11–12)

In a book about out-of-body experience, Herbert Greenhouse wrote: "A well-known long-distance swimmer . . . who prefers to be anonymous, [said] that whenever his physical body is exhausted during a marathon competition, he relaxes it by floating overhead in his double while continuing to swim. When he reenters his body, he feels refreshed and can go on for quite a while without fatigue. The man added that athletes in other sports also go out-of-body during competition, but they don't talk about it." (182: p. 339)

Charles Lindbergh described an experience which bears considerable resemblance to an out-of-body experience. During his solo flight across the Atlantic, he wrote: "For unmeasurable periods, I seem divorced from my body, as though I were an awareness spreading out through space, over the earth and into the heavens, unhampered by time or substance, free from the gravitation that binds men to heavy human problems of the world. My body requires no attention. It's not hungry. It's neither warm nor cold. It's resigned to being left undisturbed. Why have I troubled to bring it here? I might better have left it back at Long Island or St. Louis, while this weightless element that has lived within it flashes through the skies and views the planet. This essential consciousness needs no body for its travels. It needs no plane, no engine, no instruments, only the release from flesh which the circumstances I've gone through make possible." (293: pp. 352–53)

There is a substantial literature on out-of-body experiences, and the phenomenon has been studied by parapsychologists since the 1880s. It is beyond the scope of this book to summarize all the evidence for it, but further sources of information are listed in the bibliography. (See especially 99, 100, 101, 180, and 330)

AWARENESS OF THE "OTHER"

Sometimes, especially in arduous and solitary sports that tax mind and body to their limits, the athlete becomes aware of some "other"—a sense of divine presence, a source of strength outside the self, a nebulous figure, or a recognizable apparition. The athlete may even carry on a conversation with this presence or may be guided or aided by it. Explorers, sailors, and mountaineers are particularly prone to these visitations.

Phantom presences are encountered with some frequency by sailors at sea, especially when they are alone. Joshua Slocum, during his single-handed voyage around the world in the 1890s, suffered from food poisoning, became delirious, and could no longer man his sloop. When he came to his senses, the boat was plunging through a heavy sea. To his amazement he saw a foreign sailor at the helm. The phantom doffed his cap and identified himself as a member of Columbus's crew. "Lie quiet, senor Captain, and I will guide your ship tonight," the vision said. Slocum slept through the entire night, and awakened to find that his boat had covered ninety miles while holding a true course for the twenty-four hours he had been incapacitated. Feeling better, he spread his wet clothes in the sun and again fell asleep. "Then who should visit me again but my old friend of the night before, this time, in a dream. 'You did well last night to take my advice,' said he, 'and if you would, I should like to be with you often on the voyage, for the love of adventure alone.' . . . I awoke much refreshed, and with the feeling that I had been in the presence of a friend and a seaman of vast experience." (456: p. 42)

Charles Lindbergh, in his flight across the Atlantic, encountered some strange visitants: "These phantoms speak with human voices—friendly, vapor-like shapes, without substance, able to vanish or appear at will, to pass in and out through the walls of the fuselage as though no walls were there. Now, many are crowded behind me. Now, only a few remain. First one and then another presses forward to my shoulder to speak above the engine's noise, and then draws back among the group behind. At times, voices come out of the air itself, clear yet far away, traveling through distances that can't be measured by the scale of human miles; familiar voices, conversing and advising on my flight, discussing problems of my navigation, reassuring me, giving me messages of importance unattainable in ordinary life." (293: p. 389)

Sometimes the sense of presence is personified, yet remains vague and unidentifiable. One such encounter occurred during Sir Ernest Henry Shackleton's exploration of the South Pole in 1916. The following is taken from his memoirs of the trip: "When I look back at those days I have no doubt that Providence guided us, not only across those snowfields, but across the storm white sea that separated Elephant Island from our landing-place on South Georgia. I know that during that long and racking march of thirty-six hours over the unnamed mountains and glaciers of South Georgia it seemed to me often that we were four, not three. I said nothing to my companions on the point, but afterwards Worsley said to me, 'Boss, I had a curious feeling on the march that there was another person with us.' Crean confessed to the same idea. One feels 'the dearth of human words, the roughness of mortal speech' in trying to describe things intangible, but a record of our journeys would be incomplete without a reference to a subject very near to our hearts." (445: p. 211)

Shackleton's impression was shared by F. A. Worsley, who wrote: "While writing this seven years after (almost), each step of that journey comes back clearly, and even now I again find myself counting our party—Shackleton, Crean, and I and—who was the other? Of course, there were only three, but it is strange that in mentally reviewing the crossing we should always think of a fourth, and then correct ourselves." (534: p. 197) Frank Smythe, while climbing Everest in 1933, had a similar experience: "All the time that I was climbing alone, I had the feeling that there was someone with me. I felt also that were I to slip I should be held up and supported as though I had a companion above me with a rope. Sir Ernest Shackleton had the same experience when crossing the mountains of South Georgia after his hazardous open-boat journey from Elephant Island, and he narrates how he and his companions felt that there was an extra 'someone' in the party. When I reached the ledge I felt I ought to eat something in order to keep up my strength. All I had brought with me was a slab of Kendal mint cake. This I took out of my pocket and, carefully dividing it into two halves, turned round with one half in my hand to offer my 'companion.' " (499: p. 234)

The 1975 British conquest of Everest is renowned for its dramatic examples of these helpful companions. Climbers Doug Scott and Nick Estcourt both said they saw or sensed phantom climbers. Chris Bonington, the expedition leader, wrote: "Scott states that while tackling the very dangerous ridge of ice cornices he felt as if they were accompanied by another person who guided them by some sort of mental speech and warned them where the cornices, etc., were dangerous. He wrote, 'I had a mental chat with it . . . seemed like an extension of my mind outside my head. In the bivouac at 28,700 feet, on our way down from the summit, I also felt this presence, same sort of thing replied to it—it to me. Seemed quite rational then . . . a bit queer now.' " (54: p. 320)

Nick Estcourt described a similar experience, though he was not climbing with Scott. It happened early in the morning as he delivered an oxygen bottle from Camp 4 to Camp 5:

I set off on my own at about 3:30 in the morning, pulling up the fixed ropes leading up to Camp 5. . . . I was about two hundred feet above the camp when I turned around. I can't remember why, but perhaps I had a feeling that someone was following me. Anyway, I turned round and saw this figure behind me. He looked like an ordinary climber, far enough behind so that I could not feel him moving up the fixed rope, but not all that far below. I could see his arms and legs and assumed that it was someone trying to catch me up.

I stopped and waited for him. He then seemed to stop or to be moving very, very slowly; he made no effort to signal or wave; I shouted down, but got no reply, and so in the end I thought, "Sod it, I might as well press on." I wondered if perhaps it was Ang Phurba coming through from Camp 2, hoping to surprise us all by being at Camp 5 when we arrived that morning.

I carried on and turned around three or four times between there and the old site of Camp 4 . . . and this figure was still behind me. It was definitely a human figure with arms and legs, and at one stage I can remember seeing him behind a slight undulation in the slope, from the waist upwards as you would expect, with the lower part of his body hidden in the slight dip. . . .

I turned round again as I reached the old site of Camp 4, and there was no one there at all. It seemed very eerie; I wasn't sure if anyone had fallen off or what; he couldn't possibly have had time to have turned back and drop back down the ropes out of sight, since I could see almost all the way back to Camp 4. (54: pp. 176–77)

These two incidents, occurring as they did at different times and to different people during the 1975 Everest expedition, were given an even more bizarre twist. C. J. Williamson, writing in the *Journal of the Society for Psychical Research*, claimed that after a friend of his died he tried to contact him by means of automatic writing. He began to receive messages purporting to come from his deceased friend, who had been a radio operator. Many of the messages Williamson received could be verified, but he could also see that some of his own memories or thoughts could have been their source. He therefore devised a "test" for his friend, asking for information that presumably was not known to any living person. In 1974 he asked for the details of the Everest expedition of 1924, in which Mallory and Irvine disappeared. He got back several details about the expedition, including the information that the two climbers had reached the summit before they disappeared. Williamson's friend also mentioned the upcoming 1975 British expedition. Williamson wrote, "There were hints coming through . . . that something psychic was being planned to happen on the mountain during the British 1975 expedition." (523: p. 318) He immediately wrote to Chris Bonington, the leader of the expedition, asking him to make special note of anything strange that might happen to any member of the party. Then Williamson got another communication from his friend: "Finally I got a 'message' I thought of such importance that, on January 17th 1975, I lodged it in a sealed envelope with the Bank of Scotland Ltd., Lerwick, for safe keeping. This letter lay there untouched until, after the expedition had returned home again, I heard through the Press and

T.V. that something really strange had indeed been experienced by some of the climbers." (523: p. 318)

Williamson contacted the president of the Society for Psychical Research, John Beloff of the Psychology Department, Edinburgh University, asking him to open the sealed message and compare its contents with what had been reported on the 1975 expedition. Beloff did so, in the presence of a witness, and read the following message that Williamson had received through automatic writing. It went as follows: "Everest again. I know that you want to reveal to the world the survival of Mallory and Irvine. I read your thoughts and letters weeks ago. You don't have to speak or write you know. Andrew Irvine is always compliable. They will wait he says. He speaks of Smythe. Everything possible they will do to lead them or save them if need be. Bonington is cooperative—he will not be disappointed even should they not reach the summit. They will come back with better news than that. On the mountain they will see others, not of their own party, others who simply could not be there in the physical body. He will tell you all when they arrive back. Will they reach the summit you ask? Weather will be difficult and ice crevasses. Disaster to some but Bonington will come back safely. Hastie or is it Haston will be in very great danger and I doubt and trust for his safety." (523: p. 319)

The message was accurate in a number of details, but they *did* reach the summit in spite of bad weather conditions. Bonington came back safely, but one member of the expedition died. Another member, Dougal Haston, was one of the first to reach the summit, climbing with Doug Scott. On the way down they were overtaken by darkness and were forced to spend the night in the highest bivouac yet attempted, at 28,700 feet, without oxygen. Haston's life was in danger, but he survived.

Bonington rejected the possibility that Estcourt hallucinated the figure because he wasn't acclimatized to the altitude. He suggested instead that Estcourt had a psychic experience related either to the death of a member of the expedition that was to take place later that day, or to a past tragedy: Estcourt was near the spot where a Sherpa "who had worked very closely with Nick in the autumn of 1972 had perished in an avalanche in the autumn of 1973." (54: p. 177) Williamson discounted lack of oxygen and the altitude, observing that Everest had often been climbed with and without oxygen but with no reports of strange encounters except for this 1975 expedition, as had been predicted in the communication he received from his friend. After all the explanations were considered, the startling fact remained that Williamson's message, received through automatic writing, did successfully predict that "on the mountain they will see others, not of their own party."*

The same Dougal Haston (195) who took part in the 1975 Everest expedition described what may have been an apparition in his autobiography (published prior to the 1975 expedition). Climbing in the Alps, he and his companion spent the night in an empty climbers' hut. About 2 a.m. he was jerked awake by noises. He heard footsteps walking around in the room above and then descending the stairs. The door latch was rattled but not opened. Next he heard footsteps going up the stairs, followed by silence. In the morning he said nothing, but his companion mentioned that he had heard the sounds, so Haston knew he hadn't been dreaming. Together they combed the hut, but found nothing. Because of bad weather they had to spend a second night in the hut, and at 2 a.m., heard the same sounds once more. They got up and checked the corridor, finding nothing, but they didn't feel up to tackling the floor above. The following day, Haston was flipping through the climbs book and found a note in it concerning the death of the hut's guardian in an avalanche.

* See Sherrard (1380) for a discussion of alternative explanations. Psychologists Peter Suedfeld and Jane Mocellin reviewed the literature of "the 'sensed presence' in unusual environments." They used Jayne's (952) bicameral mind theory to describe it but admit that the etiology of such experience has not been adequately established. They argue that these experiences are not pathological but should be "added to . . . the recognized range of normal coping behaviors in certain unusual situations" (1430: p. 49). Izzard (941) and Ross (1314), as well as Suedfeld and Mocellin (1430) have examined the spirit or vision quest as a "sensed presence" environment. (See also 806) James Logan linked play and ordeal experiences through the concept of "flow," citing Lindbergh's transatlantic flight, solitary confinement, polar explorers, and prisoners of war. He quoted Solzhenitsyn: "Sometimes, while standing in a column of dejected prisoners, amidst the shouts of guards with machine guns, I felt such a rush of rhymes and images that I seemed to be wafted overhead. . . . At such moments I was both free and happy." (1062: p. 88) Logan observed that what all these experiences have in common is extraordinary focus accompanied by loss of a separate sense of self and merging with the environment.

In the 1972 single-handed Transatlantic yacht race, a number of hallucinations and illusions were experienced, some of them premonitions. Glin Bennet (43), who reported on the event, stresses the harmful effects of fatigue and prolonged exposure to the elements. He points out that sensory deprivation often leads to disturbances in perception and thinking. Bennet's warnings are sound, but he tells only one side, the distressful side, of what happens through stress and overexposure. Even if phantom figures perceived by explorers, mountaineers, and sailors are hallucinatory projections, they often guide the person who sees them like dreams that guide the dreamer. They sometimes act as a source of strength and insight not available to the conscious mind. While the mariner or mountaineer is unconscious, ill, or otherwise unable to cope, these figures personify inner resources that the beleaguered person cannot summon in the ordinary way.

Extraordinary conditions call forth extraordinary capabilities. What does it matter if the aid seemingly comes from "outside"? The important point is that the aid is forthcoming. If it cannot be consciously summoned, then it often breaks through from our unconscious depths. It is as if, as has been said, there is a friend behind the phenomena. A number of explorers testify to some such reality. Adventurer Wilfred Noyce (215), explaining what it is that draws some of us to the heights and depths and lonely places of the globe, said, "We go out because it is in our nature to go out, to climb the mountains and sail the seas, to fly to the planets and plunge into the depths of the oceans. By doing these things we touch something outside or behind, which strangely seems to approve our doing them." (215: p. 153) This distancing of oneself from one's daily life and the finding of a wider self beyond is described by a mountain climber who wrote psychologist James Lester: "As I climb I begin losing contact, in a physical sense, with the world below my feet, and begin to feel wafted into an ethereal 'space.' . . . The real world becomes the world above and beyond what I touch, smell, taste, feel, and see. I feel an extremely intimate oneness with the universe and all physical aspects vanish. . . . It seems that the world is all turned around and the most unreal is reality. . . . (1043: p. 38)

The altered states of perception experienced by athletes indicate that there are ways of perceiving ourselves, each other, and our world that can enable us to extend our boundaries. We can go beyond our limits, and experience a rewarding oneness both within and without. "Thou art That," the Indian sages teach. In sports, the Beyond that is within can begin to perceive its oneness with the Beyond that is without.

4

EXTRAORDINARY
FEATS

One night Bobby Orr of the Boston Bruins "took a pass from goalie Cheevers and detonated a ninety-foot shot that was so fast —despite its distance—that Detroit goalie Roger Crozier stood dumbfounded as it went by. Cheevers, who has never received a point in his career, was awarded an assist on the play. 'It's easy,' the goalie explained, 'to get an assist with Orr.' " (146: p. 7)

The literature of sport is filled with examples like this of outstanding performances turned in by a single player. For example, Julius Erving of the Philadelphia 76ers once brought his team from a 24-point deficit at the beginning of the last quarter to a victory in the final second. A reporter wrote: "It was pure magic and Philadelphia fans went nuts. This was no longer basketball, but a kind of religious exercise with Erving as shaman." (507: p. 108) In an All-Star game, Erving "stole the show with a single play, a play that had to be seen to be believed. It can best be described in words as a dunk that started near the foul line and somehow ended with Julius whipping the ball around his head and into the basket. The crowd came to its feet in disbelief, and the stomping and cheering and sounds of sheer amazement rocked the arena. The NBA Milwaukee Bucks' Oscar Robertson, who had been guarding Julius, took some time to recover from his utter bewilderment at the play. Fans who witnessed it still talk about it." (194: p. 84)

Michael Jordan, of course, often brought crowds to their feet. His ability to make clutch shots while the game was on the line was legendary. He called this ability the "extra gear," and explained that "to play better basketball I realized that I could get myself into a certain mood at certain times. It just kicked in, like a fourth gear." (1015: p. 53)

Sometimes an outstanding performance is turned in by an entire team, such as the New York Giants of 1951, who came from behind in the closing weeks of the season to win the National League pennant from their arch rivals, the Brooklyn Dodgers. Over that period of time, many extraordinary plays were made by the team, and these were climaxed by Bobby Thompson's famous home run, "the shot heard round the world." When it was over, sportswriter Red Smith wrote: "There is no way to tell it. The art of fiction is dead. Reality has strangled invention." (249: p. 150) Thomas Kiernan wrote a book about the Giants' march to victory called *The Miracle at Coogan's Bluff*, in which he insisted: "At the time Red Smith was right. There was no way to tell the story of that season and its monumental climax. People were too close to it—the players, the writers, the fans, everyone. It unfolded too quickly, too abstractly for human perception." (249: p. 150)

Throughout his book, Kiernan questions the members of the team, trying to search out the "Question"—namely, whether or not "some kind of extraterrestrial energy . . . took over the club and made it perform feats that were beyond its ordinary human capabilities." (249: p. 235) We propose that there *are* moments in sport when players tap levels of ability beyond the normal range of human accomplishment. Deep in our Western tradition is the feeling that athletes can be superhuman. "To the Greeks, the gods were athletic; then athletes must try to be godlike." (188: p. 365) Certain sport feats seem to break through into another order of existence.

EXCEPTIONAL ENERGY

The ability to call up extraordinary reserves of energy is a key to outstanding athletic performance. Jose Torres, in his book on Muhammad Ali, said of the turning point in the second Frazier fight: "He [Ali] is using those mysterious forces. I can't explain it any other way." (495: p. 212) This sense of exceptional energy is not confined to individuals. John Brodie, of the San Francisco 49ers, described "times when an entire team will leap up a few notches. Then you feel that tremendous rush of energy across the field." Brodie did not claim there is anything unusual or mystical about this. "When you have eleven men who know each other very well and have every ounce of their attention—and intention—focused on a common goal, and all their energy flowing in the same direction, this creates a very special concentration of power. Everyone feels it. The people in the stands always feel and respond to it, whether they have a name for it or not." (63: pp. 151–52)

Speed skater Barbara Lockhart's most memorable race was in a 3000-meter event, in which ordinarily one conserves energy. On this occasion, however, her skating was effortless. She wrote: "It didn't seem as if my muscles were aching or straining, but instead it felt as if I were flying across the ice: I looked toward my coach; he signified two seconds under, then the next lap, four seconds under, then five and six—it seemed as if there was no end to how fast I could go. *I could gain speed and gain speed;* I was truly exhilarated! It was at this time I felt the joy that I had never felt before, even winning national titles, setting records—I had never felt this great an exhilaration from sport." (298: 243)

Athletes often feel they are picking up energy from others. Joan Benoit described the day she ran the marathon in 2:26:11, setting a new American record. She felt she did not do it alone. "I felt the energy being passed to me from the fans. . . . I had to respond when I felt their collective emotion rise." (597: p. 161) Sometimes a particular individual galvanizes another athlete or a whole team to play at peak levels. Lionel Terray claimed that his longtime mountain climbing partner Pierre Lachenal "had a sort of hypnotic effect on his companions which made them surpass themselves." (487: p. 296) Boulderer John Gill hypothesized that the friendship that develops in a roped team "may be a manufacturer as well as a transmitter of psychic energy." (555: p. 185)

Several researchers have described a pleasant form of stress that seems to be invigorating. Some have termed it "eustress." Researcher Dorothy Harris noted that "eustress" is associated with excitement, adventure, and thrilling experiences. This stress is fun, it enhances vital sensations, it "turns us on," and in the process *it releases energy.* She also suggested that "eustress may be more than energy consuming, it may be energy mobilizing as well. . . . Most people have far more energy resources than they are aware of, and do not realize they have the capacity to *generate energy* for other activities." (190: p. 109) [Italics added.]

Athletes frequently experience these energy bursts and know that expending energy can generate higher levels of force. In the main, however, these surges occur spontaneously. Western training programs are not grounded in a philosophy that encourages the systematic development of unusual forces. The Eastern martial arts, however, have methods for mobilizing energy by uniting mind and body. Their techniques are embedded in a view that unusual energy is accessible to us all. In Japan such energy is called *ki*, in China *ch'i*, in India *prana*. Like yoga, the martial arts teach methods for deliberately tapping it. Some writers use the word *intrinsic* to differentiate this inner resource from energy that is produced by muscles. Ratti and Westbrook, a husband-and-wife team, both black belts who made intensive studies of various martial arts, wrote that by practicing Eastern methods of concentration and mind/body unification, a type of energy is produced which, if not different from, is at least "far more encompassing and comprehensive in both substance and intensity than the common type of energy usually associated with the output of man's muscular system alone." (394: p. 381)

According to some teachings, the range of this energy is infinite, and its development takes place in three stages, each encompassing more of the universe than the preceding level: The first stage, which is the one most relevant to current athletics, involves individual coordination and centralization of *ki*. In the second stage, the influence *of ki* extends beyond the individual and touches others. The final stage—rarely tapped—puts the athlete in touch with the center of life itself.

All techniques for developing *ki* have the same goal: the unity of mind and body. Aikido expert Koichi Tohei wrote: "The things that one can do when he is sincere and when his spirit and body are one are astonishing. The cornered rat has been known to turn on the cat and down him. People often display powers in time of fire that they would never dream of in ordinary life. Women have been known to lift automobiles to drag children out from under them. In desperate situations of life or death people come up with unheard-of wisdom. All of these cases involve manifestations of power made possible by the unification of the spirit and the body." (494: p. 23)

Although the methods for developing *ki* differ in some respects, most include these major elements: relaxation and letting go, concentration, breathing exercises, emptying the mind of thought, and rhythmic activity. (See 33, 174, 370, 394, and 516) Relaxation and concentration are emphasized in Western sports, but relatively few Western athletes try to evoke extraordinary energies by deliberate means such as meditation. Psychiatrist Thaddeus Kostrubala explained how both athletic activity and meditation can generate them: "I liken . . . running itself to one of the major techniques of meditation, and sometimes prayer, employed by virtually all disciplines both East and West: the constant repetition of a particular word or series of words, whether it be, "Om, na pad na, om na," or the Hail Mary. It matters little what value that particular philosophy or religion attaches to the use of the word, phrase or prayer. It is clearly intended to be an opening into another aspect of awareness. In short, by means of the repetition, the phenomenon sought—namely, the touching of another state of consciousness—is achieved. I think the same process occurs in the repetitive rhythm of slow long-distance running. Eventually, at somewhere between thirty and forty minutes, the conscious mind gets exhausted and other areas of consciousness are activated." (259: p. 103)

Breathing plays an essential role in many Eastern disciplines. W. Scott Russell noted that "when faced with stress, the karateist automatically begins his patterned breathing. And when he begins that breathing, he automatically feels calm and in control. But that's not all that happens. The karateist's controlled breathing not only keeps him calm and composed, but also gives him a tremendous surge of energy." (417: p. 55) Although Western athletes do not typically practice breathing in this way, some use similar techniques during moments of stress. Basketball's Bob Pettit wrote that he relaxed "before shooting a free throw by taking a deep breath, then slowly letting the air out of my lungs." (380: p. 128) Racing car driver Mario Andretti said, "Jackie Stewart told me he used to practice deep breathing at certain spots around the circuit." (337: p. 23)

Another method used to develop *ki* is the achievement of a detached state of mind. Karate expert Masutatsu Oyama wrote: "forget yourself, forget your enemies, forget winning and losing, and when you have done so, you will be in the spiritually unified state that is called *mu*, or nothingness, in Zen. When you have spiritually reached the state of impassivity you will have entered a corner of . . . Zen." (370: p. 320) As we saw in Chapter 2, many athletes have discovered that they perform best in a state of detachment. Tom Nieporte and Don Sauers, in a survey of professional golfers' ideas concerning the mental side of golf, conclude, "It is generally accepted among the pros that there are times when exceptionally gifted players at the top of their games can play tournament golf with 'blank minds.' Their swings and tempos are so well grooved, and their concentration is so deep, that they do everything automatically." (359: p. 64)

Another aspect of creating *ki* is the development of an effective rhythm. Sugar Ray Robinson stressed the importance of rhythm as he prepared for his first professional bout: "Now, in the minutes before I would box, I was searching for that rhythm. In some of the bootleg shows there had been a band playing between the bouts, and that music would be blaring as I came into the ring. I always wished they had continued to play while I was boxing. I think I would've boxed better. . . . Rhythm is everything in boxing. Every move you make starts with your heart, and that's in rhythm or you're in trouble. . . . Your rhythm should set the pace of the fight. If it does, then you penetrate your opponent's rhythm. You make him fight *your* fight, and that's what boxing is all about. In the dressing room that night I could feel my rhythm beginning to move through me, and it assured me that everything would be all right." (410: p. 75)

Western athletes, then, like practitioners of the martial arts, often depend on relaxation, concentration, breathing exercises, mental emptying, and rhythm to achieve exceptional performances. Even though they don't have a training system as sophisticated in this regard as yoga or the martial arts, they manage nevertheless to incorporate these elements into their practice and performance and often discover extraordinary capacities for strength, speed, balance, and ease.

Extraordinary Strength

Athletes sometimes find themselves in possession of extraordinary strength. In an unpublished term paper, a high-school wrestler describes one such experience:

> Late in that last period something strange happened. I stopped thinking about anything and just started to wrestle. Fatigue was no longer any problem. I needed a pin to win because I was too far behind in points to catch up. If I were being logical, I never could have done what I did, because I went for a reverse cradle, where the man on the bottom tries to cradle the top man—a difficult move to get. Even if one can get it, it is almost impossible to pin a man with it. Somehow I got this hold and reversed him. He was in a near-pin position but far from actually getting pinned. I should have known that I couldn't pin him. But it was as if my mind was turned off; just my body was working with strength I didn't know I had. Then it was over. I had pinned him! It was as if I had come back to reality. I couldn't believe what I had done; defeated a seemingly superior wrestler by a move that took strength and skill that I know I didn't really possess.

Seasoned golf pros have learned to adjust for abnormal strength when they are charged up. Under such conditions, Tom Weiskopf wrote: "The adrenalin gets flowing and I'll hit the ball 15 to 25 yards further than under normal conditions." (441: p. 256) Frank Beard tells how, toward the close of his first tour championship, he began to compensate deliberately according to his mental state: "I was still about two hundred yards from the middle of the green, and something popped into my mind, that good rule I still follow: when you're pumped up, always take less iron than you think you need because you'll hit it farther than you normally would. For two hundred yards, I'd normally take a three-iron. I took a five-iron. On a normal lie, under normal conditions, I couldn't hit a five-iron two hundred yards if my life depended on it. But I busted the ball right in the middle of the green, maybe twenty feet past the pin. If I'd hit a three-iron, I probably would've gone over the clubhouse." (38: p. 85)

Pittsburgh Steeler Sam Davis, talking to Roy Blount about the extraordinary strength of teammate Joe Greene, who under ordinary circumstances was not one of the team's strongest men, said, "I'm beginning to believe it's a mental thing. . . . On the pass rush [he] can lift two guys. I've seen him hit guys with one hand, rushing in, and knock them flat on the behind. If that ain't strength, I don't know what it is." (47: p. 79)

Morehei Uyeshiba, the founder of aikido, is said to have relocated a large stone that ten laborers had been unable to move. He often performed such feats, and once said, "I taught myself that an extraordinary spiritual power or soul power lies within a human body." (501: p. 153) Don Buck, karate sensei, is known for his eerie power in winning arm wrestling contests. "On at least one occasion he won such a contest using only his little finger," Glen Barclay wrote. "His explanation is that using one finger put him at an advantage because he was able to 'focus the same amount of strength into a smaller area.' " (33: pp. 47–48) John Gilbey traveled around the world in the 1960s, observing extraordinary feats of strength. In Taiwan, he "saw gifted boxers of every description. Men who could slice bricks . . . men who could lightly touch your body and bring a bright red blood line immediately to the surface; men who could support over a two-hundred-pound weight attached to their genitalia; men who could plunge their arms up to the elbow in unprepared, rather hard soil." (172: pp. 13, 14)

A book on kung fu by David Chow and Richard Spangler includes several photographs of outstanding feats they had observed. One shows an eighty-two-year-old Chinese Ch'i Kung master who drove an eight-inch nail through four inches of board with his bare forehead. (80: p. 179) Most of us have a strong impulse to reject such tales as legends or fantasies. However, there are so many stories such as these that it is difficult to believe that none of them is true. Moreover, many of these unusual feats have been witnessed by knowledgeable and skeptical observers.

Extraordinary Speed and Endurance

Sometimes athletes are able to call on level upon level of energy to achieve extraordinary endurance at exceptional speeds. Derek Sanderson insists that his (then) teammate Bobby Orr "has sixteen versions of fast." (423: p. 119) John Walker describes his win in the 1500 meters at the 1976 Olympics this way: "When I hit the front I got a flash of compelling certainty. I didn't look over my shoulder, but I sensed someone coming up on me fast. . . . I was already at full stretch. But I went into a sort of mental overdrive, and my subconscious mind took over completely—I've experienced it in races before, and I can't explain it. I burned Wohlhuter off and went to the tape with my hands over my head." (509: p. 9)

Ian Jackson describes a type of run with Rich Delgado, who was normally a faster runner than Jackson:

> I never knew how it happened. We would be easing along at 7:00 per mile and one of us (I never knew which one) would surge very slightly. Then we'd both be onto the pace of the surge. Later, there'd be another surge—just a little, almost unnoticeable increase in pace. But we kept pushing it up. Once we were moving, we didn't back off. Back and forth we'd play with the pace. He'd throw in a little more tempo. I'd match it and throw in a little of my own. Within a mile we'd go from 7:00 down to a 6:30 pace. Two miles later, we'd be under 6:00. Another mile and we'd be down to about 5:30. It was so smooth you hardly knew it was happening. Finally, we'd be flying at 5:15 or 5:10, and the miles would reel by effortlessly. (224: p. 34)

Referring to fastball pitcher Nolan Ryan, Ron Fimrite wrote: "No one can say what causes him to throw so much harder than anyone else. . . . Sheer physical strength is not the source of his speed, although at 6'2" and 198 pounds, Ryan has a good pitcher's build. . . . But muscles do not give a man arm speed. 'If they did,' said Oriole Manager Weaver, 'I'd have everybody working out with weights. No, it's not that. No one knows what it is. It's like asking what makes a man run fast.' " (144: pp. 37, 39)

Dramatic examples of extraordinary speed and endurance are provided by the *lung-gom-pa* runners of Tibet. In her book *Magic and Mystery in Tibet*, Alexandra David-Neel claimed that they undergo a special kind of training that develops "uncommon nimbleness and especially enables its adepts to take extraordinarily long tramps with amazing rapidity." (105: p. 209) She added that although many undertake the *lung-gom* training, few master it. But one day she encountered such an adept. Her companion urged her not to interrupt him, as he was running in a trance. When the man drew close, "I could clearly see his perfectly calm impassive face and wide-open eyes with their gaze fixed on some invisible far-distant object situated somewhere high up in space. The man did not run. He seemed to lift himself from the ground, proceeding by leaps. It looked as if he had been endowed with the elasticity of a ball and rebounded each time his feet touched the ground. His steps had the regularity of a pendulum." (105: pp. 202–03). According to some reports, thousands of miles are covered in this manner by *lung-gom* adepts. David-Neel takes pains to point out that the feats accomplished are more a matter of mind than of muscle. She wrote, "It must be understood that the *lung-gom* method does not aim at training the disciple by strengthening his muscles, but by developing in him psychic states that make these extraordinary marches possible." (105: p. 209)

"Setting aside exaggeration, I am convinced from my limited experiences and what I have heard from trustworthy lamas, that one reaches a condition in which one does not feel the weight of one's body. A kind of anesthesia deadens the sensations that would be produced by knocking against the stones or other obstacles on the way, and one walks for hours at an unaccustomed speed, enjoying that kind of light agreeable dizziness well known to motorists at high speed." (105: p. 215)

Lama Anagarika Govinda, a European by birth, experienced something similar to the trance of the *lung-gom-pa* runners when he was traveling in Tibet. He had spent a day far from camp painting and exploring, and did not turn toward home until dark. He had to cover many miles of boulder-covered ground at night. In spite of these obstacles, he found that "to my amazement I jumped from boulder to boulder without ever slipping or missing a foothold, in spite of wearing only a pair of flimsy sandals on my bare feet. One false step or a single slip on these boulders would have sufficed to break or to sprain a foot, but I never missed a step. I moved on with the certainty of a sleepwalker—though far from being asleep. I do not know how many miles of this boulder-strewn territory I traversed; I only know that finally I found myself on the pass over the low hills with the plain and the magnesium swamp before me. . . . Still under the influence of the 'spell' I went right across the swamp without ever breaking through." (177: p. 78)

Only later was Govinda able to find an explanation for his experience, after reading the account we quoted from David-Neel. Govinda felt that unwittingly he had followed the *lung-gom* rules: "I clearly reached a condition in which the weight of the body is no more felt and in which the feet seem to be endowed with an instinct of their own, avoiding invisible obstacles and finding footholds, which only a clairvoyant consciousness could have detected in the speed of such a movement and in the darkness of the night." (177: p. 80) He visited a place where *lung-gom-pas* in training entered meditation cubicles, which contained the necessities of life. Once they entered, the doorway was sealed. The briefest period a monk remained there was one to three months, the longest nine years. While the *lung-gom-pa* was sealed up, no one was allowed to see or speak to him. Alms, often in the form of food, were received by the *lung-gom-pas* through a nine by ten inch opening: "The same small opening . . . is said to be used as an exit by the *lung-gom-pa* after completion of his nine years' practice in uninterrupted seclusion and perfect silence." (177: p. 91)

Mountain climber Gaston Rebuffat has described an experience that resembled *lung-gom* running. In steep terrain he was threatened by an impending storm: "Horrified at the thought of a storm in this fissure, where the sheet of water would so soon be transformed into a torrent, I climbed fast, very fast, and rather roughly. Behind me the ropes were heavy with moisture. Above, the cleft was barred by vertical walls forming a difficult obstacle, demanding care and attention. Meanwhile the rock grew greasy under its film of water. It began to rain, but we seemed to be making our way through a curtain of vapour, frigid, almost tangible and hard to penetrate. There was nothing ethereal about these regions, and yet I felt myself as light as if I had abandoned my human frame; I almost ran up the rocks." (397: p. 102)

Extraordinary Balance

Peter Furst, anthropologist, tells of a shamanistic demonstration he and some students witnessed in 1966 while studying the Huichol

Indians of North Central Mexico. The shaman, Ramon Medina Silva, took the anthropologists and members of the tribe to a spectacular waterfall that he said was "specially for Shamans." He then took off his sandals and proceeded to demonstrate the meaning of balance to a shaman. Furst wrote that he "proceeded to leap—'fly' might be more appropriate—from one rock to another with arms stretched wide, often landing but a few inches from the slippery edge. . . . Or he would stand motionless at the extreme limit of a massive rock, wheel about suddenly and make a great leap to the other side of the rushing water, never showing the slightest concern about the obvious danger that he might lose his balance and fall into space." (162: p. 153) In *Tales of Power* Carlos Castaneda described a similar demonstration put on by don Genaro. On one occasion, standing on a ledge, Genaro called to Castaneda and then jumped to the ground. Castaneda said, "I saw him plummeting down from a height of fifty feet or so." (77: p. 94) These feats of don Genaro could be viewed as variations of a form of kung fu known as "leaping kung," which enables one to "leap over a car or jump across a fifteen-foot-wide mountain stream." (80: p. 154) [Richard DeMille, in *Castaneda's Journey*, suggested that Castaneda got the idea for don Genaro from Peter Furst's lecture on Ramon Medina, which Castaneda attended as a student. (110: p. 189)]

Martial arts student John Gilbey once witnessed a similar feat. An adept named Chou called to him from an open window on the third floor of a building, telling Gilbey he would leap down beside him. Gilbey said: "The next moment his small body was in flight. The next is incredible. He landed on the wooden surface without injury, but this I had seen Japanese and Thai nonboxers do. But Chou landed not only without injury but also without sound! I swear it—I saw it but I did not hear it. A physicist may be able to explain it. I own that I cannot." (172: p. 129)

One of the presently inexplicable abilities reportedly practiced in the martial arts is that of being able to walk up walls. This form of kung fu is sometimes called the "lizard technique." It "enables a student to scale a wall with nothing more than his hands and feet. Training starts with a pole inclined against a wall for assistance. Gradually, the angle of the pole against the wall is reduced until the student can scale the wall without the pole. In another version of this technique, the student stands with his back against the wall and using only his heels and hands mounts the wall." (80: p. 44)

It is also called wall climbing kung, or "gecko crawling," the gecko being a small lizard. Here is another account of this remarkable feat: "Anyone well versed in this art can, with his back against a wall, move freely on and along the surface, horizontally and vertically, by using the controlled strength of his heels and elbows. While perfection of this *Kung* is indeed similar to a Gecko darting as a matter of routine up virtually any wall, it certainly is not easy for humans to master precarious wall climbing, which often threatens to create great insecurity or instability. Generously estimating, one out of a hundred students might consummate this *Kung*." (80: p. 155)

Extraordinary Ease

A culminating experience in sport is the state of effortlessness that athletes achieve at special moments. Feats that are usually demanding and taxing are accomplished with ease. This seeming effortlessness is a feature often noted by spectators. Grantland Rice described Red Grange's running ability on the football field as follows: He "runs . . . with almost no effort. . . . There is no gathering of muscle for an extra lunge. There is only the effortless, ghostlike, weave and glide upon effortless legs." (178: p. xi)

But the case for effortlessness in peak sports performance need not rest on secondhand observations, which are often made with the proviso "He makes it *look* easy." Warren Spahn, after pitching his first no-hitter, said, "It was one of the easiest games I ever pitched. . . . Everything seemed easy. I didn't think about it until after the fifth and then I figured I'm over the hump and it's downhill." (315: p. 26) Bobby Jones, who impressed spectators by the ease with which he hit a golf ball, insisted: "Of all the times that I have struggled around the golf course, there are a few easy rounds that stand out in my memory. . . . Strangely, perhaps, one thing stands out about all these rounds: I had precisely the same feel on each occasion; I was conscious of swinging the club easily and yet without interruption. . . . I had to make no special effort to do anything." (237: pp. 184–85)

Although one might assume that to a great extent sensations of effortlessness and ease are the result of training and practice, the answer seems to be more complex. Mountain climber Lionel Terray wrote of his experience after weeks of climbing: "By this time we were so fit and acclimatized, both mentally and physically, to living in high mountains, that we had virtually overcome the normal human inadaptation to such surroundings. Our ease and rapidity of movement had become in a sense unnatural, and we had practically evolved into a new kind of alpine animal, half way between the monkey and the mountain goat. We could run uphill for hours, climb faces as though they were step-ladders, and rush down gullies in apparent defiance of the laws of gravity. The majority of climbs seemed child's play, which we could do without any particular effort in half or a third of the time taken by an ordinary good party." (487: p. 124)

ENERGY REACHING OUT: PSYCHOKINESIS

In the 1970s a number of psychics came to public attention with claims that they could perform feats of psychokinesis (PK); that is, affect objects directly by purely mental means. Uri Geller, for example, was noted for his supposed spoon-bending and watch-stopping abilities. His abilities have not been observed under strict laboratory conditions, although some reports of research with him have been published. (127, 372) Whether or not Geller's ability is genuine does not alter the fact that the *existence* of psychokinesis has been scientifically verified in several laboratories to the satisfaction of reliable witnesses. Theoretically, PK ability can provide that extra edge that might explain some otherwise inexplicable athletic feats (1270). But is there any evidence that PK occurs in sport?

Many PK laboratory experiments involve influencing the throw of dice. Subjects "will" specific die faces to turn up, or to fall to the left or the right. Willing is often mentioned by athletes. They often make statements suggesting that at times they can actually "will" things to happen. There are, for instance, golf stories about changing the flight of the ball through mental power. Don Lauck notes that for years golf galleries had believed that Jack Nicklaus "could win whenever he wanted, could will the ball into the cup if he needed a birdie at the 18th." (274: p. 3) Nicklaus's own words about Arnold Palmer show that he too prizes the power of willing.

He insisted that although Palmer possessed a fine putting touch, when at his peak, it wasn't this skill that enabled him to sink so many pressure putts. "More than anything else you get the feeling that he actually *willed* the ball into the hole." (356: p. 41) Golfer Johnny Miller wrote: "If you follow golf at all, you'll know that Bobby Nichols has a knack for holing putts in 'clutch' situations to win big money tournaments. At the Dow Jones a few years back, I was playing with him in the final group, and he needed a long putt on the last green. I remember watching his actions as he moved in to make his stroke. Everything was positive. It was apparent that there was no doubt in his mind that he'd make the putt. When he hit the ball I thought to myself, 'There is no way that ball will get to the hole,' it was going so slowly, it looked as if it would be a foot short. Then I heard Bobby say, 'Get in,' and it did. He almost willed it into the hole." (325: p. 145)

These examples cannot be attributed with certainty to PK, of course. We cannot say for sure that the golfers succeeded in getting the ball to move by any but normal means. Yet these athletes seem to feel there was an additional, psychological factor involved, one connected with the act of willing. That there is a connection in Johnny Miller's mind, at least, between what happens in golf and what parapsychologists call PK is unmistakable from the following observation: "I have a premonition that in maybe five hundred years if you want to move, say, a lamp from one part of a room to another, all you'll have to do is think of this happening and it will . . . in fact." (325: p. 179)

John Brodie once discussed a touchdown pass he threw to the 49ers' receiver, Gene Washington.

MURPHY: When the play began it looked for a moment like the safety would make an interception. But then it seemed as if the ball went through or over his hands as he came in front of Washington.

BRODIE: Pat Fischer, the cornerback, told the reporters after the game that the ball seemed to jump right over his hands as he went for it. When we studied the game films that week, it *did* look as if the ball kind of jumped over his hands into Gene's. Some of them said it was the wind and maybe it was.

MURPHY: What do you mean by *maybe?*

BRODIE: What I mean is that our sense of that pass was so clear and our *intention* so strong that the ball was bound to get there, come wind, cornerbacks, hell or high water. (343: p. 20)

In a *New York Times* article, William N. Wallace wrote that New York Giants' tight end Gary Ballman "remembers a pass coming at him overthrown so far there was no way he could catch it. So heavy was his energy flow, so intense his aspirations, that he willed the ball to hang and come down into his hands." (506: p. 3) In conversation, Ballman told Wallace: "But it happened. It was a strange feeling, I'll tell you." (506: p. 3)

In the 1976 playoffs with the Oakland Raiders, tight end Russ Francis of the New England Patriots made a one-handed catch that seemed far beyond his reach to set up the Patriots' first touchdown. To Francis, however, the play was not difficult. He said, "The ball just seemed to slow down and crawl through the air. . . . As it hit my hand, I looked down and watched it dimple my skin. It's funny, but I sometimes think I can make something happen on the football field just by picturing it in my mind." (145: p. 76)

There are also hints of possible PK in baseball. Richard Grossinger described what should have been a home run hit by Pittsburgh Pirate rookie Dave Augustine at Shea Stadium in 1973. It should have won the National League pennant. "But," Grossinger wrote, "the ball did not leave the field; its flight broke just above the grandstand and it dropped onto the railing, then bounced, not in the direction momentum should have taken it (into the stands for a home run . . .), but back into the glove of Cleon Jones, who threw out the lead run at home plate. . . . The Mets won the 1973 pennant." (185: p. 35)

If PK is a fact, there is no reason why fans cannot exercise it as well as players. Could PK be one of the many factors involved in the well-known phenomenon of the "home court advantage"? In some countries in East Africa, soccer teams pay for the services of a soothsayer, including one named Seriff, who casts spells on the opponents of the teams who hired him. Seriff noted that even if the opposing team had better players, still the ball "can be made to behave strangely—go wide, or go over or fall short of the goal." (514: p. 23)

John P. Brown, in his book on dervishes, tells of a Sufi who, while watching a wrestling match, agreed with his companion that together they would try to aid one of the contestants by means of willpower. They also agreed that, having helped the first wrestler subdue his opponent, they would then concentrate on aiding the other man to overcome the first wrestler. They succeeded both times. Brown also tells of two persons at another match who decided to help the weaker of the two wrestlers. "Immediately a wonderful occurrence took place; the thin, spare man seized upon his giant-like opponent, and threw him upon the ground with surprising force. The crowd cried out with astonishment, as he turned him over on his back, and held him down with . . . apparent ease." (67: p. 148)

Psychokinesis in the Martial Arts

In some feats performed by martial artists when physical contact is made with a person or object, the influence exerted seems greater than the degree of contact made. It appears that the "real" work is done by a force more powerful than any that muscles alone provide. For example, in the *Tameshiwari*, or breaking aspect of karate, "trained karateka can smash boards, bricks, cement blocks, ice, and roofing tiles with various parts of their body including the fists, open hands, and even their heads and fingers." (529: p. 77) In some of these breaking techniques, the effect seems to go beyond the immediate physical contact made between flesh and hard objects. Chow and Spangler (80) observed and photographed a master who struck five bricks piled on top of each other, splitting each in two except for the second from the top as he predicted he would. Bruce Lee demonstrated in public, before photographers, his capacity to deliver a punch of tremendous impact, standing right foot forward, with his almost fully extended right arm an inch away from his partner, who held a heavily padded glove against his chest for protection. In this position, from which it seeemed physically impossible to generate enough power to hurt an opponent, Lee knocked his partner flying into a waiting chair, several feet behind him. (33: p. 72)

There are eyewitness accounts "of men struck in the abdomen by blows that barely marked the skin who died later of ruptured spleens or kidneys, destroyed by the shock wave of energy dispatched by fist or foot." (233: p. 95) This "death touch" can be explained by suggestion. American psychologist Martin Seligman (443) has studied voodoo deaths among Caribbean people and concluded that the victim's faith is the cause of death. Aware of a hex and sure of its power, the victim falls into learned helplessness and slides into submissive death. But what about cases in which the victim is unaware of his intended fate? Then, if it is suggestion, it might operate by telepathy. Some writers (98, 326) suggest that the delayed death touch is an application of the principles of acupuncture. One writer said, "It stands to reason that a powerful medicine (or medical technique) can just as easily kill or cripple [as cure]." (326: p. 42)

Another technique involves the apparently simple but powerful act of expelling the breath. This has such a tenuous physical basis that it can hardly account for the results it is claimed to produce. A famous Chinese boxer, Yang Lu-ch'an, is said to have "knocked a young challenger thirty feet across a room simply by expelling his breath with a laugh when the young man let fly a punch at the famous boxer's stomach." (123: p. 38)

Two techniques in the martial arts seem to make sense only in terms of PK. One is the "*kiai* shout." E. J. Harrison tells of a master who saw "a few sparrows perched on the branch of a tall pine tree, and fixing his gaze on the birds, gave utterance to the *kiai* shout, whereupon the birds fell to the ground insensible. When he relaxed the *kiai* the birds regained consciousness and flew away." (193: p. 169) Martial artist Robert Smith tells many anecdotes about the renowned Chinese boxer Li Neng-jan'. One concerns a young man who—on the pretext of offering tea to Li— planned to attack him, as in spite of his reputation he appeared to be a harmless old man. When he did so, said Smith, "Li merely used a spirit-shout . . . that knocked the [young man] out—without spilling his tea or interrupting his conversation with another man. When asked about it, [the young man] replied: 'I heard thunder, his hands had eyes, I fell unconscious.' " (462: p. 14)

A last technique, inexplicable in ordinary physical terms, is *noi cun*, which Michael Minick describes as follows:

> More commonly known as the divine technique, this is a
> very rare form of kung fu practiced by only a handful of

adepts. It is not widely taught or particularly popular because it takes the better part of a lifetime to master. And, quite frankly, it strains the credulity of those who are asked to believe that it exists. Simply put, it is a means of generating internal power so enormous one can fell an opponent without actually touching him. As fantastic as this sounds, most kung fu masters insist that such an art exists, and many claim to have witnessed it. One modern master writing in *Karate Illustrated* stated:

Here in San Francisco lives a one-hundred-seven-year-old master who is still able to use *noi cun* (the use of internal power) despite his age and the frailty of his body. I personally have seen him demonstrate. In one of his demonstrations, he asked a young man to step to the center of the room. Then, placing himself a few yards away, he stretched forth his arm, palm pointed outward, and concentrated deeply, drawing from within that great force of his *chi*, and within a few moments the lad was staggering backward, pushed off balance by the unseen force radiating from that outstretched hand. (326: p. 41)

Minick adds that the same master gave other examples of *noi cun*, including that of a "man in Hong Kong who broke a glass vase from across a room." (326: p. 41) Chow and Spangler give a variation of it known as "red sand palm." In this variation, "without touching an assailant's body, the adept merely makes signs of rubbing or striking at him with the palm of one's hand from a distance and the receiver will be injured." (80: p. 145) They also describe "one finger Kung," in which "should the forefinger be aimed at an opponent, even though separated by a door, he still could be injured." (80: p. 147) Chow also witnessed a student who held a washboard with the corrugations facing his stomach, the skin of which was unblemished. A master, standing four feet away, meditated for half a minute and then flicked his wrist toward the board, but without touching either it or the student. When the student lowered the washboard and raised the sweater, the lines from the washboard were outlined in red across his stomach.

In all the examples given here, it is difficult or even impossible to see how ordinary physical principles could account for the feats described. In cases such as expelling breath and the red sand palm and possibly even the hand smashing of karateka, the same principle may be acting as in the spirit-shout art, about which E. J. Harrison noted: "It is not the shout itself, but the force behind it, that is really responsible for the phenomenon." (193: p. 120)

Another indication that the mind plays an essential role in the feats described is the emphasis that athletes both East and West place on confidence. Arnold Palmer told George Plimpton: "When I'm working well, I just don't think I'm going to miss a shot or a putt, and when I do I'm as surprised as hell. I can't believe it. A golfer must think that way. . . . I don't mean to suggest that it's easy. In fact, the hardest thing for a great many people is to win. They . . . *doubt*. Which gets them into trouble." (384: p. 248) Masutatsu Oyama said, "The most important thing in the stone-breaking techniques is psychological self-confidence." He adds that if you try to break a stone, no matter how small, when you are not feeling confident, "In nine cases out of ten, you will break a bone, dislocate something, or injure yourself in some other way." (370: p. 224) Yet in a confident state one can break many stones without a single bruise.

Elusiveness

The religious traditions of the East and Middle East hold the art of invisibility to be one of the *siddhis,* or extraordinary powers, that may develop in following a spiritual path. Morihei Uyeshiba, the founder of aikido, often demonstrated his ability to elude attack in this way. George Leonard quoted his teacher, Robert Nadeau, a former student of Uyeshiba. On one occasion, the Master invited Nadeau to attack him, which he did with all his strength, wanting to make a good impression. "But when I got close to him, it was like I'd entered a cloud. And in the cloud there's a giant spring that's throwing me out of the cloud. I find myself flying through the air and I come down with a hard, judo type slap-fall. Lying there, I look around for Uyeshiba, but he isn't to be seen. Finally, I turn all the way around, the one place I wouldn't have expected him to be, and there he is, standing calmly." (279: p. 253)

Leonard also described a film taken of Uyeshiba as he was attacked by two men. It shows him facing his attackers, apparently trapped. But in the next frame, he has moved two feet away and is facing in the opposite direction. According to Leonard: "While Uyeshiba appears to shift from one position to another in a fraction of a second (or in no time at all!) the oncoming movement of the attackers proceeds sequentially, a fraction of a step at a time, until the two collide and are pinned by the Master. . . . Whether or not Uyeshiba's feats can be scientifically validated, the fact remains that those who were best acquainted with the Master are convinced that he was operating "in another dimension," especially in his last years. Again and again he seems to have "just disappeared," or to have created "a warp in time and space." Such terms as these recur repeatedly in descriptions of Uyeshiba's work, and may serve to remind us of possibilities that lie beyond the . . . strictures of this culture." (279: p. 253)

In a provocative article on running back Mac Lane of the Kansas City Chiefs, Robert F. Jones wrote, "There has to be some quality of magic in the elusiveness of the best running backs. Mere physics can no more explain the missed or broken tackles that mark every long run from scrimmage than mere chemistry can explain the excitement such a performance arouses in the spectator." (236: p. 25) Pelé, the soccer great, confided that, on a day when everything was going right, suddenly he felt "a strange calmness I hadn't experienced in any of the other games. It was a type of euphoria; I felt I could run all day without tiring, that I could dribble through any of their team or all of them, that I could almost pass through them physically. I felt I could not be hurt. It was a very strange feeling and one I had not felt before. Perhaps it was merely confidence, but I have felt confident many times without that strange feeling of invincibility." (378: p. 51)

Were all these athletes and spectators deluded? Perhaps. But it is also possible that they were keying into an actual human possibility. Our seemingly impenetrable physical world may in fact be more mutable and diaphanous than we think. That the worlds of the mystic and the physicist are very alike has been pointed out by many contemporary writers. (76, 280)

Uncanny Suspension

At certain moments, as we have seen, athletes have feelings of float-ing and weightlessness; and sometimes they have out-of-body ex-periences. Now we would like to consider the possibility that some athletes literally suspend themselves in midair. We have discussed athletes' subjective feelings that they were floating or somehow outside themselves. But is there such a thing as levitation? We have collected many statements by sportswriters, coaches, and other ob-servers that attest to the fact that some athletes actually can, for brief moments, remain suspended in air.

Referring to the jumping ability of the Denver Nuggets' David Thompson, Marshall Frady used the term "uncanny suspension." (155: p. 30) Witnessing an instance of this suspension deeply af-fected author James Michener. He describes a 1941 basketball game and player Hank Luisetti in his *Sports in America*: "Some-how, Luisetti stayed up in the air, faked a shot at the basket, made the Denver center commit himself, and with a movement I had never seen before, simply extended his right arm an extra foot and banked a one-handed shot gently against the backboard and into the basket. It seemed as if he had been in the air a full minute, deceiving three different players, and ending with a delayed shot that was staggering in its beauty." (322: p. 446)

The person best known for his ability to remain suspended in air is probably Michael ("Air") Jordan, who has some interesting things to say about his levitating ability. He was not always a jumper, but only realized his extraordinary ability through prac-tice. "One day, like in a dream, he went to try a dunk and just 'exploded,' he said. 'I got up so high over the rim it scared me.' " (609: p. 4) Jordan has been awed by his ability to soar, as if it were a gift conferred upon him rather than something he does by muscle and willpower. He told Rick Telander: "I wish I could show you a film of a dunk I had in Milwaukee. . . . It's in slow motion, and it looks like I'm taking off, like somebody put wings on me. I get chills when I see it. . . . I think, when does 'jump' become 'flying'? I don't have the answer yet." (1448: p. 21) He added: "I never practice those moves. I don't know how to do them. It's amazing." (1448: p. 20)

An article in *Time* describes a performance by premier danseur Mikhail Baryshnikov:

When he launches his perfectly arched body into the arc of one of his improbably sustained leaps—high, light, the leg beats blurring precision—he transcends the limits of physique and, it sometimes seems, those of gravity itself. If one goes by the gasps in the theater or the ecstasies of the critics, such moments turn Mikhail Baryshnikov, if not into a minor god, then into a major sorcerer. . . .

He is an unbelievable technician with invisible technique. Most dancers, even the great ones, make obvious preliminaries to leaps. He simply floats into confounding feats of acrobatics and then comes to still, collected repose. He forces the eye into a double take: did that man actually do that just now? Dance Critic Walter Terry said that "Baryshnikov is probably the most dazzling virtuoso we have seen. He is more spectacular in sheer technique than any other male dancer. What he actually does, no one can really define. His steps are in no ballet dictionary. And he seems to be able to stop in mid-air and sit in space." (34: p. 44)

John Gill, a premier boulderer (one who climbs sheer walls of cliffs and large boulders), has wondered whether some climbers have psychic abilities. When interviewed by Peter Ament, he said that climbing integrates body and mind, and proposed: "If you could integrate things with a high degree of perfection, you might induce . . . telekinetic ability." One way this integration might be forwarded is through belief. If you have a positive attitude toward the climb, "perhaps with an excellent mental attitude you not only integrate your moves better, but this in turn induces a telekinetic ability to levitate you slightly, even if it is only taking off a few ounces. A few ounces can make a tremendous difference. I have seen people go beyond their limits." (555: p. 185)

If these athletes and danseurs really can remain in the air longer than is normally possible, how do they do it? Again, a possible answer may be found in the literature of the world's religions, all of which mention levitation, the ability to rise and remain in the air. Some suggest that the phenomenon is a symbol of spiritual emancipation. Ernest Wood observes, "Levitation is a universally accepted fact in India. I remember one occasion when an old yogi was levitated in a recumbent posture about six feet above the ground in an open field, for about half an hour, while the visitors were permitted to pass sticks to and fro in the space between." (466: p. 21)

Levitation in the West figures prominently in classic volumes by two scholars, Herbert Thurston (492) and Montague Summers (477), in independent works with the same title: *The Physical Phenomena of Mysticism*. Both give examples of levitation by Christian saints such as Teresa of Avila and Joseph of Copertino. James Webb, in a scholarly history of nineteenth-century occultism, notes many instances of levitation that were said to have occurred during that century. A good review of physical mediumship by a skeptical parapsychologist, J. Fraser Nicol, may be found in the *Handbook of Parapsychology*, compiled by psychiatrist Benjamin Wolman. Nicol concludes: "The overwhelming number of reports on mediumistic physical phenomena offer no valid evidence. [But] there are a few cases which the majority of critically minded students find it unreasonable to dismiss." (357: p. 311) He names the exceptions, which include Home and Palladino. Another skeptical parapsychologist, E. J. Dingwall, has written excellent surveys of the lives and phenomena of these two famous mediums. (117, 118, 368)

Levitation, if it occurs, would be a form of psychokinesis. (For a review of the evidence for laboratory PK, see the surveys by Rush [416], Schmeidler [429], and Stanford [471].) If, for purposes of discussion, we assume that it does occur, it is possible that the leaping abilities of a Michael Jordan or a Mikhail Baryshnikov may be partly empowered by it. The athlete's extreme effort to remain airborne may trigger a nonphysical factor.

Have we any clues as to how this amazing ability is induced? Nijinsky, when asked if it was difficult to remain suspended in air, "did not understand at first, and then very obligingly [replied]: 'No! No! not difficult. You have to just go up and then pause a little up there.' " (68: p. 203) Nandor Fodor, a psychoanalyst and psychical researcher, wondered if Nijinsky's ability was a rudimentary form of levitation or only an illusion. He concluded that it was indeed levitation, and suggested that Nijinsky—perhaps unconsciously—used a special technique that incorporated aspects of yoga. He was able to see himself from outside during a performance, and this suggested to Fodor that he was in a form of trance during peak performances. His technique apparently involved both breathing and muscular control. Fodor, who knew

Nijinsky's widow, asked her if her husband knew how he did it. She replied, "I often asked him how he managed to stay up in the air. He never could understand why we could not do it. He just took a leap, held his breath, and stayed up. He felt supported in the air. Moreover, he could control his descent, and could come down slower or quicker as he wished. I know he had extraordinary thigh muscles, and I know that in the matter of filling his lungs with air he has, in a friendly contest, easily beaten Caruso and Erich Schmedes." (151: p. 26) Fodor learned that it was standard technique in ballet to breathe in before a leap, to hold the breath while in the air, and to breathe out after landing. With this technique, dancers would unconsciously acquire a control over their breathing similar to that practiced by yogis.

THE INVISIBLE BARRIER

John Gilbey once saw a martial arts master use a sword to slice through a piece of wood six inches thick. He then had an assistant place the sword against his bicep and put his weight on it. No skin was broken. "There was only a slight red line caused by the pressure of the blade," Gilbey wrote. (172: p. 143–44) This form of mind over matter sometimes appears to be operative in sport—a state of invulnerability in which the athlete cannot be harmed. It seems as if an invisible wall is involved, preventing the athlete from being touched by anything harmful. The barrier appears to be mental, and if certain religious texts are to be relied on, its presence is due to the athlete's having achieved the right attitude toward his opponent and, indeed, toward life itself.

Photographs in Chow and Spangler (80) illustrate the form of *Chi Kung* that John Gilbey witnessed. In one case, Grand Master Lung Chi Cheung allowed the wheel of an automobile to run over his stomach, yet he was not injured. In another instance, five bricks were placed on the head of Shaolin Master Lung Kai Ming; his brother then broke the bricks with a blow from a sledge hammer, but Lung was not hurt. Although Western athletes do not actively cultivate invulnerability, there are scattered accounts of individuals who seem to be unusually free from injury. This is usually attributed to flexibility or reflexes that prevent harm—or simply to good fortune. It may be, however, that it is also a product of paranormal invulnerability that arises from athletic discipline.

Another kind of invulnerability involves hypnotic ability. Ratti and Westbrook point out that *ki* can be channeled by means of a magnetic personality which enables one to: "call upon strong powers of projection and suggestion, and these can often be used to prevent combat, or to win it. There is an episode . . . said to have involved a samurai who was set upon in the woods by a pack of wolves. . . . He merely kept walking straight ahead, his countenance so stable, aware, and potentially explosive that the animals were frozen in their tracks. Other episodes [involve] men lying in ambush only to confront a victim who, simply by gazing at them, terrorized them so effectively that they were immobilized." (394: p. 370)

Bobby Orr seems to have exercised a similar influence on the Chicago Black Hawks in the 1970 Stanley Cup. In trying to account for the Hawks' poor showing, sportswriter Gary Ronberg said: "Admittedly, Orr is the finest player in the game today. Does he also have hypnotic powers? In the past, respect for excellence never prevented opponents from breaking lances with a Rocket Richard or a Gordie Howe. Yet there was Orr, gliding along as if shielded by an invisible barrier as the Hawks sleep-skated sheeplike in his wake. One of the most amazing moments of any cup series came in the third game when Orr skated behind the Chicago net with three Hawks chasing after him and then leisurely set up the easiest kind of goal." (413: p. 18) Ronberg also quotes a teammate of Orr's who marveled that only a couple of Black Hawks had been willing to "mix it. . . . Hell, everybody else was just standing around watching Bobby fly, like they were in awe or something." (413: p. 21) Something unusual may have been happening in these cases, something related more to attitude and state of mind than to reflex and muscle. Though we cannot say for sure that psychokinesis was involved, we suggest that it might have been.

MIND OVER MATTER

Sport constantly shows us how the mind imposes barriers on the body. Time and again an athlete breaks through a barrier and other athletes soon follow, showing that the barrier was not physical but mental. French mountaineer René Dittert observed, "It is a strange fact, but one that has always proved true, that where one man has imposed his domination over the elements another man can pass. The way is open, because the forces of nature have waited for man to prove himself master before submitting." (215: p. 121) Arnold Beisser wrote, "The final striking impression is that when a record is finally broken by one man it opens the way for others to do the same." (39: p. 155) In this connection, sportswriter and runner Kenny Moore made an interesting point in an article on Henry Rono, the track star. He said that in Rono's native Kenya, the living conditions demand a "realism, a clarity of judgment about such things as pain and effort, that is difficult for Westerners to share." (332: p. 42) Moore proposed that this cultural factor had important implications in Rono's record-breaking: "Rono has no illusions, which is good, because the case has been made that it is our illusion that we can go no faster that holds us back." (332: p. 42)

Sometimes the barrier is associated with injury. Bernard King was, in Paul Attner's words, "a classic case of mind over matter: one of basketball's most devastating injuries overmatched by one of the game's most determined players." (567: p. 5) Attner provided a detailed account of how King came back to All-Star status over a period of six years, recovering from a snapped anterior cruciate ligament. No other basketball player had accomplished this feat, although it is now easier because of improved surgical procedures.

Robert Deindorfer observed that in fishing, "it is essential to believe, truly believe, that each trip, each hour, each cast might well produce a fish. In the words of Chris Seifert, the wish is father to the fish." (715: p. 165) If nothing else, the confident angler will perform beyond his normal capacity. Richard Reinwald caught the California state record brown trout. He picked Flaming Gorge to fish in and told many people in the nearby town of Bishop that he would hook the record fish: "Every day I actually pictured the record fish in my mind," he wrote. . . . "The picture was clear as a bell, a hen fish, the colors rather dark." (715: p. 175) And that is what he caught, a female brown trout darker than the others he had been catching.

Thirty years ago a psychologist, R. H. Thouless, and a mathematician, B. P. Wiesner, put forth an hypothesis that, if true, would provide an explanation for some of the unusual feats described in this chapter: *"I control the activity of my nervous system (and so indirectly control such activities as the movements of my body and the course of my thinking) by the same means as that by which the successful psychokinetic subject controls the fall of the dice or other object."* (491: p. 197) The famous physiologist Sir John Eccles made the same proposal. In an invited address at the 1976 convention of the Parapsychological Association, he proposed that the simple act of saying a word was actually a form of psychokinesis: "The mind has been able to work upon the brain cells, just slightly changing them. . . . The mind is making these very slight and subtle changes for hundreds of millions of cells, gradually bringing [the impulse] through and channeling it into the correct target cells to make the movement. And so there is psychokinesis, mind acting upon a material object, namely brain cells. It's extremely weak, but it's effective, because we've learned to use it." (128: pp. 257–58) We suggest that athletes learn in a similar way —haphazardly, if not by design—to extend the reach of the body beyond the confines of the flesh.

What if an athlete can control his muscles the same way that a PK subject in the laboratory can control the throw of a die? If mind is the prime mover, then the muscles are just as much "outside" the mind as a die face or the table lamp that Johnny Miller said we will one day move by mind alone. Or put the other way, the die face or lamp are no more outside the reach of the mind than one's muscles. The sports literature suggests that a few individuals who are able to perform extraordinary feats view reality in this way. Baseball enthusiast Richard Grossinger observed: "Pitchers have torn muscles, broken bones, been operated on, had ligaments grafted; they have altered everything about their delivery and rhythm that made them a pitcher in the first place. They have come back from rotary cuff surgery, from not being able to lift their arms for a year and a half, and they have won ball-games. Occasionally, like Jim Palmer and Luis Tiant, they have pitched the best baseball of their lives after the actual physical equipment was seemingly taken away. It is almost as though the outer throwing form is an illusion. If you learn how to do it in terms of a strong healthy body, the skill remains, the ability to put it over, long after the body ceases to back it. An inner image of the entire pitching sequence is regenerative, like a reptile limb." (185: p. 32)

It is not so much willpower that enables athletes to break records, although that is important. Many records fall when the athletes are involved in the sheer experience of transcending limits, doing what no one has done before. Lionel Terray said mountain climber Pierre Lachenal broke many climbing records not by setting out to do so. Rather, it happened naturally, not only through exercise of his great climbing skills, but "because he loved the feeling of etherealization, of liberation from the laws of gravity, which a perfect mastery of climbing technique can bring." (487: p. 296) Physical handicaps, too, can be transcended. Kitty O'Neil lost her hearing at age four, but she became a champion diver, set the world record as the fastest woman water-skier, became an expert in motorcycle racing, and then became a stunt person in movies, setting two records for women: a 112-foot fall and the highest fall while on fire ever attempted. She told Phil Bowie that she was motivated by a liking for danger and thrills, but added: "Mostly I want always to have a goal, some dream that I can try for." (637: p. 82)

The abilities reviewed in this chapter suggest that some of us can extend our boundaries beyond our bodily confines. The body is not the end of sport, but its beginning. It is a centering point, a place to start from, but from this sturdy base we are capable of reaching beyond—of fleshing out spirit in areas where the body cannot reach, initiating movements the eye cannot see, revealing strengths that transcend muscles, exerting energies that are not physical in the ordinary sense. Sport is not merely an end in itself, but a catalyst for human unfoldment in other areas of life.

5

SPORT AND MYSTICISM

While reading the stories we have presented so far, you may have wondered about their authenticity. How many of these accounts are like the fisherman's tale in which the fish grows larger with each telling? Does Patsy Neal, for example, sentimentalize her religious experience? (See page 28.) Did Morehei Uyeshiba's students gradually embellish their teacher's legend? Did Babe Ruth really point to those centerfield bleachers? Sometimes exaggeration is apparent in the storyteller's style, as when mountaineer Frank Smythe exclaims: "Physically you may feel but a cosmic speck of chemicalised dust, but spiritually you will feel great. For is not your vision capable in one glance of piercing the abysses of space? Is not your hearing attuned to an immortal harmony? . . . On a mountain-top a man feels himself to be an entity whose span is timeless, whose scope is magnificent beyond conception, whose birth, whose death are incidental milestones on a splendid road without beginning and without end." (464: p. 12)

Accounts of spiritual awakening can be exaggerated through inflated memory after the fact, through sentimentality, through sheer bad writing (there are volumes of purple sporting prose). But from our many interviews with sportspeople we have learned that the mystical aspects of sport can also be deflated and suppressed. The repression of the extraordinary moment is just about as common as its embellishment. In spite of the growing interest in meditation and religion among athletes, in spite of magazine articles about "sport highs" and the "inner game," people are often apprehensive about the sublime and uncanny aspects of sport. We believe that people in many fields of activity have trouble accepting such experience because they have no context, language, or philosophy to support it. The world of sport shares this general lack of understanding. Many powerful incidents slip away like Brigadoon because they find no place in the experiencer's ordinary frame of reference.

We have kept this problem in mind during our interviews and literary search. But though we are generally dealing with subjective reality—with stories that may be distorted by denial, exaggeration, or faulty memory—we do have objective corroboration of exceptional events from teammates, spectators, and sportswriters. What emerges from this wealth of material is clear: a large number of participants in a wide variety of sports have reported events remarkably similar to the ones we have described in the preceding chapters.

THE SPIRITUALLY EVOCATIVE ELEMENTS OF SPORT

What is it, then, that evokes this range of transcendent experience? What happens on playing fields, mountain heights, or ocean wildernesses that evokes the metanormal? We think there are certain elements in sport that make it a vehicle for spiritual awakening. Let's look at some of these.

The Physical and Mental Demands of Sport

As in any discipline, athletes must submit to certain rules, requirements, and ordeals, and to do this, they need to relinquish old patterns. In perfecting their skills, they have to give up habits and responses that impede their performance. To some extent they must acquire (or discover) another nature. And when they do, new powers often emerge, new energies are brought to play, new vistas begin to open. As we have seen, many people say they are renewed, even reborn, though the old self may return when the sporting event or the season is over.

Giving up old patterns—both mental and physical—is required of the sports participant. Most joggers, for example, have to resist the urge to quit as they exercise lungs, heart, and legs beyond their ordinary capacity. The impulse to stop arises after you have gone only a few hundred yards. But the compensating pleasure of exceeding a limit, the glow of fitness, the sense of pride in overcoming resistance come into play as well. Many will testify to both the pains and the joys that every sport brings from the very start.

The pains of runners come in part from the breaking down of fat, muscle, and capillaries so that the body can re-form itself for more efficient movement. Many miles of blood vessels are developed on the way to fitness, the balance of hormones is changed, and if you persist, whole groups of muscles are gradually restructured. Attitudes toward fear and discomfort change, too. Runners, like most dedicated sports participants, learn to push beyond limits and recognize the unexpected second energy that surges through them; they learn how to endure the nay-saying voices until a new-found strength arrives. "Break-down and build-up"—whether physical, emotional, mental, or spiritual—is the rule in running as it is in most sports.

Sometimes the relinquishment of old patterns involves one's entire sense of self. Mike Spino, an innovative running coach and former distance runner, described such a crisis:

In the winter of 1967, I was training on dirt and asphalt, paced by a friend who was driving a car. I had intended to run six miles at top speed, but after the first mile I was surprised at how easily I could do it. I had run the first mile in four and a half minutes with little sense of pain or exertion, as if I were carried by a huge momentum. The wet pavement and honking horns were no obstacle at all. My body had no weight or resistance. It began to feel like a skeleton—as if the flesh had been blown off of its bones. I felt like the wind. Daydreams and fantasies disappeared. The only negative feeling was a guilt for being able to do this. When the run was over conversation was impossible, because for a while I didn't know who I was. Was I the one who had been running or the ordinary Mike Spino?

I sat down by the roadway and wept. Here I was, having run the entire six miles on a muddy roadside at a four-and-a-half minute pace, which was close to the national record, and I was having a crisis deciding who I was. (468)

Spino's dilemma that day was like the problem many people have when they admit sublime or uncanny experiences into consciousness. A new self, as it were, appears before them, and their old markers of self-identification are suddenly less certain. When this happens, in sport or any activity, it is as if pins are pulled loose and floorboards give way. In this respect, sport is like profound artistic discovery or falling in love or religious awakening. Not only are particular attitudes or bodily structures stretched, but the entire self is turned over. Such openings can lead to a fuller life if the athlete surrenders to what is happening. It is possible to resist the opening, however, especially if there is no one available to support it.

Sport's Sacred Time and Space

Johan Huizinga, in his classic study of play, *Homo Ludens*, has described the role of boundaries in sport—the arena or magic circle, and the fixed duration in which a game or contest is set.

Into an imperfect world and into the confusion of life [these boundaries] bring a temporary, a limited perfection. Play demands order absolute and supreme. The least deviation from it "spoils the game," robs it of its character and makes it worthless. The profound affinity between play and order is perhaps the reason why play, as we noted in passing, seems to lie to such a large extent in the field of aesthetics. Play has a tendency to be beautiful. It may be that this aesthetic factor is identical with the impulse to create orderly form, which animates play in all its aspects. The words we use to denote the elements of play belong for the most part to aesthetics, terms with which we try to describe the effects of beauty: tension, poise, balance, contrast, variation, solution, resolution, etc. Play casts a spell over us; it is "enchanting," "captivating." It is invested with the noblest qualities we are capable of perceiving in things: rhythm and harmony. (219: p. 10)

Games often create an order that resembles the cadenced life of ashrams and monasteries, and sporting expeditions are in certain respects like religious pilgrimages. The acts they comprise are invested with special meaning and are pointed toward perfection. Athletes feel the effect of a playing field in their bones. Fenway Park or an Olympic stadium or a famous golf course like St. Andrews can bring a quickening of the spirit, a concentration of energies, a connection with heroes past and future that give performances in these places a heightened quality. And even when there is no stadium or arena involved, sport implicitly creates a sacred time and place. A mountain to be climbed, an ocean to be crossed, or a stretch of countryside to be raced on can summon up significance and power for us simply by being designated the field of adventure. The spatial and temporal boundedness of sport, by ordering and sublimating our energies and by closing off the world's drudgery and confusion, can evoke our spiritual depths like a work of art or a monastic discipline. Gaston Rebuffat wrote that as he increased his climbing skills, "little by little, in the Alps, I discovered within my innermost self the thrust of the summits towards the sky." (1284: p. 12)

Sustained and Focused Attention

Every sport requires concentration, freedom from distraction, and sustained alertness. Athletic skill depends on one's ability to focus unbroken attention on the space, objects, and other people involved, and on one's own kinesthetic sense of the body. A wandering mind diminishes athletic ability, whether you are running or bowling, playing football or chess, climbing mountains or deep-sea diving. The greatest athletes are legendary for their powers of concentration. The literature and gossip of every sport is filled with tales about the playing trances of its stars. Billie Jean King wrote that when she was playing, "It's like I'm out there by myself. I've talked with Laver and Rosewall about this, and even Court a little, and on their great days their attitude is exactly the same. I concentrate only on the ball in relationship to the face of my racket, which is a full-time job anyway, since no two balls ever come over the net the same way. I appreciate what my opponent is doing, but in a detached, abstract way, like an observer in the next room. I see her moving to her left or right, but it's almost as though there weren't any real opponent, as though I didn't know—and certainly didn't care whom I was playing against." (251: p. 197)

British golfer Tony Jacklin described the "cocoon of concentration" he sometimes found himself in: "When I'm in this state, this cocoon of concentration, I'm living *fully* in the present, not moving out of it. I'm aware of every half inch of my swing. I'm absolutely engaged, *involved* in what I'm doing at that particular moment. That's the important thing. That's the difficult state to arrive at. It comes and it goes, and the pure fact that you go out on the first tee of a tournament and say, 'I must concentrate today,' is no good. It won't work. It has to already be there." (120: p. 30) Most athletes make a distinction between their usual concentration and this special kind of playing trance. Call it the "zone," a "cocoon of concentration," or "white moment"—it brings extraordinary integration and power. The distinction athletes make between ordinary concentration and such a state resembles the distinction religious teachers make between different levels of meditation.

In Patanjali's yoga sutras, four levels of attention are described. The first, *pratyahara* (377: p. 171), is the deliberate withdrawal of attention from external objects, drawing the senses with it (Billie Jean King's blocking everything but the ball from her focus). In the second state, *dharana* (377: p. 173), the yogi holds his mind steady upon a center of consciousness within the mind or body or upon an external object (a runner focusing on his stride or a golfer concentrating on the ball). The third stage, *dhyana* (377: pp. 173–74), is "an unbroken flow of attention toward the object of contemplation," an effortless absorption beyond "brute will." This resembles the playing trance described by Jacklin and King. Many athletes, like Jacklin, distinguish ordinary concentration from this seemingly effortless state. In the fourth stage, *samadhi*, "the true nature of the object held in contemplation shines forth, undistorted by the mind of the perceiver." (377: p. 175) Here there is perfect clarity and an effortless sense of unity with whatever is perceived. Shoshin Nagamine described Okinawan Karate-do (Shorin-ryu): "The fusing of mind and body in karate is indescribably beautiful. The flow of the mind, when totally absorbed during kata practice, brings a person into contact with the essence and core of his being. One is both humbled and uplifted by this knowledge of self." (1180: p. 271)

Many experiences described by athletes share these qualities. The withdrawal of attention from distractions, the deliberate holding of a constant focus, the effortless absorption, the sense of unity and rightness of movement that Jacklin, King, and others describe are not unlike these stages of yogic meditation. The playing trance may not have the stability, penetration, and pervasiveness of the dedicated contemplative's realizations, but there are striking similarities between the two kinds of experience and between the stages in which they develop.

Another way to characterize these deepening levels of concentration is by the amount of time the mind can remain undisturbed. According to the yoga sutras: "It has been said that if the mind can be made to flow uninterruptedly toward the same object for twelve seconds, this may be called concentration [*dharana*]. If the mind can continue in that concentration for twelve times twelve seconds (i.e., two minutes and twenty-four seconds), this may be called meditation [*dhyana*]. If the mind can continue in that meditation for twelve times two minutes and twenty-four seconds (i.e., twenty-eight minutes and forty-eight seconds), this will be the lower samadhi. And if the lower samadhi can be maintained for twelve times that period (i.e., five hours, forty-five minutes, and thirty-six seconds), this will lead to nirvikalpa samadhi [the profoundest state of ecstasy]." (377: p. 179)

Like yoga, sport invites and reinforces an ever-deepening attention to the task at hand. The thousands of miles a distance runner covers, all the shots a golfer makes in practice, the hours each day a gymnast spends on each maneuver lead to moments that resemble religious ecstasy. Why does focusing our mind and energies do this? Again we turn to the yoga sutras: Ignorance and suffering come, they say, from a false identification with the passing objects of experience, through a distraction from our deepest source. By quieting the surface mind, by withdrawing our assent to the world's random turning, we can perceive our true identity with spirit. This identity transcends naming. It is something we intuitively recognize, even if we don't have words or concepts for it. An Indian story tells about a thief who, while pretending he was a yogi in order to avoid arrest, became enlightened. It didn't matter how his meditation started, only how it ended. It is like that with some athletes who concentrate simply for the sake of their sport: They catch glimpses of spiritual freedom through their discipline and feel the call of the interior life.

Detachment from Results

Because the gathering of energies we have just described takes place in the heat of competition, in the ups and downs that come with winning and losing, the sports participant often acquires a detachment from results. If an athlete cannot bear to lose or gets over-inflated from winning, he or she is less likely to succeed. Thus contests teach a centeredness in action, a grace under pressure. Such inner poise and disinterest are fundamental to every spiritual practice, for without them the richness of awareness is impeded. Detachment from the results of one's actions facilitates a quieting of the mind that makes way for the kinds of experience examined in the preceding chapters. If the mind is agitated and the emotions are in turmoil, there is little room for the extraordinary peace, the sense of power, and the transcendent joy that many sports participants report.

The concentration of will and awareness in sport is heightened, we believe, because it takes place in the midst of winning and losing, amid dramatic ups and downs. The participant who perseveres in a sport has to learn the poignant lesson—at some level at least —that there is an interior grace that transcends the world's uncertain results. Sport can teach us the ancient wisdom that by losing our lives we gain them. A famous spiritual teacher wrote: "You may take this for the truth, that when a free mind is really disinterested, God is compelled to enter it." (129: p. 84)

Sport's Creative and Integrative Power

Whether you're learning to run the mile, lower your golf score, or scale a mountain, sport demands a creative joining of various capacities. Willpower, awareness, imagination, emotion, the senses, the intellect, and motor control must be harmonized for top performance. And dreams and reveries come into play as well. New alignments of body and mind take place in the night, and the process becomes continuous through waking and sleep. (17: pp. 81–82; 46: p. 60; 89: p. 11) Successful athletes make an enormous number of psychological and physiological connections that lie beyond the scope of verbal awareness. In this regard, their creativity is close to creativity in art, science, and religion. (66: pp. 155–62) Olympic hurdle champion David Hemery wrote: "In the course of any season, the athlete will face all of the following: defeat and victory; sickness and health; tension and relaxation; degrees of pain, doubt, disappointment and despair, as well as satisfaction and ecstasy." (200: p. 186) In his book *Another Hurdle*, he described the way his sport obsessed him day and night, through winning and losing, suffering and health. He found himself perfecting his ability at home as well as on the track, in his dreams, and in his training sessions.

Jim Naughton described Michael Jordan as "one who pushes back the limits of human possibility" (1184: p. 133), who can take "to the air with nothing in mind and simply [wait] for his creativity to kick in." (1184: p. 130) He added that with Jordan on the court, there are "opportunities for the miraculous." (1184: p. 134) Bill Russell wrote that jumping "is one of the purest pleasures I know for an athlete," adding that although people the world over jump with joy, in basketball it is more likely that a player feels "happy because he is jumping." He observed: "On their way back to the floor after a particularly high leap, they bend their legs more than they need to, just to prolong the sensation." Russell wrote that the "lift" he got from jumping reinforced the new moves he was making: "I jumped higher because the moves in my mind were beginning to work on the court, and some of the moves worked better because I was jumping so high." (1320: p. 73)

Lee Evans, the 400-meters Olympic champion and world record holder, talked to us about the power of the subconscious mind to search out flaws in racing style and correct them. Working with Bud Winter, the great sprint coach at San Jose State College in the late 1960s, Evans used self-hypnosis and mental practice for several years on his way to championships and world records. In practicing for the 1968 Olympics, he visualized every step of the 400-meter race until he saw "each stride he would take." By his repeating this exercise again and again, his style and pacing improved and the overall flow of his performance was perfected. The world record he set in that race stood for twenty-three years. In dreams and waking reveries, new ideas, images, and feelings related to his running appeared, sometimes unexpectedly. His account resembled descriptions that certain artists and scientists have given of their discoveries. The French mathematician Henri Poincaré, for example, discovered part of the Fuchsian functions as he stepped onto a bus. Kekulé discovered the formula for the benzene molecule in a dream. Coleridge wrote *Kubla Khan* after hearing it in a sleep stimulated by the opiate laudanum. The history of artistic and scientific discovery is filled with insights of this kind, delivered from unconscious levels of the mind. (171, 257) The world of sport is filled with similar stories, because like art and science it can engage the imagination and the will to their deepest roots. For David Hemery, Lee Evans, and other athletes, this all-involving process is part of sport's fascination.

But psychological integration is more than intrapersonal. Even in individualistic sports such as running or mountaineering, friendship and teamwork are involved. Without them, sport loses much of its beauty. Just as it is fundamental to religious life, cooperation with others has been a prime sporting virtue. Chris Bonington had the following to say about climbing Annapurna: "I don't think any of us felt regret at leaving. . . . We had been there too long and given too much and yet we had known some of the most exciting climbing of our lives, had reached a level of unity and selflessness that had made success possible. . . . we felt . . . an extraordinary elation, not solely from our success, but also because we had managed to become such a close-knit team." (53: p. 228)

Valerie Andrews described the runner's ability "to go farther and faster than you ever have before when you link up with a group of other runners." She attributed this to "a fund of collective energy—both physical and psychological—that sustains the group as a whole and from which the weakest runner can draw new strength." (556: pp. 138–39)

Sport's Exploration of Human Limits

Sport proliferates, one can argue, out of a drive in the human race to realize more and more of its bodily possibilities. One of our most fundamental desires, it seems, is to know and dramatize the richness of physical life. So people run, jump, swim, and fly, surf on twenty-foot waves, dive to the ocean depths, glide on wings grown smaller and smaller, and climb into dangerous caves or up the most precipitous mountains. Where will this proliferation of athletics end? To what adventures and extremes will it lead us?

In this, sport is like all spiritual adventure. When you read Indian and Tibetan scriptures, for example, you find an immense variety of ways for self-exceeding. Thousands of mental states, endless varieties of love, and countless supernormal powers are dramatized in the lives of the saints. Both sport and the spiritual life grow out of our human urge to express the richness of existence.

The demands our games make on us take many forms, for each has its own set of archetypes, or ideals. Mountaineering and race car driving, for example, require very different sets of capacities. Each stretches its participants in a special way and aligns them with particular dimensions of experience. In no other field of human activity is there such a proliferation of specialized physiques. As athletics have developed in the modern world, they have required an ever greater variety of skills and bodily structure to support them—whether it is the muscular frame of a three-hundred-pound defensive tackle, the elastic joints of a gymnast, the prodigious cardiopulmonary system of a marathon runner, or the steady hand of an archer. Never before have there been so many experiments with the body's limits. This vast cultivation and redesign of the body provides an unprecedented laboratory for exploring the limits of human possibility. In this, sport points beyond itself. For it is possible to imagine an historic adventure in human transformation that might arise in part from the experiments and achievements of athletics. We will say more about this possibility in our concluding chapter.

Sport's Ability to
Command Long-Term Commitment

The long-term involvement that sport commands provides a unique basis for spiritual adventure, because without sustained commitment the far-reaching changes of mind and physique that such adventure requires are simply impossible. In most religious teachings it is said that no lasting realization can be achieved without many years of practice. Most teachers have said that enlightenment costs no less than everything. Many athletes make that kind of commitment to their sport.

The spiritually evocative elements we have discussed—long-term commitment, sustained concentration, creativity, self-integration, being in sacred times and places, and stretching to the limits of one's capacity—are common to both sport and religious discipline. These similarities between the two kinds of activity often lead to the same kinds of experience. In the pages that follow, we will explore the similarities between spiritual and athletic experience more closely.

THE PERENNIAL PHILOSOPHY

In the lore of Eastern philosophy and yoga, in the writings of mystics from every religion, and in the accounts of modern seers there exists a coherent body of insight that often corresponds with the extraordinary experiences of sports participants. The resemblance between this ancient, well-established knowledge and the stories sportspeople tell is often dramatic and compelling. Aldous Huxley (221), borrowing from the philosopher Leibnitz, called this ancient knowledge the *Perennial Philosophy*, because it has arisen repeatedly in almost every society for the past three thousand years and because rudiments exist in Stone Age cultures. It appears in the writings of Taoist, Hindu, Buddhist, Greek, Moslem, Jewish, and Christian mystics. It reappears in every century, surviving every period of skepticism and despair. It has always exhibited a core of fundamental agreement, though the intellectual forms, the language, the rituals, practices, and qualities of experience in each tradition have differed.

Let's look at some of its central tenets, for they help us understand the extraordinary aspects of sport that we are examining. This is not a complete summary of the perennial philosophy, but it is adequate, we think, to show some of the parallels that exist between the two fields of experience.

The Fundamental Reality

The central perception of the perennial philosophy is that there is a fundamental reality, godhead, or ground of existence that transcends the ordinary world, yet exists within it. However separate in appearance they may be, the individual, the universe, and transcendent divinity are essentially one. This spiritual reality is the source of all consciousness and can be known directly—either spontaneously as in sports or through deliberate practices like prayer and yoga—because we are secretly joined with It already.

> That moves and that moves not,
> That is far and the same is near.
> That is within all this and
> That is also outside all this.
> —*Isha Upanishad*

One Nature, perfect and pervading, circulates in all natures,
One Reality, all-comprehensive, contains within itself all realities.
The one Moon reflects itself wherever there is a sheet of water,
And all the moons in the waters are embraced within the one Moon.
The Dharma-body [the Absolute] of all the Buddhas enters into my own being.
And my own being is found in union with theirs. . . .

The Inner Light is beyond praise and blame;
Like space it knows no boundaries,
Yet it is even here, within us, ever retaining its serenity and fullness.
> —Yung-chia Ta-shih (221: p. 8)

These statements from Hindu and Buddhist sages reflect the eternal Reality that is all things and transcends all things. See how they resemble this account of Charles Lindbergh of his epic flight to Paris:

> While I'm staring at the instruments, during an unearthly age of time, both conscious and asleep, the fuselage behind me becomes filled with ghostly presences—vaguely outlined forms, transparent, moving, riding weightless with me in the plane. I feel no surprise at their coming. There's no suddenness to their appearance. Without turning my head, I see them as clearly as though in my normal field of vision. There's no limit to my sight —my skull is one great eye, seeing everywhere at once. . . .
>
> All sense of substance leaves. There's no longer weight to my body, no longer hardness to the stick. The feeling of flesh is gone. I become independent of physical laws—of food, of shelter, of life. I'm almost one with these vaporlike forms behind me, less tangible than air, universal as aether. I'm still attached to life; they, not at all; but at any moment some thin band may snap and there'll be no difference between us. . . .
>
> I'm on the border line of life and a greater realm beyond, as though caught in the field of gravitation between two planets, acted on by forces I can't control, forces too weak to be measured by any means at my command, yet representing powers incomparably stronger than I've ever known. . . .
>
> Death no longer seems the final end it used to be, but rather the entrance to a new and free existence which includes all space, all time.
>
> Am I now more man or spirit? Will I fly my airplane on to Europe and live in flesh as I have before, feeling hunger, pain, and cold, or am I about to join these ghostly forms, become a consciousness in space, all-seeing, all-knowing, unhampered by materialistic fetters of the world? (293: pp. 389–90)

"My skull is one great eye, seeing everywhere at once"—what a vivid image of his experience. "Am I about to . . . become a consciousness in space, all-seeing, all-knowing, unhampered by materialistic fetters of the world?"* Lindbergh's description of his experience could be a paraphrase of certain religious scriptures. The apprehension of a greater realm beyond this one, the feeling of independence from his body and physical laws, and the sense that he is acted upon by "powers incomparably stronger than I've ever known" arise from the same realization that pervades the perennial philosophy.

The Provisional Reality of the Ordinary World

Figure skater Toller Cranston described a performance when "the audience was still, watching intently, anticipating. [At one point] . . . I felt an electric shock run through the crowd. They understood. In that brief instant we fused. Reality no longer existed and time became suspended. We opened the gateway to tomorrow that night and passed through. We could feel it; we could feel the birth pangs. It was something . . . beyond reality." (365: p. 10)

Cranston's experience that night was more real, he said, than everyday existence. It was something *beyond reality*. This shift in one's apprehension and assignment of reality occurs in sport, sometimes for fleeting moments, sometimes for hours or days following an experience like Cranston's. Several people have told us that the world "seemed like a dream" after an uplifting game or sporting expedition: For a while after such events, they say, everything seemed unimportant compared to their new realizations. Listening to their accounts, we have been reminded of statements by mystics that the world seems illusory after illumination.† This sense of illusion comes in part from a spontaneous reordering of priorities

---

* Lindbergh did not describe his experience in his first book, *We, Pilot and Plane*, published in 1927, but in *The Spirit of St. Louis*, which was published in 1953, twenty-six years later. Like several athletes we have talked to, it took him many years to acknowledge the mystical dimensions of his adventure. His posthumous book *Autobiography of Values* (291) reveals more of his feelings and insights regarding these matters.

† William James, *The Varieties of Religious Experience* (227); see especially "The Sick Soul," pp. 125–63, and "The Divided Self," pp. 163–86. In *The Collected Works of Sri Aurobindo* (20), Vol. 22, pp. 39–69, Sri Aurobindo's letters describe the shifting sense of reality in the practice of yoga.

and attachments: Suddenly God or Spirit is more important than one's ordinary worldly concerns.

But as spiritual insight develops, the world comes to be seen as an aspect or manifestation of the Reality that once seemed to transcend it. In the language of Buddhism, "Samsara [the ordinary world] *is* nirvana." But in order to arrive at this sense of the Spirit in everything, one must live the right kind of life.

The Need for Discipline

Many athletes have trouble recapturing peak moments in sport because they have difficulty incorporating them into the rest of their lives. Former quarterback John Brodie described this problem: "Football players and athletes generally get into this kind of being or beingness—call it what you will—more often than is generally recognized. But they often lose it after a game or after a season is over. They often don't have a workable philosophy or understanding to support the kind of thing they get into while they are playing. They don't have the words for it. So after a game you see some of them coming down, making fools of themselves sometimes, coming way down in their tone level. But during the game they come way up. A missing ingredient for many people, I guess, is that they don't have a supporting philosophy or discipline for a better life." (343: p. 22)

To hold these realizations, this "being or beingness," we must live in tune with their truth by practicing some kind of spiritual discipline. Saint John of the Cross observed: "He who interrupts the course of his spiritual exercises and prayer is like a man who allows a bird to escape from his hand; he can hardly catch it again." (221: p. 292) Saint Francis de Sales wrote: "I am glad you make a fresh beginning daily; there is no better means of attaining . . . than by continually beginning again." (221: p. 293) And the German mystic Meister Eckhart: "I tell you that no one can experience this birth of God in the soul without a mighty effort. No one can attain this birth unless he can withdraw his mind entirely from things." (221: p. 292)

These statements resemble the praise of discipline that comes from many athletes. Yuri Vlasov, champion Russian weightlifter, told reporter Robert Lipsyte: "At the peak of tremendous and victorious effort while the blood is pounding in your head, all suddenly becomes quiet within you. Everything seems clearer and whiter than ever before, as if great spotlights had been turned on. . . . At that moment you have the conviction that you contain all the power in the world, that you are capable of everything, that you have wings. There is no more precious moment in life than this, the white moment, *and you will work very hard for years just to taste it again.*" (295: p. 280)

Surfing champion Midget Farrelly described his passion for discipline: "Maybe perfection can never be reached. But I hope that by practicing continually and by gaining more and more experience I'll get to know enough about waves to leave me free to concentrate on the board. And if I know the board, I'll be able to concentrate on what I want to do on it. And by the time I've reached the peak of my surfing life I should be able to make one movement on the board instead of two—drop down the waveface once instead of twice. . . . You've got to regulate, moderate, and keep refining everything you do. And all the time you keep pushing yourself, trying to push yourself right up to the limit, and beyond it." (141: pp. 27–28)

Champion boxer Rocky Marciano followed a very strict discipline when he was training for a fight. Joyce Carol Oates wrote that he

> was willing to seclude himself from the world, including his wife and family, for as long as three months before a fight. Apart from the grueling physical ordeal of this period and the obsessive preoccupation with diet and weight and muscle tone, Marciano concentrated on one thing: the upcoming fight. Every minute of his life was defined in terms of the opening second of the fight. In his training camp the opponent's name was never mentioned in Marciano's hearing, nor was boxing as a subject discussed. In the final month Marciano would not write a letter since a letter related to the outside world. During the last ten days before a fight he would see no mail, take no telephone calls, meet no new acquaintances. During the week before the fight he would not shake hands. Or go for a ride in a car, however brief. No new foods! No dreaming of the morning after the fight! For all that was not *the fight* had to be excluded from con-

sciousness. When Marciano worked out with a punching bag he saw his opponent before him, when he jogged he saw his opponent close beside him, no doubt when he slept he "saw" his opponent constantly—as the cloistered monk or nun chooses by an act of fanatical will to "see" only God. (1199: p. 29)

When David Smith was thrown out of college a second time, he reevaluated his life. He had been a champion swimmer in high school, but now he owned a bar, drank heavily, and lived a fast life. He stopped smoking, drinking, and gambling, and rediscovered the joy of swimming. He resolved to swim the Golden Gate, but not for mere enjoyment. "I knew that if I were to train seriously for a Gate swim," he wrote, "I would have to remove myself almost entirely from society. I would be making a journey, an essentially lonely journey, into myself, in search of something that was meaningful to me alone. In that journey my friends would be my enemies, my enjoyments would be my liabilities, and the blandishments of society in general would be impediments to any change. I had to see life differently, yet I had mixed feelings about the path I was taking." (1397: p. 16)

On the day of the Gate swim, "Almost immediately an odd thing happened to me. Just after I got into the water, my body felt possessed by a strange feeling, as if tiny charges of electricity were running through my nerve endings. At first I attributed it to excitement—I had really wanted to get swimming. But the feeling was different from any high or excitement I had felt before. It flowed through me like a powerful guidance system. . . . I thought I had been lucky enough to pick up a shore current that was helping me along toward the rip. But soon I realized it was no current. It was some power inside me." (1397: p. 22)

His swimming guide told him to slow down. But the feeling told him otherwise: "It was a message. It said that nothing could stop me; I was going to 'win.' I felt no cold. The slaps of the waves, now whipped by a sharp wind sweeping under the bridge, filled my eyes with salt under the goggles. But all I felt was exhilaration. Instead of swimming in a daze, grim and determined, I was floating along in a crystal palace of the mind." (1397: p. 22) He expected the letdown, the cold, the feeling of struggle with the current to begin at any moment, but instead, "I felt only an extraordinary focusing of effort, a compression of my whole being into a unity of action. What could it mean?" (1397: p. 23)

A rip tide caught him and he was pulled in two directions at once, then overturned. But, after what appeared to be a mere twenty seconds, he was "in the shallows at my destination. I emerged from the water like a man in a dream. . . . It felt so unreal. . . . I was . . . the possessor of some kind of secret that I felt I could not share because I did not understand what it was about." (1397: p. 23) Afterward, he felt he could account for his success because of the training he had put in, but he could not explain the exhilaration and effortlessness. Following the event, he also felt he was "high all the time. . . . an apparently continuous and different state of being. But what to do with it?" (1397: p. 24)

In the months that followed, he sold his bar and engaged in several long-distance swims, trying to repeat the experience. His first attempts did not succeed. He returned home and began reading about altered states and spiritual experiences. He practiced meditation and yoga. He had an insight that he had been trying too hard. To test it, he decided to swim the Straits of Gibralter, the site of one of his earlier failures. This time he experienced self-transcendence. "In this moment I felt a universal power—the source of all energy—passing through me. I was open to it, and I became its channel. Later I discovered that the people in the boats felt it, too." (1397: p. 42) He wrote that this swim

was not a swim as I had experienced it before. It was instead a peace. . . . Instead of journeying to Gibraltar, I was immersed in a journey that led only to the place where I already existed, in the water. This was the place! The sea smoothed itself into a great welcoming embrace. I flew toward . . . where? It didn't matter. The currents fell away. A German freighter passed close by, and the flotilla people shouted and cursed. We had to do a 360-degree turn to avoid ramming the ship, but I was like a machine, swimming through the freighter if necessary. I felt myself at the threshold of another breakthrough, another change.

It felt as if the very molecules of the Strait's waters were combining to ease my passage. I knew this was in my imagination only, but if this were truly a combination of the environment and the swimmer within it, then perhaps I was charging the waters around me with my own energy. Or the energy of the water was charging me. It really did not matter which way it was, as long as the source of the power kept sweeping me onward. (1397: pp. 41–42)

When he landed, he experienced a new identity, as an explorer of the inner life. "I had invented a quest for the source of this mysterious power, a quest I shared with nobody else." (1397: p. 44) To confirm this calling, he decided to surpass the twenty-four-hour nonstop indoor swim world record, which he did by a margin of six miles. Then, as Franklin Russell wrote in the preface to Smith's book, "he conceived and carried out a series of unique athletic adventures, using the wilderness of the earth as his settings, his arenas. He swam, walked, ran, climbed, kayaked, parachuted, and bicycled—usually in places where no one had thought to do such things. . . . for David . . . they were primarily opportunities to explore this phenomenon he called the source. Was its power a separate energy, or just his own, enhanced? Was it sprung from his discipline, or did it come from the environment? Was it a force of the wilderness?" (1397: p. 3)

An essential aspect of Smith's message, in Russell's words, was "that he has transformed the hero's journey into everyone's experience. Though his adventures may be exotic, the insights gained by them apply to all our life journeys." (1397: p. 7) In an attempt to connect others to the "source," Smith undertook what he called the Blackwater experiment, in which he took a small group of people with problems such as depression and obesity into wilderness training programs so that they could develop their own myths, new identities, and new challenges. Smith felt that they, too, experienced "the source."

In *Bone Games*, Rob Schultheis described his transformative experience during a fall on Mount Neva: ". . . the only way down was a pillar of black water ice: I shinnied down it, hands jammed between the ice and the rock face, boot heels jammed against the mountain, toes against the tissue-thin ripples in the great icicle's flank. Impossible, absurd. Then a vertical pitch of rock, nothing to hold on to and fifteen feet of it, and I clung to the *grain of the granite*—no, but I did—and moved down over it, onto more ice-scoured ledges." (1365: p. 11) He added:

> Looking back on it, I really cannot explain or describe properly that strange person I found inhabiting my body that afternoon. It was just too different from my everyday self, and I have never seen its like before, nor have I seen it since, except for a split second in Mexico in 1982, and a few strange weeks of long-distance running. . . . The person I became on Neva was the best possible version of myself, the person I *should have been* throughout my life. No regrets, no hesitation; there were no false moves left in me. I really believe I could have hit a mosquito in the eye with a pine needle at thirty paces; I couldn't miss because there was no such thing as a miss. It didn't matter whether I fell or not, because I could not fall, any more than two plus two can equal three. It was all sublime nonsense, of course, but I believed it, down in my very cells; if I hadn't believed, I would have been hurled into the Pit below. . . . Joy filled me, from the soles of my feet to the tips of the hairs on my head. (1365: pp. 12–13)

Returning home, he became his old self again. Like David Smith, he tried to reinstate the condition under which the experience had occurred, but it did not happen. As a graduate student he studied shamanism, noting the great similarity between shamans' ordeals and sports. "Many of the shamanistic training rituals," he wrote, "were really nothing more than extreme games, like mountaineering, distance running, trekking, engineered to deliberately induce the kind of power and ecstasy I had accidentally stumbled upon on Mount Neva." (1365: p. 50) However, there was one big difference: "They held on to the power they found while I lost mine." (1365: p. 54) Another difference, he noted, was that "shamans pushed their ritual games and ordeals to the very limits of possibility; if the situation wasn't drastic, the magic wouldn't come. Those power-giving gods . . . seldom appeared to anyone but the hardest-core risk takers, the exhausted ones who pushed their way through second, fifth, fiftieth winds till there were none left." (1365: p. 69)

He tried long-distance solo walking in eastern Nepal during the monsoon season, but the power did not come. He learned how body chemistry accompanies peak performance: "When the biochemistry is good, the performance and the experience are good; when it is bad, they are bad." (1365: p. 105) He hoped that by observing his biochemical responses in extreme situations he could compose his own version of the trigger mechanisms that enabled shamans to renew their metanormal experiences. He came close to a repeat experience while engaged in daily long-distance running, but the effect disappeared when he fell in love. He decided that he "would have to take the mind or spirit into account; it wasn't just an affair of the flesh." (1365: p. 131)

He then spent a week alone on Mt. Popocatépetl, aiming "not so much [at] the physical summit of the volcano as some apogee of consciousness inside myself." (1365: p. 147) Modeling his attempt after René Daumal's metaphysical novel, *Mount Analogue*, he hoped to climb "physical and metaphysical peaks simultaneously, in a holy pilgrimage." (1365: p. 148) Exhausted from dirty water and little food, he managed to crawl to the top, and then— "I felt that same sense of bliss, a joy beyond comprehension, that I had felt on Mount Neva; a feeling that all ills were healed, everything was all right, always had been, really, and always would be. There was nothing wanting in all of creation; anything less than perfection was impossible." (1365: p. 164) But in this experience he did not possess the extraordinary physical power, the strength and wondrous balance he had known the first time. Still, he felt he had "contacted something extraordinary, not of this world." (1365: p. 165) Schultheis concluded that humans lost a vital part of themselves when they let go of the "intuitive and powerful world" that we contact in high-risk sports and the passions of long-term discipline.

Knowing and Expressing the Deeper Perfection

"You will work very hard for years just to taste it again"—athletes often give this reason for training hard and long. And work they must, to achieve the prodigies of physical excellence we have described. A famous Buddhist story has it that one cannot achieve enlightenment until he wants it as badly as a person held under water wants air. Some athletes train as arduously as religious monastics. Top-flight gymnasts practice eight hours a day for decades. Distance runners run up to 200 miles a week. Many swimmers live through agonies, both in practice and in competition, and weight-lifters often measure their progress by the amount of pain they can endure.

Magic Johnson spent years off the court learning to dribble, to get what he calls "touch." He wrote: "After hours and days and months and years of dribbling all over town and every different way—behind my back, between my legs—that basketball was like a part of me, like another arm. By then, I just had the touch, and it was as if the ball wasn't there. That's what dribbling is—touch. Once I got it, I knew the game was under my control. I wanted to be able to feel the ball without looking at it. I wanted it to go where I went without fighting it or searching for it. I wanted to be able to make all my fanciest moves, spinning and twisting for the basket, and have the ball be right there in my hand. When I was coming down the floor against the defense, I wanted to keep my head up so I could see the whole floor, not looking down to search for the basketball. The only way I could do that was to have the touch." (959: p. 32)

Wayne Gretzky wrote that as a youngster the only thing he wanted to do in the winter was skate: "I'd get up in the morning, skate from 7:00 to 8:30, go to school, come home at 3:30, stay on the ice until my mom insisted I come in for dinner, eat in my skates, then go back out until 9:00. On Saturdays and Sundays, we'd have huge games, but nighttime became my time. It was sort of an un-written rule around the neighborhood that I was to be out there by myself or with my dad. I would just handle the puck in and out of these empty detergent bottles my dad set up as pylons. Then I'd set up targets in the net and try to hit them with forehands, back-hands, whatever. Then I'd do it all again, except this time with a tennis ball, which is much harder to handle. . . . I was so addicted that my dad had big kids come over to play against me. And when the kids wanted to go home, I'd beg them to stay longer. I suppose that is how I was always able to do well against bigger guys later on. That's all I could get to play against." (860: pp. 17–18)

This willingness to suffer so much for sport can be understood as a concentrated expression of our drive to express a deeper per-fection and beauty we secretly sense. That deeper perfection is more important to many athletes than prizes or applause. Billie

Jean King wrote: "It's a perfect combination of . . . violent action taking place in an atmosphere of total tranquility. . . . When it happens I want to stop the match and grab the microphone and shout, 'That's what it's all about.' Because it is. It's not the big prize I'm going to win at the end of the match, or anything else. It's just having done something that's totally pure and having experienced the perfect emotion, and I'm always sad that I can't communicate that feeling right at the moment it's happening. I can only hope people realize what's going on." (251: p. 201)

William Willis expressed a similar feeling when he tried to account for his sailing alone on a raft across the Pacific Ocean: "This was not a stunt—not merely an adventure. And I did not want to prove any scientific theory, or discover and set up any new course of any kind for others to follow. To me, this voyage was something much more—it was a pilgrimage to the shrine of my philosophy. Call it an adventure of the spirit. On this voyage I wanted to prove—had to prove to myself—that I had followed the right star throughout my life." (524: p. 15)

Ben Hogan's devotion to practice is legendary among golf professionals. His friend and fellow player Jimmy Demaret describes an episode that typified Hogan's discipline:

> He'll practice like no one else I've ever known. He loves to just stand there and hit golf balls. No man ever lived who has hit as many golf balls as Hogan. He won't think of going out for a round, even a meaningless one with friends, unless he's hit some practice shots. And practice for Hogan may mean hitting as many as a thousand balls in five or six hours. . . .
>
> In the first round of the Rochester Open in 1941, Hogan burned up the course, shooting a record 64. He had ten birdies in that score, but the poor guy took a six on the par four seventeenth. I had a 69, which I thought good enough, and I sat around with the fellows in the clubhouse until it was almost nighttime, gabbing and having a drink or two.
>
> When I went out to the car to drive home, I noticed a late evening eager beaver all alone on the practice tee hitting wood shots. I didn't have to be told it was Hogan. I walked over to him.
>
> "What are you trying to do, man?" I asked. "You had

ten birdies today. Why, the officials are still inside talking about it. They're thinking of putting a limit on you."

Ben gave me that dead-serious look of his. "You know, Jimmy, if a man can shoot ten birdies, there's no reason why he can't shoot eighteen. Why can't you birdie every hole on the course?" And then his face took on a look of real anguish and he wailed, "And how about that terrible seventeenth?" (109: pp. 159–60)

The Essential Ecstasy

To the eye of the spiritually awakened, the world is filled with beauty and adventure. In the words of the yaqui sorcerer Don Juan, ". . . it is brimming with possibility every minute." This in spite of suffering and discord, in spite of ignorance and general human failure. Sri Aurobindo, the Indian mystic and philosopher, reflected the vision of seers throughout history when he wrote: "There must be something in us—much vaster, profounder, truer than the superficial consciousness—which takes delight impartially in all experiences; it is that delight which secretly supports the superficial mental being and enables it to persevere through all labours, sufferings and ordeals. . . . In our ordinary life this truth is hidden from us or only dimly glimpsed at times or imperfectly held and conceived. But if we learn to live within, we infallibly awaken to this presence within us which is our more real self, a presence profound, calm, joyous . . . of which the world is not the master." (22: pp. 97–99) This perception, that there is something profounder in us, fits many athletes' reports of inward knowing and transcendence. They sense something that "secretly supports the superficial mental being and enables it to persevere through all labours, sufferings and ordeals." Vlasov's statement that there is no more precious moment in life than the "white moment"—and that a person will work for years to achieve it—points toward the essential joy Aurobindo described.

More than most human activities, sport reveals this essential truth of existence as it is perceived in the perennial philosophy. As one of the Indian scriptures says, "From Delight all these creatures are born; In that Delight they live and move; to that Delight they will return." Ernest Hemingway thought the bullfight dramatized this truth. He tells us of the "complete faena [the final part of the fight]; the faena that takes a man out of himself . . . that gives him an ecstasy that is, while momentary, as profound as any religious ecstasy." (201: p. 212)

The essential joy of sport, so closely allied to the secret delight that "supports the superficial being," often emerges in the athletic ordeal. A friend told us about a time he ran for five hours on the deck of a ship—a distance he later estimated to be more than 30 miles. "The discomfort grew extreme, grew into pain, but I stayed with it, said that it was all right, wondered if there was anything on the other side. After a while the pain subsided. . . . Then it returned as before, and I climbed into it again, allowed it to be OK. Then once again it slipped away. By this time I must have run at least three hours in circles on the deck of the ship. I was beginning to lose touch with my body, floating away to distant places. . . . There were thoughts of grandeur and supreme power; I could do anything. Then after a long time I began to encounter a new experience, a kind of vibrant numbness. A dull tingling throughout my whole body as if one of my limbs were coming awake after the circulation had been cut off. *There was great pain but also ecstasy.* I knew that I should stop but I couldn't: I couldn't let go of that power and joy."

Athletic ordeals, in which pain is consciously invited so that it might turn into strength and joy, often resemble the ordeals of religious contemplatives. In Zen Buddhism there are periods of practice that last for weeks, during which a monk might sit in meditation for sixteen hours a day or more. The pain and distraction that arise during these sessions are sometimes overwhelming, but depths of knowing, joy, and freedom emerge from the experience. Dervish dancing rituals sometimes last for many days. Yogis sit in the same place for months. Sport and religious practice both embrace ordeal in the service of illumination and freedom. By consciously transforming pain into delight, the athlete begins to awaken to the inner presence "of which the world is not the master."

Distance runners are notorious for the pain they go through. Champion miler Herb Elliot said that his coach, Percy Cerutty, helped him to world records "not so much by improving my technique, but by releasing in my mind and soul a power that I only vaguely thought existed. 'Thrust against pain,' Percy told me. . . . He introduced me to every book about Francis of Assisi and said, '*Walk towards suffering. Love suffering. Embrace it.*' " (133: p. 38)

It is easy to see the love of play and adventure exemplified in sport. But the athlete's love of pain and ordeal is more mysterious. One key to the mystery comes with the ancient mystical insight that a fundamental delight exists within or behind all suffering.

Knowledge by Identity

In the *Tao Te Ching*, the founding scripture of Taoism, it is said that the wise man can know the whole world without leaving his room. Teachers in many religious traditions have insisted that this is the case, that the discovery of our spiritual depths is a doorway to knowledge of the world at large. In a famous Indian metaphor, the universe is compared to the god Indra's "net of jewels," in which each jewel—that is, each facet of existence—is present in every other.*

One Reality, all-comprehensive, contains within itself all realities.
The one Moon reflects itself wherever there is a sheet of water.
And all the moons in the waters are embraced within the one Moon.
The Dharma-body [the Absolute] of all the Buddhas enters into my own being. . . . Yung-chia Ta-shih (221: p. 8)

The Roman mystic and philosopher Plotinus expressed it this way: "Each being contains in itself the whole intelligible world. Therefore All is everywhere. Each is there All, and All is each. Man as he now is has ceased to be the All. But when he ceases to be a mere ego, he raises himself again and penetrates the whole world." (221: p. 5) Because we are usually attached to ordinary appearances, we have little or no access to this fundamental order. We

---

* In every section of a hologram there exists a miniature duplicate of the entire picture. Stanford's Karl Pribram and other brain researchers believe that the brain operates largely on holographic principles. (See *The Silent Pulse* by George Leonard. [278])

need to penetrate beneath appearances if we are to find the all-encompassing knowledge we secretly possess. Meister Eckhart wrote: "When is a man in mere understanding? I answer, 'When a man sees one thing separated from another.' And when is a man above mere understanding? That I can tell you: 'When a man sees All in all, then a man stands beyond mere understanding.' (221: p. 57)

Every mystical tradition refers to a knowledge-by-identity that goes beyond particular kinds of information to an integral insight through which one knows the world's essential secrets. But there are more mundane kinds of knowledge that derive from it: some mystics, it is said, can read another person's mind and heart, can divine the secrets of nature, can sense what is happening in other times and places. To make this practical kind of knowledge accessible, however, the seer has to have a mind prepared to absorb these particular items. It takes the artist's trained sensibility or the scientist's immersion in the pertinent scientific data to translate the essential knowledge by identity into artistic or scientific discovery. Athletes, it seems, also appropriate this knowing to accomplish extraordinary feats. D. T. Suzuki, the famous Japanese scholar and translator of Zen Buddhist texts, quotes a Japanese swordsman: "When the identity is realized, I as swordsman see no opponent confronting me and threatening to strike me. I seem to transform myself into the opponent, and every movement he makes as well as every thought he conceives are felt as if they were all my own and I intuitively . . . know when and how to strike him." (479: p. 206)

In her book *Sport and Identity*, physical education professor Patsy Neal describes an experience she had competing in the Free Throw Championship at the National AAU Basketball Tournament as a college freshman. She had practiced strenuously for the event and knew she was capable of scoring well but was too nervous to do well in the early rounds of competition. On the night before the last round she prayed for help and tried to envision a sense of calm while surrounded by the spectators, but images of failure defeated her efforts. Finally, she fell asleep. She wrote:

> But then a strange thing happened in my sleep. Sometime during the night, I had a dream. I was shooting the free-throws, and each time the ball fell through the goal, the net

would change to the image of Christ. It was as though I was flowing into the basket instead of the ball. I felt endless, unhampered . . . and in some way I was connected to the image of Christ that kept flowing from the basket. The sensation was that of transcending *everything*. I was more than I was. I was a particle flowing into *all* of life. It seems almost profane to try to describe the feeling because words are so very inadequate.

The next day, I still had the feeling when I woke. I felt as though I was *floating* through the day, not just living it. That evening, when I shot my free-throws in the finals, I was probably the calmest I have ever been in my life. I didn't . . . see or hear the crowd. It was only me, the ball, and the basket. The number of baskets I made really had no sense of importance to me at the time. The only thing that really mattered was what I *felt*. But even so, I would have found it hard to miss even if I had wanted to. . . .

I know now what people mean when they speak of a "state of grace." I was in a state of grace, and if it were in my power to maintain what I was experiencing at that point in time, I would have given up everything in my possession in preference to that sensation. (350: p. 167)

Neal won the championship, missing only two baskets out of fifty. As a result of this and related experiences, she said, "*I know* God exists, regardless of the name we give Him, or the way we describe the way He works." (350: p. 169) This series of images is all the more powerful, we think, because of Neal's youthful naïveté. She flowed into the basket, which had assumed the face of Christ, and performed miraculously well. Could there be a clearer, less embellished example of knowledge by identity? But we are stretching a point, you might argue. To find union with Christ shooting baskets! We might answer with Saint Francis de Sales: "God requires a faithful fulfillment of the merest trifle given us to do, rather than the most ardent aspiration to things to which we are not called." Or with Saint Francis of Assisi, who taught that God can be served and known in our simplest act or loving gesture.

Athletes often communicate with one another in ways that seem to surpass ordinary connections, in ways that have the flavor of telepathy, or knowledge by identity. Pitching great Sandy Koufax described the extraordinary rapport he had with catcher John Roseboro. He recalled his most vivid memory of the 1963 World Series:

> As I got the ball back and began to look in for the sign, I thought to myself: I'd like to take something off my curve ball. . . .
>
> Now why does a thought like that come to you? A change-up curve is exactly what you don't throw Mantle, particularly in a spot where it can cost you a ball game. Change-up curves are what Mantle hits out of ball parks. I hadn't thrown a change-up in the entire game, as far as I could remember. And at the same moment that the thought came into my mind, there flickered the answering thought: But how will I explain why I threw it if he hits it out of here?
>
> I know it isn't brave, noble, or professional to worry about being second-guessed. It's just human.
>
> And while the thought was still half formed in my mind, I was looking down toward the plate, and John Roseboro was putting down two fingers, the sign for the curve. He was putting them down hesitantly, though, so hesitantly that I had the feeling there was something more he wanted to tell me, something that couldn't be communicated by means of a sign. Normally he'd pull the fingers right back. This time he left the fingers there for a couple of seconds and then, slowly, still hesitantly, he began to wiggle them, the sign to take something off it.
>
> As soon as I saw the fingers wiggle, I began to nod my head emphatically. I could see John begin to smile behind the mask, and then the fingers began to wiggle faster, as if he were saying to me, "Sandy baby, you don't know how glad I am that you see it this way too."
>
> As it was, I copped out just a little. I did take something off my normal curve, but I didn't throw it real slow. It was a good pitch, though. It broke right down in there for a called third strike.

As soon as we hit the clubhouse, I grabbed Roseboro. "What was the matter, John?" I said. "You seemed a little hesitant about wiggling the fingers on Mantle." And he grinned back and said, "I wanted to call it, but I was thinking: How are we ever going to explain a change-curve if he hits it out?"

That's how close the rapport between us can get. Not only did we have the same idea at the same moment, we even had the same thoughts about what could happen back in the clubhouse. (260: pp. 213–15)

There are enduring legends about uncanny rapport among skiers and climbers lost in the wilderness, among basketball players, rowers, and participants in other sports. Certain rodeo riders claim they achieve oneness with bucking bulls and horses, and race car drivers swear their cars are alive. Stirling Moss told Peter Manso that to do one's best, "you have to be part of the car. It's no longer that you're in a car and doing something with it, that's why I refer to this as a complete entity. If things are right, it *is* complete. I feel a car is an animate object." (308: p. 121)

The Richness of the Inner World

As we have seen, a wide variety of extraordinary experience emerges in sport—moments of preternatural calm and stillness, feelings of detachment and freedom, states filled with invincible force. These experiences induce a wide range of extraordinary perceptions, including changes in one's sense of time and space, apparent clairvoyance and telepathy, and glimpses of disembodied entities. This richness of experience is paralleled in the mystical traditions by the knowledge that ordinary human nature opens into vast inner worlds. Various metaphors have illustrated this fact of spiritual life. In the Greek myth of the Minotaur, the path to transformation led through the labyrinth; the seeker, like Theseus, had to find his way with the help of Ariadne's golden thread, which symbolized a teacher's leading. The soul has been pictured as a mansion (Saint Teresa's *Interior Castle*) or as a Magic Theatre (in Herman Hesse's *Steppenwolf*), in which one space opens into many others. Hindu and Buddhist writings describe a multitude of inner worlds. As Sri Aurobindo wrote, we "have not learned to distinguish the different parts of our being; for these are usually lumped together simply as 'mind.' . . . Therefore [we] do not understand our own states and actions. . . . It is part of the foundation of yoga to become conscious of the great complexity of our nature." (20: Vol. 22, p. 233)

A veteran of the National Football League, former St. Louis Cardinal linebacker David Meggyesey (317), fell into a labyrinth of the interior life during his playing days. His adventure began during a practice game against the Minnesota Vikings when he received a blow to the head. In a semidazed state, he sat on the sidelines and watched the setting sun beyond the stadium. He felt "an eerie calm and beauty," and had an impression of "outlines wavering gently in the fading light." In this pervasive sense of the uncanny and sublime, he began to see "auras around some of the players." The experience helped trigger other unusual experiences that season. On another occasion he found himself playing in "a kind of trance where I could sense the movements of the running backs a split second before they happened." With this heightened sense of anticipation, he played a brilliant game. But this state led him beyond football. His extraordinary experiences during that football season opened into a more complete understanding and practice. One inner space led to another. The spontaneous richness of these events led him into yoga and other disciplines, and he eventually evolved his own path to the inner life.

The Subtle Body

When David Meggyesey saw auras during that football game, he was beginning to perceive something that has often appeared in the work of religiously inspired artists. The golden halos and mandorlas in Christian art, the flames that encircle Japanese deities, the explosions of light from the bodies of Indian saints are all renderings of something actually seen by artists and yogis. Sri Aurobindo wrote: "The lights one sees in yogic concentration are the lights of various powers or forces of the higher consciousness. . . . They are not hallucinations. They indicate an opening of the inner vision.

Lights are very often the first things seen in yoga. They indicate the action or movement of subtle forces belonging to different planes—the nature of the force depending on the color and shade of the light." (20: vol. 23, p. 936)

Athletes—especially in the martial arts—sometimes report perceptions of subtle energy. Morehei Uyeshiba, the founder of aikido, had just settled a quarrel by fighting with a navy officer who was a fencing instructor. Every time the officer tried to strike him with his sword, Uyeshiba was able to evade it because he felt the officer's movements before they were made. The officer could not strike Uyeshiba, who then went to a nearby garden to collect himself. Suddenly he "could neither walk nor sit. He was just rooted on the ground in great astonishment." He felt that "the universe suddenly quaked, and that a golden spirit sprang up from the ground, veiled my body, and changed my body into a golden one. At the same time, my mind and body became light. I was able to understand the whispering of the birds, and was clearly aware of the mind of God." (501: 154)

Denise McCluggage, in *Centered Skiing*, described her experience of a basketball game as: "a fascinating network of visible energy, thanks perhaps in equal part to my squinting eyesight and to an intervening haze between my seat and the playing floor. . . . Bright cords of varying width connected the Golden State Warriors at their middle. The lines all emanated from Rick Barry, making him look like something straight out of Castaneda. Rick was glowingly, obviously, the hub of the team that night. The changing thicknesses of the cords extending from him indicated where his next pass was going, even when he was looking in another direction. The ball followed a remarkably predictable path down shining corridors of energy." (302: pp. 20–21)

Ian Jackson, during a period of fasting plus distance running, felt that his "very skin seemed to have opened up so that the energy of the universe could play within me, in the emptiness between the whirling atoms. . . . My body seemed insubstantial like some ethereal vehicle of awareness." (224:41)

When renowned mountain climber Walter Bonatti scaled the Matterhorn alone, he had this experience barely two hundred feet from the top: "The cross appeared to me. . . . In the sun which illumined it, it seemed incandescent. The light which emanated from it dazzled me. It was a supernatural, miraculous thing, like the haloes of the saints. . . . Then, as if hypnotized, I stretched out my arms towards the cross until I could feel its metal substance right against my chest. And I fell to my knees and wept in silence." (1283: p. 190)

In the lore of the perennial philosophy, auras, halos, filaments of energy, and similar phenomena are considered aspects of a subtle body all humans possess. Hierocles of Alexandria, a fifth-century philosopher, mentions this in commenting on Pythagorian mystical practice: "Together with the discipline (*askesis*) of virtue and the recovery of truth, he shall also be diligent in the purification of his radiant (*augoeides*) body, which the Chaldean Oracles also call the subtle vehicle of the soul." (316: p. 65) Through transformative discipline, one can learn to sense this second body and disengage it from the flesh. There is a large literature on "out-of-body" experience. As we have seen in Chapter 3, this disengagement happens in sport.

Another phenomenon related to the subtle body is the perception of disembodied entities. As related in Chapter 3, the stories of Estcourt and Scott about the British ascent of Mount Everest in 1975 include encounters with phantom climbers. Joshua Slocum, the first man to circumnavigate the globe alone, saw a phantom during his epic voyage. The loneliness, fatigue, and intensity induced by difficult voyages or climbs often trigger such visions. The strange energies some athletes feel in the midst of a game, the uncanny suspension, the out-of-body experiences, and the perceptions of disembodied entities we've described can all be understood as aspects of the subtle body as it is described in the contemplative and occult literature. (e.g., see Mead, 316) The awareness of this energy can be cultivated. Several martial arts teach us to feel and manipulate it. We will examine some of these disciplines in the next chapter.

EXTRAORDINARY POWERS

Everywhere in sport, participants are developing more advanced skills as technique improves and as more exact analysis is brought to bear on the human body and the dynamics of physical movement. Biomechanics (the study of human motion), kinesiology, filmed studies of bodily movement, and physiological analysis have grown in recent decades to further our understanding of physical development. (1445) But in spite of these new sciences, many human capacities are still poorly understood, among them the kinds we have been examining. Here, we believe, the spiritual traditions come to our aid, for they have borne witness to many of these abilities.

The Sanskrit words *siddhi* and *vibhuti* are technical terms of Hindu and Buddhist spiritual practice. The two terms are roughly synonymous—the first often translated as "power," the latter as "perfection." Both refer to capacities that spiritual discipline can evoke, from realizations of Divinity to the mastery of pain or reading minds at a distance. Taken together as they appear in the Indian scrip tures, the *vibhutis* and *siddhis* represent an immense inventory of extraordinary human potentials. They include the sporting powers we have looked at and many, many more.

Several years ago, when I (Murphy) began to see how many strange things happened in games and athletic ordeals, I began to play with the notion that sport has a genius for evoking yogic powers. By comparing lists of the traditional *siddhis* with lists of powers described by sports participants I found certain striking similarities. In the pages that follow we present the same kind of comparative list to show how suggestive the *siddhi* idea can be for our understanding of exceptional athletic abilities. In some cases, just naming these powers can lead to their recognition. The *siddhi* or *vibhuti* idea must have stimulated a similar recognition of exceptional capacity in the yogic life. Here, as everywhere, *a concept or metaphor can encourage recognition*. This has been the case in several of our interviews with sportspeople.

Hundreds of other powers could be listed in the following table, from both contemplative sources and from sports. The ones we have included are meant only to dramatize the similarities between these two fields of experience. We should mention that the terms *siddhi* and *vibhuti* refer not only to powers like the ones listed in this table, but also to cognitions of fundamental aspects of Reality. These cognitions are sometimes called *brahmasiddhis* (powers to apprehend Brahman) and are regarded as the highest of all powers that result from yogic practice. We do not include them in the following table because they fall outside the range of our inquiry. And for some of the powers listed below we have included a middle column headed "Equivalent Psychological Powers," because we are uncertain whether the *siddhi* as it has been described in Eastern scripture refers to a psychological transformation or to a bodily change.

EXTRAORDINARY POWERS IN YOGA AND SPORT

SIDDHI	EQUIVALENT PSYCHOLOGICAL POWER	ACCOMPLISHMENTS IN SPORT
• Exceptional control of bodily processes, feelings, thoughts, imagination, and other mental functions		Pulse, heartbeat, breathing, and other physiological processes come under extraordinary control when a runner does the marathon in a little over two hours (which means an average of better than a mile every five minutes for the entire 26 miles), or when underwater swimmers hold their breath for more than five minutes at depths of up to forty feet, or when a race driver makes the hairpin turns required in Grand Prix driving.
• Mastery of pain, both psychic and physical		Football players have gone through games with broken ribs, noses, toes, and fingers. Boxers have finished fights with broken hands and wrists. Often there is no pain at all during

SIDDHI	EQUIVALENT PSYCHOLOGICAL POWER	ACCOMPLISHMENTS IN SPORT
		the contest, so great is the player's concentration.
• Ability to survive with little or no oxygen, as when a yogi is buried alive		The anaerobic abilities of ocean divers and distance runners
• The Tibetan *tumo* (inner fire), which involves the ability to generate heat from within the body with little or no muscular exertion		Mountain climbers, sailors, and ocean swimmers report similar abilities to withstand freezing temperatures.
• Ability to change shape, size, and mass	Psychic mobility, altered consciousness	Morehei Uyeshiba, the inventor of aikido, seemed to change his shape and size in the swirl of a free-form match. Drastic changes in body image have been reported by golfers, football players, ocean divers, skydivers, and mountain climbers. Sometimes these changes are perceived by onlookers as actual changes in body shape and size.
• Invisibility	Ego-loss, blending, harmonizing with the elements	Uyeshiba, in a movie demonstrating aikido, seems to disappear for an instant, then reappear in another place. His followers swear the

SIDDHI	EQUIVALENT PSYCHOLOGICAL POWER	ACCOMPLISHMENTS IN SPORT
		film was never tampered with.
• Auras, halos, the odor of sanctity, emanations of extraordinary energy	A sense of inner illumination in creative moments	A skydiver saw "forms of light tumbling down the wind around her" during a jump in which she was suspended on a thermal updraft for over an hour. For Bundini Brown, Muhammad Ali glowed in the dark in certain extraordinary moments. (386)
• Levitation	The sense of being lifted up by other energies, by the *ki* or *prana* of the Eastern disciplines or by God's grace	A form of levitation appears in some of the martial arts when the participant is taught to make himself lighter at will through the manipulation of *ki.* Lee Evans and other sprinters talk about "tipping," a spontaneous lifting sprint form that carries the runner on the very tips of his toes as if he were hardly touching the track.
• Out-of-body experience,		David Smith, in his unique pentathlon, described the sensation of "rising above his body" while he was swimming. (235: p. 50) (Chapter 3 reports other out-of-body experiences.)

SIDDHI	EQUIVALENT PSYCHOLOGICAL POWER	ACCOMPLISHMENTS IN SPORT
• Stigmata, and other dramatic bodily changes		It could be argued that the sometimes radical changes of body structure an athlete goes through to perform a particular feat or to play a particular position is like this *siddhi*. The same power of mind over matter might be involved.
• Ability to pass through solids; porousness	Inner emptiness and freedom; loosening of ordinary psychic structures and boundaries; mental and emotional fluidity	Pelé: "I felt that I could dribble through any of their team or all of them, that I could almost pass through them physically." (378: p. 51) In aikido and kung fu there is something called "mesh practice" in which the participant imagines— then becomes—a net through which an opponent's energy may pass. In karate, the power to split boards and bricks is ascribed as much to *ki* as to sheer muscular force.
• Incombustibility, fire immunity, and impassability	Inner equilibrium and imperturbability; a sense of indestructibility; identification with the Eternal	In firewalking and swordswallowing— which might be classified as sports—we see this *siddhi*. In the nineteenth and early twentieth centuries there was a game that in-

SIDDHI	EQUIVALENT PSYCHOLOGICAL POWER	ACCOMPLISHMENTS IN SPORT
		volved the ducking of bullets. Some of the great heroes of this pastime, it was said, became refractory to bullets through the power of their minds.
• Freedom from the aging process	Contact with the ever-born, ever-renewed, self-existent being that is characteristic of higher states	George Blanda, at 45 was starring for the Oakland Raiders. Sam Snead was a money winner on the PGA tour at age 65. Percy Cerutty, the famous track coach, was a physical dynamo until the day he died. Bernard McFadden parachuted into the Seine and the Thames on his 85th and 86th birthdays. Track and swimming records for people over 40 are falling at a rapid rate.
• Androgyny; the 32 male and 32 female signs of the perfect Buddha; balance of the "male" and "female" characteristics		Many male athletes, even in the fiercest sports, have a strikingly feminine aspect, contrary to the old macho cliché. Freed from the need to prove themselves in this regard, they can allow a wider range of feeling and perceptions. The same can be said for many female athletes who exhibit strong "male"

SIDDHI	EQUIVALENT PSYCHOLOGICAL POWER	ACCOMPLISHMENTS IN SPORT
		characteristics. This expansion of awareness and behavioral repertoire through the dropping of defenses has been pointed out by various psychologists and sociologists.
• Precognition, prophecy, retrocognition, time travel	Freedom from tyranny of the past, present, or future; psychic mobility	David Meggyesey claims he made many tackles because he could anticipate the moves of the other team's running backs: Somehow he knew what they would do an instant before they did it. See Chapter 3 for more examples.
• Clairaudience, or hearing sounds well out of earshot, or hearing someone else's thoughts spoken in one's mind; hearing certain sounds associated with meditative states, such as a buzzing in the ears, that is not audible to others		Bobby Jones often heard a melody as he played and sometimes used it to give a rhythm to his golf swing. The sound of crickets or a subtle ringing sometimes comes to golfers and mountain climbers in the stillness of their concentration. Roscoe Newman, a retired navy captain, tells about times when he was learning to fly, when he would "climb over the haze into a different world above 5,000 feet and roll and loop until

SIDDHI	EQUIVALENT PSYCHOLOGICAL POWER	ACCOMPLISHMENTS IN SPORT
		pleasantly pooped." During these flights he would "synchronize vocally, in song, with the vibrations and noise frequencies around me to come up with all the voice parts of a great choral group and/or the various instruments of a large orchestral assembly. There was absolutely no discord in the music I heard. Every part and tone was crystal clear, true, properly amplified, and in unison." (279: pp. 43–44)
• Telepathy, clairvoyance		An extraordinary power of communication often develops between members of a team— between a quarterback and wide receiver for example—where one can anticipate the moves of the other. See Chapter 3. Skiers tell of sensing a comrade's danger or distress on the slopes. Ocean divers and skydivers tell the same kind of story.
• Synaesthesia, in which stimulation of one sense causes perception by another		Adam Smith relates that during a peak moment a diver could "hear" the grains of

SIDDHI	EQUIVALENT PSYCHOLOGICAL POWER	ACCOMPLISHMENTS IN SPORT
		sand on the ocean floor. (460: p. 37) Yacht-racer Valentin Mankin perceived every air current as having its own color. (367: p. 63)
• Transmission of energy from person to person; psychological contagion; group inspiration		Certain coaches and athletes have the power to inspire their fellows in extraordinary ways, and certain teams have been famous for their inspirational momentum.
• The ability to draw nourishment from air	Not needing to eat when one is caught up in an absorbing task or enjoying the company of a special person	John Muir and Herman Buhl could live for days in the mountains with little or no food while expending enormous amounts of energy. (70) Ian Jackson described his twenty-day fasts combined with heavy distance running in *Yoga and the* Athlete. (224)
• Spiritual healing	The ability to exert a calming effect, or instill confidence or hope in another person or a group	Many athletes have helped sports fans recover from illness. Babe Ruth was famous in this regard. (296) Improbable as it might seem to some, healing powers were ascribed to Vince Lombardi by some of his players.

SIDDHI	EQUIVALENT PSYCHOLOGICAL POWER	ACCOMPLISHMENTS IN SPORT
		(122) There are similar stories about George Best, the soccer star, and other athletes. Many athletes and sport participants have been said to possess extraordinary abilities to heal themselves, and there have been famous recoveries from injuries like Ben Hogan's.
• Control of others, through manipulation of their physiological processes, thoughts, emotions, and "bio-energetic fields"		Muhammad Ali, Jim Brown, and other athletes have been legendary for their ability to "psyche out" their opponents. Vince Lombardi and other coaches have been equally famous for their ability to inspire.
• Power of mass hypnosis	Charismatic leaders exercise a hypnotic effect on their followers.	Certain dancers—Nijinsky and Isadora Duncan, for example—have had the ability to cast a spell on the audience, an ability which dozens of authors have tried to analyze, with little success. John Brodie and other quarterbacks have talked about breaking the spell cast by an unfriendly crowd. (63) Muhammad Ali cast many a spell over an

SIDDHI	EQUIVALENT PSYCHOLOGICAL POWER	ACCOMPLISHMENTS IN SPORT
		opponent and a viewing audience.
• Immunity to harm or danger		Hockey great Bobby Orr is said to have warded off opponents merely by staring at them. Japanese samurai could train for this ability.
• Harmonizing with the elements while transcending their ordinary effects		Sailor Adrian Hayter describes his ability to blend with wind and wave during lengthy small-boat voyages. (196) Many skiers possess a similar ability.
• Heaviness and immovability	The ability to be undeterred from one's course, taking a "solid" position	This ability is encouraged in karate and other martial arts. (375: p. 59) Football players and wrestlers describe the same kind of power.
• Psychokinesis; moving objects at a distance through psychic power		Former quarterback John Brodie wrote, "I would have to say that such things seem to exist—or emerge when your state of mind is right. It has happened to me dozens of times. An intention carries a force, a thought is connected with an energy that can stretch itself out in a pass play or a golf shot or a thirty-

SIDDHI	EQUIVALENT · PSYCHOLOGICAL POWER	ACCOMPLISHMENTS IN SPORT
		foot jump shot in basketball. I've seen it happen too many times to deny it." (343) It is a legendary power among certain pool and billiard players, among golfers, and in archery and target shooting.
• Feats of extraordinary strength and endurance as with *lunggom* walkers who, it is claimed, can walk for weeks without stopping through the mountains of Tibet		Marathon running; extraordinary moments of strength in weightlifting competition, in wrestling and boxing, and in every other sport; see Chapter 4.
• Perception of internal bodily structures such as organs, cells, and molecules; clairvoyant diagnosis of disease and other ailments		Several distance runners have told us that they have caught glimpses of their own insides during a race or hard training. Some have seen capillaries break and heal over; others have reported images of particular tendons and muscles; a few have glimpsed forms that look like "cellular structures." Similar experiences have been reported to us by football players, golfers, and other athletes.

6

MIND/BODY
TRAINING

Given the similarities between sport and religious practice, the question arises whether sportspeople can deliberately promote metanormal functioning. Could the kinds of experience we have described in the preceding chapters be systematically developed? Part of the answer is clear: Coaches and athletes in many parts of the world are already using methods from yoga, the martial arts, hypnosis, meditation, and other disciplines to enrich their training programs. During the 1960s, a field of applied psychology called *psychic self-regulation* was developed in the Soviet Union. It is based on laboratory studies of our ability to control physiological processes, including pulse, muscular relaxation, blood pressure, and breathing. The methods developed in this discipline have been used in sport by some Russians and East Europeans. (411)

The United States Olympic Committee, while not making the effort that the Soviet Union and East Germany did in these areas, has instituted a few programs in biofeedback training and mental practice at their training centers at Squaw Valley, California, and elsewhere. (130) The Buffalo Bills football team has worked with clinical psychologist Robert Nideffer on mental practice, relaxation, and concentration. (358; 192: p. 4) The Detroit Tigers have worked with biofeedback, and the Philadelphia Phillies have used transcendental meditation. Ken Norton employed hypnosis before several fights, including the one in which he beat Muhammad Ali.

Lee Pulos, a Canadian clinical psychologist, helped the Canadian National Women's Volleyball team and other world-class athletes by getting them to practice their sports both mentally and physically. His general method is simple. In volleyball, for example, he encouraged players to imagine a particular shot several hundred times until they saw it vividly. When the image is powerfully established, the athlete practices that shot on the court, bringing his body into alignment with his inner vision. Periods of physical practice alternate with periods of mental practice until the athlete clearly sees what he wants to do—and then does it to his or his coach's satisfaction. Billie Jean King, Olympic 400-meters champion Lee Evans, high jumper Dwight Stones, and bodybuilders Frank Zane and Arnold Schwarzenegger have used mental techniques. The list could go on and on. Many coaches and athletes pay attention to the mental aspects of their training. The question is: How far might this be developed? What could be done to bring the metanormal dimensions of athletes into the open and nurture them more fully?

ELEMENTS OF A MIND/BODY TRAINING PROGRAM

What follows is a preliminary answer, a set of suggestions for anyone who wants to explore these possibilities. We are not talking about specific athletic skills. The practices we describe embrace capacities that operate not only in sports but the rest of our lives. Some of these methods—like meditation and biofeedback—are relatively familiar and are used to some extent in training programs now. Others, like "inner seeing" and developing the "energy body," may seem strange, but are promising enough, we believe, to include in this review. There are probably as many ways to combine these approaches as there are coaches and athletes. Their effectiveness depends in large part upon the special situations and makeup of the people involved.

Meditation

As we have seen, sport depends largely upon focusing one's attention, whether on the sporting arena, on one's teammates and opponents, on the ball, or on the functioning of one's own body. Success depends in large part on the steadiness and clarity of the participant's awareness. We have also seen that ordinary focusing can grow into something more, into something athletes have called "the zone" and others have labeled the "playing trance." This "something more" resembles the advanced meditation states we have described—the *dhyana* or *samadhi* of Patanjali's yoga sutras, for example, in which "the true nature of the world shines forth, not distorted by the mind of the perceiver." (377: p. 175)

Sport by its very nature promotes this heightened concentration, but formal meditation practice can help it develop. Several well-known athletes, among them Bill Walton, Joe Namath, rodeo rider Larry Mahan, and Billie Jean King, have testified to the help meditation has given them. The Detroit Tigers, the Philadelphia Phillies, and other teams have encouraged their members to use it. Running coach Mike Spino (467, 469), tennis teacher Tim Gallwey (164, 165), and other instructors have described meditative approaches in their books. The practices these athletes and coaches advocate can improve both performance and enjoyment in sport because they help bring the participant to a deeper center, a more effective level of personal functioning.

Describing the action of the mind, yogic commentators often employ the image of a lake. If the surface of a lake is lashed into waves, the water becomes muddy and the bottom invisible. In this metaphor the lake represents the ordinary mind with its usual agitations, while its bottom represents one's essential self. After hours of hitting golf shots or watching a fishing fly dance on a stream, you might discover the depths of your own mind as if you had been meditating. But the formal practice of meditation can quicken the process.

Meditation is profoundly simple in method. Zen sitting, for example, involves simple attention to breath or to the passing contents of your mind. In another Buddhist practice, you simply attend to the sensations of walking. (This practice resembles the steady attention required for distance running, swimming, cross-country skiing, and other endurance sports.) Many forms of meditation involve the observation of the mind's subtle turns. The Christian "prayer of quiet" requires a simple focus on the light or form of God, without elaborate imagery. In these and other contemplative methods there is only the barest, most focused activity of mind, a constant indwelling so that a deeper consciousness might emerge, bringing with it a more spontaneous and harmonious action and a growing union with our deepest resources. The "noise" that intervenes between our deeper self and ordinary consciousness is partially or largely eliminated in these practices. Identification with the mind's superficial movements gives way to a sense of something free and eternal.

Meditation practice need not be limited to a quiet retreat. Its use by professional rodeo riders (who practice meditation before entering the chutes with Brahma bulls and bucking horses) and among professional football players attests to its power in the midst of the most tumultuous sports. Basketball star Bill Walton wrote: "I try to do some form of meditation every day. . . . The nicest thing about meditation is that it puts your body in harmony with your surroundings. And that can be real helpful, because when you're a professional athlete, your surroundings can get pretty unharmonious." (32: p. 84) Or golf professional Jane Blalock: "I go into the locker room and find a corner by myself and just sit there. I try to achieve a peaceful state of nothingness that will carry over onto the golf course. If I get that feeling of quiet and obliviousness within myself, I feel I can't lose." (131: p. 174)

There are many ways to set up meditation practice. But most important are patience and regularity. In an old religious metaphor, the act of meditation is compared to the ringing of a bell, in which the afterglow of the experience is like the dying sound. It is crucial to hit the bell (meditate again) before the ringing (the afterglow) stops. By practicing at regular intervals, the insight and calm of meditation are maintained and amplified. Gradually those qualities become second nature. The specific method you use is less important than faithfulness of practice. Whether you simply attend to your thoughts, count breaths, repeat a prayer, or focus on a point, the important thing is persistence. Two sessions a day—one in the morning and another in the afternoon or evening—will have their effect if you are patient.

Biofeedback

Some athletic programs already use biofeedback. It was incorporated, for example, into the training of prospective Olympic athletes by the United States Olympic Committee. (130) The method works as follows: An instrument attached to the body gives a continuous record of one or more physiological processes so that the subject can alter those processes directly. If someone wants to lower his pulse, for example, a record of it is presented to him as a sound or a squiggle on a moving graph. By watching the record, the subject gradually learns what thoughts, images, feelings, moods, muscular contractions, and other factors are associated with the fluctuations of his pulse. With this growing awareness, he can learn to modify his thoughts and feelings so that his pulse drops or rises at will. Biofeedback is now being used to help people control pulse, blood pressure, electrical activity in the brain, muscular tension, stomach acidity, and other bodily processes.

Visualization and Mental Practice

We often picture an activity in our mind before we undertake it. Most of us do this every day, though typically in a haphazard way. Reflect for a moment on your own experience. Haven't you seen yourself meeting someone or accomplishing a task or trying some impossible feat? Images of future action pass in and out of awareness without our willing them—sometimes showing us performing to perfection, sometimes anticipating defeat. Our imagination can be either helpful or discouraging when it begins to anticipate a course of action. It is a force that can encourage or defeat us.

This anticipatory power of the imagination has been utilized in many sports, and scientific research has established its effectiveness for athletes. This research has shown that by picturing the successful completion of moves they want to make, athletes can improve their performance, especially if the mental picture is accompanied by physical practice. (358, 405, 406, 472, 766a) Merely imagining a good round of golf or a successful race is ineffective without hitting shots or going through the necessary conditioning.

Top athletes are good at both mental and physical self-control.

Think of Jack Nicklaus, Chris Evert, Billie Jean King, Bill Russell, or Arnold Schwarzenegger. These champions have described how they picture the moves they want to make. Jack Nicklaus, for example, claimed that hitting good shots depends 10 percent on his swing mechanics, 40 percent on his setup and stance, and 50 percent on his mental picture. In his book *Golf My Way* he described how he visualizes a shot before he makes it:

> I never hit a shot, not even in practice, without having a very sharp, in-focus picture of it in my head. It's like a color movie. First I "see" the ball where I want it to finish, nice and white and sitting up high on the bright green grass. Then the scene quickly changes and I "see" the ball going there: its path, trajectory, and shape, even its behavior on landing. Then there is sort of a fadeout, and the next scene shows me making the kind of swing that will turn the previous images into reality. . . . It may be that handicap golfers also "go to the movies" like this before most of their shots, but I somehow doubt it. Maybe . . . they see only pictures of the swing, rather than of what it's supposed to achieve. If that's true in your case, then I believe a few moments of movie-making might work some small miracles in your game. Just make sure your movies show a perfect shot. We don't want any horror films of shots flying into sand or water or out of bounds. (355: pp. 79–80)

In rodeo riding—a sport very different from golf—meditation and visualization have become popular. Champion bronco and bull rider Larry Mahan said, "I try to picture a ride in my mind before I get on the bull. Then I try to go by the picture." (299: p. 212) Francis Tarkenton, the famous quarterback, visualized upcoming games as follows:

> On this week, for example, he must think Pittsburgh and nothing else. He must see that Steeler defense in his dreams, every one of them, knowing their names, numbers, bodies, moves. He must be able to tell who is chasing him by the sound of the footsteps, and which way to turn to evade him, for every man has his weakness. He must see those linebackers eyeing him as they backtrack into pass coverage,

know their relative speed and effectiveness, know just how many steps each one will take on specific defensive calls so that he can find the right hole at the right time. "Sometimes I think I'm going into a . . . quandary trying to anticipate what's going to happen. By Friday, I'm running whole blocks of plays in my head. . . . I'm trying to visualize every game situation, every defense they're going to throw at me. I tell myself, 'What will I do on their five-yard line and it's third and goal to go, and our short passing game hasn't been going too well and their line looks like a wall and we're six points behind?' I walk around on another planet and I'm not much fun to live with." (17: p. 81)

Basketball great Bill Russell discovered the value of mental rehearsal when he was made a member of a post-high-school All-Star team. He wrote in his autobiography, *Second Wind*, that on that All-Star tour something happened that "opened my eyes and chilled my spine." (1320: p. 66) He was tutored by two of the stars on his team, Bill Treu and Eural McKelvey, who were interested in the way a basketball moves. They would experiment and unselfishly share what they learned. Russell studied them. On one occasion he had been trying to copy the way McKelvey took an offensive rebound and turned it into a basket. He had an accurate image of McKelvey making the play, and he replayed the picture with himself making parts of it. "Finally I saw myself making the whole move, and I ran this over and over. When I went into the game, I grabbed an offensive rebound and put it into the basket just the way McKelvey did. It seemed natural, almost as if I were just stepping into a film and following the signs. When the imitation worked and the ball went in, I could barely contain myself. I was so elated I thought I'd float right out of the gym. . . . for the first time I had transferred something from my head to my body. It seemed so easy. My first dose of athletic confidence was coming to me when I was eighteen years old." (1320: p. 67)

It is interesting that when Russell was younger he had wanted to be an architect and would study the paintings of Michelangelo. He would memorize them, then try to reproduce them, but without success. In a flash he knew he could accomplish through basketball what he could not do with painting. Now he found he "got the details right, and repeatedly they fell into place." (1320: p. 68) He developed this technique further so that when he tried, say, to mimic one of McKelvey's moves, he would redo the play in his mind, and if he had made an extra move or incorrect twist, he would replay it and try to perform it correctly. "The important thing was that I could see what was wrong and what was right, and that my body responded to what I saw." (1320: p. 68)

Russell became one of the first name players to emphasize defense. When he replayed Treu's moves in taking the ball up court, he imagined himself defensively shadowing the smaller man. He saw himself as a mirror image of Treu, as if they were dancing together. "Any way he bent, I'd bend with him." (1320: p. 70) He was ecstatic the first time he tried one of the defensive moves that he had mentally invented. He made them real: "They grew out of my imagination." (1320: p. 70)

Research about visualization's effectiveness combined with these endorsements by sporting champions makes a strong case for this kind of practice. The method is simple in principle: just picture the move you want to make until you see it clearly, then imagine how that action would feel. Repeat the procedure until the perfected move comes naturally to you, then take the image and your feeling of it into physical practice. But a warning here: Though practiced images of desired performance can help us, at times they must give way to better ones that arise spontaneously. In *Golf in the Kingdom*, the narrator describes such a process: "I saw the path of my ball on the first hole at Burningbush going down the right side of the fairway with a draw, not down the middle as I might have seen it, and so it flew—to the best part of the fairway for an approach to the green. Some invisible radar had superseded my ordinary judgment. This has happened to me many times. Through experience you can learn when to stay with your original image and when to yield to the new one." (340: p. 180)

Sometimes our mind and body unconsciously make adjustments that are superior to the first image we have. When we become aware of the readjusted image, we have to go with it. Maybe our first image didn't anticipate all the variables in a given situation. Whatever the case, we should surrender to the spontaneous maneuver, as it is the result not only of mental preparation and physical practice but also of on-the-spot intuition.

And sometimes, images arise that might be trying to deliver a message that goes beyond our sports activity. Quoting again from *Golf in the Kingdom*:

> Many thoughts that arise as you are playing must be brushed aside. But certain ones that will not be brushed aside must be understood, otherwise they will haunt you until your golf game and your disposition suffer. Some years ago a thought like that began to torment me.
>
> It began entering my mind when I was putting. It said, "You are not lined up straight, line up again." It occurred to me over and over that the angle of my putter face was slightly askew. I would stand back and try to line up at a better angle, but still the thought was there. It kept coming back through the entire round. When I played again, a week or so later, the same voice began again. "You are not lined up straight, line up again," it said, creeping into my mind on every green and eventually as I was addressing the longer shots. I adjusted and readjusted my stance, waggled the club endlessly, the greens and fairways began to look like cubistic drawings as I surveyed them for a better line. Then it slowly dawned upon me that the thought was coming from some deep recess of my mind, that it was one of those thoughts Shivas had said I should listen to. What did it have to say? I let it run through my mind after that second round, let it play itself out, "You are not lined up straight, line up again." Slowly, inexorably, the meaning came clear: indeed I was not lined up straight, in my work, with my friends, during most of the day. I was sleeping in my office then, rising to telephone calls, . . . doing business over every meal. I was as disorganized as I had ever been and my unconscious knew it, and now it was speaking to me clearly on the golf course. I needed to realign my life, it said, not just my putt or my drive. Only during a round of golf did I slow down enough for the word to get through. (340: pp. 173–74)

An athlete can find visualization effective not only in improving performance but also in reshaping the body. There are many ways, large and small, gross and subtle, in which a body can change in the course of a training routine. Muscles may be recontoured, fat may disappear, new capillaries may develop, organelles may be added to cells, tendons may be stretched and made more flexible. This happens naturally, of course, through physical exercise. Each sport or training regimen determines what the athlete's body will be like. But the process can be aided by suggestion, visualization, and other mental techniques.

Bodybuilders use mental imaging to facilitate their physical development. The two greatest bodybuilders of the 1970s, Arnold Schwarzenegger (437) and Frank Zane (1533), have said that visualizing a particular muscle's contour somehow speeds the process of acquiring it. "A pump when I see the muscle I want," Schwarzenegger told us, "is worth ten with my mind drifting." He talked about sculpting his body in the movie *Pumping Iron:* He would first plan the kind of physique he wanted—aiming for values like symmetry, definition, and elegance—then work to achieve it. Like a sculptor, he followed his artistic conception, working with his own living flesh. First he saw what he wanted, then he maintained that image during his workouts. The process began and was maintained by the image of his inner eye. There is evidence from other fields as well that mind can affect the body in dramatic ways. We will review some of this evidence in the following chapter.

Visualization, then, can give power to performance, reveal the mind's workings, help remold our physique, and catalyze spontaneous powers. Russian coaches have also incorporated it into "rejuvenation" exercises. These involve guided visualization after hard practice or competition in which the athlete imagines his body recovering from the stress it has suffered.

Some athletes use hypnotic and suggestive techniques as an adjunct to visualization and mental practice. There are more methods of hypnosis than we can usefully summarize here, but in general, hypnotic suggestion is used only to support the kind of mental practice we have already described. The hypnotist-trainer helps athletes make their own images more vivid and certain. Most coaches and sports psychologists say it is better if athletes learn to visualize on their own. Hypnosis should lead the player toward an independent ability to imagine desired outcomes without the need of external support.

Dreaming

Many artists, poets, and scientists have made discoveries in a dream. The same kind of inspiration comes to athletes. Jack Nicklaus described one that helped him recover from a slump in tournament play. He had "been trying everything to find out what [was] wrong. It was getting to the place where I figured a 76 was a pretty good round. But last Wednesday night I had a dream and it was about my golf swing. I was hitting them pretty good in the dream and all at once I realized I wasn't holding the club the way I've actually been holding it lately. I've been having trouble collapsing my right arm taking the club head away from the ball, but I was doing it perfectly in my sleep. So when I came to the course yesterday morning, I tried it the way I did in my dream and it worked. I shot a 68 yesterday and a 65 today and believe me it's a lot more fun this way. I feel kind of foolish admitting it, but it really happened in a dream. All I had to do was change my grip just a little." (108: p. 101)

As we have seen, dreams can also carry a message about the future. After his devastating premonition of his fight with Jimmy Doyle, Sugar Ray Robinson said he never again disregarded dreams with warnings (see Chapter 3). Bruce Jenner told Tony Kornheiser that he used to dream of the Olympics constantly—especially of crossing the finish line victoriously in the 1500 meters at the end of the decathlon. (258: p. 6) We suggest that you can learn from your dreams—about new techniques, perhaps, or situations to avoid. They might deliver new perspectives on your sport or on your life in general.

Inner Seeing

There is a mental ability which we will call "inner seeing" that goes beyond visualization as we have described it. This capacity involves images that are not deliberately constructed like the mental pictures Nicklaus and Schwarzenegger (437) have recommended. Unlike ordinary visualization, this power appears to involve a direct perception of structures or processes that are usually invisible to us.

Some distance runners, for example, have told us that they sometimes see organs, muscles, and blood vessels—and even forms that look like cells. Following a hard workout, one runner was flooded with images of breaking capillaries. He had lain down to rest when, in his mind's eye, he suddenly saw red cells spurting from broken vessels. The perception was frightening, but there was a sensation of healing in his chest and a pervasive sense of well-being. A few nights later he had the same kind of vision in a dream, and guessed that through this imagery he was gaining a closer rapport with the process of breakdown and buildup in his training. Stories like his have led us to ask other runners if they have had similar episodes, and we have found that some have. During talks on these subjects, I (Murphy) have sometimes asked if anyone in the audience might have had this kind of experience. Generally, about a quarter of those present have said that they have. This consistent finding plus stories of similar phenomena among athletes leads us to believe that many, if not most, people possess a latent power through which they can directly perceive their body structures. Evidence from other fields of experience supports this belief. For example:

- Many people say that they have seen internal body structures during meditation, psychotherapy, or other transformative disciplines. Such glimpses often come during exercises in which they are imagining what the inside of their bodies looks like.
- As we have seen in Chapter 5, this kind of power has been recognized by yogis and contemplatives for thousands of years.
- The literature on psychedelic and hallucinogenic drugs is filled with similar accounts. (184, 314)

So the phenomenon as it appears in sport finds parallels in yoga, psychotherapy, and research with psychedelic drugs. But does this prove that people can actually *see* their hearts or lungs or capillaries? Aren't such experiences simply the product of people's imaginations? At present we have no certain proof that these perceptions are of actual body structures. But we can say this: (1) the experience often carries a sense of conviction with it, (2) it is sometimes accompanied by a sense of healing, which indicates some degree of self-mastery, (3) this kind of power has been described in the yogic and shamanistic traditions for some three thousand years or more, and (4) a few of these perceptions have been verified, as we will see in the next chapter. Taken together, this evidence is certainly suggestive. At the very least, "inner seeing" vivifies one's bodily awareness, and if it is a real power, it could be harnessed to help us achieve increasing rapport with our body's processes. Maybe we possess a rudimentary scanning device—something like a built-in microscope complete with zoom lens and television screen for easy readout—by which we can zero in on whatever ails us or on whatever body part we want to change. In that case, bodybuilders and runners who have glimpsed their own insides might be learning how to use this instrument. Perhaps they have unknowingly discovered a great human capacity.

But how do we incorporate this power into a training program? That's a difficult question, for this ability is harder to develop than ordinary introspection, imagination, or self-suggestion. Wait until it happens. Sometimes it appears in meditation, sometimes in the course of visualization exercises, and at times it comes unexpectedly, during a workout, or in a dream, or while you are absorbed in a game. When it comes, let it happen: That is the best advice we have to give. See what it wants to reveal and where it wants to take you.

Sensory and Kinesthetic Awareness

Various methods of sensory and kinesthetic training go under names like *sensory awareness, sensory awakening,* or *body awareness.* These disciplines aim to promote a more open, sensitive, untroubled contact with both the internal and external worlds.* There are problems in describing them, however, for they depend much more on the nonverbal, artistic, and unique characteristics of their practitioners than they do on automatically repeatable techniques or formulas. Charles Brooks, who with his wife Charlotte Selver pioneered this kind of work in the United States, wrote:

* See studies of the Alexander Technique by Brown (653) and Myers (1178), and the interesting application of the method in the act of splitting firewood described by Tresmer. (1465)

"Like Zen meditation, sensory awareness is not a teaching but a practice. . . . We have no real theoretical framework, and our experiments are entirely empirical. Our aim is not the acquisition of skills, but the freedom to explore sensitively and to learn from that exploration. We work toward an adult version of the open, curious attitude which healthy children have to the world they are born into. Charlotte Selver has been working for more than forty years with this approach, but she is constantly improvising and coming on approaches that she has not tried before." (64: p. 14)

One experiences a cumulative effect in a sensory awareness workshop, an atmosphere and caring that are more important than any technique. If you want to explore this kind of approach, you will find that, like meditation, it requires patience and persistence. And like meditation, the various exercises involved are simple. Brooks described the way one might learn about standing in a Charlotte Selver workshop:

> We sit down and explore our feet directly. With our own hands we go deeply into them, discovering and enlivening the many joints and ligaments of which a foot consists. How far and deep must one go to follow the identity of a given toe until it becomes lost in the interior? What can we feel of the architecture of the arch? How does the heel seem to our palm and our fingers, in its aspect as bone and its aspect as padding? . . .
>
> Now come back to standing. . . . Take time to feel where the floor is. How do we relate to it? Many people now feel that they *are* relating to the floor. They no longer stand on their feet but on something which they feel really supports them from below. The feet feel flexible and alive, not stood on but free to explore what they touch, as the hands a moment ago were exploring them.
>
> Now the leader may ask, "Do you allow the connection with the floor upward into you?" And a little later, "Do you allow it through your knees?" Afterward, a number of people may well report that they found their knees were locked. When they gave up this locking, readjustments could be felt taking place in the ankles or the pelvis or higher. . . .

As thighs and calves wake up, slight changes may occur spontaneously. Or we may deliberately tighten our buttocks or our stomach muscles, taking time to notice how this affects our relation to the support under us, and noticing the changes as we gradually give up the constriction to allow more connection through. Reports often follow of an opening, resulting in a sense of contact with the floor throughout the organism. Changes may be felt as far away as in neck, eyes, and lips, together with an increased sense of standing altogether, which is no longer just a gap in living but is now becoming a positive activity. Very often breathing changes, as one release triggers another, or perhaps sets up a constriction somewhere else.

Such deliberate tensing of muscle constellations, when followed by a very gentle and conscious release—quite different from the nerveless "letting go" so often practiced for relaxation—can be very valuable in bringing habitual contractions to consciousness, where they may slowly dissolve as the vital processes which they are inhibiting begin to be felt and permitted. This requires a fresh and new exploration on each occasion, as opposed to the technique or exercise which is repeated always with the same objective in view. For we are working not with ideas, but with consciousness itself.

Still standing, let us bring our hands gently to resting on the top of our heads. Through palms and fingers we can feel, if we are sensitive, not only our hair but also the temperature and perhaps the animation of living tissue underneath. This is as far up as we extend, just as the soles of our feet delimit our extension downward. What is alive in between? Is there some sense of our existing altogether between the meeting of hands and scalp at the top and of soles and floor at the bottom?

Somewhere in this extent air enters, penetrates to a constantly varying distance, and leaves; weight is passed on from bone to bone and muscle to muscle; fluids circulate; metabolic processes generate ever-changing energies. Everywhere sensory nerves are interwoven and there is the possibility of more awakeness. Our standing is an endless readjustment of these happenings to one another, depending on the clear functioning of our proprioceptive nervous system and on the flexibility of our musculature.

In such trips through one's interior there is always a likelihood of getting stalled; so many toll gates and barricades have been set up over the years. Now and then, however, a new path opens: sensation and energy flood through; consciousness expands to regions heretofore out of bounds. One has a new and full recognition: I am alive there too! I exist: and I am standing on something which exists also. (64: pp. 42–46)

Many sportspeople find their way naturally to the "open, curious attitude which healthy children have"—but others do not. Many of us were discouraged by the competitiveness and drudgery of those gym classes we suffered through in grammar school and high school. Who can forget the tough-looking coach bawling us out because we weren't doing our push-ups fast enough? Or the teacher ridiculing the fat girl who was last in the sprints? Physical education courses, all too often, were lessons in how *not* to enjoy the body and its senses. Various practices to cultivate sensory and kinesthetic awareness can help to right the balance.

The Energy Body

As we saw in Chapter 4, exceptional physical feats are possible when athletes deliberately develop *ki*, or subtle energy. *Ki* (*chi* in Chinese, *prana* in Sanakrit) is an aspect of our body that is, in a sense, both separate from and intimately connected with our physical frame.

An approach has been developed in the West that draws on the martial arts to cultivate awareness and control of this subtle energy. Some of this work has been pioneered by Robert Nadeau and George Leonard, black belt experts in aikido. The main ingredient in their teaching is permission. Leonard described this kind of training in his book *The Ultimate Athlete*:

Energy Body workshops begin with the assumption that a field of energy exists in and around each human body. . . .

The individual is viewed as an *energy being,* a center of vibrancy, emanating waves that radiate . . . through space and time, waves that respond to and interact with myriad other waves. The physical body is seen as one manifestation of the total being, coexisting with the Energy Body. Its reality and importance is in no way denied. It provides us with the most reliable information as to the condition of the total being. The Energy Body, on the other hand, is less reliable and more difficult for us to perceive at this stage in our development. But it is far less limiting than the physical body. It can change shape, size, density, intensity, and other qualities. Each of these changes influences the physical body to some extent. In some mysterious way that we can't yet fully understand, the Energy Body also seems to transcend space and time, connecting each human consciousness to all of existence. (279: pp. 68–71)

Some fifty thousand people have attended programs based on these premises conducted by Leonard during the past twenty years. Participants in these programs are frequently able to sense the location of other people in the room with their eyes closed, create an "energy flow" by which they can resist force with considerable ease, transmute pain and shock into positive feelings of being energized, resist being lifted or become effectively lighter. Leonard introduces beginners to this kind of experience through exercises in balance and centering, soft eye focus, energy sensing, and energy flow. Here is a description of one of his exercises:

First have someone try to bend your extended arm at the elbow.

Then stretch and shake your hand with wrist limp. Breathe deeply, allowing the abdomen to swell. Relax. Now stand with your right foot slightly in front of the left, weight evenly distributed on both feet, knees neither locked nor bent. Let your right arm rise to a horizontal position in front of you, hand open, thumb up. Elbows should not be locked.

Now imagine that your arm is part of a beam of pure, smooth, unbendable energy. Your arm is in the center of this beam which extends a few inches all around it. With eyes soft (that is, not sharply focused on any specific object), imagine the beam of which your arm is a part extending through any object in front of you—the wall or whatever —across the horizon to the ends of the universe. Your arm is part of the beam. The beam is like a laser. It cannot be bent but it takes no effort on your part to keep it from being bent. All you have to do is concentrate on its extension.

Now have the same person try to bend your arm at the elbow, using the same amount of force as he used before. Have him use more force. Note the difference. (279)*

By combining the approaches we have reviewed in this chapter with regular physical practice, you can enhance athletic enjoyment. This kind of training needn't be limited to championship athletics; it can be applied to any sport program. But just as conventional sports training must fit the physique and temperament of the athlete, so these approaches must be adapted to your readiness and ability. You will have to experiment and try different combinations of them. You may want to find teachers to help you with particular aspects of one approach or another. If you want to read more about any of these training dimensions, we have included books and articles about them in the bibliography.

---

* In *The Ultimate Athlete* (279) Leonard outlines ways in which the energy body comes into play during conventional athletics (see Chapter 6, pp. 110–22), and in *The Silent Pulse* (278) he develops a theory that may help account for these phenomena. In *Golf in the Kingdom* (340) I (Murphy) relate some of these phenomena to golf and other sports (see especially "The Pleasures of Practice," pp. 166–80).

7

EVOLUTIONARY
POSSIBILITIES

Is there a limit to how fast the mile or the marathon can be run? How much further can swimming records be lowered? How difficult will future ascents in climbing be, or maneuvers in gymnastics? Records fall in some sport each week, it seems, and athletes constantly attempt the impossible. Our human ability to surpass apparent limits is dramatized in sport in a way that has caught the world's imagination. As we begin to perceive the spiritual side of athletic self-surpassing, as we begin to comprehend the range of inward knowing and metanormal power that sport evokes, we can also wonder how far body and mind might develop in contexts other than sport.

Is there a significant frontier here? In gathering material for this book, we have found ourselves frequently asking this question. Could the extraordinary capacities we have explored be more fully developed in the culture at large? Do the metanormal aspects of sport point to similar possibilities in all of us, whether we are athletes or not? We believe that they do. Indeed, many programs to explore these possibilities are emerging in different parts of the world. The immense interest in Buddhist, Yogic, Sufi, Christian, and Jewish mysticism; the popularity of experimental psychotherapies; work with biofeedback and hypnosis; the development of disciplines like psychic self-regulation in Russia; and the growing fascination with altered states of consciousness demonstrates a readiness in modern culture to explore the kinds of experience this book illustrates.

Sports provide a strong, compelling focus for an exploration of mental and physical transformation, but extraordinary human capabilities emerge in other fields as well, of course, lending further weight to the proposition that we possess enormous untapped potentials. For example:

Placebo Research

A placebo is a sugar pill or inert substance that is given to a patient who believes it is a medicine or drug. By accepting the authority of the doctor or experimenter, persons taking the pill often produce changes they have been led to expect. Placebos, for example, have helped people lower the amount of fat and protein in their blood, change their white cell count, reduce the trembling associated with Parkinson's disease, relieve depression, reduce post-operative wound pain, relieve symptoms of arthritis, eliminate symptoms of withdrawal from morphine, and produce various specific effects of both stimulant and depressant drugs. Through placebos we are authorized to mobilize our self-regenerative powers.

The placebo effect often produces astonishing results. Changing our blood cell count is usually considered to be a feat for yogis, yet unsuspecting patients have done it. Placebo research shows how specific and how effective our powers of self-surpassing can be. (See 1516)

Hypnosis and Suggestion

Hypnosis and suggestion have proven to be effective for a variety of problems from shyness to serious illness. Researchers have successfully used hypnotic induction, for example, to alleviate congenital ichthyosis, a devastating disease characterized by skin that is black, horny, and covered with scales. (248, 312, 432, 530) It has also been shown that women can successfully use suggestive techniques to increase their breast size. In one study (275), Leslie M. LeCron hypnotized twenty women and suggested that their "inner mind" restart the pubescent process of breast growth. Twelve of the twenty increased their bust line by one to one-and-a-half inches, and five of the remaining eight women increased theirs by two inches. In another study (521), thirteen women who wanted larger breasts were given weekly hypnotic suggestions to reexperience the sensations of puberty. After twelve weeks, their average bust measurement increased 2.1 inches as compared with control measurements of the rib cage just below the bust, which showed no change over the same period.

Using hypnosis, James Esdaile, a Scottish surgeon, performed several hundred operations without anesthesia in India during the mid-nineteenth century. These operations included the amputation of arms, fingers, and toes; the removal of tumors internally and externally; the extraction of teeth; and the removal of cataracts. His patients not only felt less pain, but their wounds healed faster than those of patients who were not hypnotized. Esdaile's operations were observed and described by many reliable witnesses, including British government officials. (135, 136)

Results like these have been achieved in many experiments during the past 150 years.* Such studies clearly demonstrate that through hypnosis many people can win significant freedom from pain, disease, and allergy, change the structure of their body, and increase certain skills and capacities.

Spiritual or Mind-Assisted Healing

Dr. Carl Simonton and his wife, Stephanie Matthews, pioneered a cancer treatment based on the premise that an individual's mental and emotional processes are significant contributors to the disease. Their treatment program consisted of regular exercise, psychological counseling, radiation therapy, and mental self-healing. Participants in it visualized a scenario in which their natural immune systems were seen fighting the cancer as a healthy body does. One

---

* We recommend F. W. H. Myers's *Human Personality* (344), Ernest R. Hilgard's *Hypnotic Sensibility* (210), and *Hypnosis: Research Developments and Perspectives*, edited by Erika Fromm and Ronald E. Shor (159; 818, 2nd ed.), for reviews of hypnosis experiments during the nineteenth and twentieth centuries.

of the Simontons' patients was a sixty-one-year-old man with extensive throat cancer. By using mental imagery and radiation therapy, he was healed after a year and a half. In the course of his remission, he drew pictures to represent the state of his disease, and Dr. Simonton was amazed to observe his accurate representation of the cancer's size and shape. The patient seemed to see internally what Dr. Simonton could only see with an instrument. After his cancer was gone, this man used the mental techniques he had learned to eliminate arthritis and sexual impotence. (454)

There have always been gifted individuals who appear to possess healing abilities. Drs. Elmer and Alyce Green have studied some of them at the Menninger Foundation in Topeka, Kansas. Healer Jack Schwartz, for example, was able to stop bleeding from puncture wounds in his arms and hands, at will, in the Greens' laboratory.* The work of the Simontons, the Greens, and other researchers is breaking new ground in the scientific study of mind-assisted healing.

Biofeedback

Mental exercises combined with biofeedback help patients control heart rate, muscle tension, lymph flow, blood flow, blood pressure, gastrointestinal functions, air flow in bronchial tubes, and electrical characteristics of the skin and brain. These generalized tasks have been effectively applied to the treatment of Raynaud's disease, Parkinson's disease, migraine and tension headaches, hypertension, spastic colon, asthma, neuromuscular problems, epilepsy, and cerebral palsy. (181) Torrey (1463) described recent technology such as miniaturized electronics and advanced materials engineering that make possible portable high-speed training equipment capable of providing instant feedback.

John Basmajian explored the voluntary control of single nerve fibers through auditory and visual feedback from electrodes placed in a thumb muscle. His subjects learned such delicate control that they could produce neural rhythms such as "doublets, triplets, gallop rhythms, and drum rolls," at will, after sixty to ninety minutes

---

* The Greens have reported the results of their studies in numerous articles and in their book, *Beyond Biofeedback* (181).

of training. (35, 36) Bernard Engel showed that some people can learn to control individual sections of the heartbeat. (134) Laboratory studies have demonstrated a person's ability to influence blood sugar levels at will. These various investigations suggest that any aspect of a person's physiology that can be brought to awareness, either directly or through instruments, can become accessible to conscious control.

Russian "Psychic Self-Regulation" (PSR)

PSR is defined by its Russian authors as "a directed, purposeful regulation of the various actions, reactions, and processes of an organism realized by means of its own psychic (mental) activity." The system combines yoga, hypnosis, autogenic training, and the martial arts. In it, mastery of muscle relaxation and breathing rhythms, achievement of temperature changes in the arms, chest, abdomen, and head, and control of heart rate are developed in preparation for more selective control of various psychological and physiological processes.

Russian researchers report that they have found a normal distribution curve for this self-transformative capacity in the general population. Everybody, they say, has it to some degree. But because most people are unaware of it, it is usually used nonconsciously, often contributing to the development of disease. PSR researchers maintain that mental self-influence occurs through normal physiological pathways, such as the central nervous system, and at the micromolecular level down to the most fundamental structures within living organisms. Published research from the Russian medical and sport communities suggests that PSR techniques can help increase the growth of muscle fiber and affect cellular and subcellular processes. (282, 283, 411, 412)

Psychokinesis and Telepathic Suggestion

The ability to affect physical objects, including one's own body and the bodies of others, without the mediation of any known physical medium has been studied by psychical researchers since the 1880s. If such a power exists, it would help explain many of the phenomena we have examined in this book.

There is a class of event in which it is not always clear whether psychokinesis or telepathic suggestion is the mediating factor. F. W. H. Myers, a founder of the (British) Society for Psychical Research and the author of the field's great classic, *Human Personality and Its Survival of Bodily Death*, described several experiments in which a subject was hypnotized telepathically and commanded to perform certain actions. One such experiment was witnessed by Myers and Pierre Janet, Freud's famous contemporary. Janet and Myers watched while their colleague Dr. Gibert, a physician of Le Havre, induced an unsuspecting patient to leave her home at night and walk across town to Gibert's house—a highly unusual excursion. Myers, Janet, and Gibert conducted twenty-five such experiments between October 1885 and May 1886, of which they deemed nineteen to be successful. (344)

Similar experiments in "suggestion at a distance" have been conducted by many researchers since then. The Russian physiologist L. L. Vasiliev, who established the former Soviet Union's first parapsychology laboratory, studied the phenomenon in the 1930s. His experimenters used telepathic suggestion to induce people miles away to sway back and forth. In other experiments, sleep and arousal were telepathically induced in unsuspecting subjects. Vasiliev's experiments led to further work in Russia along these lines. (74, 505, 520) Several experiments have been reported in which a person psychokinetically influenced bacteria, plants, or mice. (51, 68, 303, 512) And experimenters have developed a teaching mechanism using feedback for the distant influence of another person's physiology. William Braud and Marilyn Schlitz have reported efforts to influence the galvanic skin response (GSR) of another person while receiving continuous feedback of the target person's GSR activity. They found a significant correlation between attempts to increase or decrease the subjects' GSR and the actual GSR fluctuations. (58) Braud and Schlitz (640; see also 641) have reviewed recent research with biological systems as targets.

In 1970, Helmut Schmidt introduced a reproducible and consistent approach to the scientific study of psychokinesis. He designed and built a random event generator triggered by the radioactive decay of strontium-90 nuclei. The electron emission from such decay is one of nature's most random processes. Since then many psychokinesis studies using this device or similar equipment have been reported in the scientific literature. In most of these studies, subjects were able to influence random process mentally, primarily by getting sensory feedback whenever a decrease in the randomness occurred. Generally, experienced meditators learned the task more easily than nonmeditators. Charles Honorton, in a presidential address to the Parapsychological Association, characterized the process as an ability to bring "order out of disorder, as a function of intention." (214) For a review of random event generators and PK research, see Radin and Nelson (1270). In our opinion, these studies confirm the human capacity for intentional psychokinesis. (214, 430, 431) In showing that order can be imposed on randomness by meditation or mere intention, they dramatize the mind's role in self-transformation.

The extensions of human capacity that we have reviewed in these last few pages come from established fields of research and have been demonstrated in many clinical and experimental settings. There is a growing scientific literature about them. But there are also more exotic phenomena that reveal extraordinary powers that are latent in human nature. Some of these phenomena have not been scrutinized in scientific laboratories like the ones we have just reviewed, but they have been observed by reliable witnesses for centuries and have been attested to in the religious traditions. They include the following.

Religious Stigmata and Tokens of Espousal

Bleeding wounds on hands and feet, apparent lance wounds in the abdomen, bruises on the shoulders, chafing of wrists and ankles, punctures on the forehead simulating the crown of thorns—all these have appeared on the bodies of devotees during contemplation of Christ's crucifixion. They demonstrate how specific and elaborate the mind's effect on the body can be. Apparently, the body will dramatize any image that is passionately embraced by the mind.

It is generally thought that St. Francis of Assisi was the first to exhibit the stigmata. Thomas de Celano, in the first biography of St. Francis, wrote: "Marks of nails began to appear in his hands and feet. . . . These marks were rounded on the inner side of the hands and elongated on the outer side, and certain small pieces of flesh were seen like the ends of nails bent and driven back, projecting from the rest of the flesh. So also the marks of nails were imprinted in his feet, and raised above the rest of the flesh." (492: pp. 45–46) Since St. Francis, over three hundred stigmatics have borne the marks of the crucifixion. Certain wounds suggest that the stigmatic's imagination is influenced by his or her surroundings during the wound-forming process. Catherine Emmerich (1774–1824), for example, had a Y-shaped cross on her chest that resembled the unusual Y-shaped cross in the church in which she prayed.

Allied to stigmata is the token of espousal, a ring-shaped modification of flesh that forms around a nun's finger as a symbol of her betrothal to Christ. At the beatification of Catherine de Ricci (1522–89) in 1614, eyewitnesses described "a ring on the index finger of the left hand made entirely of flesh raised up like a ridge." (492: pp. 135–36) The French stigmatic Marie-Julie Jahenny was studied by Dr. Imbert Gourbeyre, a French physician, who observed the "appearance of a mystical ring, that is, a hoop of vivid red encircling the ring finger of the left hand." (492: p. 132) Twenty years later Gourbeyre wrote, "Marie-Julie's ring remains to the present day . . . still a ring made in the fleshy tissues, like a hoop of red coral which had sunk into the skin." (492: pp. 131–33) Like stigmata, this bodily change symbolizes a crucial event in the imaginative life of the devotee—in this case the spiritual marriage to Christ. It is another dramatic example of the specificity with which body structures can be altered through internal processes without external intervention or manipulation.

Incendium Amoris and the Tibetan Tumo

Some contemplatives exhibit an extreme body heat (*incendium amoris*) that they attribute to the fire of their love for God. Padre Pio of Foggia, Italy (1887–1968), who was stigmatic from 1915 until his death, had a temperature of 112° Fahrenheit at times, reported doctors who studied him. The Dominican nun Suor Maria Villani of Naples (1584–1670) was "continually consumed by an almost unsupportable flame of love." (492: p. 219) When a surgeon opened her body nine hours after her death, smoke issued forth and the heat prevented him from placing his hand in the abdominal cavity. In Tibetan Buddhism, the "warmth of spiritual devotion" is called *tum-mo*, the "Inner Fire." In certain exercises the devotee contemplates this energy, "which radiates light as well as warmth," and makes it possible to endure the cold of Tibetan snow and ice. (177: p. 165) In the Sufi tradition, there is an equivalent phenomenon, which is called the "fire of separation." (44, quoted in 425: p. 17)

Bodily Luminosity

Father Francis Suarez, the famous Jesuit theologian, was observed by a lay brother while encompassed in a radiant light. In the words of Jerome da Silva: "I perceived that a blinding light was coming from the crucifix. . . . This light streamed from the crucifix upon the face and breast of Father Suarez." (492: p. 166) Thomas à Kempis, in a biography of St. Lydwina of Schiedam, described some of the luminous phenomena around her: "She was discovered . . . surrounded by so great a divine brightness . . . although she always lay in darkness and material light was unbearable to her eyes, nevertheless, the divine light was very agreeable to her. . . . Her cell was often so wondrously flooded by light that to the beholders the cell itself appeared full of material lamps or fires." (492: p. 167) Similar events were observed in the presence of St. Philip Neri, St. Charles Borromeo, St. Ignatius of Loyola, St. Francis of Sales, and Ramana Maharshi, a modern Indian saint. (492)

Incorruptibility After Death

St. Madeline Sophie Barat, founder of the Society of the Sacred Heart, died in 1865. Twenty-eight years later her body was found almost perfectly intact, though her coffin was partly decayed and covered with mildew. St. Bernadette of Lourdes was buried in

1879. Thirty years later her body was exhumed during her beatification process. An eyewitness described the event: "Not the least trace of corruption nor any bad odour could be perceived in the corpse. . . . Even the habit in which she was buried was intact. The face was somewhat brown, the eyes slightly sunken." (492: p. 235)

The body of Paramahansa Yogananda, founder of the Self-Realization Fellowship, is reputed to have been perfectly preserved twenty days after his death. In a notarized letter, Harry Rowe, mortuary director at Forest Lawn Memorial Park in Los Angeles, wrote: "No physical disintegration was visible in his body even twenty days after death. . . . No indication of mold was visible on his skin, and no visible desiccation took place in the bodily tissues. . . . The physical appearance of Yogananda on March 27, just before the bronze cover of the casket was put into position, was the same as it had been on March 7th [the date of his death]." (536: p. 575)

The human organism can work wonders of self-transformation. Sometimes it is tricked into assuming this power, as in the placebo effect. Sometimes it is guided, as in the hypnotic removal of allergies, or assisted with instruments, as in biofeedback. Or it can work with self-reliant awareness, as it does in yoga or psychic self-regulation. This transformative power can be specific enough to alter the blood cell count, powerful enough to remove cancer, or sufficiently elaborate to cause wounds in the hands and feet that bleed only on Good Friday. It can also touch others in mysterious ways, if we can believe the evidence we have just reviewed.

Such powers, which are generally unknown to modern psychology and physical science, are often involved in the dramatic experiences we have described in this book—and sometimes seem to mediate them. We have mentioned the distance runner, for example, who saw images of his capillaries breaking while healing sensations passed through his chest, and bodybuilders who have vivid pictures of the muscles they are training. Another such power is a subtle internal hearing that accompanies moments of surpassing performance. The sounds heard in this way may be loud or faint, harsh or musical, human or unearthly. One champion bodybuilder, for example, said that he heard his muscles growing in his sleep when he was training heavily. They sounded like "cornflakes poured into a bowl." (163: p. 72) Bobby Jones claimed he heard a melody as he approached a round of golf and that if he swung the club to its rhythm he would play his best game. Barbra Streisand described a similar though more painful kind of internal hearing in a *Playboy* interview:

> I had clicks in my ears. I told my mother and she said, "Well, sleep on a hot-water bottle." She never asked me about it again. From that day, I led a secret life. . . . Two years later, I developed a high-pitched noise that I have heard all my life. I never hear the silence. When I used to have my ears examined, it turned out I had supersonic hearing. I hear high-range, high-pitch noises off the machine.
>
> When I was a kid, I used to go around with scarves to try to cut out the noise, which only made it worse, because it drives it more inside your head. I had this secret, I never told anybody. I didn't want to be different. I felt totally abnormal.

PLAYBOY: How do you connect that with your musical talent?
STREISAND: Strange connection. It made me listen very carefully to life. I would listen like nobody listened. But it's not good, it's not fun. I'm like inside my body, I hear my body. I'm very aware of my body's functions. It's very frightening. I see many colors.
PLAYBOY: In your head?
STREISAND: In my eyes. When I look at a wall, I don't just see a white wall. I see other things.
PLAYBOY: Textures or colors?
STREISAND: Textures *and* colors. It's like overemphasizing the processes of being alive.
PLAYBOY: Is it like being stoned?
STREISAND: I don't know. That's what people talk about. Maybe I'm stoned all the time. (382)

Subtle hearing and seeing, clairvoyant sensing or "touching," and the ability to affect one's environment by a power like psychokinesis might look like symptoms of disease if they come uninvited.

Disembodied voices or glimpses of your own insides can be profoundly disturbing. But the very fact that such powers arise spontaneously in many people suggests that they are a fundamental part
of human nature. The fact that they burst in upon so many of us
might indicate that we are designed to use them. Perhaps these
strange abilities are part of a larger awareness and capacity that is
pressing to be born in the human race.

This is the belief of many sacred traditions. In some schools of
yoga, Sufism, Buddhism, and Taoism, the aspirant is taught the
meaning of subtle sounds and sights that lead to larger realms of
consciousness and beauty. Such leadings were honored by shamans
thousands of years ago. The same can be said for almost all the
capacities we have looked at here: Nearly all of them were cultivated somewhere, at some period in the human past. And nearly
all of them arise spontaneously in people who do not expect or
welcome them. Apparently they cannot be suppressed completely,
even in a culture that is generally blind to their existence. Taken
as a whole, they shadow forth a vast unexplored realm. Cultivated
wisely, they may lead us to a new evolutionary adventure.

The exploration of human nature's further reaches has already
been joined on several fronts. Research in biofeedback, hypnosis,
and meditation; the psychic self-regulation developed in Russia; the
dissemination of Eastern religions in the West; the growing interest
in altered states of consciousness—all are openings onto a great
frontier. We suspect that still bolder explorations will follow. Like
all advances in human knowledge, these developments will have
practical by-products, we think—ways to make education more
effective and to help cure disease.

If a large-scale enterprise were mounted to explore these immense potentials of human nature, who knows what discoveries
we might make? Couldn't we support highly trained researchers
who would investigate the openings we have looked at in these
pages? It would bring a new zest to us all, we believe, just to know
that such attempts were being made. It is even conceivable that we
might win radical new insights not only into the structure of the
mind but also into the most fundamental processes of the physical
universe.

The extraordinary capabilities in sport that we have described
in this book are only a glimmer of what humans can realize. We

simply do not know the limits of long-term research into these phenomena. But if the pattern we have seen so often in human history holds, every new opening to knowledge and mastery will reveal further vistas to engage those who want to explore the limits of human nature.

BIBLIOGRAPHY

The bibliography follows in two parts, entitled "First Edition," which corresponds to the bibliography from the 1978 publication of this book (*The Psychic Side of Sports*), and "Second Edition," which is a new bibliography for this 1995 edition. Each bibliography is listed alphabetically by author's last name (or by title, in the rare cases where no author is given). The items in both bibliographies are listed in *one* numerical order, from 1 to 538 in the first edition and from 539 to 1545 in the second. These numbers are used in the text to cite references. Even though there are two bibliographies, because references are listed in one numerical order the reader can pinpoint a citation by looking up its number.

DIFFERENCES IN THE ARRANGEMENT OF THE BIBLIOGRAPHIES

The format of the bibliography of the first edition has been changed so that where possible it is the same as that of the second edition. However, the principles determining the order in which the items are listed in the bibliography of the first edition could not be changed without changing all the numbers in the bibliography and in the text. In the first bibliography, when a given author has more than one title listed, the various titles are arranged alphabetically (not counting "a," "the," and "an"). Also, in the first bibliography the older custom of alphabetizing Mc and Mac as if they were "Mac" is followed. In the bibliography of the *second* edition, however, the authors are arranged strictly alphabetically, including Mac and Mc. When a given author has more than one title listed, the titles are arranged *chronologically,* giving the earliest date first. If more than one item was published in the same year, they are arranged alphabetically by title with letters following the year (e.g., 1990a for the first title, 1990b for the second title, etc.).

The bibliography of the first edition emphasized classical works on sport, play, and adventure, and first-person accounts by athletes or works about individual athletes. The new bibliography emphasizes books and articles of interest to serious students and reflects the burgeoning literature on peak and flow experience in sports. Some of the items in the new bibliography have been annotated, and we have gone back and annotated some of the key items in the first bibliography, especially the classic books, articles of interest to students, and sources of multiple first-person accounts of the extraordinary sports experience.

Both bibliographies include not only the references cited in the text but additional books and articles we recommend for further reading on aspects of the extraordinary sports experience. Sometimes these recommended titles are not about sport per se, but are listed because they provide background information on the unusual states and capacities we have discussed in this book. A boldface letter following a citation refers to one of the ten subject categories listed below. These categories are not exclusive. Although only one subject category has been assigned to an entry, many titles fit two or more categories. The letters for each category are as follows:

A Altered states of consciousness
B Biographies and autobiographies containing unusual sports experiences
C Creativity in athletics
E "Extraphysical" and parapsychological energies, and out-of-body experiences
G General works on the extraordinary sports experience
I Works on individual sports containing material on the extraordinary sports experience
M Martial arts
O The ordeal in sport
P Psychology and sports
T Theoretical and philosophical issues related to the extraordinary sports experience
Y Yoga and yogic aspects of sports

First Edition

1. Alderman, R. B. (1974). *Psychological Behavior in Sport*. Philadelphia: Saunders. **P**

2. Alderman, R. B. (1970, Mar.). A sociopsychological assessment of attitude toward physical activity in champion athletes. *Research Quarterly, 41:* 1–9. **P**

3. Algonzin, Keith. (1976, Fall). Man and sport. *Philosophy Today, 20:* 190–95. **G**
Algonzin attempts a philosophical explanation of the universal human fas-

cination with sport, suggesting that it involves "our human aspiration for un-alienated action" (p. 192).

4. Ali, Muhammad, with Durham, Richard. (1975). *The Greatest*. New York: Random House. B

5. Allen, Jim. (1970). *Locked In: Surfing for Life*. New York: Barnes & Noble. I

6. Allen, Woody. (1977). A fan's notes on Earl Monroe. *Sport*, 65(5): 20–21+. I

7. Anderson, Dave. (1976, Jan. 11). Ali's radar waves. *New York Times*. B

8. Andretti, Mario. (1970). *What's It Like Out There?* Chicago: Regnery. B

9. Andrews, Peter. (1976). Sooner or later, the altitude gets you. *Signature*, 11(3): 34–37+. A

10. Andrews, Valerie. (1976). The joy of jogging. *New York*, 10(1): 60–63. I

11. Angell, Roger. (1975). The sporting scene: Down the drain. *New Yorker*, 51(18): 42–59. A

12. Angell, Roger. (1974, Oct. 13). Still getting the ink. *New York Times Book Review*, 6–8. B

13. Aran, Gideon. (1974). Parachuting. *American Journal of Sociology*, 80(1): 124–52. I

14. Arens, William. (1975). Great American football ritual. *Natural History*, 84(8): 72–81. Y

15. Ashe, Arthur. (1976). Catching Connors in the stretch. *Sports Illustrated*, 45(6): 20–21. A

16. Ashe, Arthur, with DeFord, Frank. (1975). *Arthur Ashe: Portrait in Motion*. Boston: Houghton Mifflin. B

17. Asinof, Eliot. (1968). *Seven Days to Sunday*. New York: Simon & Schuster. I

18. Assagioli, Roberto. (1965). *Psychosynthesis*. New York: Hobbs Dorman. Y

19. Aultman, Dick. (1973). Gain more leverage—start down slow. *Golf Digest*, 24(9): 28–33. I

20. Aurobindo, Sri. (1970). *The Collected Works of Sri Aurobindo*, Vol. 22. Pondicherry, India: Sri Aurobindo Ashram Trust. Y
Collected letters of the famous Indian philosopher and mystic Sri Aurobindo, about his philosophy of integral yoga, and the different levels and dimensions of human nature.

21. Aurobindo, Sri. (1970). *The Collected Works of Sri Aurobindo*, Vol. 23. Pondicherry, India: Sri Aurobindo Ashram Trust. Y
More letters by Sri Aurobindo on yoga through work, meditation, devotion, human relationships in yoga, and different kinds of spiritual experience.

22. Aurobindo, Sri. (1951). *The Life Divine*. New York: Dutton, 1951. Y

23. Avalon, Arthur (Sir John Woodruffe). (1974). *The Serpent Power*. New York: Dover. E

24. Axthelm, Pete. (1970). *The City Game: Basketball in New York*. New York: Harper's Magazine Press. B

25. Axthelm, Pete. (1973, Nov. 26). O.J.—The juice really flows. *Newsweek*, *82*: 67–70. **B**

26. Axthelm, Pete. (1976). Sky king. *Newsweek*, *87*(21): 55. **C**

27. Axthelm, Pete. (1972). The year of the runner. *Newsweek*, *80*(23): 76–84. **O**

28. Bach, Richard. (1972). *Stranger to the Ground*. New York: Avon Books. **I**

29. Banner, Bob. (1977). Physical exercises: An overview. *Preparation*, *1*(1): 14–21. **Y**

30. Bannister, Roger. (1955). *The Four-Minute Mile*. New York: Dodd, Mead. **B**

Bannister's poetic description of his training and record-breaking race, the beauty of running, and the thrill of doing what no one else had done before.

31. Bannister, Roger. (1973). The meaning of athletic performance. In John Talamini & Charles H. Page (Eds.), *Sport and Society* (pp. 325–35). Boston: Little, Brown. **G**

32. Barbieri, Ralph. (1975). A visit with Bill Walton . . . and from FBI. *Sport*, *61*(2): 74–76+. **B**

33. Barclay, Glen. (1973). *Mind Over Matter*. Indianapolis: Bobbs-Merrill. **M**

34. Baryshnikov: Gotta dance. (1975). *Time*, *105*(21): 44–50. **B**

35. Basmajian, John V. (1963, Aug. 21). Control and training of individual motor units. *Science*, *41*: 440–41. **P**

A landmark study of biofeedback training, in which it was shown that subjects can be trained to control a single nerve cell.

36. Basmajian, John V. (1962). *Muscles Alive: Their Functions Revealed by Electromyography*. Baltimore: Williams & Wilkins. **P**

37. Baumbach, Jonathan. (1970, Jan.). Aesthetics of basketball. *Esquire*, *73*: 140–46. **I**

38. Beard, Frank, & Schaap, Dick. (1970). *Pro: Frank Beard on the Golf Tour*. Cleveland: World. **B**

39. Beisser, Arnold. (1967). *The Madness in Sport*. New York: Appleton-Century-Crofts. **P**

See 589 for annotation of second edition.

40. Bell, Marty. (1974). Hypnosis in sports. *Sport*, *57*(3): 92–95+. **A**

41. Bell, Marty. (1975). *The Legend of Dr. J*. New York: Coward-McCann. **B**

42. Belmonte, Juan. (1937, Feb.). The making of a bullfighter. *Atlantic*, *159*: 129–48. **B**

43. Bennet, Glin. (1973, Oct. 6). An account of medical and psychological problems during the 1972 single-handed transatlantic yacht race. *Lancet*, *2*: 747–54. **O**

44. Bhavan, B. (1971). *Sufis, Mystics and Yogis of India*. Bombay: Bankey Behari. **Y**

45. Block, Alex Ben. (1974). *The Legend of Bruce Lee*. New York: Dell. **Y**

46. Blofeld, John. (1973). *The Secret and Sublime*. London: Allen & Unwin. Y

47. Blount, Roy, Jr. (1974). *About Three Bricks Shy of a Load*. Boston: Little, Brown. I

48. Bodo, Peter, & Hirshey, David. (1977). *Pelé's New World*. New York: Norton. B

49. Bolt, Tommy. (1971). *The Hole Truth*. Philadelphia: Lippincott. B

50. Bonatti, Walter. (1964, ©1961). *On the Heights*. London: Rupert Hart-Davis. B
Autobiography of a legendary mountain climber with descriptions of his major climbs from 1949–61, and some of his extraordinary sports experiences.

51. Bond, Donald. (1952). *The Love and Fear of Flying*. New York: International Universities Press. P

52. Bongartz, Roy. (1977). The $100,000 bowling machine. *Sports Illustrated*, 46(11): 66–76. I

53. Bonington, Chris. (1971). *Annapurna South Face*. New York: McGraw-Hill. B

54. Bonington, Chris. (1976). *Everest the Hard Way*. New York: Random House. B

55. Borden, Charles A. (1967). *Sea Quest: Global Blue-Water Adventuring in Small Craft*. Philadelphia: Macrae Smith. I

56. Bradley, Bill. (1976). *Life on the Run*. New York: Quadrangle/New York Times Book Co. B

57. Bradshaw, Terry, & Conn, C. (1973). *No Easy Game*. Old Tappan, NY: H. Fleming Revell. B

58. Braud, William. (1978). Allobiofeedback: Immediate feedback for a psychokinetic influence upon another person's psychology. *Research in Parapsychology 1977*. Metuchen, NJ: Scarecrow. E

59. Breslin, Jimmy. (1975). A day with the doctor. *Sport*, 60(3): 28–32. B

60. Brier, Robert M. Personal communication. B

61. Brier, Robert M. (1969, Sep.). PK on a bio-electrical system. *Journal of Parapsychology*, 33: 187–205. E

62. Brock, Lou, & Schulze, Franz. (1976). *Stealing Is My Game*. Englewood Cliffs, NJ: Prentice-Hall. B

63. Brodie, John, & Houston, James D. (1974). *Open Field*. New York: Bantam. B

64. Brooks, Charles V. W. (1974). *Sensory Awareness: The Rediscovery of Experiences*. New York: Viking. Y

65. Brown, Barbara B. (1977). *Stress and the Art of Biofeedback*. New York: Harper & Row. A

66. Brown, George I., & Gaynor, Donald. (1967). Athletic action as creativity. *Journal of Creative Behavior*, 1(2): 155–62. C
Brown and Gaynor recommend that coaches and physical educators consider not only an athlete's physical ability but also his or her creative ability.

67. Brown, John Porter. (1868, ©1927). *The Darvishes: or Oriental Spiritualism* (2nd ed.). London: Frank Cass. E

68. Buckle, Richard. (1971). *Nijinsky 1909*. New York: Simon & Schuster, 1971. B

69. Budge, E. A. Wallis (Ed.). (1967). *The Egyptian Book of the Dead.* New York: Dover. E

70. Buhl, Hermann. (1956). *Lonely Challenge.* New York: Dutton, 1956. O

Autobiography of a mountain climber who began as a weakling but became a climber of great renown, possessed "not only of fantastic skill but of superhuman energy and endurance" (p. 6).

71. Butt, Dorcas Susan. (1976). *The Psychology of Sport.* New York: Van Nostrand Reinhold. P

The author was an international tennis circuit player and Canada's first-ranked player for three years. She was also one of the first clinical psychologists to investigate the flow experience in sport, under the name of "competence motivation." Athletes who engage in sport because of competence motivation do so for play's intrinsic rewards and the "feelings of self-fulfillment" they experience in their quest for excellence. This can be experienced in two forms—the overall experience of engaging over a period of several years in a particular sport that is inherently rewarding and in special moments or specific performances in which there is effortlessness, altered perceptions of space and time, elation, and beauty. Butt discusses ways in which society could change in order for competence motivation and flow to be the primary aims of sport, instead of ruthless competition.

72. Byrd, Richard E. (1938). *Alone.* New York: Putnam's. O

73. Cahill, Tim. (1977, Sep. 8). A man for off season. *Rolling Stone,* 247: 24–30. B

74. Caldwell, Carol. (1978). Beyond ESP. *New Times,* 10(7): 42–50. E

75. Campbell, Gail. (1977). *Marathon: The World of Long-Distance Athletes.* New York: Sterling. O

76. Capra, Fritjof. (1975). *The Tao of Physics: An Exploration of the Parallels Between Modern Physics and Eastern Mysticism.* Berkeley, CA: Shambhala. E

77. Castaneda, Carlos. (1974). *Tales of Power.* New York: Simon & Schuster. A

78. Cath, S. H., Kahn, A., & Cobb, N. (1977). *Love and Hate on the Tennis Court.* New York: Scribner's. I

79. Chouminard, Yvan. (1977, Dec.). Chouminard on ice. *Outside,* 1: 30–33. I

80. Chow, David, & Spangler, Richard. (1977). *Kung Fu: Philosophy and Technique.* Garden City, NY: Doubleday. M

81. Cleary, William. (1967). *Surfing: All the Young Wave Hunters.* New York: New American Library. I

82. Cochran, Jacqueline, with Odlum, Floyd. (1954). *The Stars at Noon.* Boston: Little, Brown. B

83. Cohen, Marvin. (1919, Jul. 26). Baseball and religion. *Dial,* 67: 57–59. G

84. Cohen, Marvin. (1974). *Baseball the Beautiful.* New York: Link Books. I

Poetic tribute to the beauty and significance of baseball and nostalgia for youthful playing days.

85. Colbert, Jim. (1975, Jun.). Fine-tuning your concentration. *Golf Magazine*, 17(6): 54–58. **Y**

86. Coleman, Kate. (1955, Sep.). Because it's there . . . Outward bound: Not for the social climber. *WomenSports*, 2(9): 30–33+. **O**

87. Colletto, Jerry, with Sloan, Jack L. (1975). *Yoga Conditioning and Football*. Millbrae, CA: Celestial Arts. **Y**

88. Collins, Larry, & Lapiere, Downe. (1968). *Or I'll Dress You in Mourning*. New York: Simon & Schuster. **B**

89. Columbo, Franco, & Fels, George. (1977). *Winning Bodybuilding*. Chicago: Regnery. **I**

90. Connolly, Olga. (1968). *Rings of Destiny*. New York: David McKay. **B**

91. Cooper, Kenneth. (1968). *Aerobics*. New York: M. Evans. **Y**

92. Cooper, Kenneth. (1977). *The Aerobics Way*. New York: M. Evans. **Y**

93. Cooper, Linn F., & Erickson, Milton H. (1954). *Time Distortion in Hypnosis*. Baltimore: Williams & Wilkins. **A**

94. Cousteau, Jacques Y., with Dumas, Frederic. (1953). *The Silent World*. New York: Harper & Row. **I**

95. Cousy, Bob, as told to Hirshberg, Al. (1958). *Basketball Is My Life*. Englewood Cliffs, NJ: Prentice-Hall. **B**

96. Cousy, Robert. (1964). *The Last Loud Roar*. Englewood Cliffs, NJ: Prentice-Hall. **B**

97. Cratty, Bernard J. (1973). *Psychology in Contemporary Sport*. Englewood Cliffs, NJ: Prentice-Hall. **P**

98. Crompton, Paul H. (1975). *Kung Fu: Theory and Practice*. Toronto: Pagurian Press. **M**

99. Crookall, Robert. (1972). *Casebook of Astral Projection*. Secaucus, NJ: University Books. **E**

100. Crookall, Robert. (1966, ©1960). *The Study and Practice of Astral Projection*. Secaucus, NJ: University Books. **E**

101. Crookall, Robert. (1964). *The Techniques of Astral Projection*. New York: Samuel Weiser. **E**

102. Csikzentmihalyi, Mihalyi. (1976). *Beyond Boredom and Anxiety*. San Francisco: Jossey-Bass. **A**

A study of autotelic activities, or those that are engaged in because of their intrinsic value. Describes research interviews with nearly sixty persons, including college hockey and soccer players, spelunkers and explorers, a mountain climber of international repute, a champion handball player, and a world-record long-distance swimmer. Csikzentmihalyi developed a model of intrinsic rewards to explain the responses based on the "flow" experience, which he felt is the crucial component of enjoyment in sport and other activities. Several accounts of flow experiences are provided.

103. Csikzentmihalyi, Mihalyi. (1975). Play and intrinsic rewards. *Journal of Humanistic Psychology*, 15(3): 41–63. **A**

104. Csonka, Larry, & Kiick, Jim. (1973). *Always on the Run*. New York: Random House. **B**

105. David-Neel, Alexandra. (1965, ©1956). *Magic and Mystery in Tibet.* Secaucus, NJ: University Books. **E**

106. Davidson, Art. (1969). *Minus 148: The Winter Ascent of Mt. McKinley.* New York: Norton. **O**

107. Delatire, Edwin J. (1975, Sep.). Some reflections on success and failure in competitive athletics. *Journal of the Philosophy of Sport,* 2: 133–39. **P**

108. Dement, William C. (1974). *Some Must Watch While Some Must Sleep.* San Francisco: W. H. Freeman. **A**

109. Demaret, Jimmy. (1954). *My Partner, Ben Hogan.* New York: McGraw-Hill. **B**

110. DeMille, Richard. (1976). *Castaneda's Journey.* Santa Barbara, CA: Capra Press. **E**

111. DeMott, Benjamin. (1962–63, Win.). An unprofessional eye . . . Suspended youth. *American Scholar,* 32: 107–12. **G**

112. Dennis, Larry. (1973, Nov.). Weiskopf walking slower and swinging smoother. *Golf Digest,* 24(11): 80–81. **B**

113. Devaney, John. (1965). *Bob Cousy.* New York: Putnam's. **B**

114. Devaney, John. (1973). *The Bobby Orr Story.* New York: Random House. **B**

115. Diaz-Canabate, Antonio. (1956). *The Magic World of the Bullfighter.* London: Burke. **I**

116. Dickinson, Mary Lindsay. Personal communication. **B**

117. Dingwall, Eric J. (1962). D. D. Home: Sorcerer of kings. In E. J. Dingwall, *Some Human Oddities* (pp. 91–128). Secaucus, NJ: University Books. **E**

118. Dingwall, Eric J. (1962). Eusapia Palladino: Queen of the cabinet. In E. J. Dingwall, *Very Peculiar People* (pp. 178–217). Secaucus, NJ: University Books. **E**

119. Dobereiner, Peter. (1976, Nov.). The day Joe Ezar called his shots for a remarkable 64. *Golf Digest,* 27(11): 66–67. **B**

120. Doust, Dudley. (1973, Nov. 4). Opening the mystical door of perception in sport. *The Sunday Times.* **G**

121. Doust, Dudley. (1974, Apr.). Tony Jacklin, mystical perception in sport. *Intellectual Digest,* 4: 32–33. **B**

122. Dowling, Tom. (1970). *Coach! A Season with Lombardi.* New York: Norton. **B**

123. Draeger, Donn F., & Smith, Robert W. (1974, ©1969). *Asian Fighting Arts.* New York: Berkley. **M**

124. Duncan, Isadora. (1928). *The Art of the Dance.* New York: Theatre Arts. **B**

125. Duncan, Isadora. (1927). *My Life.* New York: Boni & Liveright. **B**

126. Dürckheim, Karlfried. (1975). *Hara: The Vital Centre in Man.* New York: Weiser. **M**
Dürckheim develops the Eastern concept of the hara, or center of power, its general human significance, its ways of expression, and the principle of its practice.

127. Ebon, Martin (Ed.). (1975). *The Amazing Uri Geller.* New York: New American Library. **E**

128. Eccles, Sir John. (1977). The human person in its two-way relationship to the brain. In *Research in Parapsychology 1976* (pp. 251–62). Metuchen, NJ: Scarecrow Press. E

129. Eckhart, Meister. (1941). *Meister Eckhart; a Modern Translation* (Raymond Bernard Blakney, Trans.). New York: Harper & Row. Y

130. Editorial. (1977, Jul./Aug.). *Olympian, 1*(10): 13–15. G

131. Edmiston, Susan. (1976, Sep.). Winners and how they win. *Woman's Day, 33:* 174+. G

132. Ellen, Arthur, with Jennings, Dean. (1968). *The Intimate Casebook of a Hypnotist*. New York: New American Library. A

133. Elliot, Herb. (1961). *The Herb Elliot Story*. New York: Thomas Nelson. B

134. Engel, Bernard T. (1975). Visceral control: Some implications for psychiatry. Paper presented at the American Psychiatric Association Conference, Anaheim, CA, 1975. P

135. Esdaile, James. (1976, ©1846). *Mesmerism in India*. New York: Arno Press A

In this book, nineteenth-century Scottish physician James Esdaile described his use of mesmerism to amputate limbs, remove cataracts and tumors, and perform other surgeries without anesthesia. Esdaile's work was observed for many years by other physicians, journalists, and British government officials, and was generally deemed to be highly successful.

136. Esdaile, James. (1975, ©1852). *Natural and Mesmeric Clairvoyance*. New York: Arno Press. A

Esdaile's descriptions of clairvoyant experiences that he observed in the course of his medical practice, some of which were induced by mesmeric trance.

137. Evans, Jay, & Anderson, Robert R. (1975). *Kayaking: The New White Water Sport for Everybody*. Brattleboro, VT: Stephen Greene Press. I

138. Evans, Lee. Personal communication. A

139. Fairfax, John. (1971). *Britannia: Rowing Alone Across the Atlantic*. New York: Simon & Schuster. B

140. Falls, Joe. (1977). *The Boston Marathon*. New York: Macmillan. I

141. Farrelly, Midget, as told to McGregor, Craig. (1967). *The Surfing Life*. New York: Arco. I

142. Ferguson, Marilyn. (1973). *The Brain Revolution*. New York: Taplinger. P

143. Fessier, Michael, Jr. (1976, Jul.). Transcendental running. *Human Behavior, 5*(7): 17–20. I

144. Fimrite, Ron. (1975, Jun. 16). Bringer of the big hit. *Sports Illustrated, 42*(24): 33+. B

145. Fincher, Jack. (1977, Oct.). If Russ Francis can't beat you, his "kahuna" can. *Sport, 65*(4): 76+. B

146. Fischler, Stan. (1969). *Bobby Orr and the Big, Bad Bruins*. New York: Dodd, Mead. B

147. Fixx, James. (1977). *The Complete Book of Running*. New York: Random House. I

148. Floyd, Keith. (1973–74, Win.). Of time and the mind. *Fields Within Fields Within Fields*, No. 10: 47–57. **P**

149. Fluegelman, Andrew. (1976). *The New Games Book*. Garden City, NY: Doubleday. **A**

150. Flying Magazine Editors. (1976). *Sport Flying*. New York: Scribner's. **I**

151. Fodor, Nandor. (1964). The riddle of Nijinsky. In his *Between Two Worlds* (pp. 24–29). West Nyack, NY: Parker. **B**

152. Ford, Whitey; Mantle; Mickey; & Durso, Joseph. (1977). *Whitey and Mickey*. New York: Viking. **B**

153. Fox, Matthew. (1976). *Whee! We, Wee All the Way Home*. Gaithersburg, MD: Consortium Books. **E**

154. Fox, Oliver (1963). *Astral Projection*. Secaucus, NJ: University Books. **E**

155. Frady, Marshall. (1975, Feb.). The little man is a big man on the N.C. State campus. *Sport, 60*(2): 30+. **B**

156. Frager, Robert. (1969, Jan.). Psychology of the samurai. *Psychology Today, 2*: 48–53+. **M**

157. Frazier, Walt. (1974). *Rockin' Steady*. Englewood Cliffs, NJ: Prentice-Hall. **B**

158. Frazier, Walt, & Jares, Joe. *Clyde*. (1970). New York: Holt, Rinehart & Winston. **B**

159. Fromm, Erika, & Shor, Ronald E. (Eds.). (1972). *Hypnosis: Research Developments and Perspectives*. Chicago: Aldine. **A**

160. Furlong, William B. (1969, Jan. 27). Danger as a way of joy. *Sports Illustrated, 30*: 52–53. **A**

161. Furlong, William Barry. (1976, Jun.). The fun in fun. *Psychology Today, 10*(1): 35+. **A**

162. Furst, Peter. (1972). *Flesh of the Gods*. New York: Praeger. **A**

163. Gaines, Charles, & Butler, George. (1974). *Pumping Iron*. New York: Simon & Schuster. **I**

164. Gallwey, Timothy. (1974). *The Inner Game of Tennis*. New York: Random House. **I**
Gallwey's first attempt to "explore the limitless potential within the human body" (p. 13) via the "inner game." It consists of exercises to induce performances in which one's limits are surpassed repeatedly.

165. Gallwey, Timothy. (1976). *Inner Tennis*. New York: Random House. **I**
Sequel to *The Inner Game of Tennis*. Concentrates on overcoming mental obstacles to peak performance, which Gallwey views in terms of self 1, the interfering conscious mind that creates obstacles, and self 2, body consciousness, which "shows a talent so great that we are often afraid even to identify with it" (p. 9). The play of self 2 is "in the zone," or "unconscious."

166. Gallwey, Timothy, & Kriegel, Bob. (1977). *Inner Skiing*. New York: Random House. **I**
Here Gallwey applies his "inner game" principles to skiing. The authors claim that skiing (or any other sport) can provide the athlete with firsthand

knowledge of levels of awareness that "are more beneficial and deeply satisfying than we ordinarily reach in our daily lives" (p. 141).

167. Gaskins, G., & Masterson, D. W. (1974, Sep.). The work of art in
sport. *Journal of the Philosophy of Sport, 1:* 36–66. **C**

168. Genasci, James E., & Klissouras, Vasillis. (1966, Feb.). The Delphic
spirit in sports. *Journal of Health, Physical Education, and Recreation, 37*(2):
43–45. **G**

The Delphic spirit exists in sport when "the athlete does not retreat from
life but immerses himself completely. He experiences a revival of spirit, mind,
and body that provides joy of self-discovery and reflects the integrated
[person]."

169. Gerber, Dan. (1978, May). The way it feels: Sailfishing off Key West.
Outside, 1: 53–54. **I**

170. Gerber, Ellen W. (Ed.). (1972). *Sport and the Body: A Philosophical
Symposium.* Philadelphia: Lea & Febiger. **G**

Anthology of sixty-three philosophical writings on sport and the body.
There are sections on the nature of sport, sport and metaphysical speculations,
the body and being, sport as a meaningful experience, sport and value-oriented
concerns, and sport and aesthetics. Each section has its own bibliography and
a useful introductory review by Gerber.

171. Ghiselin, Brewster (Ed.). (1955, ©1952). *The Creative Process: A
Symposium.* New York: New American Library. **C**

172. Gilbey, John. (1963). *Secret Fighting Arts of the World.* Rutland, VT:
Tuttle. **M**

173. Glasser, William. (1976). *Positive Addiction.* New York: Harper &
Row. **P**

Puts forth the idea that people can form "positive" addictions—to sports,
meditation, and other activities. Glasser describes how these addictions develop
and their role in one's life, including combatting negative addictions.

174. Gluck, Jay. (1962). *Zen Combat.* New York: Ballantine Books. **M**

175. Golf Digest's Professional Teaching Panel. (1973, Nov.). How your
game can brighten under pressure. *Golf Digest, 26*(11): 85–88. **I**

176. Gott, Jim, with Smith, Norman Lewis. (1976). *Amphibian.* Chicago:
Playboy Press. **B**

177. Govinda, Lama Anagarika. (1969). *Foundations of Tibetan Mysticism.* New York: Samuel Weiser. **Y**

178. Grange, Red, as told to Morton, Ira. (1953). *The Red Grange Story.*
New York: Putnam's. **B**

179. Greeley, Andrew, & McCready, William C. (1975, Jan. 26). Are we
a nation of mystics? *New York Times Magazine,* 12–13. **E**

180. Green, Celia. (1968). *Out-of-the-Body Experiences.* Oxford: Institute
of Psychophysical Research. **E**

181. Green, Elmer, & Green, Alyce. (1977). *Beyond Biofeedback.* New
York: Dial Press. **Y**

182. Greenhouse, Herbert. (1974). *The Astral Journey.* Garden City, NY:
Doubleday. **E**

183. Gregg, Jearald. (1971). A philosophical analysis of the sports experience. Unpublished doctoral dissertation, University of Southern California. **G**

184. Grof, Stanislav. (1975). *The Realms of the Human Unconscious*. New York: Viking. **A**

185. Grossinger, Richard. (1976). *The Unfinished Business of Doctor Hermes*. Plainfield, VT: North Atlantic Books. **I**

186. Gutkind, Lee. (1973). *Bike Fever*. Chicago: Follett. **I**

187. Hagen, Walter, as told to Heck, Margaret S. (1956). *The Walter Hagen Story*. New York: Simon & Schuster. **B**

188. Hano, Arnold. (1971). John F. Kennedy: His legacy to sports. In Al Silverman (Ed.), *The Best of Sport*. New York: Viking. **G**

189. Harper, William. (1969, May). Man alone. *Quest, 12:* 57–60. **G**

190. Harris, Dorothy V. (1973). *Involvement in Sport*. Philadelphia: Lea & Febiger. **P**

191. Harris, Dorothy V. (1978, Jan.). Sports science: The happy addict. *WomenSports, 5*(1): 53. **P**

192. Harris, T. George. (1975, Oct.). Why pros meditate. *Psychology Today, 9*(5): 4. **P**

193. Harrison, E. J. (1955). *The Fighting Spirit of Japan*. New York: Foulsham. **M**

194. Haskins, James. (1975). *Doctor J.* Garden City, NY: Doubleday. **B**

195. Haston, Dougal. (1972). *In High Places*. New York: Macmillan. **B**

196. Hayter, Adrian. (1959). *The Long Voyage*. New York: Harper & Row. **B**

197. Heinz, William C. (1976). The ghost of the gridiron. In Red Smith (Ed.), *Press Box* (pp. 45–59). New York: Norton. **B**

198. Heller, Peter. (1973). *In This Corner*. New York: Simon & Schuster. **I**

199. Hellison, Donald. (1973). *Humanistic Physical Education*. Englewood Cliffs, NJ: Prentice-Hall. **C**

200. Hemery, David. (1976). *Another Hurdle*. New York: Taplinger. **B**

201. Hemingway, Ernest. (1932). *Death in the Afternoon*. New York: Scribner's. **I**

202. Hemingway, Patricia Drake. (1975). *Transcendental Meditation Primer*. New York: David McKay. **Y**

203. Herrigel, Eugen. (1953). *Zen in the Art of Archery*. New York: Pantheon. **Y**

In Japan and other Far Eastern countries, martial arts are a means of training the mind and bringing "it into contact with the ultimate reality" (p. 9). Herrigel presents the introspective stages involved as the pupil progresses from learning how to move to performing "the unmoved movement, the undanced dance [which] passes over into Zen" (p. 91).

204. Herrington, Nancy. (1978). Body work: A guide to the new physical therapies. *New Age, 3*(8): 48–53+. **Y**

205. Herzog, Maurice (1952). *Annapurna*. New York: Dutton. **O**

206. Hickman, James C.; Murphy, Michael; & Spino, Michael. (1977). Psychophysical transformations through meditation and sport. *Simulational Games, 8*(1): 49–60. **Y**

Description of a workshop in which mental and physical disciplines were taught to a group of runners.

207. Hicks, Gail F. (1974). *Creativity and Body Awareness.* Unpublished doctoral dissertation, Washington State University. **C**
Concludes that "creativity is an emergent property of a cycle of sensitivity to body changes during movement, relaxation, and the rhythmic alternation" between all three. It can be enhanced by means of focus and concentration.

208. Higdon, Hal. (1978). Can running cure mental illness? [Part 1]. *Runner's World, 13*(1): 36–43. **P**

209. Higdon, Hal. (1978). Can running put mental patients on their feet?" [Part 2]. *Runner's World, 13*(2): 36–43. **P**

210. Hilgard, Ernest R. (1965). *Hypnotic Susceptibility.* New York: Harcourt, Brace & World. **A**

211. Hoffman, S. J. (1976, Sep.). Athletae dei: Missing the meaning of sport. *Journal of the Philosophy of Sport, 3:* 42–51. **G**

212. Hogan, Ben. (1955). This is my secret. *Life, 39*(6): 60–63. **B**

213. Honig, Donald. (1976). *Baseball Between the Lines.* New York: Coward, McCann & Geoghegan. **I**

214. Honorton, Charles R. (1976). Has science developed the competence to confront claims of the paranormal? *Research in Parapsychology* 1975 (pp. 199–223). Metuchen, NJ: Scarecrow Press. **E**

215. Hornbein, Thomas F. (1965). *Everest—The West Ridge.* San Francisco: Sierra Club. **I**

216. Horwitz, Tom, & Kimmelman, Susan, with Lui, H. H. (1976). *Tai Chi Ch'uan: The Technique of Power.* Chicago: Chicago Review Press. **M**

217. Houston, Charles S. (1968). The last blue mountain. In Samuel S. Klausner (Ed.), *Why Men Take Chances* (pp. 48–58). Garden City, NY: Doubleday/Anchor. **O**

218. Houts, Jo Ann. (1972). Feeling and perception in the sport experience. *Journal of Health, Physical Education, and Recreation, 111*(8): 71–72. **A**
One of the first studies to identify the sport experience as consisting of many of Maslow's characteristics of peak experiences.

219. Huizinga, Johan. (1950). *Homo Ludens.* Boston: Beacon Press. **G**

220. Hunter, Catfish, as told to Vass, George. (1973). The game I'll never forget. *Baseball Digest, 32*(6): 35–37. **B**

221. Huxley, Aldous. (1945). *The Perennial Philosophy.* New York: Harper & Row. **Y**

222. Ismail, A. H., & Trachtman, L. E. (1973). Jogging the imagination. *Psychology Today, 6*(10): 78–82+. **P**

223. Jacklin, Tony. (1970). *Jacklin.* New York: Simon & Schuster. **B**

224. Jackson, Ian. (1975). *Yoga and the Athlete.* Mountain View, CA: World Publications. **Y**
The author describes peak moments that occurred as he immersed himself in surfing, running, long-distance running, fasting, and yoga. In the final chapter, his yoga teacher Joel Kramer describes yoga as adult play, saying, "like child's play, it involves a great amount of energy, but no effort" (p. 87). He also describes it as a way of playing physically, mentally, and spiritually, "with the edges or frontiers of one's being" (p. 91).

225. Jackson, Marni. (1978). Wheeling for distance. *Outside,* 1(7): 49–54. I

226. James, William. (1908). *The Energies of Men.* New York: Moffat, Yard. A

James proposes that there may be "beyond the very extremity of fatigue-distress, amounts of ease and power that we never dreamed ourselves to own—sources of strength habitually not taxed at all, because habitually we never push through the obstruction, never pass those early critical points" (pp. 7–8).

227. James, William. (1902). *The Varieties of Religious Experience.* New York: Modern Library. A

A comparative study of religious experience by America's most prominent psychologist-philosopher. James combines appreciation of metanormal experience with critical distance from theological and philosophic interpretations of it. His approach constitutes a "natural history" of extraordinary functioning.

228. Jenner, Bruce. (1976). It was too easy. *Sport,* 63(5): 67–78. B

229. Jenner, Bruce, & Finch, Philip. (1977). *Decathlon Challenge.* Englewood Cliffs, NJ: Prentice-Hall B

230. Jennings, Melchior. (1965). *Instinct Shooting.* New York: Dodd, Mead. I

231. Jerome, John. (1978). Frank Shorter: The man who invented running. *Outside,* 1(8): 33–37. B

232. Johansson, Ingemar. (1959). New challenger scouts a fight. *Life,* 46(19): 40+. B

233. Johnston, Richard W. (1976, Oct. 18). Dangerous delusion. *Sports Illustrated,* 45: 88–92+. O

234. Jolivet, Regis. (1961, Sum.). Work, meditation, play, contemplation. *Philosophy Today,* 5: 114–20. Y

235. Jones, Robert F. (1970, May 11). The world's first peace pentathlon. *Sports Illustrated,* 32: 50–58+. I

236. Jones, Robert F. (1970, Nov. 16). You learn the art of invisibility. *Sports Illustrated,* 33: 23–25. B

237. Jones, Robert Tyre, Jr. (1966). *Bobby Jones on Golf.* Garden City, NY: Doubleday. I

238. Jones, Robert Tyre, Jr. (1960). *Golf Is My Game.* Garden City, NY: Doubleday. I

239. Jordan, Pat. (1977). *Broken Patterns.* New York: Dodd, Mead. G

240. Kaelin, Eugene F. (1968, May). The well-played game: Notes toward an aesthetics of sport. *Quest,* 10: 16–28. C

241. Kahn, Roger. (1971). *The Boys of Summer.* New York: Harper & Row. I

242. Kahn, Roger. (1960). Stan Musial: Pride of the St. Louis Cardinals. In Ed Fitzgerald (Ed.), *Heroes of Sport* (pp. 5–22). New York: Bartholomew House. G

243. Keen, Sam, & Murphy, Michael. (1978). Our bodies, our souls: A New Age interview. *New Age,* 3(8): 34–37+. G

244. Kellogg, Curtiss. (1977). Running loose. *Runner's World,* 12(8): 64. I

245. Kenn, C. W. (1949). *Firewalking From the Inside.* Los Angeles: Franklin Thomas. E

246. Kenyon, Gerald S. (1968, May). A conceptual model for characterizing physical activity. *Research Quarterly,* 39(1): 96–105. G

247. Kerley, M. R. (1977). Kitty O'Neil: a deaf stunt woman races the speed of sound. *WomenSports,* 4(4): 17–19. B

248. Kidd, C. (1966). Congenital *Ichthyosiform Erythroermia* treated by hypnosis. *British Journal of Dermatology,* 78: 101–05. A

249. Kiernan, Thomas. (1975). *The Miracle at Coogan's Bluff.* New York: Crowell. I

250. Kilner, Walter J. (1965). *The Human Aura.* Secaucus, NJ: University Books. E

251. King, Billie Jean, with Chapin, Kim. (1974). *Billie Jean.* New York: Harper & Row. B

252. Kirkpatrick, Harvey. (1975, Feb.). Wayne Estes' final game. *Sport,* 60(2): 25–26. E

253. Kirshenbaum, Jerry (1969, Jul. 21). They're all out to launch. *Sports Illustrated,* 31: 38–41. I

254. Kleinfield, Sonny. (1977). *A Month at the Brickyard.* New York: Holt, Rinehart & Winston. I

255. Kleinman, Seymour. (1975, Sep.). The nature of a self and its relation to an other in sport. *Journal of the Philosophy of Sport,* 2: 45–50. A

256. Klobucher, Jim, & Tarkenton, Fran. (1976). *Tarkenton.* New York: Harper & Row. B

257. Koestler, Arthur. (1964). *The Act of Creation.* New York: Macmillan. C

258. Kornheiser, Tony. (1977, Mar. 13). Bruce Jenner: Apple pie hero. *New York Times.* B

259. Kostrubala, Thaddeus. (1976). *The Joy of Running.* Philadelphia: Lippincott. P

260. Koufax, Sandy, with Linn, Ed. (1966). *Koufax.* New York: Viking. B

261. Kram, Mark. (1972, Mar. 27). All the best [George Best]. *Sports Illustrated,* 36(13): 60–69. B

262. Kram, Mark. (1976, Mar. 8). The face of pain. *Sports Illustrated,* 44(10): 58–66. O

263. Kram, Mark. (1969, Apr. 7). The not-so-melancholy Dane [Torben Ulrich]. *Sports Illustrated,* 30: 78–86. B

264. Krikler, Bernice. (1965, Feb.). A preliminary psychological assessment of the skills of motor racing drivers. *British Journal of Psychiatry,* 3: 192–94. P

265. Krippner, Stanley, & Rubin, Daniel. (Eds.). (1975). *The Energies of Consciousness.* New York: Gordon & Breach. E

266. Krippner, Stanley, & Rubin, Daniel. (Eds.). (1974). *The Kirlian Aura.* Garden City, NY: Doubleday. E

267. Krumdick, Victor F., & Lumian, Norman C. (1963, Sep.). The psychology of athletic success. *Athletic Journal,* 44(1): 52+. P

268. Kupfer, Joseph. (1975, Sep.). Purpose and beauty in sport. *Journal of the Philosophy of Sport, 2:* 83–90. G

269. Lampe, David. (1977, Dec. 19–26). Yesterday. *Sports Illustrated, 47:* E6+. O

270. Lance, Kathryn. (1977). *Running for Health and Beauty.* Indianapolis: Bobbs-Merrill. A

271. Lang, Andrew. (1900, Feb.). The fire walk. *Proceedings of the Society for Psychical Research, 15*(Part 36): 2–15. E

272. Larned, Dorothy. (1976, Mar.). Fantasies and fatigue: Diana Nyad floats alone. *WomenSports, 3*(3): 36–39. O

273. Laski, Marghanita. (1961). *Ecstasy.* Bloomington: University of Indiana Press. A

A pioneering study of religious and secular forms of ecstasy. Part I describes a questionnaire Laski developed, as well as her methods of analysis. Part II describes many types of ecstasy, illustrated by examples from informants and literature. In Part III, Laski discusses beliefs that arise from ecstatic experiences. Her theories are presented in Part IV. In voluminous appendices, she presents literary and religious texts, the analyses she performed, specific triggers, and ideas for further research.

274. Lauck, Dan. (1977, Aug. 21). Has the king's crown slipped? *Newsday:* 10–11. B

275. LeCron, L. (1969). Breast development through hypnotic suggestion. *Journal of the American Society of Psychosomatic Dentistry and Medicine, 6:* 58–61. A

276. Leonard, George B. (1973, Jun.). Aikido and the mind of the West. *Intellectual Digest, 4:* 17–20. M

277. Leonard, George. (1976, Aug. 16). Running for life: How the masters are redefining human potential. *New West, 1:* 34–45. I

278. Leonard, George. (1978). *The Silent Pulse: A Search for the Perfect Rhythm That Exists in Each of Us.* New York: Dutton. E

279. Leonard, George. (1975). *The Ultimate Athlete.* New York: Viking. G

280. LeShan, Lawrence. (1974). *The Medium, the Mystic, and the Physicist.* New York: Viking. E

281. Leuchs, Arne, & Skulka, Patricia. (1976). *Ski with Yoga.* Matteson, IL.: Greatlakes Living Press. Y

Includes yoga and skiing lessons that involve physical, mental, and spiritual conditioning to improve concentration, self-control, and well-being.

282. Lewis, A. J. (1976). Influence of self-suggestion on the human organism. Los Angeles: Garrett AiResearch Corp. P

283. Lewis, A. J. (1977). Psychic self-regulation. Paper presented at the Fourth Annual Western Regional Association for Humanistic Psychology Conference, San Diego, CA. G

284. Lewis, Jesse Francis. (1974). *Ecstatic Experience: A Classification.* Unpublished doctoral dissertation, University of Arizona. A

285. Libby, Bill. (1975). *Bud Harrelson.* New York: Putnam's. B

286. Libby, Bill. (1974). *Foyt.* New York: Hawthorn Books. B

287. Libby, Bill. (1970, Jan.). Jack is nimble, Jack is quick. *Sport, 49*(1): 48–49+. B

288. Libby, Bill. (1974). *O. J.* New York: Putnam's. B

289. Libby, Bill. (1969). *Parnelli.* New York: Dutton. B

290. Libby, Bill, with Petty, Richard. (1977). *King Richard.* Garden City, NY: Doubleday. B

291. Lindbergh, Charles. (1977). *Autobiography of Values.* New York: Harcourt Brace Jovanovich. G

292. Lindbergh, Charles. (1969). Man's potential. In Charles Musés (Ed.), *Consciousness and Reality* (pp. 304–12). New York: Outerbridge & Lazard. C

Lindbergh speculates on the future of science and suggests that humankind will explore galaxies and know the interior of atoms by a combination of perception and extrasensory perception.

293. Lindbergh, Charles. (1953). *The Spirit of St. Louis.* New York: Scribner's. B

Lindbergh's account of his epic crossing of the Atlantic in 1927, with descriptions of his spiritual experiences during the flight.

294. Linn, Ed. (1971, Sep.). Warm breeze from the past. *Sport, 52*(3): 50–52+. G

295. Lipsyte, Robert. (1975). *Sportsworld.* New York: Quadrangle/New York Times Book Co. G

296. Lloyd, F. R. (1976, Spr.). The home run king. *Journal of Popular Culture, 9*(4): 983–95. B

297. Loader, W. R. (1961). *Sprinter.* New York: Macmillan. B

298. Lowe, Benjamin. (1977). *The Beauty of Sport.* Englewood Cliffs, NJ: Prentice-Hall. G

299. Ludwig, Jack. (1976). *Games of Fear and Winning.* Garden City, NY: Doubleday. O

300. Lunn, Sir Arnold. (1957). *A Century of Mountaineering, 1857–1967.* London: Allen & Unwin. O

A history of mountaineering, written as "a part of the story of [human] self-conquest" (p. 6).

301. McClintock, Jack. (1977). *The Book of Darts.* New York: Random House. I

302. McCluggage, Denise. (1977). *The Centered Skier.* Vermont Crossroads: Vermont Crossroads Press. Y

Applies the Eastern concepts and practices of t'ai chi and aikido, especially centeredness and energy flow, to skiing. Of special interest is a chapter on how learning the Chinese language helped McCluggage view the world, and especially skiing, in a new way, and another on the uses of anxiety entitled "The Energy in Fear."

303. MacDonald, R. G.; Hickman, J. L.; & Dakin, H. S. (1976). Preliminary physical measurements of psychophysical effects associated with three alleged psychic healers. Mimeograph. San Francisco: 3101 Washington St. E

304. McKinney, Steve. (1975, Spr.). How I broke the world's speed ski record. *Ski Magazine, 39*(7): 36–39+. B

305. McPhee, John. (1965). *A Sense of Where You Are.* New York: Farrar, Straus. B

306. Maheu, Rene. (1963, Oct.). Sport and culture. *Journal of Health, Physical Education and Recreation,* 34(8): 30–32+. G

307. Manry, Robert. (1966). *Tinkerbelle.* New York: Harper & Row. B

308. Manso, Peter. (1969). *Vroom! Conversations with Grand Prix Champions.* New York: Funk & Wagnalls. I

A race car aficionado asked some questions about racing he had pondered for several years by interviewing Grand Prix drivers. Manso tried to "get some notion of who they think they are and why they do what they do" (p. xii). He calls racing "a colloquy of imagination and control" (p. xiii). The text consists of interviews with eleven champion race car drivers: Joakim Bonnier, Dan Gurney, Jack Ickx, Innes Ireland, Bruce McLaren, Stirling Moss, Jochen Rindt, Pedro Rodriguez, Jackie Stewart, and John Surtees. The interviews were unstructured, and all dealt with motivation, the element of risk, and the relationship of the driver to other racers and to his racing car and team. The drivers' remarks frequently hint at an element beyond simple competition, fame, and glory, such as feeling "destined" to race or "an endless belief" in one's ability as a racing car driver, or feeling it "inside you," or experiencing the car as "part of your body . . . like one person altogether."

309. Maravich, Pete, with Kirkpatrick, Curry. (1969, Dec. 1). I want to put on a show. *Sports Illustrated, 31:* 39+. B

310. Marcus, Joe. (1976). *The World of Pelé.* New York: Mason/Charter. B

311. Maslow, Abraham. (1954). *Motivation and Human Personality.* New York: Harper & Row. G

312. Mason, A. (1952). A case of congenital ichthyosiform erythrodermia of brocq treated by hypnosis. *British Medical Journal, 2:* 422–23. A

313. Masters, Robert. (1975, Feb. 22). Psychophysical education: Recovering the body. *Saturday Review, 2(2):* 30–31. Y

314. Masters, Robert E. L., & Houston, Jean. (1966). *The Varieties of Psychedelic Experience.* New York: Holt, Rinehart & Winston. A

315. Maule, Tex. (1961, May 8). Masterpiece in Milwaukee. *Sports Illustrated, 14:* 24–27. I

316. Mead, George R. (1967). *The Doctrine of the Subtle Body in Western Tradition* (2nd ed.). Wheaton, IL: Theosophical Publishing House. G

317. Meggyesey, David. Personal communication. B

318. Merrien, Jean. (1954). *Lonely Voyagers.* New York: Putnam's. O

319. Meryman, R. (1970, Mar. 6). The flake and the old man. *Life, 68(8):* 54–56+. B

320. Messner, Reinhold. (1974). *The Seventh Grade.* New York: Oxford University Press. B

321. Metheny, Eleanor. (1968). *Movement and Meaning.* New York: McGraw-Hill. C

Sets forth a philosophy of sport in which potential champions are seen "as creative people who extend the limits of human performance, even as the creative scientist or artist may extend the limits of human understanding" (p. 74).

322. Michener, James A. (1976). *Sports in America.* New York: Random House. **G**

323. Middlecoff, Cary. (1956, Apr.). The winning feeling. *Esquire, 45*(4): 67+. **A**

324. Miller, David L. (1970). *Gods and Games.* Cleveland: World. **G**

325. Miller, Johnny, with Shanklin, Dean, (1976). *Pure Golf.* Garden City, NY: Doubleday. **I**

326. Minick, Michael. (1974). *The Wisdom of Kung Fu.* New York: Morrow. **M**

327. Mishima, Yukio. (1970). *Sun and Steel.* Palo Alto, CA: Kodansha International. **B**

328. Mishra, Rammurti S. (1973). *Yoga Sutras.* Garden City, NY: Doubleday. **Y**

329. Monkerud, Donald. (1977). Aikido, art of the velvet fist. *New Realities, 1*(1): 26–31. **M**

330. Monroe, Robert. (1971). *Journeys Out of the Body.* Garden City, NY: Doubleday. **E**

331. Moody, Raymond A., Jr. (1975). *Life after Life.* Atlanta: Mockingbird Books. **E**

332. Moore, Kenny. (1978, Jun. 5). The Kenya connection. *Sports Illustrated, 48:* 40–42+. **I**

333. Moore, Kenny. (1977, May 23). A night for stars, both born and reborn. *Sports Illustrated, 46:* 32–34. **I**

334. Morgan, William P. (1978, Apr.). The mind of the marathoner. *Psychology Today, 11*(2): 38–49. **P**
Contrasts the physical and mental practices of merely competent long-distance runners with those strategy of world-class runners. Morgan considers the latter to be less dangerous than the former.

335. Morgan, William P. (1974, Dec.). Selected psychological considerations in *Sport. Research Quarterly, 45:* 374–90. **P**

336. Morley, David C. (1976). *The Missing Links: Golf and the Mind.* New York: Atheneum/SMI. **P**

337. Moses, Sam. (1977, May 30). Suddenly Mario is the magician again. *Sports Illustrated, 46:* 22–23. **B**

338. Moss, Stirling, with Purdy, Ken. (1963). *All But My Life.* New York: Dutton. **B**

339. Muldoon, Sylvan, & Carrington, Hereward. (1956). *The Projection of the Astral Body.* London: Rider. **E**

340. Murphy, Michael. (1972). *Golf in the Kingdom.* New York: Viking. **I**

341. Murphy, Michael. (1977). *Jacob Atabet: A Speculative Fiction.* Millbrae, CA: Celestial Arts. **E**

342. Murphy, Michael. (1977, Fall). Sport as yoga. *Journal of Humanistic Psychology, 17*(4): 21–33. **Y**
Presents a list of altered states of consciousness and extraordinary powers in sport.

343. Murphy, Michael, & Brodie, John. (1973, Jan.). I experience a kind of clarity. *Intellectual Digest, 3*(5): 19–22. **G**

344. Myers, Frederic W. H. (1903; 1954). *Human Personality and Its Survival of Bodily Death*. New York: Longmans, Green. (2 vols.) E
Pioneering and enduring work of psychology and parapsychology that classifies and illustrates a wide range of extraordinary experiences, including multiple personality, dissociation, genius, hypnosis, automatisms, apparitions, trance, possession, and ecstasy. Two thirds of the work consists of case studies.

345. Mystery of firewalking. (1978, Mar.). *Human Behavior,* 7(3): 51+. E

346. Namath, Joe, with Oates, Bob, Jr. (1973). *A Matter of Style*. Boston: Little, Brown. I

347. Namath, Joe, with Schaap, Dick. (1969). *I Can't Wait Until Tomorrow 'Cause I Get Better-Looking Every Day*. New York: Random House. B

348. Naruse, Gosaku. (1965, Jan.). The hypnotic treatment of stage fright in champion athletes. *International Journal of Clinical and Experimental Hypnosis.* 13: 63–70. A

349. National Football League. Properties, Inc. The Creative Staff. (1969). *The First Fifty Years*. New York: Ridge Press/Benjamin Co. C

350. Neal, Patsy. (1972). *Sport and Identity*. Philadelphia: Dorrance. G
One of the best books on the extraordinary sports experience and the role it plays in the identity of the athlete. Neal writes both as a champion athlete and physical educator.

351. Neale, Robert E. (1967). Play and the sacred. In Ralph Slovenko & James A. Knight (Eds.), *Motivation in Play, Games and Sport* (pp. 148–57). Springfield, Ill.: Charles C. Thomas. G
Defines play as participation in an event that occurs by chance, involves risk, and "is of remarkable import" (p. 149). One who plays takes part in a drama. Religion would do well to encourage play, thereby enhancing "the physical response to the sacred" (p. 156).

352. Netto, Aranio, & Souza, Claudio Melloe. (1964, Oct.). King of the booters. *Reader's Digest, 43*: 203–09. B

353. Neumann, Randy. (1974, Jul.). Randy Neumann. *Sport, 58*: 85–89+. B

354. Newman, Roscoe Lee. (1975). Personal communication. In George Leonard, *The Ultimate Athlete,* New York: Viking. B

355. Nicklaus, Jack. (1974). *Golf My Way*. New York: Simon & Schuster. I

356. Nicklaus, Jack. (1977, Mar.). Nicklaus psychoanalyzes the superstars. *Golf Digest, 28*(3): 38–41. P

357. Nicol, J. Fraser. (1977). Historical background. In Benjamin B. Wolman (Ed.), *Handbook of Parapsychology* (pp. 305–23). New York: Van Nostrand Reinhold. E

358. Nideffer, Robert M. (1976). *The Inner Athlete*. New York: Crowell. G
Describes techniques for developing mind/body awareness and exceptional performance in sport, among them relaxation, hypnosis, Transcendental Meditation, mental rehearsal, and biofeedback.

359. Nieporte, Tom, & Sauers, Don. (1968). *Mind Over Golf*. Garden City, NY: Doubleday. I

360. Nishiyama, Hidetaka, & Brown, Richard C. (1960, ©1959). *Karate: The Art of "Empty Hand" Fighting.* Rutland, VT: Tuttle. M

361. Nitschke, Ray, as told to Wells, Robert W. (1953). *Mean on Sunday.* Garden City, NY: Doubleday. B

362. Novak, Michael. (1976). *The Joy of Sports.* New York: Basic Books. G
Proposes that in following their favorite sport, sports fans participate in a kind of sacrament, allowing them to enter sacred space and time and to engage in self-discovery. He also argues that leisure activities civilize human beings by providing first-hand experience of beauty, truth, and the transcendence of limits.

363. Noyce, Wilfred. (1958). *The Springs of Adventure.* Cleveland: World. G
Examines the motives behind adventure, with examples from many types of endeavor. Noyce defines adventure as "a novel enterprise undertaken for its own sake" (p. 16) as expressed in "physical adventure on land and sea or in the air" (p. 19). Noyce limits himself to the end of the 1700s and the beginning of the 1800s because this is when the concept of adventure "for its own sake" crystallized in the Western mind.

364. Nyad, Diana. (1975, Oct.). Mind over water. *Esquire, 84*(4): 132–39. O

365. Oglanby, Elva. (1976). *Toller.* New York: Vanguard. B

366. Otto, Rudolf. (1950). *The Idea of the Holy* (2nd ed.). London: Oxford University Press. E

367. Our Olympic hopes. (1976, Aug.). *Soviet Life, 8*(239): 60–65. G

368. Owen, A. R. G. (1970). Stigmata. In Richard Cavendish (Ed.)., *Man, Myth & Magic* (Vol. 20) (pp. 2647–2703). New York: Marshall Cavendish. E

369. Oxendine, Joseph B. (1968). *The Psychology of Motor Learning.* New York: Appleton-Century-Crofts. P

370. Oyama, Masutatsu. (1965). *This Is Karate.* Rutland, VT.: Japan Publications. M

371. Palmer, Arnold. (1973). *Go for Broke.* New York: Simon & Schuster. I

372. Panati, Charles. (Ed.). (1976). *The Geller Papers.* Boston: Houghton Mifflin. E

373. Papanek, John. (1976, Feb. 9). Strutting their stuffs. *Sports Illustrated, 44:* 50–52. I

374. Park, Roberta. (1973, Win.). Raising the consciousness of sport. *Quest, 19:* 78–82. A
Describes Aurobindo's concept of *body consciousness* and relates Maslow's peak experiences to sport.

375. Parker, Edmund K. (1963). *Secrets of Chinese Karate.* Englewood Cliffs, NJ: Prentice-Hall. M

376. Parr, Jeanne. (1976). *The Superwives.* New York: Coward, McCann & Geoghegan. G

377. Patanjali. (1953). *How to Know God, the Yoga Aphorisms of Patan-*

jali (Trans. and with a new commentary by Swami Prabhavananda & Christopher Isherwood). New York: Harper & Row. Y

378. Pelé, with Fish, Robert L. (1977). *My Life and the Beautiful Game.* Garden City, NY: Doubleday. B

379. Peterson, Robert. (1970). *Only the Ball Was White.* Englewood Cliffs, NJ: Prentice-Hall. I

380. Pettit, Bob, with Wolff, Bob. (1966). *Bob Pettit.* Englewood Cliffs, NJ: Prentice-Hall. B

381. Pirie, Gordon. (1961). *Running Wild.* London: W. H. Allen. B

382. Playboy interview: Barbra Streisand. (1977, Oct.). *Playboy, 24:* 79+. B

383. Player, Gary. (1967). *Positive Golf.* New York: McGraw-Hill. I

384. Plimpton, George. (1968). *The Bogeyman.* New York: Harper & Row. I

385. Plimpton, George. (1971, Jul. 5). In the mind's eye. *Sports Illustrated, 35:* 50–52+. P

386. Plimpton, George. (1970, Nov. 23). Watching the man in the mirror. *Sports Illustrated, 33:* 80–83+. G

387. Plimpton, George, & Curry, Bill. (1977). *One More July.* New York: Harper & Row. B

388. Ponsonby, David. (1973, May 29). Soccer in the kingdom. Part 1. *Soccer America, 4*(22): 12+. I

389. Ponsonby, David. (1973, Jun. 5). Soccer in the kingdom. Part 2. *Soccer America, 4*(23): 17. I

390. Powell, Arthur E. (1973). *The Astral Body.* Wheaton, IL: Theosophical Publishing House. E

391. Powell, Arthur E. (1969). *The Etheric Double.* Wheaton, IL: Theosophical Publishing House. E

392. Proxmire, William. (1973). *You Can Do It.* New York: Simon & Schuster. G

393. Pye, David. (1927). *George Leigh Mallory: A Memoir.* London: Oxford University Press. B

394. Ratti, Oscar, & Westbrook, Adde. (1973). *Secrets of the Samurai.* Rutland, VT: Tuttle. M

395. Ravizza, Kenneth. (1977, Fall). Peak experiences in sport. *Journal of Humanistic Psychology, 17*(4): 35–40. A

By means of the interview technique, Ravizza investigated peak experiences in sport.

396. Ravizza, Kenneth. (1973). A study of the peak experiences in sport. Unpublished doctoral dissertation, University of Southern California. A

Eleven athletes described peak experiences associated with team sports and nine with individual sports. Of Maslow's nineteen qualities of peak experience, the following recurred in the athletes' experiences: Most felt a strong feeling of belonging to the situation, or a harmony with the world, fearlessness, a feeling of control, time-space disorientation, fusion of the self on all levels, awe and wonder at the "perfection" of the experience, total concentration on the sport activity, and effortlessness. The experience was self-validating for the individuals regardless of the outcome of their competitions. Ravizza concluded that the peak experience in sport is a unique, nonvoluntary, transient, spontaneous experience. This can result in a temporary transcendence of the usual self, which is replaced by a sense of union or harmony with the environment. The athletes also felt that someone or something was "moving" them.

397. Rebuffat, Gaston. (1968, ©1957). *Starlight and Storm*. New York: Oxford University Press. **B**

398. Reich, Leonard. (1974, Feb.). Try not to think about it. *Runner's World, 9:* 17. **Y**

399. Reid, Ron. (1972, Oct. 16). Handy pair of brainy Bengals. *Sports Illustrated, 37:* 46–51. **B**

400. Rhine, Louisa E. (1954, Jun.). Frequency of types of experience in spontaneous precognition. *Journal of Parapsychology, 18:* 93–123. **E**

401. Rhine, Louisa E. (1953, Jun.). Subjective forms of spontaneous psi experiences *Journal of Parapsychology, 17:* 77–114. **E**

402. Rice, Grantland. (1954). *The Tumult and the Shouting*. New York: A. S. Barnes. **G**

403. Richard, Colette. (1967). *Climbing Blind*. New York: Dutton. **B**

404. Richards, Bob. (1973). *Heart of a Champion*. Old Tappan, NY: Fleming H. Revell. **B**

405. Richardson, Alan. (1967, Mar.). Mental practice: A review and discussion, Part 1. *Research Quarterly, 38:* 95–107. **P**

406. Richardson, Alan. (1967, May). Mental practice: A review and discussion, Part 2. *Research Quarterly, 38:* 263–73. **P**

407. Rickard, Rodger S. (1970). An explication of the role of aesthetic value in American physical education. Unpublished doctoral dissertation, Stanford University. **G**
Historical review of the role of aesthetic value in American physical education from 1885 to 1970, showing how it related to historic events and trends. Notes that a future trend of American society is increased leisure, with the younger segment searching for meaning. Rickard urges physical educators to provide students with "an experience . . . of the fullness that meaningful human movement can provide" (p. 116).

408. Robinson, Doug. (1969). The climber as visionary. *Ascent, 9:* 4–10. **I**
Describes the intensity of vision that emerges spontaneously when one is immersed in a concentrated task, such as mountain climbing, that takes one's personal skills to one's limits. Gives several examples of the experience, its qualities, and the conditions under which it is likely to occur.

409. Robinson, Doug. (1977, Dec.). Ice nine. *Outside, 1:* 26–29. **B**

410. Robinson, Sugar Ray, with Anderson, Dave. (1970). *Sugar Ray*. New York: Viking. **B**

411. Romen, A. S., et al. (Eds.) (1974). *Psychical Self-Regulation*. (Vols. 1 & 2). Alma-Alta, U.S.S.R. **P**

412. Romen, A. S., et al. (1974). *Psychical Self-Regulation*. Alma-Alta, U.S.S.R. **P**

413. Ronberg, Gary. (1970, May 4). Tea party for Bobby's Bruins. *Sports Illustrated, 32:* 18–21. **I**

414. Rosenthal, Saul R. (1975). Risk exercise and the physically handicapped. *Rehabilitation Literature, 36*(5): 144–49. O

415. Rush, Joseph. (1964). *New Directions in Parapsychological Research.* New York: Parapsychology Foundation. E

416. Rush, Joseph H. (1977). Problems and methods in psychokinesis research. In Stanley Krippner (Ed.), *Advances in Parapsychological Research* (Vol. 1, pp. 15–78). New York: Plenum. E

417. Russell, W. Scott. (1976). *Karate; The Energy Connection.* New York: Delacorte Press/Eleanor Friede. M

418. Ruth, Babe, as told to Considine, Bob. (1948). *The Babe Ruth Story.* New York: Dutton. B

419. Ryback, Eric. (1971). *The High Adventure of Eric Ryback.* San Francisco: Chronicle Books. B

420. Saal, Herbert. (1974). The great leap. *Newsweek, 84*(7): 84. B

421. Sadler, William A. (1966). Creative existence: Play as a pathway to personal freedom and community, *Review of Existential Psychology and Psychiatry, 6:* 237–45. C
Argues that play is a form of creativity that can foster personal growth and a sense of communion with others.

422. Sage, George H. (1974). Humanistic theory, the counter-culture, and sport. In *Sport and American Society* (2nd ed.) (pp. 415–29). Reading, MA.: Addison-Wesley. G
One of the first applications of the principles of humanistic psychology to sport emphasizing the role sport plays in "human growth and self-fulfillment" (p. 427) rather than on performance criteria and social adjustment.

423. Sanderson, Derek, with Fischler, Stan. (1970). *I've Got to Be Me.* New York: Dodd, Mead. B

424. Sanford, Bob. (1972). *Riding the Dirt.* Newport Beach, CA: Bond/ Parkhurst Books. I

425. Sannella, Lee. (1976). *Kundalini: Psychosis or Transcendence?* San Francisco: H. S. Dakin. E

426. Sawyer, Benjamin, & Dorbin, Sandy. (1973). Athletics as art: Bibliographic essay on the potentiality of sport. *Synergy,* No. 41: 19–30. C

427. Schaap, Dick. (1976). *The Perfect Jump.* New York: New American Library. B

428. Schaap, Dick. (1972, Dec.). The second coming of St. Francis. *Sport, 54:* 84–94. B

429. Schmeidler, Gertrude R. (1977). Research findings in psychokinesis. In Stanley Krippner (Ed.), *Advances in Parapsychological Research* (vol. 1) (pp. 79–132). New York: Plenum. E

430. Schmidt, Helmut. (1970, Sep.). A PK test with electronic equipment. *Journal of Parapsychology, 34:* 175–81. E

431. Schmidt, Helmut. (1970, Feb.). Quantum-mechanical random number generator. *Journal of Applied Physics, 41:* 462–68. E

432. Schneck, Jerome. (1966). Hypnotherapy of ichthyosis. *Psychosomatics, 7:* 233–35. A

433. Schofield, Len J., & Abbuhl, Stephanie. (1975). The stimulation of insight and self-awareness through body-movement. *Journal of Clinical Psychology, 31*(4): 745–46. C

434. Schollander, Don. (1971). *Deep Water.* New York: Crown. B

435. Schultheis, Rob. (1977, Nov.). Skiing out of bounds. *Outside, 1:* 38–41. I

436. Schutz, William C. (1971). *Here Comes Everybody.* New York: Harper & Row. G

437. Schwarzenegger, Arnold, & Hall, Douglas Kent. (1977). *Arnold— The Education of a Bodybuilder.* New York: Simon & Schuster. I

438. Scorecard: The sporting look. (1969, Nov. 24). *Sports Illustrated, 31:* 14. G

439. Scott, Jack. (1971). *The Athletic Revolution.* New York: Free Press. C

440. Seaver, Tom, with Schapp, Dick. (1970). *The Perfect Game.* New York: Dutton. B

441. Seitz, Nick. (1975). Is this the man to succeed Palmer? In Irving T. Marsh & Edward Ehre (Eds.), *Thirty Years of Best Sports Stories* (pp. 252– 59). New York: Dutton. B

442. Seitz, Nick. (1976). What makes a golfer unique in pro sports? The onlyness. *Golf Digest, 27*(1): 52–55. I

443. Seligman, Martin E. P. (1974). Submissive death: Giving up on life. *Psychology Today, 7*(12): 80–85+. P

444. Sevier, Vernon A. (1974). Physical fitness and the integrated personality. *Journal of Physical Education, 71:* 145+. C

445. Shackleton, Ernest H. (1947, ©1920). *South.* New York: Macmillan. O

446. Sharman, Bill. (1965). *Sharman on Basketball Shooting.* Englewood Cliffs, NJ: Prentice-Hall. I

447. Shaw, Gary. (1972). *Meat on the Hoof.* New York: St. Martin's. I

448. Sheehan, George. (1977, Aug.). Basics of jogging. *Runner's World, 12:* 34–37. I

449. Sheehan, George. (1975). *Dr. Sheehan on Running.* Mt. View, CA: World Publications. G

450. Sheehan, George. (1978). I found it in running. *New Times, 10*(7): R22-R23. C

451. Sheehan, George. (1978). *Running and Being: The Total Experience.* New York: Simon & Schuster. G
Autobiographical account of the personal meaning Sheehan found in running, with the emphasis on self-identity.

452. Shoemaker, Willie. (1976). *The Shoe.* Chicago: Rand McNally. B

453. Silverman, Al (Ed.). (1971). *The Best of Sport 1946–71.* New York: Viking. G

454. Simonton, Carl, & Simonton, Stephanie. (1978). *Getting Well Again.* Los Angeles: J. P. Tarcher; distributed by St. Martin's. E

455. Singer, Robert R. (1975). *Myths and Truths in Sport Psychology.* New York: Harper & Row. P

456. Slocum, Joshua. (1963, ©1900). *Sailing Alone Around the World.* New York: Sheridan House. B

Joshua Slocum made the first solo voyage around the world, in the 1890s. In this book, he told the story of his adventure, which included a vivid encounter with a "phantom sailor."

457. Slovenko, Ralph, & Knight, James (Eds.). (1967). *Motivation in Play, Games and Sports.* Springfield, IL: Charles C Thomas. **G**

458. Slusher, Howard. (1967). *Man, Sport and Existence.* Philadelphia: Lea & Febiger. **G**

Emphasizes sport's quality of providing athletes with the opportunity to open themselves up, "and in the process, transcend the self" (p. 11). There are chapters on sport and being, purpose, meaning, the religious, existence and death.

459. Smith, Adam. (1975, Oct.). Sport is a Western yoga. *Psychology Today, 9:* 48–51+. **Y**

460. Smith, Adam. (1973). Trying the dance of Shiva. *Sports Illustrated, 39*(7): 36–38+. **Y**

461. Smith, Marshall. (1951). Wary old devil [Juan Fangio]. *Life, 43*(6): 82–90. **B**

462. Smith, Robert W. (1974). *Hsing-I.* Tokyo & New York: Kodansha International. **M**

463. Smythe, Frank. (1940). *The Adventures of a Mountaineer.* London: J. M. Dent. **B**

464. Smythe, Frank. (1949). *The Mountain Vision.* London: Hodder & Stoughton. **I**

465. Sollier, Andre, & Gyorbiro, Zsolt. (1969). *Japanese Archery: Zen in Action.* New York: Walker/Weatherhill. **Y**

466. Solomon, Ted J. (1964). "Para" normal powers actually normal. *Gateway, 9*(2): 21–23. **E**

467. Spino, Mike. (1976). *Beyond Jogging: The Innerspaces of Running.* Millbrae, CA: Celestial Arts. **I**

Presents running as art and outlines an integral training program that combines physical conditioning techniques and self-awareness exercises to help athletes achieve new levels of physical accomplishment and psychological well-being.

468. Spino, Mike. (1971). Running as a spiritual experience. Appendix B in Jack Scott, *The Athletic Revolution* (pp. 222–25). New York: Free Press. **I**

Account of Spino's own extraordinary sport experience.

469. Spino, Mike. (1977). *Running Home.* Millbrae, Calif.: Celestial Arts. **I**

Includes accounts of extraordinary experiences associated with running, some negative.

470. Spino, Mike, & Hickman, James. (1977). Beyond the physical limits. *Runner's World, 12*(3): 52–53. **Y**

Describes a program to develop mind/body unity.

471. Stanford, Rex G. (1977). Experimental psychokinesis. In Benjamin B. Wolman (Ed.), *Handbook of Parapsychology* (pp. 324–81). New York: Van Nostrand Reinhold. **E**

472. Start, Kenneth B., & Richardson, Alan. (1964). Imagery and mental practice. *British Journal of Educational Psychology, 34*(3): 280–84. **P**

473. Stebbins, R. J. (1938, Oct.). A comparison of effects of physical and mental practice in learning a motor skill. *Research Quarterly, 39:* 714–20. **P**

474. Stewart, Jackie, & Manso, Peter. (1972). *Faster: A Racer's Diary.* New York: Farrar, Straus. **I**

475. Stone, Roselyn E. (1970). *Meanings Found in the Acts of Surfing and Skiing.* Unpublished doctoral dissertation, University of Southern California. **G**

This study grew out of two questions: What is it that the performer finds meaningful in the nonutilitarian activity called sport? What is it that sustains the interest of athletes? Stone reviewed the English-language skiing and surfing literature for the period 1945 to 1969 looking for answers.

476. Suinn, Richard M. (1976). Body thinking: Psychology for Olympic champs. *Psychology Today, 10*(2): 38–41+. **P**

477. Summers, Montague. (1950). *The Physical Phenomena of Mysticism.* New York: Barnes & Noble. **E**

478. Sutton, Don. (1975). Hypnosis snapped my slump. *Sport, 60*(2): 62–65. **A**

479. Suzuki, Daisetz T. (1959). *Zen and Japanese Culture.* New York: Pantheon. **Y**

480. Swedenborg, Emanuel. (1873). *The Heavenly Arcana.* New York: American Swedenborg Publishing Society. **E**

481. Tansley, David V. (1977). *Subtle Body.* London: Thames & Hudson. **E**

482. Tarshis, Barry. (1977). *Tennis and the Mind.* New York: Atheneum. **I**

483. Tart, Charles T. (1975). *States of Consciousness.* New York: Dutton. **A**

484. Tech talk: East German secrets? (1976, Nov.). *Track and Field News, 29*(10): 32. **I**

485. Tekeyan, Charles. (1975, Dec. 28). The athlete and death: Immortality wrestles with reality. *New York Times,* V, 2. **O**

Athletes, in their invincibility, get a taste of immortality.

486. Telander, Rick. (1976). *Joe Namath and the Other Guys.* New York: Holt, Rinehart & Winston. **I**

487. Terray, Lionel. (1964). *The Borders of the Impossible.* Garden City, NY: Doubleday. **B**

World-famed mountaineer Terray writes poetically about the meaning of his vocation and moments of transcendence he experienced when climbing. Alone with a companion in the mountains, he felt that "a mineral silence entered into us. In the enormous peace, I felt that somehow nothing else would truly ever matter for me" (p. 22). Terray describes extraordinary climbing moments, including "the sensation of superhuman powers which enables one to confront risks" (p. 158).

488. Thomas, Caroline. (1972). *The Perfect Moment.* Unpublished doctoral dissertation, Ohio State University. **G**

Attempts to show that engagement in sport can be a "valid and genuine aesthetic experience" (p. 4). Examples are provided from self-reports of athletes.

489. Thomas, Caroline. (1974, Sep.). Toward an experiential sport aesthetic. *Journal of the Philosophy of Sport. 1:* 67–91. G

490. Thomas, Vaughn. (1970). *Science and Sport.* Boston: Little, Brown. P

491. Thouless, R. H., & Wiesner, B. P. (1948). The psi processes in normal and "paranormal" psychology. *Journal of Parapsychology, 12*(3): 192–212. E

492. Thurston, Herbert. (1952). *The Physical Phenomena of Mysticism.* London: Burns, Oates & Washbourne. E

493. Tiller, William A. (1975). *Kirlian Photography: Its Scientific Foundations and Future Potentials.* Stanford, CA: Stanford University Press. E

494. Tohei, Koichi. (1966). *Aikido in Daily Life.* Tokyo; Rikugei Publishing House. M

495. Torres, Jose. (1970). *Sting Like a Bee.* New York: Abelard-Schuman. B

496. Trias, Robert A. (1973). *The Hand Is My Sword—A Karate Handbook.* Rutland, VT: Charles E. Tuttle. M

497. Trippett, Frank. (1969). The ordeal of fun. *Look, 33*(15): 24–34. O

498. Twining, Wilbur E. (1949, Dec.). Mental practice and physical practice in learning a motor skill. *Research Quarterly, 20:* 432–35. P

499. Ullman, James Ramsay. (1947). *Kingdom of Adventure: Everest.* New York: William Sloane. O

500. Ullyot, Joan. (1976). *Women's Running.* Mt. View, CA: World Publications. I

501. Uyeshiba, Kisshomaru. (1974). *Aikido.* Tokyo: Hozansha. M
This is a combined version of two books written by the author, the son of the founder of aikido, Morihei Uyeshiba. In aikido, the younger Uyeshiba wrote, "there is no duality, no struggle, no opponent. There is only a harmonious action of our own spirit with the spirit of the universe. The techniques of Aikido are the bodily realization of this harmony" (p. 14).

502. Vandell, Roland A.; Davis, Robert A.; & Clugston, Herbert A. (1943, Oct.). The function of mental practice in the acquisition of motor skills. *Journal of General Psychology, 29:* 243–50. P

503. Vanderzwaag, Harold J. (1972). *Toward a Philosophy of Sport.* Reading, MA: Addison-Wesley. G

504. Vanek, M., & Cratty, B. (1970). *Psychology and the Superior Athlete.* New York: Macmillan. P

505. Vasiliev, Leonid L. (1963). *Experiments in Mental Suggestion.* Church Crookham, Hampshire, England: Institute for the Study of Mental Images. E

506. Wallace, William N. (1973, Aug. 25). Psychic phenomena on the ball field. *New York Times.* E

507. Ward, Robert. (1977). The mutilation of a work of art. *Sport, 64*(5): 96–104+. B

508. Watanabe, Jiichi, & Avakian, Lindy. (1960). *The Secrets of Judo.* Rutland, VT: Charles E. Tuttle. M

509. Watts, Barrie. (1976, Aug. 31). World's fastest miler says: "My psychic powers help me to win." *The Star.* B

510. Webb, James. (1974). *The Occult Underground.* LaSalle, IL: Open Court. E

511. Weiss, Paul. (1969). *Sport: A Philosophic Inquiry.* Carbondale: Southern Illinois University Press. G

512. Wells, Roger, & Klein, Judith. (1972, Jun.). A replication of a "psychic healing" paradigm. *Journal of Parapsychology, 36:* 144–49. E

513. Wentz, Walter Yeeling Evans (Ed.). (1960). *The Tibetan Book of the Dead.* London: Oxford University Press. E

514. Wepukhulu, Hezekiah. (1973, Nov./Dec.). Seriff, soccer soothsayer. *Africa Report, 18:* 22–23. E

515. West, Jerry, with Libby, Bill. (1969). *Mr. Clutch.* Englewood Cliffs, NJ: Prentice-Hall. B

516. Westbrook, Adde, & Ratti, Oscar. (1970). *Aikido and the Dynamic Sphere.* Rutland, VT: Charles E. Tuttle. M

517. White, David A. (1975, Sep.). Great moments in sport: The one and the many. *Journal of the Philosophy of Sport, 2:* 124–32. A

518. White, Rhea A. (Ed.). (1976). *Surveys in Parapsychology.* Metuchen, NJ: Scarecrow Press. E

519. White, Rhea A., & Dale, Laura A. (1973). *Parapsychology: Sources of Information.* Metuchen, NJ: Scarecrow Press. E

520. Wilhelm, John L. (1977, Aug. 7). Psychic spying? *Washington Post.* E

521. Williams, J. (1974). Stimulation of breast growth by hypnosis? *Journal of Sex Research, 10:* 316–26. A

522. Williams, Ted, with Underwood, John. (1969). *My Turn at Bat.* New York: Simon & Schuster. B

523. Williamson, C. J. (1976). The Everest message. *Journal of the Society for Psychical Research, 48:* (769): 318–20. E

524. Willis, William. (1955). *The Gods Were Kind.* New York: Dutton. B

525. Willis, William. (1967). *Whom the Sea Has Taken.* New York: Meredith. B

526. Wills, Maury, & Freeman, Don. (1976). *How to Steal a Pennant.* New York: Putnam's. B

527. Wind, Herbert Warren (Ed.). (1961). *The Gilded Age of Sport.* New York: Simon & Schuster. G

528. Wind, Herbert Warren (Ed.). (1966). *The Realm of Sport.* New York: Simon & Schuster. G

529. Winderbaum, Larry. (1977). *The Martial Arts Encyclopedia.* Washington, DC: Inscape Publishers. M

530. Wink, C. (1961). *Congenital ichthyosiform erthrodermia* treated by hypnosis: Report of two cases. *British Medical Journal, 2:* 741–43. A

531. Wolf, David. (1972). *Foul! The Connie Hawkins Story.* New York: Holt, Rinehart & Winston. B

532. Wolman, Benjamin B. (Ed.). (1977). *Handbook of Parapsychology.* New York: Van Nostrand Reinhold. E

533. Wolters, Richard A. (1971). *The Art and Technique of Soaring.* New York: McGraw-Hill. I

534. Worsley, F. A. (1977). *Shackleton's Boat Journey*. New York: Norton. O

535. Wraparound: High: What's up there? (1973, Oct.). *Harper's, 247*: 3–10. A

536. Yogananda, Paramahansa. (1969). *The Autobiography of a Yogi* (10th ed.). Los Angeles: Self-Realization Fellowship. Y

537. Zimmer, Heinrich. (1946). *Myths and Symbols in Indian Art and Civilization*. New York: Pantheon. Y

538. Zimmerman, Paul. (1970). *A Thinking Man's Guide to Pro Football*. New York: Dutton. I

Second Edition

In this, the bibliography of the second edition, we have tried to cover a good portion of the burgeoning literature on sport psychology published since 1977, the cutoff point for the first edition, that emphasizes peak and flow experiences in sport and, more broadly, sport and altered states of consciousness and ways of inducing and extending such states. We have also included citations on the psychology of peak and flow experiences even if they do not deal with athletics or sport.

We have also included a number of religious and philosophical works on sport and the wider concepts of play, adventure, recreation, and leisure because they help widen and deepen our conception of these subjects. Many items address the aesthetic aspect of sport not only because a sense of beauty—for both player and spectator—is an integral component of the extraordinary sport experience, but because looking at sport from the aesthetic viewpoint can suggest new approaches and ways of thinking about sport.

Ranging beyond these studies like a mountain mass hidden by mist are metanormal aspects of sport seldom touched on in sport psychology: the association between elements of sport and yoga, hints of psychic ability, and mystical experiences that transcend what many accept as peak experiences or "happiest moments." Here also are phenomena of energy, strength, and timing that to psychology are quirks and aberrations—anomalous phenomena, plays too far off the bell-shaped curve of probability to be credible. We cite material that deals with such experiences from philosophy, religion, parapsychology, and firsthand accounts of athletes themselves. Implicit in sportspeople's sometimes trite and even inchoate phrases is the message: "It is there."

The arrangement of this bibliography is alphabetical by author, and when the same author has more than one title listed, it is further arranged by year, starting with the earliest. (The bibliography of the first edition was alphabetically arranged by title under each author.) Here, if there is more than one item in a given year, it is further arranged alphabetically by the first word of the title (excepting "a," "an," and "the"), and a letter follows the year, as in 1990a for the author's first title in that year, 1990b for his/her second 1990 title, and so forth. In a few cases, such as 630a, items were added after the bibliography number system was set. These items were inserted in the correct alphabetical order and were assigned the number each would have followed, with an "a" added. (See 630a for an example.)

539. Abe, Shinobu. (1986). Zen and sport. *Journal of the Philosophy of Sport, 13:* 45–48. Y

540. Abe, Shinobu. (1987). Modern sports and the Eastern tradition of physical culture: Emphasizing Nishida's theory of the body. *Journal of the Philosophy of Sport, 14:* 44–47. Y

541. Abraham, H. (1985, Mar.). Peak performance. *JPSCI: Journal of Professional Ski Coaching and Instruction, 14:* 32–33. P

542. Ackerman, Diane. (1985). *On Extended Wings.* New York: Atheneum. B

Exciting and lyrical account of a woman's adventures in learning to fly and of the highs involved in risk activities.

543. Adler, Peter, & Adler, Patricia A. (1978). The role of momentum in sport. *Urban Life, 7:* 1153–76. P

Deals with pre-game and game factors, momentum starters, maintaining momentum, momentum breakers, seasonal factors, and presents a general theory of momentum.

544. Ahrabi-Fard, Iradge. (1974). *Implications of the Original Teachings of Islam for Physical Education and Sport.* Unpublished doctoral dissertation, University of Minnesota. Y

545. Aitken, Brian W. W. (1989). The emergence of born-again sport. *Studies in Religion, 18:* 391–405. In Charles S. Prebish, *Religion and Sport: The Meeting of the Sacred and Profane* (pp. 197–214). Westport, CT: Greenwood. G

546. Alexander, Franz. (1978). A contribution to the theory of play. *Psychoanalytic Quarterly, 27:* 175–93. T

Examines the ideas about play of Schiller, Sartre, Groos, Freud, Waelder, Erikson, Roheim, and Huizinga. Considers play an important culture-building faculty.

547. Allard, F., Graham, S., & Poarsaler, M. E. (1980). Perception in sports: Basketball. *Journal of Sport Psychology, 2:* 14–21. I

548. Allen, Dorothy J., & Fahey, Brian. (Eds.). (1977). *Being Human in Sport.* Philadelphia: Lea & Febiger. G

549. Allen, Dorothy J., & Thomas, C. (1977). Sport experience and the experience of self. In Dorothy J. Allen & B. W. Fahey (Eds.), *Being Human in Sport.* Philadelphia: Lea & Febiger. G

550. Allen, R. M.; Haupt, T. D.; & Jones, W. (1964). An analysis of peak experiences reported by college students. *Journal of Clinical Psychology, 20:* 207–12. G

Used Thorne's classification of peak experiences for accounts of 214 college students.

551. Allen, Thomas. (1988). The cognitive bases of peak performance: A classroom intervention with student-athletes. *Journal of Counseling and Development, 67:* 202–04. G

Drawing upon self-efficacy theory (e.g., *see* Feltz), or more popularly, "self-psyching," a class of seventeen undergraduates used techniques based on books by Gallwey, Garfield, and Oh to improve their sports performance. Many did so. They completed the Psychological Performance Inventory developed by Loehr and kept journals. Some began applying the principles to life situations.

552. Alt, John. (1982). Sport and cultural reification: From ritual to mass consumption. *Theory, Culture, and Society, 1:* 93–107. T

553. Alvarado, Carlos. (1994). Synesthesia and claims of psychic experiences: An exploratory study. *Proceedings of Presented Papers: The 37th Annual Convention of the Parapsychological Association,* pp. 11–17. E

554. Alvarez, A. (1967, Sep. 9). I like to risk my life. *Saturday Evening Post, 240:* 10–12. B

555. Ament, Pat. (1977). *Master of Rock: The Biography of John Gill.* Boulder, CO: Alpine House. B

Story of the bouldering life and feats, witnessed in part by the author, of climber/mathematics professor John Gill. Includes an interview with Gill in which he touches on intuition and bouldering, being in the zone, merging body and mind, and the possible role of psychic ability (ESP and PK) in performing beyond one's limits. He speculates that slight levitations may occur in bouldering.

556. Andrews, Valerie. (1978). *The Psychic Power of Running: How the Body Can Illuminate the Mysteries of the Mind.* New York: Rawson, Wade. I

On "inner-directed running: jogging for personal growth and self-expansion," with chapters on running and meditation, the runner's high, running and psychic healing, the cosmology of runners, creativity and running, running and personal growth for women, and running as a means of forwarding human evolution.

557. Anthony, D. W. J. (1968, Mar.). Sport and physical education as a means of aesthetic education. *Physical Education, 60:* 1–6. T

558. Are sports good for the soul? (1971, Jan. 11). *Newsweek, 77:* 52. T

559. Arkina, Natalia. (1977). Sport and art: Figure-skating and classical ballet. *Cultures, 4(2):* 123–36. C

Proposes that art and sport are coming together to create a new form of human expression. In particular, music can unify sport and art.

560. Arnold, Peter J. (1978). Aesthetic aspects of sports. *International Review of Sport Sociology, 13:* 45–61. C

561. Arnold, Peter J. (1979a). Agency, action, and meaning "in" movement: An introduction to three new terms. *Journal of the Philosophy of Sport, 6:* 49–57. T

The terms are "Movistruct," "Movicept," and "Movisymbol."

562. Arnold, Peter J. (1979b). Intellectualism, physical education and self-actualization. *Quest, 31:* 87–96. T

563. Arnold, Peter J. (1979c). *Meaning in Movement, Sport and Physical Education.* London: Heinemann. T

564. Arnold, Peter J. (1985). Aesthetic aspects of being in sport: The performer's perspective in contrast to that of the spectator. *Journal of the Philosophy of Sport, 12:* 1–7. C

565. Aspin, David N. (1974). Sport and the concept of "the aesthetic." In

H. T. A. Whiting & Don W. Masterson (Eds.), *Readings in the Aesthetics of Sport*. London: Lepus Books. T

566. Atkins, Chandler W. (1990). A comparative analysis of peak experience performance and non-peak experience performance in professional actors and actresses [Summary]. *Dissertation Abstracts International, 51*(4-B): 2096. G

567. Attner, Paul. (1991, Feb. 25). The king of comebacks. *Sporting News, 211:* 5–7. B

568. Austin, J. S., & Pargman, D. (1981). The inner game approach to performance and skill acquisition. *Motor Skills: Theory Into Practice, 5:* 3–12. T

569. Bäck, Allan, & Kim, Daeshik. (1979, Fall). Towards a Western philosophy of the Eastern martial arts. *Journal of the Philosophy of Sport, 6:* 19–28. M

The authors put the more mystical aspects of the Eastern martial arts into a Western philosophical framework. They examine the following claims in particular: that the martial arts (1) promote moral character, (2) foster nonviolence, and (3) lead to enlightenment.

570. Back, Allan, & Kim, Daeshik. (1984). The future course of the Eastern martial arts. *Quest, 36:* 7–14. M

Tae kwon do and other Eastern martial arts taught in the U.S. today emphasize full contact with the goal of "winning," rather than artistic excellence and spiritual development. The authors ask if this Western version of Eastern philosophy is having a positive influence on American society.

571. Bain, L. (1989). Interpretive and critical research in sport and physical education. *Research Quarterly, 60:* 21–24. P

Brief overview of critical qualitative research and its application to sport.

572. Bakker, Frank C.; de Koning, Joseph J.; van Ingen Schenau, Gert Jan; & de Groot, Gert. (1993, Oct./Dec.). Motivation of young elite speed skaters. *International Journal of Sport Psychology. 24:* 432–42. P

573. Ballatore, R. (1981). Workshop: Team spirit and team unity. In *American Swimming Coaches Association World Clinic Yearbook* (pp. 251–54). Fort Lauderdale, FL: The Association. P

574. Bammel, E., & Bammel, L. L. (1975, Dec.). Aesthetics of play. *Physical Educator, 32:* 192–93. T

575. Bandy, Susan. (1986). A humanistic interpretation of the mind/body problem in Western thought. In Seymour Kleinman (Ed.), *Mind and Body: East Meets West*. Champaign, IL: Human Kinetics. T

576. Banham, Charles. (1965, Aug.). Man at play. *Contemporary Review, 207:* 61–64. T

577. Banks, Gary C. (1966). *The Philosophy of Friedrich Nietzsche as a Foundation for Physical Education*. Unpublished master's thesis, University of Wisconsin. T

578. Bannister, Roger. (1964, Mar.). What makes the athlete run? *Australian Journal of Physical Education:* 31–36. B

579. Bate, R. (1979). Developing aesthetic awareness. *Momentum, 4*(1): 29–39. G

580. Bate, R. (1982a). Developing aesthetic awareness. *Journal of Psych-Social Aspects, 8:* 1–10. G
Combines extraordinary sports experience, aesthetic experiences, and sensory awareness technique.

581. Bate, R. (1982b). Enlightenment intensive. *Journal of Psych-Social Aspects, 8,* 27–33. G

582. Bate, R. (1982c). Physical education and enlightenment. *Journal of Psych-Social Aspects, 8,* 34–55. G

583. Batten, Jack. (1977). Jogging and the inner life. In his *The Complete Jogger* (pp. 78–85). New York: Harcourt Brace. I
On certain benefits of running: it can sharpen thinking, ease depression, quicken brain processes, improve sleep, and alleviate anxiety.

584. Bazzara, Carmelo. (1986). The body's role in the philosophy of the Renaissance man. In Seymour Kleinman (Ed.), *Mind and Body: East Meets West.* Champaign, IL: Human Kinetics. T

585. Becker, Carl B. (1982). Philosophical perspectives on the martial arts in America. *Journal of the Philosophy of Sport, 9,* 19–29. M

586. Beets, N[icholas]. (1964). The experience of the body in sport. In E. Jokl & E. Simon (Eds.), *International Research in Sport and Physical Education.* Springfield, IL: Charles C Thomas. P

587. Beets, Nicholas. (1966, Spr.). Historical actuality and bodily experience. *Humanitas, 2:* 15–28. T

588. Begel, Daniel. (1992). An overview of sport psychiatry. *American Journal of Psychiatry, 149:* 606–14. P
Provides a framework for understanding the developmental, occupational, pathological, therapeutic, and research aspects of sport psychiatry.

589. Beisser, Arnold. (1979). *The Madness in Sports* (2nd ed.). Bowie, MD: Charles Press. P
Beisser, a psychiatrist specializing in sport, views sport as a secular religion. His last chapter, "Beyond the Game," is devoted to the extraordinary sports experience, including his own. He warns that although sports are "a source of recreation, renewal, and transcendent experiences" (p. 207), the forces that are disintegrating society have also diminished the opportunity to experience spiritual moments in sports. He thinks increased public involvement in sport will benefit society as a whole.

590. Belaief, Lynn. (1977). Meanings of the body. *Journal of the Philosophy of Sport, 4:* 50–68. In David L. Vanderwerken & Spencer K. Wertz (Eds.), *Sport Inside Out: Readings in Literature and Philosophy* (pp. 414–34). Fort Worth, TX: Texas Christian University Press, 1985. T
Argues that sport is the expression "of a new living myth for a new society, namely, that individual human power can be positive rather than destructive." This power can be "positively actualized as power over oneself and for one's creativity" (p. 66). It is learned through participating in sport.

591. Bell, James W. (1976). An investigation of the concept—Sport as art. *Physical Educator, 33:* 81–84. T

592. Bellafante, Ginia. (1992, May/Jun.). Taking the bungee plunge: Are high-risk sports an inexpensive form of therapy? *Utne Reader,* 22–23. T

593. Bench, Johnny, & Brashler, William. (1979). *Catch You Later*. New York: Harper & Row. B

594. Bennett, James G., & Pravitz, James E. (1982). *The Miracle of Sport Psychology*. Englewood Cliffs, NJ: Prentice-Hall. P

595. Bennett, Jeff, & Downey, Scott. (1994). *The Complete Snowboarder*. New York: Ragged Mountain/McGraw-Hill. I

596. Bennett, M. Jeanine. (1975). *Sport Fans and Others: A Comparison of Personality Characteristics of Sports Fans Who Attend Professional Games with Persons with Religious Attendance and Persons Who Indicate No Formal Social Affiliations* [Summary]. Unpublished doctoral dissertation, Ohio State University. *Dissertations Abstracts International*, 1976 (Feb.), *36B*: 4221. P

597. Benoit, Joan, with Baker, Sally. (1987). *Running Tide*. New York: Knopf. B

598. Berger, Bob. (1990). Road warrior. *Omni, 12*(6): 62–71. B
First-person account of the author's visits with masters of "martial and mystical arts . . . seeking the invisible essence of energy called *ch'i, ki,* or *prana.*"

599. Berger, Bonnie G. (1980). The meaning of regular jogging: A phenomenological approach. In R. Cox (Ed.), *American Alliance for Health, Physical Education, and Recreation Research Consortium Symposium Papers* (Vol. 2, Book 2). Washington, DC: American Alliance for Health, Physical Education, Recreation, and Dance. P

600. Berger, Bonnie G. (1982). Fact and fantasy: Mood alteration through exercise. *Journal of Physical Education, Recreation, and Dance, 53*(9): 47–48. P
Brief survey of findings regarding exercise and mental health.

601. Berger, Bonnie G. (1983/1984). Stress reduction through exercise: The mind/body connection. *Motor Skills Theory Into Practice, 7*: 31–46. T

602. Berger, Bonnie G. (1984). Running toward psychological well-being: Special considerations for the female client. In M. L. Sachs & G. Buffone (Eds.), *Running as Therapy: An Integrated Approach* (pp. 172–97). Lincoln: University of Nebraska Press. P

603. Berger, Bonnie G., & Hecht, L. (1989). Exercise, aging, and psychological well-being: The mind/body question. In A. C. Ostrow (Ed.), *Aging and Motor Behavior* (pp. 117–57). Indianapolis, IN: Benchmark Press. T

604. Berger, Bonnie G., & Mackenzie, M. M. (1980). A case study of a woman jogger: A psychodynamic analysis. *Journal of Sport Behavior, 3*: 3–16. P

605. Berger, Bonnie G., & McInman, Adrian. (1993). Exercise and the quality of life. In R. N. Singer, M. Murphey, & L. K. Tennant (Eds.), *Handbook of Research on Sport Psychology* (pp. 729–60). New York: Macmillan. P

606. Berger, Bonnie G., & Owen, David R. (1983). Mood alteration with swimming—swimmers really do "feel better." *Psychosomatic Medicine, 45*: 425–33. P

607. Berger, Bonnie G., & Owen, David R. (1986). Mood alteration with

swimming: A re-evaluation. In L. Vander Velden & J. H. Humphrey (Eds.), *Current Selected Research in the Psychology and Sociology of Sport* (Vol. 1, pp. 97–114). New York: AMS. P

608. Berger, Bonnie G., & Owen, David R. (1988). Stress reduction and mood enhancement in four exercise modes: Swimming, body conditioning, hatha yoga, and fencing. *Research Quarterly for Exercise and Sport, 59:* 148–59. P

609. Berkow, Ira. (1988, May 8). Jordan hovers above the rest. *New York Times:* 1, 4. B

610. Berman, Neil. (1980). Zen and the art of basketball in Lawrence Shainberg's *One on One. Critique, 22:* 5–20. I
Describes how Shainberg's novel about basketball captures "the metaphorical texture and significance of sport" (p. 51), including mystical aspects and self-actualization.

611. Berman, Ronald. (1977, Jul. 23). Track at the middle distance. *New Republic, 177:* 19–21. I
On the training effect in running, which Berman singles out as one of the few sports in which a mutation in bodily ability can occur.

612. Bernstein, N. (1967). *The Coordination and Regulation of Movements.* Oxford, England: Pergamon Press. P

613. Best, David. (1974). The aesthetic in sport. *British Journal of Aesthetics, 14:* 197–213. Reprinted in *Journal of Human Movement Studies, 1975, 1:* 41f. In William J. Morgan & Klaus V. Meier (Eds.), *Philosophic Inquiry in Sport* (pp. 477–93). Champaign, IL: Human Kinetics, 1988. C

614. Best, David. (1974). *Expressions in Movement and the Arts.* London: Lepus. C

615. Best, David. (1978). *Philosophy and Human Movement.* London: George Allen and Unwin. T

616. Best, David. (1980). Art and sport. *Journal of Aesthetic Education, 14:* 69–80. C

617. Bickel, Lennard. (1977). *Mawson's Will: The Greatest Survival Story Ever Written.* New York: Stein & Day. B

618. Billing, J. E. (1975, Jan.). A taxonomy of sport forms. *Proceedings of the National College Physical Education Association for Man:* 34–39. P

619. Bindrim, Paul. (1968). Facilitating peak experiences. In Herbert A. Otto & John Mann (Eds.), *Ways of Growth: Approaches to Expanding Awareness* (pp. 115–27). New York: Simon & Schuster. G

620. Blackburn, Dan, & Jorgenson, Maryann. (1976). *Zen and the Cross-Country Skier.* Pasadena, CA: Ward Ritchie Press. I

621. Blackmore, Susan J. (1982). *Beyond the Body: An Investigation of Out-of-the-Body Experiences.* London: Heinemann. E

622. Blanchard, Kendall. (1986). *The Many Forces of Play.* Champaign, IL: Human Kinetics. T

623. Blanchard, Kendall, & Cheska, A. (1985). *The Anthropology of Sport.* South Hadley, MA: Bergin & Garvey. T

624. Blanchard, William H. (1969). Psychodynamic aspects of the peak experience. *Psychoanalytic Review, 56:* 87–112. G
Questions whether peak experiences are always positive or more prevalent

in self-actualizers. Blanchard views them as an aspect of creative possibility, which can be fulfilling or destructive. An element of danger and risk, he suggests, is as integral to the peak experience as beauty and pleasure.

625. Blum, Arlene. (1980). *Annapurna: A Woman's Place*. San Francisco: Sierra Club Books. **B**

626. Blumenfield, Walter. (1941, Jun.). Observations concerning the phenomenon and origin of play. *Philosophy and Phenomenological Research, 1:* 470–78. **T**

627. Blundell, N. (1989). Psychological aspects of peak performance in sport. In *Coaching Women: A Proceedings Booklet* (pp. 28–29). Victoria, Australia: Consultative Committee of Women on Leisure and Recreations. **P**

627a. Boardman, Peter. (1982). *Sacred Summits*. Seattle: The Mountaineers. **B**

628. Bompa, T. (1984, Apr.). Peaking for the major competition(s). Part one. *Sports: Science Periodical on Research and Technology in Sport:* 1–6. **P**

629. Bompa, T. (1984, May). Peaking for the major competition(s). Part two. *Sports: Science Periodical on Research and Technology in Sport:* 1–6. **P**

630. Bonington, Chris. (1981). *Quest for Adventure*. Sevenoaks, England: Hodder & Stoughton. **G**
Accounts of different kinds of adventure in various settings: oceans, deserts, rivers, mountains, the poles, air, space, and beneath the earth. Contains an interesting chapter entitled "Facets of Adventure," in which Bonington generalizes about the qualities of adventure.

630a. Bonington, Chris. (1986). *The Everest Years: A Climber's Life*. New York: Viking. **B**

631. Bosga, Steve. (1988). *Risk! An Exploration into the Lives of Athletes on the Edge*. Berkeley, CA: North Atlantic Books. **G**
Ten top athletes were interviewed about their motivation and the risk factors in their sport. Bosga found that they experienced "intense rushes of exhilaration, even euphoria, when they break through the risk barrier" (p. xiii).

632. Bouet, M. (1973). Basic principles of an interpretation of high-performance sport. In Ommo Grupe, Dietrich Kurz, & Johannes Teipel (Eds.), *Sport in the Modern World—Chances and Problems*. New York: Springer-Verlag. **T**

633. Bouet, M. (1973). The phenomenology of aesthetics of sport. In Ommo Grupe, Dietrich Kurz, & Johannes Teipel (Eds.), *Sport in the Modern World—Chances and Problems*. New York: Springer-Verlag. **T**

634. Boutcher, Steve. (1993). Emotion and aerobic exercise. In Robert N. Singer, Milledge Murphy, & L. Keith Tennant (Eds.), *Handbook of Research on Sport Psychology* (pp. 799–814). New York: Macmillan. **P**

635. Boutilier, Mary A., & San Giovanni, Lucinda. (1983). Alternative approaches to sport sociology and feminism. In Mary A. Boutilier & Lucinda San Giovanni, *The Sporting Woman* (pp. 5–22). Champaign, IL: Human Kinetics. **T**
Notes that in the 1970s and early 1980s, scholarship in psychology and sociology had begun to incorporate research and theory about sport health and recreation. The authors examine why, criticize the approaches that have been taken to women in sport, and offer alternatives.

636. Boutilier, Mary A., & San Giovanni, Lucinda. (1983). *The Sporting Woman*. Champaign, IL: Human Kinetics. T

This groundbreaking book attempts to correct some of the primary weaknesses of social science, such as insistence on value-neutralist and normative consensus, the deterministic view of individuals, and the predominance of quantitative research techniques. The book is based on a humanistic sociology and the use of qualitative approaches, such as participant observation and interviews, as applied to the sociology of women's participation in sport.

637. Bowie, Phil. (1977, Mar.). Fastest woman on earth. *Saturday Evening Post, 249:* 42–43, 82–83. Abridged in *Reader's Digest,* 1978 (Jun.), *112:* 127–29. B

638. Boxill, J. M. (1988). Beauty, sport, and gender. In William J. Morgan & Klaus V. Meier (Eds.), *Philosophic Inquiry in Sport* (pp. 509–18). Champaign, IL: Human Kinetics, 1988. T

639. Bradburn, N. (1969). *The Structure of Psychological Well-Being.* Chicago: Aldine. G

640. Braud, William G., & Schlitz, Marilyn J. (1991). Consciousness interactions with remote biological systems: Anomalous intentionality effects. *Subtle Energies, 2:* 1–46. E

641. Braud, William G.; Schlitz, Marilyn; & Schmidt, Helmut. (1989). Remote mental influence of animate and inanimate target systems: A method of comparison and preliminary findings. *Proceedings of Presented Papers: The Parapsychological Association 32nd Annual Convention:* pp. 12–25. E

642. Bregman, Lucy. (1976). Maslow as theorist of religion: Reflections on his popularity and plausibility. *Soundings, 59:* 139–63. G

Views Maslow's religious writings as folk-science aimed at "finding something 'true' in an age of relativism and awareness of cultural multiplicity" (p. 145). Characterizes Maslow's thinking as "authentically post-industrial and peculiarly American." Raises important considerations for anyone interested in peak experience and self-actualization in contemporary America, including those who are researching the interface between peak experience, self-actualization, and sport.

643. Bressan, Elizabeth. (1978). *The Generation of a Theoretical Framework for Physical Education from Frank Lloyd Wright's Theory of Organic Architecture.* Unpublished doctoral dissertation, Micrographics Dept., Doheny Library, University of South California. T

644. Bressan, Elizabeth S., & Pieter, Willy. (1985). Philosophic processes and the study of human moving. *Quest, 37:* 1–15. T

The authors propose that the philosophic processes of edification and theory building be applied to sport, dance, and exercise. Of special interest is the section on the intuitive modes of inquiry.

645. Britt, Steuart Henderson, & Janus, Sidney Q. (1941). Toward a social psychology of human play. *Journal of Social Psychology, 13:* 351–84. P

Historical review of empirical studies of play from 1890 to 1939, noting that the experimental and social psychology of play had come into its own by 1939. Covers theoretical considerations, representative empirical studies, and outlines nineteen problem areas for future study.

646. Broad, William J. (1979, Apr.). Focus or fantasize? Techniques produce differing results. *Science Digest, 85:* 57–61. P

Reviews William P. Morgan's studies of average marathon runners who were able to get through pain, and especially the "wall," by dissociating from it through fantasy, or consciously attending to something else. When Broad interviewed world-class marathoners, he found they associated to, rather than dissociated from, their bodies, and they experienced little pain and no wall. They treat "pain and body sensations as vital information about how the web of muscles, fibers, and tendons is taking the strain. The . . . elite runner attempts to 'read' the body and modulate the pace accordingly. . . . They stayed glued to an inner sense that set the pace" (p. 58).

647. Brooks, George A. (1987). The exercise physiology paradigm in contemporary biology: To molbiol or not to molbiol—That is the question. *Quest, 39:* 231–42. P

Describes recent findings in molecular biology regarding the regulation of essential cellular processes. Exercise physiologists can contribute to molecular biology in the areas of "adaptation to environmental stressors, resistance to degenerative diseases, and expansion of the limits to human performance" (p. 231).

648. Brooks, George A., & Fahey, T. D. (1984). *Exercise Physiology: Human Bioenergetics and Its Applications.* New York: Macmillan. P

649. Brosnan, Jim. (1985). The fantasy world of baseball. In David L. Vanderwerken & Spencer K. Wertz (Eds.), *Sport Inside Out: Readings in Literature and Philosophy* (pp. 636–43). Fort Worth, TX: Texas Christian University Press. T

650. Brown, David F. (1977). Inner skiing: Skiing out of your mind. *New Realities, 1*(4): 8–14. I

651. Brown, E. Y.; Morrow, J. R., Jr.; & Livingston, S. M. (1982). Self-concept changes in women as a result of training. *Journal of Sport Psychology, 4:* 354–63. P

652. Brown, J. C. (1979). *The Therapeutic Mile.* Irmo, SC: Human Growth and Development Books. P

653. Brown, Richard Alvin. (1977). Kinesthetic and cognitive determinants of emotional state: An investigation of the Alexander technique [Summary]. *Dissertation Abstracts International,* 38(9B): 4–99. P

Brown investigated the claim that control of postural sets in the Alexander technique changes emotional well-being. His study suggests that the Alexander technique is effective in altering kinesthetic experience and that "kinesthesis can play an important role in the production of emotional states" (p. 4499-B).

654. Bruya, L. D. (1977). Effect of selected movement skills on positive self-concept. *Perceptual and Motor Skills, 45:* 252–54. P

655. Buffone, Gary W. (1980). Exercise as therapy: A closer look. *Journal of Counseling and Psychotherapy, 3*(2): 101–15. P

656. Bunn, Curtis G. (1990, Jun. 15). Johnson's shot in final second secures 2nd title. *Newsday,* 159. B

657. Bunting, Camille J. (1982). Managing stress through challenge activ-

ities. *Journal of Physical Education, Recreation and Dance, 53*(7): 48–49. P
Examines the possibility that activities involving real or perceived risk can be beneficial because they provide emotional release, social interaction, expanded perspective, and expanded personalities.

658. Burke, Richard J. (1988). Taking play seriously. In William J. Morgan & Klaus V. Meier (Eds.), *Philosophic Inquiry in Sport* (pp. 159–67). Champaign, IL: Human Kinetics. T

659. Burkett, D. (1979). Centered athlete: An examination of altered states of consciousness and peak experiences in the racquet sports. In J. L. Groppel (Ed.), *Proceedings of a National Symposium on the Racquet Sports: An Exploration of Research Implications and Teaching Strategies*. Urbana-Champaign: University of Illinois Press. A

660. Buskirk, E. R. (1981). The emergence of exercise physiology in physical education. In George A. Brooks (Ed.), *Perspectives on the Academic Discipline of Physical Education: A Tribute to G. L. Patrick* (pp. 56–74). Champaign, IL: Human Kinetics. P

661. Butt, Dorcas Susan. (1980a). Perspectives from women on sport and leisure. In C. S. Adamec (Ed.), *Sex Roles: Origins, Influences and Implications for Women* (pp. 70–88). Montreal: Eden. T

662. Butt, Dorcas Susan. (1980b). What can psychology offer the athlete? In Richard M. Suinn (Ed.), *Psychology in Sports: Methods and Applications* (pp. 78–85). Minneapolis: Burgess. P

663. Butt, Dorcas Susan. (1985). Psychological motivation and sports performance in world class women field hockey players. *International Journal of Women's Studies, 8*: 328–37. P

664. Butt, Dorcas Susan. (1987). *Psychology of Sport: The Behavior, Motivation, Personality, and Performances of Athletes* (2nd ed.). New York: Van Nostrand Reinhold. P

665. Butt, Dorcas Susan. (1991). Psychological motivation in sports, exercise, and fitness. In Lewis Diamint (Ed.), *Mind-Body Maturity: Psychological Approaches to Sports, Exercise, and Fitness* (pp. 213–36). New York: Hemisphere. P
A discussion of health psychology and competence development in sport.

666. Byrd, Oliver E. (1963). The relief of tension by exercise: A survey of medical viewpoints and practices. *Journal of School Health, 33*: 238–39. P

667. Byrne, Peter. (1978). Running the Thula Bheri: White-water adventure on Nepal's wildest river. *Quest, 2*: 29–34, 36. I
Account of a wild whitewater raft adventure after which the principals involved concluded that the experience would enhance and expand their future lives.

668. Cady, Edwin H. (1978). *The Big Game: College Sports and American Life*. Knoxville: University of Tennessee Press. T

669. Cady, Edwin H. (1985a). Pop art and the American dream. In David L. Vanderwerken & Spencer K. Wertz (Eds.), *Sport Inside Out: Readings in Literature and Philosophy* (pp. 197–207). Fort Worth, TX: Texas Christian University Press. T

670. Cady, Edwin H. (1985b). The sort of sacred, sometimes ritual. In David L. Vanderwerken & Spencer K. Wertz (Eds.), *Sport Inside Out: Read-*

ings in Literature and Philosophy (pp. 308–18). Fort Worth, TX: Texas Christian University Press. G

671. Caillois, Roger. (1957, Fall). Unity of play; diversity of games. *Diogenes, 19:* 92–121. T

672. Caillois, Roger. (1959). Play and the sacred. In Roger Caillois, *Man and the Sacred.* (Meyer Barash, Trans.). Glencoe, IL: Free Press of Glencoe. T

673. Caillois, Roger. (1961). *Man, Play, and Games* (Meyer Barash, Trans.). New York: Free Press of Glencoe. T

674. Caillois, Roger. (1988). The structure and classification of games. In William J. Morgan & Klaus V. Meier (Eds.). (1988). *Philosophic Inquiry in Sport* (pp. 7–15). Champaign, IL: Human Kinetics. T

675. Cantelon, H. (1980). The reproductive and transformative potential of sport: Comparative analyses utilizing the Weberian concept of domination and rationalization. In John Pooley (Ed.), *Proceedings of the Second International Seminar on Comparative Physical Education and Sport.* Halifax: Delhousie Printing Center. T

676. Caputo, John D. (1970). Being, ground and play in Heidegger. *Man and World, 3:* 26–48. T

677. Carlisle, Robert. (1974). Physical education and aesthetics. In H. T. A. Whiting & Don W. Masterson (Eds.), *Readings in the Aesthetics of Sport.* London: Lepus Books. T

678. Carmack, M. A., & Martens, R. (1979). Measuring commitment to running: A survey of runners' attitudes and mental states. *Journal of Sport Psychology, 1:* 25–42. P

679. Carron, A. V. (1980). *Social Psychology of Sport.* Ithaca, NY: Movement. P

680. Chace, M. (1964, Jul.). Dance alone is not enough. *Dance Magazine, 38:* 46–47, 58. I

681. Chambers, D. (1979). Developing a cohesive team spirit. *Hockey Scope, 2(1):* 10–11. P

682. Chase, W. H., & Simon, H. A. (1973). Perception in chess. *Cognitive Psychology, 4:* 55–81. P

683. Cherry, Christopher. (1976). Games and the world. *Philosophy, 51:* 57–61. T

684. Christina, Robert W., & Eckert, Helen M. (Eds.). (1992). *Enhancing Human Performance in Sport: New Concepts and Developments.* Champaign, IL: Human Kinetics. P

685. Claeys, Urbain. (1985, Sep.). Evolution of the concept of sport and the participation/nonparticipation phenomenon. *Sociology of Sport Journal, 2:* 233–39. T

686. Coe, George Albert. (1956, May/Jun.). A philosophy of play. *Religious Education, 51:* 220–22. T

687. Cohen, Ted. (1988). Sports and art: Beginning questions. In Jonathan Dancy (Ed.), *Human Agency* (pp. 258–73). Stanford, CA: Stanford University Press. T

688. Cohn, Patrick J. (1991). An exploratory study on peak performance in golf. *Sport Psychologist, 5,* 1–14. I

Cohn interviewed nineteen professional and collegiate golfers regarding the qualities of peak performance, including immersion in task, effortless performance, calmness, relaxed state, feeling of self-control, high self-confidence, fun, fearlessness. These qualities were determined by content analysis. Several athletes' descriptions are included.

689. Collier, John. (1917). Recreation. *Homilectic Review*, 74: 44–50. T

690. Conry, Barbara J. (1974). *An Existential Phenomenological View of the Lived Body.* Unpublished doctoral dissertation, Ohio State University. T

691. Cooper, W. E. (1978). Do sports have an aesthetic aspect? *Journal of the Philosophy of Sport, 5:* 51–55. C

692. Cordner, C. D. (1984). Grace and functionality. *British Journal of Aesthetics, 24:* 301–13. C

693. Cordner, Christopher. (1988). Differences between sport and art. *Journal of the Philosophy of Sport, 15:* 31–47. C

693a. Costa, D. Margaret, & Guthrie, Sharon R. (Eds.). (1994). *Women and Sport: Interdisciplinary Perspectives.* Champaign, IL: Human Kinetics. P

A discussion of women in sport, including history, Olympic competition, biomedical considerations, and psychological and social dimensions. Gender issues are discussed throughout.

694. Coutts, Curtis A. (1968, May). Freedom in sport. *Quest, 10:* 68–71. T

695. Cowan, Ed. (1979, Nov./Dec.). Why sport? *Humanist, 39:* 22–28. T

696. Cox, Harvey. (1969). Faith as play. In *The Feast of Fools: A Theological Essay on Festivity and Fantasy* (pp. 142–49). Cambridge, MA: Harvard University Press. T

Argues that faith and prayer are related to play. The common factor in each "is to yield oneself to a kind of magic" (p. 147).

697. Cratty, Bernard J. (1968). *Psychology and Physical Activity.* Englewood Cliffs, NJ: Prentice-Hall. P

698. Critcher, Charles. (1986). Radical theorists of sport: The state of play. *Sociology of Sport Journal, 3:* 333–43. T

699. Crocitto, J. A. (1982). Jogging: A holistic integrative experience. *Journal of Humanistic Education and Development, 21*(2): 58–64. I

700. Csikszentmihalyi, Mihalyi. (1992). A response to the Kimiecik & Stein and Jackson papers. *Journal of Applied Sport Psychology, 4:* 181–83. P

701. Csikszentmihalyi, Mihalyi, & Csikszentmihalyi, Isabella Selega. (Eds.). (1988). *Optimal Experience: Psychological Studies of Flow in Consciousness.* New York: Cambridge University Press. P

702. Cureton, Thomas K. (1963). Improvement of psychological states by means of exercise-fitness programs. *Journal of the Association of Physical and Mental Rehabilitation, 17:* 14–[unknown]. P

703. Curtis, J., & McTeer, W. (1981). Toward a sociology of marathoning. *Journal of Sport Behavior, 4*(2): 67–81. I

704. Dailey, Richard Lee. (1977). Higher consciousness through sports [Summary]. *Dissertations Abstracts International, 38*(6B): 2853–54. G

Dailey examined the effects of techniques set forth in Gallwey's *Inner Game of Tennis,* and found that participants underwent greater psychological growth and more improved tennis abilities than those using a more conventional method.

705. Danehy, Elisabeth. (1980). Centering movement and the visualization of transformational imagery. In J. E. Shorr, G. E. Sobel, P. Robin, & J. A. Connella (Eds.), *Imagery: Its Many Dimensions and Applications* (pp. 243–50). New York: Plenum. **P**

706. Daniels, Frederic S., & Landers, Daniel M. (1981). Biofeedback and shooting performance: A test of disregulation and systems theory. *Journal of Sport Psychology, 3,* 271–82. **P**

707. Daumal, René. (1992). *Mount Analogue: A Novel of Symbolically Authentic Non-Euclidian Adventures in Mountain Climbing* (Rose Shattuck, Trans.). Boston: Shambhala. **I**

708. Davidson, Ben. (1976). *The Skateboard Book.* New York: Grosset & Dunlap. **I**

709. Davidson, Julian M. (1976). The physiology of meditation and mystical states of consciousness. *Perspectives in Biology and Medicine, 19:* 345–79. **P**
Reviews physiological and psychological aspects of meditation and prospects for future research.

710. Davis, John Eisele. (1936, Jan.). The utilization of play in the construction of healthy mental attitudes. *Mental Hygiene, 20:* 49–54. **P**

711. Davis, John; Lockwood, Linda; & Wright, Charles. (1991). Reasons for not reporting peak experiences. *Journal of Humanistic Psychology, 31*(1): 86–94. **G**
Two hundred forty-six eighteen- to sixty-four-year-olds were surveyed as to whether they had had a peak experience and whether or not they told others about it. Peak experiences were reported by 79 percent, but most of them had told only a few people about their experience, because it was too intimate or unusual, or they feared having the experience denigrated, or they felt unable to describe the experience adequately.

712. DeCauluwe, Goederoen. (1979). *Theology of Play: A Conceptual Analysis.* Unpublished master's thesis, University of Western Ontario. **T**

713. Deci, E. L. (1975). *Intrinsic Motivation.* New York: Plenum. **P**

714. Deford, Frank. (1985). Religion in sport. In David L. Vanderwerken & Spencer K. Wertz (Eds.), *Sport Inside Out: Readings in Literature and Philosophy* (pp. 319–50). Fort Worth, TX: Texas Christian University Press. **G**

715. Deindorfer, Robert G. (1981). *Positive Fishing.* New York: Seaview Books. **I**
On flow experience in anglers, or the "Zen of fishing."

716. Dendinger, Rose A. (1980). Imagination and movement therapy. In J. E. Shorr, G. E. Sobel, P. Robin, & J. A. Connella (Eds.), *Imagery: Its Many Dimensions and Applications* (pp. 237–41). New York: Plenum. **P**

717. Derry, L. (1980). Study of peak experience in sport. *Momentum, 5*(2): 21–35. **G**

718. Desensi, J. T. (1980). *A Story of Martin Buber's I-Thou and I-It Relationship in Sport.* Unpublished doctoral dissertation, University of North Carolina at Greensboro. **T**

719. Desmonde, William H. (1952, Jun.). The bull-fight as a religious ritual. *American Imago, 9:* 173–95. **I**

720. DeVries, H. A. (1981). Tranquilizer effect of exercise: A critical review. *Physician and Sports Medicine, 9*(11): 48–49, 52–53, 55. **P**

721. Dewar, Alison. (1991, Aug.). Feminist pedagogy in physical education: Promises, possibilities, and pitfalls. *Journal of Physical Education, Recreation and Dance, 62:* 68–77. **P**

Describes Dewar's experiences in developing a feminist approach to teaching physical education, which she defines as creating "ways of learning where theory and practice are integrated and where learning is designed to allow students to be critical of, and reflect about, the knowledge that they are learning and the conditions under which they are learning it" (p. 70). This is relevant to the study of the extraordinary sport experience, which might get the attention it merits if "theory and practice" were geared to experience instead of making athletes' experiences fit a predetermined methodology or theoretical structure.

722. Diamant, Leif Robert, & Baker, Richard M. (1991). Mental states and physical performance. In Louis Diamant (Ed.), *Mind-Body Maturity: Psychological Approaches to Sports, Exercise, and Fitness* (pp. 255–64). New York: Hemisphere. **P**

Reviews the following aspects of preparation for peak performance: development of psychomotor competence; relaxation and psyching up; self-hypnosis; imagery; rehearsal; mechanisms for enhancing body/mind performance; and the inner game.

723. Diamant, Louis. (Ed.). (1991a). *Mind-Body Maturity: Psychological Approaches to Sports, Exercise, and Fitness.* New York: Hemisphere. **P**

State-of-the-art chapters on various reports on aspects of the psychology of sport and health.

724. Diamant, Louis. (Ed.) (1991b). *Psychology of Sports, Exercise and Fitness: Social and Personal Issues.* New York: Hemisphere. **P**

725. Diamant, Louis. (1991c). Theory and research in sports, exercise, and fitness psychology. In Louis Diamant (Ed.), *Psychology of Sports, Exercise, and Fitness: Social and Personal Issues* (pp. 5–16). New York: Hemisphere. **P**

726. Dickinson, Jo Leissa, & Travis, Fiona. (1977). Movement as dance: A journey backward [Dickinson]; A journey forward [Travis]. *Theory into Practice, 16*(3): 211–14. **I**

Explores the value of dance for knowing the self and Dickinson's experiences in teaching it. Theorizes that although creative dance is a journey back to childhood pleasures, it is also "a journey forward into new sensory awareness of self and environment" (p. 213).

727. Diener, Ed. (1984). Subjective well-being. *Psychological Bulletin, 95:* 542–75. **G**

Reviews theories and problems of measurement of the experience of well-being, which is one aspect of the extraordinary sports experience.

728. Dienstbier, Richard A. (1974). The effect of exercise on personality. In Michael L. Sachs & Gary W. Buffone (Eds.), *Running as Therapy: An Integrated Approach* (pp. 253–72). Lincoln: University of Nebraska Press. **P**

729. Dishman, Rod K. (1980). Overview of ergogenic properties of hypnosis. *Journal of Physical Education and Recreation, 51:* 52–54. **A**

730. Dishman, Rod K. (1993). Exercise adherence. In Robert N. Singer,

Milledge Murphy, & L. Keith Tennant (Eds.), *Handbook of Research on Sport Psychology* (pp. 779–98). New York: Macmillan. P

731. Dishman, Rod K.; Ickes, W. J.; & Morgan, William P. (1980). Self-motivation and adherence to habitual physical activity. *Journal of Applied Psychology, 10:* 115–31. P

732. Dodds, Patt. (1979). Creativity in movement: Models for analysis. *Journal of Creative Behavior, 12:* 264–73. C

Several creativity factors were applied to movement responses, and a behavioral model was used to describe them.

733. Doherty, J. Kenneth. (1964, Apr.). Why men run. *Quest, 2:* 61–66. I

734. Donnelly, P., & Young, K. M. (1985). Reproduction and transformation of cultural forms in sport: A contextual analysis of rugby. *International Review of Sport Sociology, 20:* 20–38. I

735. Dosamantes-Alperson, E. (1974a). Carrying experiencing forward through authentic body movement. *Psychotherapy: Theory, Research and Practice, 11:* 211–14. P

736. Dosamantes-Alperson, E. (1974b). The creation of meaning through body movement. In A. I. Rabin (Ed.), *Clinical Psychology: Issues of the Seventies.* East Lansing: Michigan State University Press. P

737. Dosamantes-Alperson, E. (1974c). Process for facilitating body-mind integration. *JSAS Catalog of Selected Documents in Psychology, 4*(83): (Ms. No. 688). P

738. Dosamantes-Alperson, E. (1976). Experiential movement psychotherapy. *Art Psychotherapy, 3:* 1–5. P

739. Dosamantes-Alperson, E. (1977). Nonverbal and verbal integration. In W. Anderson (Ed.), *Therapy and the Arts.* New York: Harper & Row. P

740. Dosamantes-Alperson, Erma. (1980). Contacting bodily-felt experiencing in psychotherapy. In J. E. Shorr, G. E. Sobel, P. Robin, & J. A. Connella (Eds.), *Imagery: Its Many Dimensions and Applications* (pp. 223–36). New York: Plenum. P

741. Dossey, Larry. (1982). Time and athletic achievement. In *Space, Time and Medicine* (pp. 169–74). Boulder, CO: Shambhala. G

Describes nonordinary time experiences of athletes that resemble the experience of meditators and mystics. Cites former Dallas Cowboy defensive end Pat Toomay's theory that the extraordinary sports experience occurs when one goes beyond what David Bohm called the "explicate order" and participates in the perfection of the "implicate order" where the athlete does not so much *do* as *be* (p. 172).

742. Douglas, David. (1983). The spirit of wilderness and the religious community. *Sierra, 68*(3): 56–57. T

Criticizes religious institutions for not being identified with wilderness conservation. Describes spiritual values of wilderness such as silence, solitude, and awe.

743. Drengson, Alan R. (1985). Wilderness travel as an art and as a paradigm for outdoor education. In David L. Vanderwerken & Spencer K. Wertz (Eds.), *Sport Inside Out: Readings in Literature and Philosophy* (pp. 363–75). Fort Worth, TX: Texas Christian University Press. T

744. DuBois, P. E. (1974). The aesthetic of sport and the athlete. *Physical Educator, 31:* 198–201. C

745. Duncan, Margaret Carlisle. (1986). A hermeneutic of spectator sport: The 1976 and 1984 Olympic games. *Quest, 38:* 50–77. P

746. Duncan, Margaret Carlisle, & Brummett, Barry. (1987). The mediation of spectator sport. *Research Quarterly for Exercise and Sport, 58:* 168–77. T
The authors propose that "what sports *are* for people [including how they *experience* them] is determined by the nature of the medium through which they are experienced" (p. 178). This fact must be considered in investigations of sports that are presented to the public via TV or any other media form.

747. Dunning, E. (1967). Notes on some conceptual and theoretical problems in sociology of sport. *International Review of Sport Sociology, 2:* 143–53. T

748. Durrant, S. M. (1976). *State of Consciousness and the Sport Experience.* Unpublished doctoral dissertation, Ohio State University. G

749. Dustin, Daniel L., & Rentschler, Gary J. (1980). Magical outcomes of organized camping. *Journal of Physical Education and Recreation, 51*(6): 46. T
The authors apply principles derived from General Systems Theory, especially that of synergy, to account for the seemingly "magical" therapeutic success of their summer camp programs.

750. Dyer, John B., & Crouch, Joyce G. (1988). Effects of running and other activities on moods. *Perceptual and Motor Skills, 67*(1): 43–50. P
Comparison of the effects of exercise on runners, aerobic dancers, weightlifters, and nonexercising controls. The first two groups experienced not only improved stress tolerance but a more positive sense of well-being.

751. Dyskstra, Lenny, with Noble, Marty. (1987). *Nails: The Inside Story of an Amazin' Season.* Garden City, NY: Doubleday. B

752. Earls, N. (1986). Naturalistic inquiry: Interactive research and the insider-outsider perspective (Special Monograph). *Journal of Teaching in Physical Education, 6:* 1–108. P

753. Ebersole, Peter. (1972). Effects and classification of peak experiences. *Psychological Reports, 30:* 631–35. G
Survey of eighty-eight college students, 55 percent of whom reported no lasting effect of peak experiences. The peak experiences reported were distributed evenly over Thorne's categories of peak experience.

754. Edwards, John. (1979). The home-field advantage. In Jeffrey H. Goldstein (Ed.), *Sports, Games and Play: Social and Psychological Viewpoints* (pp. 409–38). Hillsdale, NJ: Erlbaum. P
Examines statistics from various sports that bear on the hypothesis of the home-field advantage and its possible limitations.

755. Egger, G. (1979). *Running High.* Melbourne, Australia: Sun Books. I

756. Egger, G. (1981). *The Sport Drug.* Sydney, Australia: Allen & Unwin. G

757. Ehrmann, Jacques. (1971). Homo ludens revisited. In Jacques Ehrmann (Ed.), *Game, Play, Literature.* Boston: Beacon Press. T

758. Eischens, Roger R., & Greist, John H. (1974). Beginning and contin-

uing running: Steps to psychological well-being. In Michael L. Sachs & Gary W. Buffone (Eds.), *Running as Therapy: An Integrated Approach* (pp. 63–82). Lincoln: University of Nebraska Press. I

Outline of a treatment plan to promote psychological fitness.

759. Eischens, Roger R.; Greist, John H.; & McInvaille, T. (1978). *Run to Reality.* Madison, WI: Madison Running Press. I

760. Eitzen, Stanley, & Sage, George H. (1978). *Sociology of American Sport.* Dubuque, IA: William C. Brown. T

761. Elena, Lugo. (1969). *Jose Ortega y Gasset's Sportive Sense of Life: His Philosophy of Man.* Unpublished doctoral dissertation, Georgetown University. I

762. Elias, Norbert, & Dunning, Eric. (1970). The quest for excitement in unexciting societies. In G. Luschen (Ed.), *The Cross-Cultural Analysis of Sports and Games.* Champaign, IL: Stipes. T

763. Ellis, G. D.; Witt, P. A.; & Aguilar, T. (1983). Facilitating "flow" through therapeutic recreation services. *Therapeutic Recreation Journal, 17*(2): 6–15. G

764. Ellis, M. J. (1972). *Why People Play.* Englewood Cliffs, NJ: Prentice-Hall. T

765. Ellis, M. J. (1981). Motivational theories of play: Definitions and explanations. In G. Luschen & G. H. Sage (Eds.), *Handbook of Social Science of Sport* (pp. 479–91). Champaign, IL: Stipes. P

766. Epstein, Joseph. (1976, Jul.). Obsessed with sport. *Harper's, 253:* 67–72. In David L. Vanderwerken & Spencer K. Wertz (Eds.), *Sport Inside Out: Readings in Literature and Philosophy* (pp. 109–18). Fort Worth, TX: Texas Christian University Press, 1985. T

766a. Ericsson, K. Anders, & Charness, Neil. (1994). Expert performance: Its structure and acquisition. *American Psychologist, 49:* 725–47. P

767. Erikson, Erik H. (1972). Play and actuality. In M. W. Piers (Ed.), *Play and Development.* New York: Norton. T

768. Ermler, K. L. (1980). *Relationship of Existential Freedom to Symbolic Death in Sport.* Unpublished doctoral dissertation, State University of New York at Buffalo. T

769. Esposito, Joseph L. (1974). Play and possibility. *Philosophy Today, 18:* 137–46. In William J. Morgan & Klaus V. Meier (Eds.), *Philosophic Inquiry in Sport* (pp. 175–81). Champaign, IL: Human Kinetics, 1988. T

770. Ewert, Alan W. (1994, Jan.). Playing the edge: Motivation and risk taking in a high-altitude wilderness-like environment. *Environment and Behavior, 26*(1): 3–24. G

771. Ewert, Alan, & Hollenhorst, Steve. (1989). Testing the adventure model: Empirical support for a model of risk recreation participation. *Journal of Leisure Research, 21:* 124–39. G

Investigates "type and level of risk, social orientation, locus of decision-making, frequency of participation, and preferred environment in the adventure recreation setting" (p. 124).

772. Fahey, Brian. (1977). The passionate body. In Dorothy J. Allen & Brian Fahey (Eds.), *Being Human in Sport.* Philadelphia, PA: Lea & Febiger. P

773. Fahlberg, Larry L. (1990). *A Hermeneutical Study of Meaning in Health Behavior: Women and Exercise.* Unpublished doctoral dissertation, University of Utah, Salt Lake City. P

774. Fahlberg, Larry L., & Fahlberg, Lauri A. (1994). A human science for the study of movement: An integration of multiple ways of knowing. *Research Quarterly for Exercise and Sport, 65*(2): 100–109. P
Points to limitations in the physical science approach in movement studies. "The human world of movement, in addition to relating to the material realm, also includes meaning" (p. 100).

775. Fahlberg, Larry L.; Fahlberg, Lauri A.; & Gates, W. (1992). Exercise and existence: Exercise behavior from an existential-phenomenological perspective. *Sport Psychologist, 6:* 172–91. T

776. Fairchild, David. (1978). Man, mind and matter: Toward a philosophy of sport. *Journal of Thought, 13:* 225–34. Provides philosophical definitions of play, games, and sport. T

777. Fairchild, David L. (1979). What we are and what we may be: Reflections on technology, play and the meaning of contemporary life. In William J. Morgan (Ed.), *Sport and the Humanities: A Collection of Original Essays.* Knoxville: University of Tennessee Press. T

777a. Falkus, Hugh. (1981). *Sea Trout Fishing: A Guide to Success* (rev. 2nd ed.). London: H. F. & G. Witherby. I
For examples of possible ESP in fishing, see pp. 152–57.

778. Fardun, Edrie, & Felshin, Jan. (1982). The stress mess: From management to engagement. *Journal of Physical Education, Recreation and Dance, 53*(7): 46. P

779. Farrell, J. E. (1975). The classification of physical education skills. *Quest, 24:* 63–68. P

780. Feezell, Randolph. (1981a). Play, freedom and sport. *Philosophy Today, 25:* 166–75. T

781. Feezell, Randolph M. (1981b). Sport: Pursuit of bodily excellence of play—An examination of Paul Weiss' account of sport. *Modern Schoolman, 58:* 257–70. T

782. Feezell, Randolph. (1984). Play and the absurd. *Philosophy Today, 28:* 319–28. T

783. Feldenkreis, Moise. (1972). *Awareness Through Movement.* New York: Harper & Row. P

784. Fell, Joseph P. (1979). The ethics of play and freedom: Conversion. In *Heidegger and Sartre: An Essay on Being and Place* (pp. 129–51). New York: Columbia University Press. T
Explanation of Sartre's view of *lucid play,* which would give birth to an ethics of play that involves deliverance and salvation, a "genuinely 'radical' conversion" (p. 141).

785. Felshin, Jan. (1969, May). Sport and modes of meaning. *Journal of Health, Physical Education, and Recreation, 40:* 43–44. T

786. Felshin, Jan. (1972). *More than Movement: An Introduction to Physical Education.* Philadelphia: Lea & Febiger. T

787. Feltz, D. L. (1984). Self-efficacy as a cognitive mediator of athletic

performance. In W. F. Straub & J. M. Williams (Eds.), *Cognitive Sport Psychology* (pp. 191–98). Lansing, NY: Sport Science Association. P

788. Feltz, D. L. (1987). Advancing knowledge in sport psychology: Strategies for expanding our conceptual frameworks. *Quest, 39*: 243–54. P

Briefly describes the evolution of some current paradigms in sport psychology and provides strategies for expanding the field's conceptual frameworks.

789. Feltz, D. L., & Landers, D. M. (1983). The effects of mental practice on motor skill learning and performance: A meta-analysis. *Journal of Sport Psychology, 5*: 25–57. P

790. Fensterheim, Herbert. (1980, Mar.). A behavioral method for improving sport performance. *Psychiatric Annals, 10*(3): 54–63. P

791. Fenz, W. D., & Jones, G. B. (1972). Individual differences in physiological arousal and performance in sport parachutists. *Psychosomatic Medicine, 29*: 1–8. P

792. Fetters, Janis L. (1976). *The Aesthetic Experience of the Body in Sport.* Unpublished doctoral dissertation, Ohio State University. C

793. Fetters, Janis L. (1977). The body aesthetic: A symbolic experience. *Proceedings of the National College Physical Education Association for Men/ National Association for Physical Education of College Women Conference,* Orlando, Florida, Jan. 6–9, 1977. C

794. Fetters, Jan. (1978). Somatic unity in the movement experience. *Somatics, 2*(1): 22–26. G

Fetters examined experiences of "athletes' perceptions, feelings and body attention patterns" (p. 22) and interpreted them according to "an existential phenomenological interpretation of spatiality and temporality" (p. 22).

795. Figler, Stephen K. (Ed.). (1979). *Sport and Play in American Life: A Textbook in the Sociology of Sport.* Madison, WI: Brown & Benchmark. T

796. Fine, Gary A. (1979). Small groups and culture creation: The idioculture of Little League baseball teams. *American Sociological Review, 44*: 733–45. T

797. Fine, Gary A. (1986). Small groups and sport: A symbolic interactionist perspective. In C. R. Rees & A. W. Miracle (Eds.), *Sport and Social Theory* (pp. 159–69). Champaign, IL: Human Kinetics. T

798. Fink, Eugen. (1960, Sum.). The ontology of play. *Philosophy Today, 4*: 95–110. In William J. Morgan & Klaus V. Meier (Eds.), *Philosophic Inquiry in Sport* (pp. 145–57). Champaign, IL: Human Kinetics, 1988. T

799. Fisher, A. C. (1976). *Psychology of Sport: Issues and Insights.* Palo Alto, CA: Mayfield. P

800. Fisher, A. C. (1984). New directions in sport personality research. In J. M. Silva & R. S. Weinberg (Eds.), *Psychological Foundations of Sport* (pp. 70–80). Champaign, IL: Human Kinetics. P

801. Fisher, Marjorie. (1972). Sport as an aesthetic experience. In Ellen W. Gerber (Ed.), *Sport and the Body: A Philosophical Symposium* (pp. 315–22). Philadelphia, PA: Lea & Febiger. C

802. Fogelin, Robert. (1972). Sport: The diversity of the concept. In Ellen W. Gerber (Ed.), *Sport and the Body: A Philosophicial Symposium* (pp. 58–61). Philadelphia: Lea & Febiger. T

803. Folkins, Carlyle H. (1976). Effects of physical training on mood. *Journal of Clinical Psychology, 32:* 385–88. **P**

804. Folkins, Carlyle H.; Lynch, S.; & Gardner, M. M. (1972). Psychological fitness as a function of physical fitness. *Archives of Physical Medicine and Rehabilitation, 53:* 503–08. **P**

805. Folkins, Carlyle H., & Sime, Wesley E. (1981). Physical fitness training and mental health. *American Psychologist, 36:* 373–89. **P**

806. Foster, Stephen, with Little, Meredith. (1980). *The Book of the Vision Quest: Personal Transformation in the Wilderness.* Covelo, CA: Island Press. **I**

807. Fowler, Corky, & Smith, Christopher. (1977). *The Hidden Skier.* Chicago: Contemporary Books. **I**
On the joy of skiing and the process of discovering one's hidden talents. The authors emphasize the process of self-discovery.

808. Fox, Karen M. (1994). Negotiating in a world of change: Ecofeminist guideposts for leisure scholarship. *Journal of Leisure Research, 26:* 39–56. **T**

809. Fox, Richard M. (1982). The so-called unreality of sport. *Quest, 34:* 1–11. **T**

810. Fraleigh, Sondra H. (1975, Jan.). Man creates dance. *Quest, 23:* 20–27. **C**

811. Fraleigh, Warren P. (1973a). The moving "I." In Robert G. Osterhoudt (Ed.), *The Philosophy of Sport: A Collection of Original Essays* (pp. 108–29). Springfield, IL: Charles C Thomas. **G**
Identifies certain experiences that occur in dance, aquatics, exercise, and sport in general and examines some possible meanings that are an aspect of such experiences.

812. Fraleigh, Warren P. (1973b). On Weiss on records, athletic activity and the athlete. In Robert G. Osterhoudt (Ed.), *The Philosophy of Sport: A Collection of Original Essays* (pp. 29–38). Springfield, IL: Charles C Thomas. **T**

813. Fraleigh, Warren P. (1973c). Some meanings of the human experience of freedom and necessity in sport. In Robert G. Osterhoudt (Ed.), *The Philosophy of Sport: A Collection of Original Essays* (pp. 130–48). Springfield, IL: Charles C Thomas. **T**
Through interpretation of the meaning of the lived body in sport, Fraleigh shows how one's self-identity can be clarified, especially as regards necessity and freedom.

814. Fraleigh, Warren P. (1975). Sport-purpose. *Journal of the Philosophy of Sport, 2:* 74–82. **T**

815. Fraleigh, Warren. (1984). *Right Actions in Sport.* Champaign, IL: Human Kinetics. **T**

816. Franke, E. (1973). Sporting action and its interpretation. In Ommo Grupe, Dietrich Kurz, & Johannes Teipel (Eds.), *Sport in the Modern World —Chances and Problems.* New York: Springer-Verlag. **T**

817. Freischlag, J., & Freischlag, T. (1993, Mar.). Selected psycho-social, physical, and technical factors among rock climbers: A test of the flow paradigm. *Applied Research in Coaching and Athletics Annual,* 109–22. **I**

818. Fromm, Erika, & Shor, Ronald E. (Eds.). (1979). *Hypnosis: Devel-*

opment in Research and New Perspectives (rev. 2nd ed.). New York: Aldine. **A**

819. Furlong, William. (1979, May). Coping: The power of imagination. *Quest, 27*: 95–96. **P**

820. Gabbard, Glen O., & Twemlow, Stuart W. (1984). *With the Eyes of the Mind: An Empirical Analysis of Out-of-Body States.* New York: Praeger. **E**

821. Gabriel, Trip. (1984). The eminently practical Robby Naish. *Outside, 9*(8): 32–37, 63–65. **B**

822. Galvin, Richard F. (1985). Aesthetic incontinence in sport. In David L. Vanderwerken & Spencer K. Wertz (Eds.), *Sport Inside Out: Readings in Literature and Philosophy* (pp. 519–24). Fort Worth, TX: Texas Christian University Press. **T**

823. Garfield, Charles A. (1985). Peak performance: Do limits really exist? *Women's Sport and Fitness, 7*(8): 60–61. **G**

824. Garfield, Charles A. (1986). *Peak Performers.* New York: William Morrow. **G**

825. Garfield, Charles A., & Bennett, Hal Z. (1984). *Peak Performance: Mental Training Techniques of the World's Greatest Athletes.* New York: Warner Books. **G**
Garfield interviewed athletes who described their peak performances as being characterized by physical and mental relaxation, confidence, high energy and awareness, being in control and focused in the present moment.

826. Garrett, Roland. (1985). The metaphysics of baseball. In David L. Vanderwerken & Spencer K. Wertz (Eds.), *Sport Inside Out: Readings in Literature and Philosophy* (pp. 643–63). Fort Worth, TX: Texas Christian University Press. **T**
Offers a social and metaphysical view of baseball.

827. Gaucon, E. F. (1985). Peak performance: Peak performance means getting it all together. *Wrestling USA, 21*(4): 6, 11–14. **G**

828. Gauron, E. (1984). *Mental Training for Peak Performance.* Lansing, NY: Sport Science Associates. **G**

829. Geertz, Clifford. (1972). Deep play: Notes on the Balinese cock fight. *Daedalus, 101*: 1–37. **I**

830. Gendlin, Eugene T. (1973). Experiential psychotherapy. In R. Corsini (Ed.), *Current Psychotherapies.* Itasca, IL: Peacock. **P**

831. George, T. R. (1989). *Mental Preparation Strategies and Peak Performance Among Intercollegiate Baseball Players: An Exploratory Study.* Unpublished master's thesis, Miami University, Oxford, OH. **I**
George interviewed ten college baseball players who characterized themselves in peak moments as mentally prepared, highly aware, in control, confident, focused, and time/space disoriented.

832. Gerber, Ellen W. (1967, May). Identity, relation and sport. *Quest, 8*: 90–97. **P**

833. Gerber, Ellen W. (1972a). Arguments on the reality of sport. In Ellen W. Gerber (Ed.), *Sport and the Body: A Philosophical Symposium* (pp. 68–69). Philadelphia: Lea & Febiger. **T**

834. Gerber, Ellen W. (1972b). Commitment to self. In D. J. Allen &

B. W. Fahey (Eds.), *Being Human in Sport*. Philadelphia: Lea & Febiger. I

835. Gerber, Rudolph J. (1964). Marcel's phenomenology of the human body. *International Philosophical Quarterly, 4:* 443–63. I

836. Giddens, Anthony. (1964, Mar.). Notes on the concept of play and leisure. *Sociological Review, 12:* 73–89. I

837. Gill, D. L.; Gross, J. B.; & Huddleston, S. (1983). Participation motivation in youth sports. *International Journal of Sport Psychology, 14:* 1–14. P

838. Glassford, R. Gerald. (1987). Methodological reconsiderations: The shifting paradigms. *Quest, 39:* 295–312. T
Compares research methods of the positivist/behaviorist paradigm and those of interpretivism or antipositivism.

839. Glisson, Charles A. (1973). Abraham Maslow's theory of self-actualization applied to the sensitivity training group. *Group Psychotherapy and Psychodrama, 26:* 77–87. G
Presents potential links between Maslow's peak experience, self-actualization, and sensitivity groups that may be applicable to team sports.

840. Goldstein, Jeffrey H. (1979a). Outcomes in professional team sports: Chance, skill, and situational factors. In Jeffrey H. Goldstein (Ed.), *Sports, Games and Play: Social and Psychological Viewpoints* (pp. 401–08). Hillsdale, NJ: Erlbaum Associates. T
Proposes that the outcome of team sports, especially professional ones, "may be based on chance and situational variables" (p. 407). But if this lessens the interest of participants in winning, it should also facilitate "a corresponding increase in the intrinsic motivations and satisfactions inherent in sports" (p. 407).

841. Goldstein, Jeffrey H. (Ed.). (1979b). *Sports, Games and Play: Social and Psychological Viewpoints*. Hillsdale, NJ: Erlbaum Associates. P

842. Goldstein, Jeffrey H. (1985). Athletic performance and spectator behavior: The humanistic concerns of sports psychology. In Wiley Lee Umphlett (Ed.), *American Sport Culture: The Humanistic Dimensions* (pp. 159–79). Lewisburg, PA: Bucknell University Press. P

843. Gontang, A.; Clitsome, T.; & Kostrubala, Theodore. (1977). A psychological study of fifty sub-three-hour marathoners. *Annals of the New York Academy of Sciences, 301:* 1020–28. P

844. Gould, Daniel. (1993). Goal setting for peak performance. In J. M. Williams (Ed.), *Applied Sport Psychology: Personal Growth to Peak Performance* (2nd ed., pp. 158–69). Palo Alto, CA: Mayfield. G

845. Gould, Daniel; Eklund, Robert C.; & Jackson, Susan A. (1992a). 1988 U.S. Olympic wrestling excellence: I. Mental preparation, precompetitive cognition, and affect. *Sport Psychologist, 6:* 358–82. P

846. Gould, Daniel; Eklund, Robert C.; & Jackson, Susan A. (1992b). 1988 U.S. Olympic wrestling excellence: II. Thoughts and affect occurring during competition. *Sport Psychologist, 6*(4): 383–402. P

847. Gould, Daniel; Eklund, Robert C.; & Jackson, Susan A. (1993). Coping strategies used by more versus less successful U.S. Olympic wrestlers. *Research Quarterly for Exercise and Sport, 64:* 83–93. P
Report of in-depth interviews with all twenty members of the 1988 U.S.

Olympic wrestling team in regard to their coping with stress at the Seoul Olympics.

848. Gould, Daniel; Feltz, D.; & Weiss, M. (1985). Motives for participating in competitive youth swimming. *International Journal of Sport Psychology, 16:* 126–40. **P**

849. Gould, Daniel; Finch, Laura M.; & Jackson, Susan A. (1993a, Sep./Oct.). Coaching national champions: A skater's perspective. *Professional Skater Magazine,* 32–33. **P**

850. Gould, Daniel; Finch, Laura M.; & Jackson, Susan A. (1993b). Coping strategies used by national champion figure skaters. *Research Quarterly for Exercise and Sport, 64:* 453–68. **P**

The authors investigated seventeen of twenty senior U.S. National champion figure skaters 1985–1990 to identify and describe their coping strategies and examine the relationship between these strategies and specific sources of stress.

851. Gould, Daniel; Hodge, Ken; Peterson, Kirsten; Giannini, John. (1989). An exploratory examination of strategies used by elite coaches to enhance self-efficacy in athletes. *Journal of Sport & Exercise Psychology, 11:* 128–40. **P**

852. Gould, Daniel, & Horn, T. (1984). Participation motivation in youth sports. In John M. Silva & R. S. Weinberg (Eds.), *Psychological Foundations of Sport* (pp. 359–70). Champaign, IL: Human Kinetics. **P**

853. Gould, Daniel; Jackson, Susan A.; & Finch, Laura M. (1993). Life at the top: The experiences of U.S. national champion figure skaters. *Sport Psychologist, 7:* 354–74. **P**

854. Gould, Daniel; Jackson, Susan A.; & Finch, Laura M. (1993). Sources of stress in national champion figure skaters. *Journal of Sport and Exercise Psychology, 15:* 134–59. **P**

855. Gould, Daniel; Weiss, M.; & Weinberg, R. S. (1981). Psychological characteristics of successful and nonsuccessful Big Ten wrestlers. *Journal of Sport Psychology, 3:* 69–81. **P**

856. Graves, H. (1900, Dec.). A philosophy of sport. *Contemporary Review, 78:* 877–93. **T**

857. Gray, Miriam. (1966, Dec.). The physical educator as artist. *Quest, 7:* 18–24. **T**

858. Greenwald, H. (1968). Play and self-development. In Herbert Otto & John Mann (Eds.), *Ways of Growth: Approaches to Expanding Awareness* (pp. 16–24). New York: Simon & Schuster. **T**

859. Greist, John H.; Klein, M. H.; Eischens, Roger R.; Faris, J.; Gorman, A. S.; & Morgan, William P. (1978). Running through your mind. *Journal of Psychosomatic Research, 22:* 259–94. **G**

860. Gretzky, Wayne, with Reilly, Rick. (1990). *Gretzky: An Autobiography.* New York: HarperCollins. **B**

861. Groos, Karl. (1901). *The Play of Man.* New York: D. Appleton. **T**

862. Gross, Albert C. (1986). *Endurance: The Events, the Athlete, the Attitude.* New York: Dodd, Mead. **P**

863. Grout, William. (1981, Sep.). How skiing changed her life. *Skiing, 34*(1): 33. **B**

Reproduces letter from Susan Olney, who tells how she was empowered by skiing to apply for law school and how she has applied lessons learned in skiing to her school assignments and life activities.

864. Gruneau, Richard. (1980). Freedom and constraint: The paradoxes of play, games and sports. *Journal of Sport History, 7:* 68–86. T

865. Guba, E. (1981). Criteria for assessing the trustworthiness of naturalistic inquiries. *Educational Communications and Technology, 29:* 75–81. T

866. Gulick, Luther Halsey. (1899). Psychological, pedagogical, and religious aspects of group games. *Pedagogical Seminary* (now *Journal of Genetic Psychology*), *6:* 135–51. P

867. Gulick, Luther Halsey. (1920). *A Philosophy of Play.* New York: Scribner's. T

868. Gunter, B. G. (1987). The leisure experience: Selected properties. *Journal of Leisure Research, 19*(2): 115–30. T

869. Guttmann, Allen. (1978). *From Ritual to Record: The Nature of Modern Sport.* New York: Columbia University Press. T

870. Guttmann, Allen. (1981). Introduction. In B. Rigauer (Ed.), *Sport and Work.* New York: Columbia University Press. G

Writes of the "exhilaration and joy of self-realization" that are significant and important aspects of sport.

871. Guttmann, Allen. (1985). The sacred and the secular. In David L. Vanderwerken & Spencer K. Wertz (Eds.), *Sport Inside Out: Readings in Literature and Philosophy* (pp. 298–308). Fort Worth, TX: Texas Christian University Press. G

872. Hall, M. A. (1985). Knowledge and gender: Epistemological questions in the social analysis of sport. *Sociology of Sport Journal, 2:* 25–42. T

873. Hammer, W. M., & Wilmore, J. H. (1973). An exploratory investigation in personality measures and physiological alterations during a ten-week jogging program. *Journal of Sports Medicine and Physical Fitness, 13:* 231–37. P

874. Hanna, Thomas. (1973). The project of somatology. *Journal of Humanistic Psychology, 13*(3): 3–14. T

875. Hans, James S. (1980). Hermeneutics, play, deconstruction. *Philosophy Today, 24:* 299–317. T

876. Hardy, Lew, & Nelson, Dave. (1988). Self-regulation training in sport and work. *Ergonomics, 31:* 1573–78. P

Describes "the state of the art of self-control or self-regulation training procedures as they are used in sport, including goal setting, activation control, imagery, and attention control" (p. 1573).

877. Harper, F. D. (1979). *Jogotherapy: Jogging as a Therapeutic Strategy.* Alexandria, VA: Douglass. P

878. Harper, William A. (1982). The philosopher in us. *Journal of Physical Education, Recreation and Dance.* In David L. Vanderwerken & Spencer K. Wertz (Eds.), *Sport Inside Out: Readings in Literature and Philosophy* (pp. 449–54). Fort Worth, TX: Texas Christian University Press, 1985. T

879. Harper, William A. (1983, Spr.). On playing sport. *Physical Education Review, 6:* 52–57. T

880. Harper, William. (1986). Freedom in the experience of leisure. *Leisure Sciences, 8*(2): 115–30. T

881. Harris, Dorothy V. (1980). On the brink of catastrophe. In Richard M. Suinn (Ed.), *Psychology in Sports: Methods and Applications* (pp. 112–18). Minneapolis: Burgess. P

Isolates *eustress-seeking* as a common factor in sport motivation or any adventurous activity. Eustress means "pleasant stress" (as opposed to unpleasant or "dys-stress"). Suggests that "eustress may be a factor in physical activity that 'turns on' many individuals" (p. 113). Describes the characteristics of eustress, the factors that influence eustress-seeking, and supporting theories. Notes that "sports and participation in physical activity appear to serve as one of the few socially accepted avenues left for eustress seeking," unlike drugs, crime, and violence. "The problem is one of channeling and providing suitable modes of expression, not suppressing . . . eustress-seeking" (p. 117).

882. Harris, Dorothy V. (1982). Maximizing athletic potential: Integrating body and mind. *Journal of Physical Education, Recreation, and Dance, 53*(3): 31–33. P

On the need for coaches to prepare athletes mentally.

883. Harris, Dorothy V., & Harris, B. L. (1984). *The Athlete's Guide to Sports Psychology: Mental Skills for Physical People.* West Point, NY: Leisure Press. P

884. Harris, Janet C. (1981). Hermeneutics, interpretive cultural research, and the study of sports. *Quest, 33:* 72–86. P

Emphasizes the need to "learn about the meanings of sports for those who are involved with them" (p. 85).

885. Harris, Janet C. (1983). Broadening horizons: Interpretive cultural research, hermeneutics, and scholarly inquiry in physical education. *Quest, 35:* 82–96. T

886. Harris, Janet C. (1987). Social contests, scholarly inquiry, and physical education. *Quest, 39:* 282–94. T

Calls for the investigation of sport and exercise within the social contexts in which they are most often embedded—health, leisure, and education. Sociocultural researchers are the ones best suited for this task.

887. Harris, M. B. (1981a). Runners' perceptions of the benefits of running. *Perceptual and Motor Skills, 52:* 153–54. I

888. Harris, M. B. (1981b). Women runners' views of running. *Perceptual and Motor Skills, 53:* 395–402. I

889. Hart, M. (1972). *Sport in the Sociocultural Process.* Dubuque, IA: William C. Brown. T

890. Harter, S. (1981). The development of competence motivation in the mastery of cognitive and physical skills: Is there still a place for joy? In Glyn C. Roberts & D. M. Landers (Eds.), *Psychology of Motor Behavior and Sport—1980* (pp. 3–29). Champaign, IL: Human Kinetics. G

891. Hatfield, Brad D. (1991). Exercise and mental health: The mechanisms of exercise-induced psychological states. In Louis Diamant (Ed.), *Psychology of Sports, Exercise, and Fitness: Social and Personal Issues* (pp. 17–50). New York: Hemisphere. P

892. Haverland, Lillian Edith Hite. (1953). *The Effects of Relaxation Training on Certain Aspects of Motor Skill.* Unpublished doctoral dissertation, University of Illinois. **P**

893. Healy, John William. (1977). *Art and Sport: A Comparison.* Unpublished doctoral dissertation, Columbia University Teachers College. **T**

894. Heaps, R. A. (1978). Relating physical and psychological fitness: A psychological point of view. *Journal of Sports Medicine, 18:* 399–408. **P**

895. Hearn, Francis. (1976–77). Toward a critical theory of play. *Telos, 40:* 145–60. **T**

896. Heckler, Richard S. (Ed.). (1985). *Aikido and the New Warrior.* Berkeley, CA: North Atlantic Books. **M**
Anthology of eighteen pieces on the application of the principles of aikido to psychology, health, education, law enforcement, business, and sports (a chapter each on baseball and basketball). There are two chapters by the founder of aikido, Morihei Uyeshiba, who taught that in life and in sport the opponent is within ourselves, so "we must first work within our own minds and bodies instead of trying to correct others" (p. 112).

897. Hein, Hilde. (1968, Fall). Play as an aesthetic concept. *Journal of Aesthetics, 27:* 67–71. Also *Humanitas,* 1969 (Spr.), *5:* 21–29. **T**

898. Hein, Hilde. (1970, Spr.). Performances as an aesthetic category. *Journal of Aesthetics and Art Criticism, 28:* 381–86. **C**

899. Hekman, Susan. (1984). Action as a text: Gadamer's hermeneutics and the social scientific analysis of action. *Journal for the Theory of Social Behaviour, 14:* 333–54. **T**

900. Hendricks, Gay, & Carlson, J. (1982). *The Centered Athlete.* Englewood Cliffs, NJ: Prentice-Hall. **G**

901. Henning, Joel. (1978). *Holistic Running: Beyond the Threshold of Fitness.* New York: New American Library. **I**
Contains some lyrical descriptions of runner's high and how it alters one's conception of the self.

902. Herman, Daniel J. (1975). Mechanism and the athlete. *Journal of the Philosophy of Sport, 2:* 102–10. **T**

903. Heyman, S. R. (1982). Comparisons of successful and unsuccessful competitors: A reconsideration of methodological questions and data. *Journal of Sport Psychology, 4:* 295–300. **P**

904. Higgs, Robert J. (1983, Fall). Muscular Christianity, holy play, and spiritual exercises: Confusion about Christian sports and religion. *Arete: The Journal of Sport Literature, 1:* [pages unknown]. **T**

905. Higgs, Robert J., & Isaacs, Neil D. (Eds.). (1977). *The Sporting Spirit: Athletes in Literature and Life.* New York: Harcourt Brace Jovanovich. **G**

906. High risk, high thrill fitness: These exercises work on your brain as well as your body. (1994, Apr.). *Mademoiselle,* 182–84. **G**

907. Highlen, P. S., & Bennett, B. B. (1979). Psychological characteristics of successful and nonsuccessful elite wrestlers: An exploratory study. *Journal of Sport Psychology, 1:* 123–37. **P**

908. Highlen, P. S., & Bennett, B. B. (1983). Elite divers and wrestlers: A comparison between open- and closed-skill athletes. *Journal of Sport Psychology, 5:* 390–409. **P**

909. Hinman, Lawrence M. (1974, Sum.). Nietzsche's philosophy of play. *Philosophy Today, 18:* 106–24. T

910. Hinman, Lawrence M. (1975). On work and play: Overcoming a dichotomy. *Man and World, 8:* 327–46. T

911. Hissinson, T. W. (1984). Saints and their bodies. In Steven A. Riess (Ed.), *The American Sporting Experience: A Historical Anthology of Sport in America.* West Point, NY: Leisure Press. G

912. Hoffman, Edward. (1992). *Visions of Innocence.* Boston: Shambhala. G

913. Hoffman, Shirl J. (1986a, Apr. 4). The sanctification of sport: Can the mind of Christ coexist with the killer instinct? *Christianity Today, 30:* 17–21. T

914. Hoffman, Shirl J. (1986b, Apr. 4). The stadium as cathedral. *Christianity Today, 30:* 19. T

914a. Hoffman, Shirl J. (Ed.). (1992). *Sport and Religion.* Champaign, IL: Human Kinetics. T

Anthology of twenty-five previously published articles and chapters (several listed separately in this bibliography) on the relationship between religion and sport in America. There are four parts, each with a full introduction. They cover Sport as Religion; Sport as Religious Experience; Religion in Sport; and Sport, Religion, and Ethics.

915. Hohler, V. (1974). The beauty of motion. In H. T. A. Whiting & Don W. Masterson (Eds.), *Readings in the Aesthetics of Sport.* London: Lepus Books. C

916. Holbrook, Leona. (1963, Dec.). A teleological concept of the physical qualities of man. *Quest, 1:* 13–17. T

917. Hollands, Robert G. (1984). The role of cultural studies and social criticism in the sociological study of sport. *Quest, 36:* 66–79. T

918. Holtzworth, John. (1980). Peak performance and flow: "Being on." *Handball, 30*(6): 40–43. I

Describes the flow experience in handball and presents several sensory awareness exercises to increase its likelihood. Proposes that "sensory awareness is a means to finer muscular control, as well as increased flow opportunities because the player's senses, perceptions, and action become totally immersed in the game" (p. 41).

919. Hood, Ralph W. Jr. (1975). Construction and preliminary validation of a measure of reported mystical experiences. *Journal for the Scientific Study of Religion, 14:* 29–41. G

919a. Horn, Thelma S. (Ed.). (1992). *Advances in Sport Psychology.* Champaign, IL: Human Kinetics. P

Up-to-date review of the major issues in sport psychology.

920. Horne, Herman H. (1910, Jun.). The principle underlying modern physical education. *American Physical Education Review, 15:* 433–39. T

The "principle" is mind/body unity.

921. Howley, E. T. (1967). *Study of the Second Wind Phenomenon.* Unpublished master's thesis, University of Wisconsin. P

922. Huelster, L. (1965). The body of knowledge in physical education—philosophical. *Physical Educator, 22:* 6–8. T

923. Humphrey, N. R., & Ruhling, R. O. (1975). Second wind—trying to catch it in the lab. *Physician and Sports Medicine, 3*(5): 74–76. P

924. Hussey, Christopher. (1929). *R. Tait McKenzie: A Sculptor of Youth.* London: Country Life. G

925. Hutslar, Jack. (1981). This thing that we do: A model for sport and dance. *Quest, 33:* 87–95. T

926. Hyland, Drew A. (1972). Athletic angst: Reflections on the philosophical relevance of play. In Ellen W. Gerber (Ed.), *Sport and the Body: A Philosophical Symposium* (2nd ed.; pp. 87–94). Philadelphia, PA: Lea & Febiger. T

927. Hyland, Drew A. (1974). Modes of inquiry in sport, athletics, and play. *Journal of the Philosophy of Sport, 1:* 123–28. T

928. Hyland, Drew A. (1977). "And that is the best part of us": Human being and play. *Journal of the Philosophy of Sport, 4:* 36–49. T
Views play existentially as a mode of being in the world, after a quotation from Plato. He views play "as a stance or orientation" that humans take, upon occasion, toward the world and other humans.

929. Hyland, Drew A. (1980, Fall). The stance of play. *Journal of the Philosophy of Sport, 7:* 87–99. T
Clarifies the "stance" of play, which involves an openness to the environment not usually present in nonplay situations and a responsiveness to the possibilities such openness elicits. It is precisely this "responsive openness" that results in the "well-known experience of immersion. . . . of being totally involved in an activity" (p. 90). Also discusses the play properties of finitude, value, and fun, adding that these are not peculiar to play but are present in nonplay activities. Stresses that one of the values of play is that certain issues and themes, present but often hidden in everyday life, are brought forth to a central position, "which they should perhaps have for us always" (p. 98).

930. Hyland, Drew A. (1984a). Opponents, contestants, and competitors: The dialectic of sport. *Journal of the Philosophy of Sport, 11:* 63–70. T

931. Hyland, Drew A. (1984b). *The Question of Play.* Lanham, MD: University Press of America. T
On responsiveness in play and the kinship between philosophy and play.

932. Ingham, A. (1978). Dance and sport. *International Journal of Sport Sociology, 13:* 85–97. P

933. Ingham, A. (1979). Methodology in the sociology of sport: From symptoms of malaise to Weber for a cure. *Quest, 31:* 187–215. T

934. Ingham, Alan G., & Loy, John W., Jr. (1973). The social system of sport: A humanist perspective. *Quest, 19:* 3–23. T

935. Ingham, Alan G., & Loy, John W. (Eds.). (1993). *Sport in Social Development: Traditions, Transitions, & Transformations.* Springfield, IL: Charles C Thomas. T

936. Ingram, Anne. (1973, Feb.). Art and sport. *Journal of Health, Physical Education and Recreation, 44:* 24–27. G

937. International Center for Aquatic Research. (1991). Peak performance in elite swimmers: Case study analysis. In John D. Troup (Ed.), *International Center for Aquatic Research Annual: Studies by the International Center for*

Aquatic Research 1990–91 (pp. 163–69). Colorado Springs, CO: United States Swimming Press. **P**
   Report that elite swimmers believe the following factors contributed to their success: high self-confidence, self-controlled arousal, holistic mind set, high concentration, and belief in previous training.
   938. Irwin, Harvey J. (1985). *Flight of Mind: A Psychological Study of Out-of-Body Experience.* Metuchen, NJ: Scarecrow Press. **E**
   939. Ismail, A. H., & Young, R. J. (1977). Effect of chronic exercise on the personality of adults. *Annals of the New York Academy of Sciences, 301:* 958–69. **P**
   940. Iso-Ahola, Seppo E., & Mobily, Ken. (1980). "Psychological momentum": A phenomenon and an empirical (unobtrusive) validation of its influence in a competitive sport tournament. *Psychological Reports, 46:* 391–401. **P**
   Report of a field study of the psychological edge in sports.
   941. Izzard, R. (1954). *The Innocent on Everest.* London: Hodder. **I**
   942. Jackson, Susan A. (1988). *Positive Performance States of Athletes: Toward a Conceptual Understanding of Peak Performance.* Unpublished master's thesis, University of Illinois, Champaign. **G**
   943. Jackson, Susan A. (1992). Athletes in flow: A qualitative investigation of flow states in elite figure skaters. *Journal of Applied Sport Psychology, 4:* 161–80. **P**
   A pioneer study of flow states in sixteen former U.S. National champion figure skaters (1985–1990) during an optimal skating experience, using an interpretive qualitative approach with in-depth interviews and inductive analyses. The report also provides a good overview of qualitative methodology in sport. Illustrative quotations from the interviews with the (unidentified) athletes are presented. Suggestions are made for future research.
   944. Jackson, Susan A. (1992). *Elite Athletes in Flow: The Psychology of Optimal Sport Experience.* Unpublished doctoral dissertation, University of North Carolina, Greensboro. **G**
   945. Jackson, Susan A. (1993). Understanding flow state and factors influencing the occurrence of flow in elite athletes. *ASASP Newsletter, 8(2):* 25–27. **P**
   946. Jackson, Susan A., & Roberts, Glyn C. (1992). Positive performance states of athletes: Toward a conceptual understanding of peak performance. *Sport Psychologist, 6:* 156–71. **P**
   947. Jacobs, L. W. (1980). *Running as an Addiction Process.* Unpublished doctoral dissertation, University of Alberta, Canada. **I**
   948. Jacobson, E. (1967). *Biology of Emotions.* Springfield, IL: Charles C Thomas. **P**
   949. James, C. L. R. (1974). The relationship between popular sport and fine art. In H. T. A. Whiting & Don W. Masterson (Eds.), *Readings in the Aesthetics of Sport.* London: Lepus Books. **C**
   950. Jasnoski, M. L., & Holmes, D. S. (1981). Influence of initial aerobic fitness, aerobic training and changes in aerobic fitness on personality function. *Journal of Psychosomatic Research, 25:* 553–56. **P**
   951. Jaspers, Karl. (1957). Sport. In *Man in the Modern Age* (pp. 68–71). Garden City, NY: Doubleday. (Original work published 1930) **T**

Sport offers modern people a means of keeping fit bodies, a way of "soaring upward in vital courage," and a means of overcoming the danger of losing the sense of self. "Through bodily activities subjected to the control of the will, energy and courage are sustained, and the individual seeking control with nature draws nearer to the elemental force of the universe" (p. 68).

952. Jaynes, Julian. (1976). *The Origin of Consciousness in the Breakdown of the Bicameral Mind*. Boston: Houghton Mifflin. T

953. Jerome, John. (1978). *On Mountains*. New York: Harcourt Brace Jovanovich. G

On "heights" within and without associated with mountain climbing and skiing.

954. Jerome, John. (1980a). *The Sweet Spot in Time*. New York: Summit Books. G

Motivated by "the haunting power I felt on that occasional throw [in youth] when I knew as the stone left my hand that it was going to hit its target" (p. 14), Jerome presents a biomechanical theory to account for it, which he calls "The Sweet Spot Theory of (Sports) Performance." Jerome also theorizes that athletes—and magicians—have more room in time than most people, in part because they can find the right rhythm within themselves. He concentrates on those sports that people engage in "for the sheer pleasure of the act" (p. 25). He proposes that deliberately stretching a particular muscle can be "therapeutic, relaxing, and restorative," almost yogalike (p. 303). He eschews mystical explanations: For him the experience of his own muscle fibers, "the athletic process, the miracle of use, is wondrous in itself." He celebrates the "capacity of the cell to flout the laws of entropy: to steal energy out of stress, and with it to construct new health" (p. 332).

955. Jerome, John. (1980b, Oct.). The sweet spot in time. *Playboy, 27*: 137–38, 156, 217–22. G

Proposes that humans engage in play, competitively and noncompetitively, for "the sheer pleasure of the act" and "a momentary healing of the mind-body split" (p. 218).

956. Jerome, John. (1984). *Staying With It*. New York: Viking. P

Recounts his first-person study of the "training effect," when at forty-seven he decided to become an athlete, hoping that in learning more about his own exercise physiology he would retard the effects of aging. He logs various changes, physiological and psychological, as he progressed, using swimming as his main exercise. He became conscious of his kinesthetic sense, and recognized that it was the "organizing principle of childhood" (p. 122). Training leads to "new states of mind, new modes of concentration" (p. 129), but one has to keep increasing the *discomfort* to keep on growing. He took up Masters swimming, and at fifty placed in the top ten of his age group. He realized that peak performance, whether in the "click" of an idea or a personal best, is the same—"seeing a new potential, which is the best antidote to aging there is" (p. 223).

957. Jeu, Bernard. (1972). What is sport? *Diogenes, 80*: 150–63. T

958. Johns, David. (1985). Body awareness and the gymnastic movement. *Phenomenology and Pedagogy, 3*: 116–25. P

959. Johnson, Earvin "Magic," Jr., & Johnson, Roy S. (1989). *Magic's Touch*. Reading, MA: Addison-Wesley. **B**

960. Johnson, William (1972, Jul. 17). After the golden moment. *Sports Illustrated, 37:* 28–41. **B**
Follow-up on some Olympic champions.

961. Jokl, Ernst. (1974). Art and sport. In H. T. A. Whiting & Don W. Masterson (Eds.), *Readings in the Aesthetics of Sport*. London: Lepus Books. **C**

962. Jokl, Ernst. (1977). Running, psychology, and culture. *Annals of the New York Academy of Sciences, 301:* 970–1001. **T**

963. Jokl, Ernst. (1983). Brain, mind and movement. In H. Lenk (Ed.), *Topical Problems of Sport Philosophy*. Koln: Bundesinstitut für Sports Wissenschaft. **T**

964. Jones, J. M., & Williamson, S. A. (1976). A model of athletes' attitudes toward sports performance. *International Journal of Sport Psychology,* 7(2): 82–106. **P**

965. Kaelin, Eugene F. (1972). Being in the body. In Ellen W. Gerber (Ed.), *Sport and the Body: A Philosophical Symposium* (pp. 165–74). Philadelphia, PA: Lea & Febiger. **C**
On transcendence and creativity in movement.

966. Kahn, Roger. (1957, Sum.). Intellectuals and ballplayers. *American Scholar, 26:* 342–49. **T**

967. Kaplan, Max. (1960). Games and sport as leisure. In *Leisure in America: A Social Inquiry*. New York: Wiley. **T**

968. Kapreliam, Mary Haberkorn. (1969). *A Comparison of Two Aesthetic Theories as They Apply to Modern Dance*. Unpublished doctoral dissertation, University of Wisconsin. **T**

969. Keenan, Francis W. (1973). The athletic contest as a "tragic" form of art. In Robert G. Osterhoudt (Ed.), *The Philosophy of Sport: A Collection of Original Essays* (pp. 309–26). Springfield, IL: Charles C Thomas. **T**
Points out why athletic contests are potentially dramatic and shows how sports are like the arts, with the emphasis on the process rather than a quantitative result.

970. Keleman, Stanley. (1972). The body is all. In J. B. Grant & R. Welch (Eds.), *The Geocentric Experience*. Los Gatos, CA: Lamplighters Roadway Press. **T**

971. Kellar, Hans. (1974). Sports and art—The concept of mastery. In H. T. A. Whiting & Don W. Masterson (Eds.), *Readings in the Aesthetics of Sport*. London: Lepus Books. **T**

972. Kelly, Darlene Alice. (1970). *Phenomena of the Self-Experienced Body*. Unpublished doctoral dissertation, University of Southern California. **T**

973. Kent, Norman. (1968, Mar.). Art in sports. *American Artist, 32:* 45–47, 55. **G**

974. Kenyon, Gerald S. (1969). Sport involvement: A conceptual go and some consequences thereof. In Gerald S. Kenyon (Ed.), *Aspects of Contemporary Sport Sociology* (pp. 77–84). Proceedings of C.I.C. Symposium on the Sociology of Sport. Chicago: The Athletic Institute. **T**

975. Kenyon, Gerald S., & Loy, John W. (1965, May). Toward a sociology of sport. *Journal of Health, Physical Education, and Recreation, 36:* 24–25, 68–69. T

976. Kenyon, Gerald S., & Loy, John W. (1969). Toward a sociology of sport. In John W. Loy & Gerald S. Kenyon (Eds.), *Sport, Culture and Society* (pp. 36–43). Toronto: Macmillan. T

977. Kew, F. C. (1978). Values in competitive games. *Quest, 29:* 103–12. T

978. Keyes, Ralph. (1985). *Chancing It: Why We Take Risks.* Boston: Little, Brown. T

979. Kimiecik, Jay C., & Stein, Gary L. (1992). Examining flow experiences in sports contexts: Conceptual issues and methodological concerns. *Journal of Applied Sport Psychology, 4:* 144–60. G

The authors address the nature of flow, how flow states occur, and the pros and cons of conducting qualitative and quantitative research on athletic flow experience.

980. King, J. R. (1986). The moment as a factor in emotional well-being. *Journal of Religion and Health, 25:* 207–20. G

Explores the value of momentary experience in various human endeavors, including sports. They are characterized by a heightened sense of presentness and are often associated with "kinetic experiences in sports."

981. Kirk, D. (1986). The aesthetic experience in sport. *Journal of Human Movement Studies, 12:* 99–111. G

982. Klausner, Samuel Z. (Ed.). (1968). *Why Man Takes Chances.* New York: Anchor. T

983. Klavetter, Robert E., & Mogar, Robert E. (1967). Peak experiences: Investigation of their relationship to psychedelic therapy and self-actualization. *Journal of Humanistic Psychology, 7:* 171–77. G

The authors administered Peak Experience/Self-Actualization scales to seventy-seven males and forty-two females who had participated in a fourteen-month LSD program to test whether peakers would experience increased self-actualization following LSD whereas nonpeakers would not. This hypothesis was confirmed. This study is cited for theoretical and research reasons. First, the authors view peak experiences not as discrete events but in the experiencer's life context. They describe peakness *as a process variable.* Their Peak Experience/Self-Actualization Scales are given in Tables I and II.

984. Kleiber, Douglas A., & Fiscella, Joan. (1982). Leisure as interlude. *Journal of Physical Education, Recreation and Dance, 53*(7): 46. T

985. Kleinman, Seymour. (1964). The significance of human movement: A phenomenological approach. In National Association for Physical Education of College Women, *Report of the Ruby Anniversary Workshop.* Interlochen, MI. T

986. Kleinman, Seymour. (1968). Toward a non-theory of sport. *Quest, 10:* 29–34. T

987. Kleinman, Seymour. (1972). The significance of human movement: A phenomenological approach. In Ellen W. Gerber (Ed.), *Sport and the Body: A Philosophical Symposium* (pp. 175–78). Philadelphia, PA: Lea & Febiger. T

988. Kleinman, Seymour. (1973, Jan.). Is sport experience? (Part IV of "Sport: Whose bag?"). *Quest, 19:* 93–96. T

989. Kleinman, Seymour. (1977). Effort/shape: Heightening aesthetic awareness of the self and the other. *Proceedings of the National College Physical Education Association for Men/National Association for Physical Education of College Women National Conference,* Orlando, Florida, Jan. 6–9, 1977. T

990. Kleinman, Seymour. (1980). Art, sport, and intention. *National Association for Physical Education in Higher Education Proceedings.* Champaign, IL: Human Kinetics. T

991. Kleinman, Seymour. (1986). *Mind and Body: East Meets West.* Champaign, IL: Human Kinetics. T

992. Klint, K. A., & Weiss, M. R. (1986). Dropping in and dropping out: Participation motives of current and former youth gymnasts. *Canadian Journal of Applied Sport Sciences, 11:* 106–14. P

993. Klint, K. A., & Weiss, M. R. (1987). Perceived competence and motives for participating in youth sports: A test of Harter's competence motivation theory. *Journal of Sport Psychology, 9:* 55–65. P

994. Knowlton, E. E. (1968). *Study to Determine the Location of Peak Performance Data for College Women in Three Measures of All-Out Performances.* Unpublished doctoral dissertation, University of Wisconsin. P

995. Koizumi, Tetsunori. (1986). The importance of being stationary: Zen, relativity, and the aesthetics of no-action. In Seymour Kleinman (Ed.), *Mind and Body: East Meets West.* Champaign, IL: Human Kinetics. T

996. Koppett, Leonard. (1981). *Sports Illusion, Sports Reality.* Boston, MA: Houghton Mifflin. T

997. Kosiewicz, J. (1984, Win.). Physical activity and human well-being. *Dialectics and Humanism, 11:* 175–78. T

998. Kostrubala, Thaddeus. (1974). Running and therapy. In Michael L. Sachs & Gary W. Buffone (Eds.), *Running Therapy: An Integrated Approach* (pp. 112–24). Lincoln: University of Nebraska Press. P
Psychiatrist Kostrubala contrasts "the couch, the chair, and running as therapeutic tools" (p. 113). Using running as a tool, he observed "the apparently spontaneous appearance of transcendent belief systems," which is often an indication that therapy is approaching completion. Two cases of running therapy are described. Although running is seen as only one of many tools used in psychotherapy, he raises the possibility that it may change psychotherapy as such and the therapist as well.

999. Kostrubala, Thaddeus. (1978). The training of a running therapist. *Medicine and Sport, 12:* 111–15. P

1000. Kostrubala, Thaddeus. (1981). Running: The grand delusion. In Michael H. Sacks & Michael L. Sachs (Eds.), *Psychology of Running.* Champaign, IL: Human Kinetics. P

1001. Kovich, Maureen. (1971, Oct.). Sport as an art form. *Journal of Health, Physical Education, and Recreation, 42:* 42. T

1002. Krell, David Farrell. (1972). Towards an ontology of play. *Research in Phenomenology, 2:* 63–93. T

1003. Kretchmar, R. Scott. (1971). *A Phenomenological Analysis of the Other in Sport.* Unpublished doctoral dissertation, University of Southern California. T

1004. Kretchmar, R. Scott. (1972). Ontological possibilities: Sport as play. *Philosophic Exchange, 1:* 113–22. In Robert G. Osterhoudt (Ed.), *The Philosophy of Sport: A Collection of Original Essays* (pp. 64–78). Springfield, IL: Charles C Thomas, 1973. T

1005. Kretchmar, R. Scott. (1973). Phenomenology of sport. In Ommo Grupe, Dietrich Kurz, & Johannes Teipel (Eds.), *Sport in the Modern World —Chances and Problems.* New York: Springer-Verlag. T

1006. Kretchmar, R. Scott. (1974). Modes of philosophic inquiry and sport. *Journal of the Philosophy of Sport, 1:* 129–31. T

1007. Kretchmar, R. Scott. (1975, Sum.). Meeting the opposition: Buber's "will" and "grace" in sport. *Quest, 24:* 19–27. T

1008. Kretchmar, R. Scott. (1980). Philosophical academy. *Journal of Physical Education and Recreation, 51*(5): 40–41. T
On the ways in which philosophy is of relevance to sport and physical education.

1009. Kretchmar, R. Scott. (1982a). Athletic courage and heart: Two ways of playing games. *Journal of the Philosophy of Sport, 7:* 107–16. P

1010. Kretchmar, R. Scott. (1982b). Never mind about that: How do good athletes think? *Somatics, 3*(4): 55–61. C
Discusses the possibility of creativity and genius in sports.

1011. Kretchmar, R. Scott. (1985). "Distancing": An essay on abstract thinking in sport performances. In David L. Vanderwerken & Spencer K. Wertz (Eds.), *Sport Inside Out: Readings in Literature and Philosophy* (pp. 87–103). Fort Worth, TX: Texas Christian University Press. T

1012. Kretchmar, R. Scott. (1988). From test to contest: An analysis of two kinds of counterpoint in sport. In William J. Morgan & Klaus V. Meier (Eds.), *Philosophic Inquiry in Sport* (pp. 223–29). Champaign, IL: Human Kinetics. T

1013. Kretchmar, R. Scott, & Harper, William A. (1969, Mar.). Must we have a rational answer to the question why does man play? *Journal of Health, Physical Education, and Recreation, 40:* 57–58. T

1014. Krotee, M. L. (1979). *The Dimensions of Sport Sociology.* West Point, NY: Leisure Press. T

1015. Krugel, Mitchell. (1994). *Jordan: The Man, His Words, His Life.* New York: St. Martin's. B

1016. Kuntz, Paul Grimley. (1973). The aesthetics of sport. In Robert G. Osterhoudt (Ed.), *The Philosophy of Sport: A Collection of Original Essays* (pp. 305–09). Springfield, IL: Charles C Thomas. C
Points out ways in which sporting and artistic performances, and athlete and artist, are similar.

1017. Kuntz, Paul Grimley. (1974). Aesthetics applies to sports as well as to the arts. *Journal of the Philosophy of Sport, 1:* 6–35. T

1018. Kuntz, Paul Grimley. (1976, Fall). Paul Weiss: What is a philosophy of sport? *Philosophy Today, 20:* 170–89. Also in Thomas Krettek (Ed.), *Cre-*

ativity and Common Sense (pp. 162–87). Albany: State University of New York Press, 1987. T

1019. Kuntz, Paul Grimley. (1977, Jun.). Paul Weiss on sports as performing arts. *International Philosophical Quarterly, 17:* 147–65. T

Explicates, criticizes, and extends Weiss' classification of sport with art. Kuntz subsumes both art and sport under performance.

1020. Kuntz, Paul Grimley. (1979). From Ziff to zen: A defense of the aesthetics of sport. *Philosophy in Context, 9:* 22–32. T

1021. Kuntz, Paul Grimley. (1985). Aesthetics applies to sports as well as to the arts. In David L. Vanderwerken & Spencer K. Wertz (Eds.), *Sport Inside Out: Readings in Literature and Philosophy* (pp. 492–509). Fort Worth, TX: Texas Christian University Press. T

1022. Kupfer, Joseph. (1975). Purpose and beauty in sport. *Journal of the Philosophy of Sport, 2:* 83–90. C

1023. Kupfer, Joseph. (1988). A commentary on Jan Boxill's "Beauty, Sport, and Gender." In William J. Morgan & Klaus V. Meier (Eds.), *Philosophic Inquiry in Sport* (pp. 519–22). Champaign, IL: Human Kinetics. T

1024. Kupfer, Joseph H. (1988). Sport—the body electric. In William J. Morgan & Klaus V. Meier (Eds.), *Philosophic Inquiry in Sport* (pp. 455–75). Champaign, IL: Human Kinetics. T

1025. Kwant, Remy. (1966, Spr.). The human body as the self-awareness of being. *Humanitas, 2:* 43–62. T

1026. Laither, P. (1986). Issues of validity in openly ideological research: Between a rock and a soft place. *Interchange, 17*(4): 63–84. T

1027. Landers, Daniel M. (1982). Arousal, attention, and skilled performance: Further considerations. *Quest, 33:* 271–83. P

Selective review of the literature of arousal, attention, and skilled performance. Concludes that in order to design effective programs using techniques such as biofeedback and relaxation it is necessary to understand the complex relations between one's levels of attention, arousal, and performance.

1028. Landsman, T. (1967). One's best self. In S. Jourard (Ed.), Existential psychological studies of the self. *Social Science Monograph, 34.* T

1029. Landsman, T. (1969). The beautiful person. *Futurist, 3*(3): 41–42. P

1030. Lawrence, Andrea Mead, & Burnaby, Sara. (1980). *A Practice of Mountains.* New York: Seaview. B

World champion skier Andrea Lawrence calls skiing a means of exploring and extending awareness. Mountains are a challenge, not only to physical mastery but "to spiritual possibility."

1031. Lawrence, E. A. (1982). *Rodeo: An Anthropologist Looks at the Wild and the Tame.* Knoxville: University of Tennessee Press. I

1032. Lawton, Philip. (1976, Fall). Sports and the American spirit: Michael Novak's theology of culture. *Philosophy Today, 20:* 196–208. T

1033. Lea, V. C. (1985). Peak performance: Will you recognize it when it happens? *Melpomene Institute Report, 4*(3): 4–7. G

1034. Lee, C. (1982). Self-efficacy as a predictor of performance in competitive gymnastics. *Journal of Sport Psychology, 4:* 405–09. P

1035. Lefcoe, N. M., & Yuhasz, M. S. (1971). Second wind phenomenon in constant load exercise. *Journal of Sports Medicine and Physical Fitness, 4*(3): 135–38. P

1036. Leimroth, C., & Stevens, S. F. (1984). *Peak Experience at the San Fermin.* San Jose, CA: Caislan Press. I
On peak experiences of participants at the San Fermin festival in Pamplona, Spain, with bullfights, drinking, and wild abandon.

1037. Lenk, Hans. (1976). Herculean "myth" aspects of athletics. *Journal of the Philosophy of Sport, 3:* 11–21. In David L. Vanderwerken & Spencer K. Wertz (Eds.), *Sport Inside Out: Readings in Literature and Philosophy* (pp. 435–47). Fort Worth, TX: Texas Christian University Press, 1985. G
Discusses mythic interpretations of sports from the viewpoint of both spectator and athlete.

1038. Lenk, Hans. (1985a). Action theory and the social scientific analysis of sport actions. In David L. Vanderwerken & Spencer K. Wertz (Eds.), *Sport Inside Out: Readings in Literature and Philosophy* (pp. 480–86). Fort Worth, TX: Texas Christian University Press. T

1039. Lenk, Hans. (1985b). Prolegomena toward an analytic philosophy of sport. In David L. Vanderwerken & Spencer K. Wertz (Eds.), *Sport Inside Out: Readings in Literature and Philosophy* (pp. 474–77). Fort Worth, TX: Texas Christian University Press. T
Deals critically with some earlier attempts to define sports, paying special heed to their contexts and taking pains not to confound definitions and explications.

1040. Lenk, Hans. (1988). Toward a social philosophy of achievement and athletics. In William J. Morgan & Klaus V. Meier (Eds.), *Philosophic Inquiry in Sport* (pp. 393–402). Champaign, IL: Human Kinetics. T

1041. Lenk, Hans. (1989). Sport between Zen and the self. In Gregory Baum & John Coleman (Eds.), *Sport* (pp. 79–92). Edinburgh, Scotland: T & T Clark. T

1042. Leonard, George B. (1968). *Education and Ecstasy.* New York: Dodd. G

1043. Lester, James T. (1983). Wrestling with the self on Mount Everest. *Journal of Humanistic Psychology, 23*(2): 31–41. P
The author was a psychologist in the 1963 American Everest expedition. He reports on a summit climber who had a mystical experience.

1044. LeUnes, Arnold; Wolf, Paula; Ripper, Natalie; & Anding, Kathy. (1990). Classic references in *Journal of Sport Psychology*, 1979–87. *Journal of Sport and Exercise Psychology, 12:* 74–81. P

1045. Lever, J. (1983). *Soccer Madness.* Chicago: University of Chicago Press. I

1046. Levey, Joel. (1990, Sep./Oct.). Sports: A western yoga. *New Realities, 11:* 24–28. Y

1047. Levy, Joseph. (1983). Towards a humanistic approach to sports and leisure: Implications beyond 2001. *Journal of Physical Education, Recreation and Dance, 54:* 12–14. T
Levy argues that without breadth of vision, leisure is only a superficial and

fleeting diversion. Sport and leisure together with other community and personal values can contribute to an optimal quality of life.

1048. Lilliefois, J. (1978). *The Running Mind*. Mountain View, CA: World Publications. **I**

1049. Lincoln, C. E. (1987). In search of the second wind: Beyond fatigue but before exhaustion lies a hazy state of athletic renewal. *Sport, 78*(7): 87–88. **P**

1050. Lincoln, Yvonna S., & Guba, Egon. (1985). *Naturalistic Inquiry*. Beverly Hills, CA: Sage. **P**

1051. Linden, Paul. (1984). Aikido: A movement awareness approach to physical education. *Journal of Physical Education Recreation and Dance, 55*(7): 64–65. **Y**

Aikido teaches that "proper practices" teach students "how to become aware of themselves" and achieve "freedom as moving beings" (p. 65).

1052. Lion, Lionel S. (1978). Psychological effects of jogging: A preliminary study. *Perceptual and Motor Skills, 47*: 1215–18. **P**

1053. Lipsky, Richard. (1981). *How We Played the Game: Why Sports Dominate American Life*. Boston: Beacon Press. **T**

On the personal meaning of sport and its social ramifications. Lipsky notes how changes in society are reflected in sports.

1054. Littlewood, P. K. (1981). *An Inquiry Into the Aesthetic Nature of Play: Philosophic Bases and Current Concepts*. Unpublished master's thesis, Washington State University. **T**

1055. Livingston, Michael K. (1989). *Mental Discipline: The Pursuit of Peak Performance*. Champaign, IL: Human Kinetics. **G**

Livingston, a former Harvard crew man, attempts to show that "every act of mind and body potentially can be styled and gauged as a performance, and the quality of that performance invariably can be enhanced through right practice" (p. vi). The purpose of the book is to show how a road to peak performance can be formed within virtually *any* discipline of body or mind. He draws on the disciplines of neurophysiology, exercise physiology, quantum physics, and forms of Eastern meditation.

1056. Locke, Lawrence F. (1989). Qualitative research as a form of scientific inquiry in sport and physical education. *Research Quarterly for Exercise and Sport, 60*(1): 1–20. **P**

Locke appraises the strengths and limitations of qualitative research, in particular as compared with the conventional physical education model of inquiry. He discusses complex issues that may control the future application of qualitative methods in physical education, as well as ground rules for conducting a dialogue on qualitative forms of inquiry.

1057. Lockhart, Barbara. (1973, Spr.). The joy of effort. *The Foil, 52*: pages unknown. **I**

1058. Loehr, James E. (1982). *Mental Toughness for Sports: Achieving Athletic Excellence*. New York: Forum. **G**

Loehr interviewed hundreds of athletes and found that their peak performance was characterized by physical relaxation, high energy, low anxiety, mental focus, and a feeling of control.

1059. Loehr, James E. (1983, Jan.). Ideal performance state. *Sport: Science Periodical on Research and Technology in Sport:* 1–8. **G**

1060. Loehr, James E. (1994). *The New Toughness Training for Sports.* New York: Dutton. **P**

1061. Logan, Richard D. (1980). The solitary ordeals of Lindbergh, Chichester and Byrd. *Psychological Perspectives, 11:* 172–87. **G**
Suggests that Lindbergh, Chichester, and Byrd, in venturing into " 'realms beyond'—danger, new places, far horizons, fear, death—actually sought their own other sides" (p. 182), as well as balance and spiritual unity.

1062. Logan, Richard D. (1985). The "flow experience" in solitary ordeals. *Journal of Humanistic Psychology, 25:* 79–89. **G**

1063. Lowe, Benjamin. (1970). *The Aesthetic Sensitivity of Athletes.* Unpublished doctoral dissertation, University of Wisconsin. **C**

1064. Lowe, Benjamin. (1971a, Jun.). The aesthetics of sport: The statement of a problem. *Quest, 16:* 13–17. **T**

1065. Lowe, Benjamin. (1971b). A theoretical rationale for investigation into the relationship of sport and aesthetics. *International Review of Sport Sociology, 8:* 95–102. **T**

1066. Lowen, Alexander. (1970). The body in therapy. *Proceedings, Fifth Annual Conference, American Dance Association:* 1–9. **T**

1067. Lowen, Alexander. (1975). *Bioenergetics.* New York: Penguin Books. **T**

1068. Loy, John W., Jr. (1968). The nature of sport: A definitional effort. *Quest, 10:* 1–15. **G**

1069. Loy, John W. (1980). The emergence and development of the sociology of sport as an academic speciality. *Research Quarterly, 51:* 91–108. **T**

1070. Loy, John W.; Birrell, S.; & Rose, D. (1976). Attitudes held toward agonetic activities as a function of selected social identities. *Quest, 26:* 81–93. **P**

1071. Loy, John W., Jr., & Kenyon, Gerald S. (Eds.). (1969). *Sport, Culture, and Society: A Reader on the Sociology of Sport.* London: Macmillan. **T**

1072. Lucas, John A., & Smith, Ronald A. (1985). Sport for all. In Wiley Lee Umphlett (Ed.), *American Sport Culture: The Humanistic Dimensions* (pp. 305–14). Lewisburg, PA: Bucknell University Press. **G**

1073. Lüschen, G. (1976). The interdependence of sport and culture. In M. Hart (Ed.), *Sport in the Sociocultural Process* (pp. 96–109). Dubuque, IA: William M. Brown. **T**
Discusses the concept of the postself, or "concern of a person with the presentation of his or her self in history" (p. 1088) as it applies to sport.

1074. Lüschen, G., & Sage, George H. (Eds.). (1981). *Handbook of Social Science of Sport.* Champaign, IL: Stipes. **T**

1075. Macaloon, J., & Csikszentmihalyi, M. (1983). Deep play and the flow experience of rock climbing. In J. C. Harrins & R. J. Park (Eds.), *Play, Games and Sports in Cultural Contexts* (pp. 361–84). Champaign, IL: Human Kinetics. **I**

1076. MacLean, M. E. (1978). Moments of transcendence. *Gamon Yachting,* 22(7): 14–15. **I**

1077. Madden, C. C., Kirkby, R. J., & McDonald, D. (1989). Coping styles of competitive middle distance runners. *International Journal of Sport Psychology, 20:* 287–96. **P**

1078. Madden, C. C.; Summers, J. J.; & Brown, D. F. (1990). The influence of perceived stress on coping with competitive basketball. *International Journal of Sport Psychology, 21:* 21–35. **P**

1079. Mahoney, M. J., & Avener, M. (1977). Psychology of the elite athlete: An exploratory study. *Cognitive Therapy and Research, 1:* 135–41. **P**

1080. Mahoney, M. J.; Gabriel, T. J.; & Perkins, R. S. (1987). Psychological skills and exceptional athletic performance. *Sport Psychologist, 1:* 181–99. **P**

1081. Mandell, Arnold J. (1977). *Coming of Middle Age: A Journey.* New York: Summit. **G**

1082. Mandell, Arnold J. (1978a). Psychoanalytic narcissism projected. *Journal of Nervous and Mental Disease, 166:* 369–73. **T**

1083. Mandell, Arnold J. (1978b). Toward a psychobiology of transcendence: God in the brain. In Julian M. Davidson & Richard J. Davidson (Eds.), *The Psychobiology of Consciousness* (pp. 379–464). New York: Plenum Press. **T**

A review of neurochemical mechanisms and systems neurophysiology, inspired by William James's *Varieties* and the hope that attention to "background feelings of self may make possible new hypotheses about brain-biogenic amine regulation" (p. 382).

1084. Mandell, Arnold J. (1979). The *second* second wind. *Psychiatric Annals, 9*(3): 57, 61–63, 66–69. **O**

A psychiatrist and long-distance runner describes his experiences of first and *second* winds and reviews relevant neurochemical and physiological studies. He describes psychiatric treatment "designed to normalize brain function by 'transcendence training' " (p. 67) so that patients will have healthier brain functioning and be able to cope with their problems. He connects this transcendental therapy with kundalini and the "new narcissism."

1085. Mandell, Richard D. (1984). Joyous sport, beautiful sport. In *Sport: A Cultural History* (pp. 282–304). New York: Columbia University Press. **C**

Proposes that the nearly worldwide advocacy of physical fitness is "evidence of deeper forces that encourage all of us constructively to pursue our limits in self-realization" (p. 303). He adds that sport today "provides not only physical release" but "is a force for spiritual assurances as well. The creative possibilities are far from being exhausted" (pp. 303–04).

1086. Mannell, Roger C. (1979a). Conceptual and experimental basis for research in the psychology of leisure. *Loisir et Societ/Society and Leisure, 2*(1): 179–96. **T**

1087. Mannell, Roger C. (1979b). Social psychological techniques and strategies for studying leisure experiences. In S. Iso-Ahola (Ed.), *Social Psychological Perspectives on Leisure and Recreation.* Springfield, IL: Charles C Thomas. **P**

1088. Mannell, Roger C.; Zuzanek, J.; & Larson, Rad. (1988). Leisure states and "flow" experiences: Testing perceived freedom and intrinsic motivation hypotheses. *Journal of Leisure Research, 20:* 289–304. **G**

1089. Marburger, Donna R. (1988). Peak experiences: Helping students reach beyond themselves. *Journal of Physical Education, Recreation, and Dance, 59*(1): 72–73. G

Suggests ways in which physical education teachers can set the stage for students to have peak experiences, which "may be as important as teaching motor skills and developing fitness, for it may provide the motivation for lifelong participation in [physical] activity" (p. 73).

1090. Margoshes, A., & Litt, S. (1966). Vivid experiences: Peak and nadir. *Journal of Clinical Psychology, 22*: 175. G

1091. Marinier, J. L. (1979). Judo: The phenomenon of second wind. *Judo Digest, 9*(5): 5, 22. I

1092. Markus, Hazel, & Nurius, Paula. (1986). Possible selves. *American Psychologist, 41*: 954–69. T

1093. Markus, Hazel, & Wurf, Elissa. (1987). The dynamic of self-concept: A social psychological perspective. *Annual Review of Psychology, 38*: 299–37. T

1094. Martens, R. (1975). The paradigmatic crisis in American sport personology. *Sport-Wissenschaft, 1*: 9–24. P

Review of the sport personology literature from 1950 to 1973. Martens discusses the paradigms of trait, situationism, and interactionism, and advocates the latter.

1095. Martens, R. (1978). *Peak Experience as it Relates to Sport: A Philosophic Inquiry.* Unpublished master's thesis, University of North Carolina, Greensboro. G

1096. Martens, R. (1987). Science, knowledge, and sport psychology. *Sport Psychologist, 1*: 29–55. P

1097. Martland, T. R. (1985). Not art and play, mind you, nor art and games, but art and sports. *Journal of Aesthetic Education, 19*: 65–71. T

1098. Maslow, Abraham H. (1959a). Cognition of being in the peak experience. *Journal of Genetic Psychology, 94*: 43–66. G

"Peak experiences" are defined and described as they occur in different activities, including "certain forms of athletic fulfillment" (p. 62). Maslow describes seventeen characteristics of peak experiences, or "moments of highest happiness and fulfillment," and defines self-actualization as "an episode, or a sport in which the powers of the organism come together in a particularly efficient and intensely enjoyable way" (p. 62). Persons undergoing peak experience feel they are actualizing their potentialities more perfectly than usual. Seven aftereffects are noted.

1099. Maslow, Abraham H. (1959b). Critique of self-actualization: To some dangers of being-cognition. *Journal of Individual Psychology, 15*: 24–32. G

1100. McBride, Frank. (1975, Sep.). Toward a non-definition of sport. *Journal of the Philosophy of Sport, 2*: 4–11. T

1101. McBride, Peter. (1932). *The Philosophy of Sport.* London: Heath Cranton. T

1102. McClain, Edward W., & Andrews, Henry B. (1969). Some personality correlates of peak experiences—a study in self-actualization. *Journal of Clinical Psychology, 25*: 36–38. G

1103. McColl, Sharon Lee. (1979). Dance as aesthetic education. *Journal of Physical Education and Recreation, 50:* 44–46. T

1104. McGirr, M. B. (1979). *Women Professional and Amateur Golfers' Self-Perceptions with Respect to Flow Theory.* Unpublished master's thesis, University of North Carolina, Greensboro. I

1105. McInman, Adrian D., & Grove, J. Robert. (1991). Peak moments in sports: A literature review. *Quest, 43:* 333–51. G
Examination of four models of peak moments (those proposed by Landsman, Panzarella, Thorne, and Privette/Bundrick), with emphasis on the latter. Includes a detailed discussion of peak experience, peak performance, and flow. The characteristics of peak moments in sport are described, and personal factors associated with the capacity for peak experience and the optimal conditions for such experiences are reviewed. Particular attention is given to how interference with peak experiences can be minimized.

1106. McKay, D. (1981). The problem of rehearsal of mental practice. *Journal of Motor Behavior, 13:* 274–85. P

1107. Mead, George H. (1959). Play, the game, and the generalized other. In Charles W. Morris (Ed.), *Mind, Self and Society From the Standpoint of a Social Behaviorist.* Chicago, IL: University of Chicago Press. T

1108. Meakin, Derek C. (1980, Spr.). Aesthetic appraisal and human movement. *Physical Education Review, 3:* 41–49. C

1109. Meichenbaum, D. (1985). *Stress Inoculation Training.* Elmsford, NY: Pergamon. P

1110. Meier, Joel F. (1978). Is the risk worth taking? *Journal of Physical Education and Recreation, 49*(4): 31–33. G

1111. Meier, Klaus V. (1975a). *Authenticity and Sport: A Conceptual Analysis.* Unpublished doctoral dissertation, University of Illinois, Urbana-Champaign. T

1112. Meier, Klaus V. (1975b). Cartesian and phenomenological anthropology: The radical shift and its meaning for sport. *Journal of the Philosophy of Sport, 2:* 51–73. T

1113. Meier, Klaus V. (1976). The kinship of the rope and the loving struggle: A philosophic analysis of communication in mountain climbing. *Journal of the Philosophy of Sport, 3:* 52–64. I

1114. Meier, Klaus V. (1977). The pineal gland, "mu," and the "body subject": Critical reflections on the interdependence of mind and body. In Shinobu Abe (Ed.), *The Philosophy of Physical Education* (6th ed.). Tokyo: Shoyo-Shoin. T

1115. Meier, Klaus. (1979). Embodiment, sport, and meaning. In Ellen Gerber & William J. Morgan (Eds.), *Sport and the Body: A Philosophical Symposium* (2nd ed., pp. 192–98). Philadelphia: Lea & Febiger. T

1116. Meier, Klaus V. (1980, Fall). An affair of flutes: An appreciation of play. *Journal of the Philosophy of Sport, 7:* 24–45. G
An appreciation of and apology for play, which Meier views as "an activity voluntarily undertaken for intrinsic purposes." He champions play as "a singularly fulfilled, liberating experience" that opens doors for humans that are normally closed and enables them to alter their accustomed modes of percep-

tion and refuse "to tolerate premature and limiting closures," to view "the naked simplicity of the world and entities within it," and to initiate various actions and processes that involve "creative and novel transformation" (p. 31). Moreover, "the player, through exuberant, delightful, joyous and spontaneous movement, gestures, and actions, confronts the world in a fresh manner, engages in dialogue with it, and explores it and himself in a manner pregnant with individual significance" (p. 32). Play satisfies creative imagination and emotions, "excites the soul, and satisfies the senses" (p. 35). It provides a milieu in which "new paths to understanding and meaning are nurtured in an open field of free expression" (p. 35). It is liberating and revelatory, enabling humans to affirm their sensual nature and "luxuriate in the intense, fully-lived release, if not explosion of [their] subjectivity" (p. 38).

1117. Meier, Klaus V. (1985). Restless sport. *Journal of the Philosophy of Sport, 12:* 64–77. T

1118. Meier, Klaus V. (1986). Play and paradigmatic integration. In Kendall Blanchard (Ed.), *The Many Faces of Play.* Champaign, IL: Human Kinetics. T

1119. Memmott, A. James. (1982). Wordsworth in the bleachers: The baseball essays of Roger Angell. *Journal of American Culture, 5*(4): 157–65. In David L. Vanderwerken & Spencer K. Wertz (Eds.), *Sport Inside Out: Readings in Literature and Philosophy* (pp. 157–65). Fort Worth, TX: Texas Christian University Press, 1985. T

1120. Meredith, Lawrence. (1984). Why do we care who wins any contest? *Arete: The Journal of Sport Literature, 1:* [pages unknown]. T

1121. Mermin, N. D. (1989). Can you help your team tonight by watching TV? More experimental metaphysics from Einstein, Podolsky, and Rosen. In *Boojums All the Way Through.* Cambridge, England: Cambridge University Press. T

A physicist baseball fan argues that fans can't help players by ESP or PK.

1122. Messenger, Christian K. (1979). Introduction to *Sport and the Spirit of Play in American Fiction: Hawthorne to Faulkner.* In Wiley Lee Umphlett (Ed.), *American Sport Culture: The Humanistic Dimensions* (pp. 197–211). Lewisburg, PA: Bucknell University Press. G

1123. Messner, Reinhold. (1977). *The Challenge.* New York: Oxford University Press. B

1124. Messner, Reinhold. (1978). *The Big Walls.* New York: Oxford University Press. B

Account of his odyssey climbing the highest mountains, and the lessons he has learned, including that it was not simply new successes that made him climb but the experience of the "soothing 'White Loneliness' of the Big Walls," where he "found a door to freedom" (p. 143).

1125. Messner, Reinhold. (1991). *Free Spirit: A Climber's Life.* Seattle, WA: Mountaineers Books. B

1126. Metheny, Eleanor. (1965). *Connotations of Movement in Sport and Dance.* Dubuque, IA: William C. Brown. T

1127. Metheny, Eleanor. (1967). Physical education as an area of study and research. *Quest, 9:* 73–78. T

1128. Metheny, Eleanor (1969, Mar.). This "thing" called sport. *Journal of Health, Physical Education, and Recreation, 40:* 59–60. **T**

1129. Metheny, Eleanor. (1972). The symbolic power of sport. In Ellen W. Gerber (Ed.), *Sport and the Body: A Philosophical Symposium* (pp. 221–26). Philadelphia, PA: Lea & Febiger. **C**

1130. Metheny, Eleanor, & Ellfeldt, Lois. (1958). Movement and meaning: Development of a general theory. *Research Quarterly, 29:* 264–73. **T**

1131. Metzl, Ervine. (1962, Nov.). Art in sports. *American Artist, 26:* 30–37. **C**

1132. Metzner, Ralph. (1963). The subjective aftereffects of psychedelic experiences: A summary of four recent questionnaire studies. *Psychedelic Review, 1:* 18–26. **G**

1133. Meyer, Jeffrey F. (1991). The right place is here, the right time is now: Taiji as mental and physical therapy. In Louis Diamant (Ed.), *Psychology of Sports, Exercise, and Fitness: Social and Personal Issues* (pp. 153–62). New York: Hemisphere. **M**

1134. Meyers, A. W.; Cook, A. J.; Cullen, J.; & Liles, L. (1979). Psychological aspects of athletic competitors: A replication across sports. *Cognitive Therapy and Research, 3:* 361–66. **P**

The more successful athletes who were interviewed in this study had greater self-confidence, were better at imaging successful performances, and had more daily thoughts and dreams about their sport.

1135. Meyers, Barbara A. (1978). Being in movement. *Physical Educator, 35:* 191–94. **G**

A physical education teacher calls for a holistic approach in all the "movement professions" based on the tenet that mind and body, as well as person and environment, are one. The experience of this unity, she says, is the "essence of movement." She points to the need for research on why some people can engage in one or more activities for their intrinsic worth whereas others "view life with boredom or anxiety" (p. 193).

1136. Miller, David. (1971). Theology and play studies: An overview. *Journal of the American Academy of Religion, 39:* 349–54. **T**

1137. Miller, Peter. (1981, Jan. 25). Skiing the steeps. *New York Times Magazine:* 18–20. **I**

On the rise of steep skiing, primarily in Europe, which is conducive to the extraordinary sports experience.

1138. Miller, Stephen. (1973). Ends, means, and galumphing: Some leitmotifs of play. *American Anthropologist, 75:* 87–98. **T**

1139. Millman, Dan. (1979). *The Warrior Athlete: Body, Mind & Spirit.* Walpole, NH: Stillpoint. **M**

Describes methods of systematically integrating body, mind, and emotions to bring out the "inner athlete." In the last of four parts, "Achieving Unity," Millman views the development of athletic training from an Eastern viewpoint and integrates sport with insights gained in meditation and spiritual experience.

1140. Mills, Stephanie. (1983). Spiritual swimming. *New Age, 8*(12): 48–49. **I**

1141. Min, K. (1981). Martial arts in the American educational setting. *Quest, 31:* 97–106. **M**

1142. Mitchell, Brian. (1976). *Running to Win.* Newton Abbot, England: David & Charles. I

On racing psychology.

1143. Mitchell, Janet Lee. (1981). *Out-of-Body Experiences: A Handbook.* Jefferson, NC: McFarland. E

1144. Mitchell, Richard G. (1982). The benefits of leisure stress. *Journal of Physical Education, Recreation, and Dance, 53*(7): 50–51. G

For some, stress is an "essential ingredient that provides meaning and clarity to social experience" (p. 51).

1145. Mitchell, Richard G., Jr. (1983). *Mountain Experience: The Psychology and Sociology of Adventure.* Chicago: University of Chicago Press. I

Sociological approach to the experience of climbing mountains. Mitchell discusses the climbing experience, which involves every task from the initial idea through its execution; the climber's identity, including organizations; and the motivation for climbing, which involves "historical accounts, psychological rewards, and social pressures" (p. xv). Although elite mountain climbers were part of the study, Mitchell was more concerned with representative conventional climbers. Includes a chapter on the flow experience.

1146. Mitchell, Robert Thomas. (1974). *A Conceptual Analysis of Art as Experience and Its Implications for Sport and Physical Education.* Unpublished doctoral dissertation, University of Northern Colorado. C

1147. Mitchell, Robert Thomas. (1975, Sum.). Sport as experience. *Quest, 24:* 28–33. G

1148. Miura, Yuichiro, with Perlman, Eric. (1978). *The Man Who Skied Down Everest,* New York: Harper & Row. B

Speed skier Miura skiied down the South Col of Everest using a parachute to stop himself before reaching an ice crevasse. This is a journal of his feat. His experience induced something ineffable, having to do with love: "something very gentle and sweet. I feel totally alive" (p. 167).

1149. Moltmann, Jurgen. (1972). *Theology of Play* (Reinhard Ulrich, Trans.). New York: Harper & Row. T

1150. Monkerud, Donald. (1978a, Aug. 17). The running high: The power known as the positive addiction. *On the Run,* 22–23. I

Applies William Glasser's theory of positive addiction to running.

1151. Monkerud, Donald. (1978b). Running into consciousness. *New Realities,* 2(3): 48–53. I

Offers suggestions for how to develop more (and higher) consciousness through the discipline of running.

1152. Moore, R. A. (1966). *Sports and Mental Health.* Springfield, IL: Charles C Thomas. P

1153. Moore, William E., & Stevenson, John R. (1994). Training for trust in sport skills. *Sport Psychologist, 8,* 1–12. P

1154. Morgan, William J. (1973). An existential phenomenological analysis of sport as a religious experience. In Robert G. Osterhoudt (Ed.), *The Philosophy of Sport: A Collection of Original Essays* (pp. 78–100). Springfield, IL: Charles C Thomas. G

Proposes that the sport quest expresses an aspiration of being itself and is revealed best by cultivating the religious inclinations that are fundamental to sport. Sport involves a self-surrender to the forces of being that is religious in nature.

1155. Morgan, William J. (1975). *Sport and Temporality: An Ontological Analysis.* Unpublished doctoral dissertation, University of Minnesota. G

1156. Morgan, William J. (1976a). An analysis of the futural modality of sport. *Man and World, 9:* 418–34. G

Following Heidegger, Morgan proposes that "the 'letting-be' quality of man's involvement in sport, . . . which owes its form and substance to sport's particular way of futurizing its possibilities, suggests a possible kinship between sport and the humanistic endeavors of life—most notably the fine arts and philosophy" (p. 429).

1157. Morgan, William J. (1976b). On the path towards an ontology of sport. *Journal of the Philosophy of Sport, 3:* 25–34. T

Brings together Huizinga's ideas on play, Gerber's examination of the mythology of sport, and Heidegger's views on ontology to provide the foundation for a sport ontology.

1158. Morgan, William J. (1977). Some Aristotelian notes on the attempt to define sport. *Journal of the Philosophy of Sport, 4:* 15–35. T

Argues that it is possible to define sport as long as the "conceptual model we employ . . . includes Aristotle's doctrine of "focal meaning."

1159. Morgan, William J. (1978). The lived time dimensions of sportive training. *Journal of the Philosophy of Sport, 5:* 11–26. G

1160. Morgan, William J. (1978, Aug.). A preliminary discourse concerning sport and time. *Journal of Sport Behavior, 3:* 139–46. T

1161. Morgan, William J. (Eds.). (1979). *Sport and the Humanities: A Collection of Original Essays.* Knoxville: University of Tennessee Press. T

1162. Morgan, William J. (1980). Sport personology: The credulous-skeptical argument in perspective. In W. Straub (Ed.), *Sport Psychology: An Analysis of Athlete Behavior* (pp. 330–39). Ithaca, NY: Movement. T

1163. Morgan, William J. (1983). Toward a critical theory of sport. *Journal of Sport and Social Issues, 7:* 24–35. T

1164. Morgan, William J. (1985a, Mar.). "Radical" social theory of sport: A critique and a conceptual emendation. *Sociology of Sport Journal, 2:* 56–71. T

1165. Morgan, William J. (1985b). Social philosophy of sport: A critical interpretation. *Journal of the Philosophy of Sport, 10:* 33–51. T

1166. Morgan, William J., & Goldston, S. E. (Eds.). (1987). *Exercise and Mental Health.* New York: Hemisphere. P

1167. Morgan, William J., & Meier, Klaus V. (Eds.). (1988). *Philosophic Inquiry in Sport.* Champaign, IL: Human Kinetics. T

Anthology of fifty-five recent and classic documents on the philosophy of sport arranged in six sections: "The Nature of Sport, Play, and Games"; "Sport and Embodiment"; "Sport, Play, and Metaphysics"; "Sport and Ethics"; "Sport and Social-Political Philosophy"; and "Sport and Aesthetics."

1168. Morgan, William P. (1969). Physical fitness and emotional health: A review. *American Corrective Therapy Journal, 23:* 124–27. P

1169. Morgan, William P., & Pollock, M. L. (1977). Psychological characterization of the elite distance runner. *Annals of the New York Academy of Sciences, 301:* 382–402. P

1170. Morgan, William P.; Roberts, J. A.; & Feinerman, A. D. (1971). Psychological effect of acute physical activity. *Archives of Physical Medicine and Rehabilitation, 52:* 422–25. P

1171. Morinis, A. (1985). The ritual experience: Pain and the transformation of consciousness in ordeals of initiation. *Ethos, 13:* 150–74. O

1172. Morris, A. F.; Lussier, L.; Vaccaro, P.; & Clarke, D. H. (1982). Life quality characteristics of national-class women masters long-distance runners. *Annals of Sports Medicine, 1:* 23–26. P

1173. Murphy, Michael. (1992). *The Future of the Body: Explorations Into the Further Evolution of Human Nature.* Los Angeles, CA: Tarcher. T
Digest of evidence and theory in many of the physical, biological, and human sciences as well as religion and sport on extraordinary (metanormal) physical, mental, and spiritual capacities. In addition to noting and classifying human transformative abilities, Murphy devotes three chapters to transformative practices, which may be used to develop metanormal abilities.

1174. Murphy, Shane M. (1990). Models of imagery in sport psychology: A review. *Journal of Mental Imagery, 14(3/4):* 153–72. P
Reviews and criticizes theories of mental practice in sport because they ignore the meanings of images for athletes. Proposes new research approaches for dealing with imaginal processes in the psychology of sport.

1175. Murphy, Shane M. (1994). Imagery interventions in sport. *Medicine & Science in Sports & Exercise, 26:* 486–94. P
Argues that the findings of research on mental practice in sports are equivocal. Provides guidelines for productive imagery research in sports.

1176. Myers, Martha. (1980a). Body therapies and the modern dancer: Dance training's new frontier. *Dancemagazine, 54(7):* 78–82. C

1177. Myers, Martha. (1980b). Body therapies and the modern dancer: Moshe Feldenkrais's awareness through movement. *Dancemagazine, 54(5):* 136–40. T

1178. Myers, Martha. (1980c). Body therapies and the modern dancer: The Alexander technique. *Dancemagazine, 54(4):* 90–94. T

1179. Myers, Martha. (1980d). Body therapies and the modern dancer: Todd, Sweigard, and ideokinesis. *Dancemagazine, 54(6):* 90–94. T

1180. Nagamie, Shoshin. (1976). *The Essence of Okinawan Karata-Do (Shorin-ryu).* Rutland, VT: Charles E. Tuttle. M

1181. Nahm, M. C. (1942, Mar.). Some aspects of the play-theory of art. *Journal of Philosophy, 39:* 148–59. T

1182. Nash, J. E. (1976). The short and the long of it: Legitimizing motives for running. In J. E. Nash and J. P. Spradley (Eds.), *Sociology: A Descriptive Approach.* Chicago: Rand McNally. T

1183. Natale, M., & Hantas, M. (1982). Effects of temporary mood states on selective memory about the self. *Journal of Personality and Social Psychology, 42:* 927–34. P

1184. Naughton, Jim. (1992). *Taking to the Air: The Rise of Michael Jordan.* New York: Warner Books. B

1185. Neal, Patsy. (1974). *So Run Your Race.* Grand Rapids, MI: Zondervan. G

1186. Neale, Robert E. (1969). *In Praise of Play.* New York: Harper & Row. G

1187. Neiss, Rob. (1988). Reconceptualizing arousal: Psychobiological states in motor performances. *Psychological Bulletin, 103:* 345–66. P

1188. Nettleton, B. (1983). Fostering team spirit. *Sports Coach,* 7(2): 11–13. P

1189. Nicol, C. W. (1975). *Moving Zen.* New York: William Morrow. M
Account of an American's experiences in Japan, where he went to learn karate. Nicol worked with several masters who performed feats that appear to have involved some form of PK (pp. 48, 84–85).

1190. Nideffer, Robert M. (1976). Test of attentional and interpersonal style. *Journal of Personality and Social Psychology, 34:* 397–404. P

1191. Nideffer, Robert M. (1986). *An Athlete's Guide to Mental Training.* Champaign, IL: Human Kinetics. P

1192. Nideffer, Robert M. (1987). Psychological preparation of the highly competitive athlete. *Physician and Sports Medicine,* 16(10): 85–92. P
Offers a mental skills program for coaches and athletes with behavioral definitions of concentration, peak or "flow" experience, mental toughness, and concentration goals. Notes that concentration demands differ according to the competitive setting. The roles of sport psychologist and coach are illustrated by two cases.

1193. Nixon, J. E. (1967). The criteria of a discipline. *Quest, 9:* 42–48. T

1194. Norbeck, Edward. (1969, Spr.). Human play and its cultural expression. *Humanitas, 5:* 43–55. T

1195. Novak, Michael. (1979a). American sports. American virtues. In Wiley Lee Umphlett (Ed.), *American Sport Culture* (pp. 34–49). Lewisburg, PA: Bucknell University Press. T

1196. Novak, Michael. (1979b). The natural religion. In D. S. Eitzen (Ed.), *Sport in Contemporary Society: An Anthology* (pp. 335–41). New York: St. Martin's. G

1197. Nygaard, Gary. (1976, Nov./Dec.). Sport in contemporary literature. *Journal of Physical Education and Recreation, 47,* 20–23. T
Categorizes schools of sport literature and presents a good reading guide of approximately 150 books on sports, mostly nonfiction. He notes sports literature's rapid growth since the 1960s.

1198. Oates, Bob, Jr. (1980). *The Winner's Edge: What the All-Pros Say About Success.* New York: Mayflower. G

1199. Oates, Joyce Carol. (1987). *On Boxing,* Garden City, NY: Doubleday. I
In this beautiful work, Oates expresses an intimate appreciation of boxing and its meaning in our culture. She thinks that "boxing has become America's tragic theater" (p. 116).

1200. Oglesby, Carole A. (1993). Changed times or different times— What's happening with "women's ways" of sport? *Journal of Physical Education, Recreation and Dance,* 64(3): 60–62. T
Oglesby presents the classic mechanistic versus the organicist philosophy

of science debate in terms of movement/sport science. She "recasts the issue within the unique and peculiar gender polarity" of physical education.

1201. Oglesby, Carole, & Shelton, C. (1992). Exercise and sport studies. In *The Knowledge Explosion: Generations of Feminist Scholarship*. New York: Teachers College Press. T

1202. Oh, Sadaharu, & Faulkner, David. (1984). *Sadaharu Oh: A Zen Way of Baseball*. New York: Times Books. M

Sadaharu Oh tells how he became a leading home run hitter by learning martial arts techniques when studying under Hiroshi Arakawa, who became his lifelong mentor. He developed his home run skill by learning to concentrate on his "one point," or *hara*, two inches below the navel. According to Arakawa, Sadaharu progressed to the third stage of the four stages of martial arts training, the fourth being the Way itself.

1203. Okwumabua, T. M.; Meyers, A. W.; & Santille, L. (1987). A demographic and cognitive profile of master runners. *Journal of Sport Behavior*, *10*: 212–20. P

1204. Oliver, Pater. (1990). Extreme explained: An inside look at extreme skiing: Its roots, its meaning, its devotees. *Skiing*, *43*(3): 109–13, 116. I

1205. O'Neil, John. (1974). The spectacle of the body. *Journal of the Philosophy of Sport*, *1*: 110–22. T

1206. Orlick, Terry. (1980). *In Pursuit of Excellence: How to Win in Sport and Life Through Mental Training*. Champaign, IL: Human Kinetics. (2nd ed. published in 1990) P

1207. Orlick, Terry, & Partington, J. (1988). Mental links to excellence. *Sport Psychologist*, *2*: 105–30. P

1208. Orringer, Nelson Robert. (1969). *Sport and Festival: A Study of Ludic Theory in Ortega y Gasset*. Unpublished doctoral dissertation, Brown University. T

1209. O'Shea, P. (1990/1991). The science of cross-training: Theory and application for peak performance. *National Strength and Conditioning Association Journal*, *12*(6): 40–44. P

1210. Osterhoudt, Robert G. (1973a). An Hegelian interpretation of art, sport, and athletics. In Robert G. Osterhoudt (Ed.), *The Philosophy of Sport: A Collection of Original Essays* (pp. 326–59). Springfield, IL: Charles C Thomas. T

Discusses what might be made of athletics and sport as an art form founded on Hegelian philosophy. Suggests that at base the disposition of sports is idealistic and spiritual.

1211. Osterhoudt, Robert G. (1973b). *The Philosophy of Sport: A Collection of Original Essays*. Springfield, IL: Charles C Thomas. T

Anthology of twenty-two chapters not previously published dealing with philosophy and sport. There are sections on the ontological, ethical, and aesthetic status of sport. Osterhoudt provides introductory overviews for each section.

1212. Osterhoudt, Robert G. (1973c). A taxonomy for research concerning the philosophy of physical education and sport. *Quest*, *20*: 87–91. T

1213. Osterhoudt, Robert G. (1978). *An Introduction to the Philosophy of Physical Education and Sport*. Champaign, IL: Stipes. T

1214. Osterhoudt, Robert G. (1979). Prolegomenon to a philosophical anthropology of sport. *Philosophy in Context, 9:* 95–101. **T**

1215. Osterhoudt, Robert G. (1982). *Sport: A Humanistic Overview.* Tempe: Arizona State University. **T**

1216. Osterhoudt, Robert G. (1984). Empiricistic dualism: The paradoxical basis/nemesis of modern physical education. *Quest, 36:* 61–65. **T**

Dualistic philosophies and empiricism are too one-sided to provide a balanced interpretation of humanity's intellectual and physical parts or an adequate physical education.

1217. Overdorf, Virginia G. (1990). Timing—in life and in sports—is everything. *Journal of Physical Education, Recreation, and Dance, 62*(7): 66–69. **T**

Describes internal timing, external timing, their interaction, and their role in motor performance.

1218. Oxendine, J. B. (1970). Emotional arousal and motor performance. *Quest, 13:* 23–32. **P**

1219. Paffard, M. K. (1970). Creative activities and peak experiences. *British Journal of Educational Psychology, 40:* 283–290. **G**

1220. Pargman, D. (1980). The way of the runner: An examination of motives for running. In Richard M. Suinn (Ed.), *Psychology in Sports: Methods and Applications* (pp. 90–98). Minneapolis: Burgess. **I**

1221. Park, R. J. (1986). Hermeneutics, semiotics, and the nineteenth-century quest for a corporeal self. *Quest, 38:* 33–49. **T**

1222. Passer, M. W. (1982). Children in sport: Participation motives and psychological stress. *Quest, 33:* 231–44. **P**

1223. Patrick, G. T. W. (1921, Oct.). The play of a nation. *Scientific Monthly, 13:* 350–62. **T**

1224. Payne, Peter. (1981). *Martial Arts: The Spiritual Dimension.* New York: Crossroad. **M**

This book explores "how a physical activity, seemingly closely related to the fields of pure sport such as prizefighting or wrestling, can come to deal with . . . psychospiritual transformation and the nature of reality" (p. 5).

1225. Peak performance in elite swimmers: Case study analysis. (1991). In John D. Troup (Eds.), *International Center for Aquatic Research Annual: Studies by the International Center for Aquatic Research 1990–1991* (pp. 163–69). Colorado Springs, CO: United States Swimming Press. **P**

1226. Peele, Stanton. (1979). Redefining addiction II: The meaning of addiction in our lives. *Journal of Psychedelic Drugs, 11:* 289–97. **G**

1227. Peele, Stanton. (1980). Addiction to an experience (Comment). *American Psychologist, 35:* 1047–48. **G**

1228. Peele, Stanton, & Brodsky, Archie. (1976). *Love and Addiction.* New York: Signet. **G**

1229. Perkins, K., & Epstein, L. (1988). Methodology in exercise adherence research. In R. Dishman (Ed.), *Exercise Adherence* (pp. 399–416). Champaign, IL: Human Kinetics. **T**

1230. Perkins, Richard Donald. (1977). *Prolegomena to the Study of Play in Nietzsche.* Unpublished doctoral dissertation, State University of New York, Buffalo. **T**

1231. Perry, R. Hinton. (1902). The relations of athletics to art. *Outing, 49:* 456–63. **T**

1232. Phelan, Jacquie, & Gabriel, Trip. (1986). Riding the steeps. *Outside, 11*(6): 75. **I**

1233. Phillips, Patricia A. (1975, Jan.). The sport experience in education. *Quest, 23:* 94–97. **G**

1234. Pieper, Josef. (1963). *Leisure: The Basis of Culture.* New York: New American Library. (Original work published 1952). **T**

Pieper views leisure not as a means of refreshment, but as an opportunity for celebration and worship, as an end in itself. It is a time for play, creativity, spontaneity, and above all, openness to wonder and "a deepened sense of mystery" (p. 102).

1235. Pieper, Josef. (1965). *In Tune With the World: A Theory of Festivity.* New York: Harcourt, Brace & World. **T**

1236. The poetry of football. (1967). In Derek Stanford (Ed.), *The Arts of Sport and Recreation.* London: Thomas Nelson. (Reprinted from *The Times,* October 23, 1962.) **I**

1237. Pool, Robert. (1989). Can you help the Mets by watching on TV? *Science, 244:* 773–74. **T**

According to quantum physicist N. D. Mermin, no.

1238. Porter, J., & Foster, J. (1987). In your mind's eye: The process of visualization can improve your game. *World Tennis, 8:* 35. **P**

1239. Porter, Kay, & Foster, Judy. (1986). *The Mental Athlete: Inner Training for Peak Performance.* Dubuque, IA: William C. Brown. **P**

Two runners, one a psychologist and the other an artist, describe methods they use for improving athletic performance. They emphasize relaxation, imagery, and positive attitudes, and devote a chapter to "psychological issues of the female athlete."

1240. Postow, Betsy C. (Ed.). (1983). *Women, Philosophy, and Sport: A Collection of New Essays.* Metuchen, NJ: Scarecrow Press. **T**

1241. Postow, Betsy C. (1984). Sport, art and gender. *Journal of the Philosophy of Sport, 11:* 52–55. **T**

1242. Prebish, Charles. (1982, Jan. 17). Spirit of sports inspires new faith. *New York Times, 5:* 2. **G**

Argues that sport is a religion in its own right and the ultimate sports experience is transformative.

1243. Prebish, Charles S. (1984). "Heavenly father, divine goalie": Sport and religion. *Antioch Review, 42:* 306–18. **G**

Philosopher Prebish holds that if sport can provide an experience of the ultimate, and "this is expressed through a formal series of public and private rituals requiring a symbolic language and space deemed sacred by its worshipers," then it is appropriate to call sport a religion—the "newest and fastest-growing" religion (p. 318).

1244. Prebish, Charles S. (1993). *Religion and Sport: The Meeting of the Sacred and Profane.* Westport, CT: Greenwood. **G**

Contains a discussion of the nature of religion, of sport, and whether sport is a religion. Parts 1 and 3 are by Prebish, and explore the nature of sport, which he argues is religious in nature. Part 2 is an anthology of chapters by

D. Stanley Eitzen and George Sage, William J. Morgan, Michael Novak, Howard Slusher, and Brian Aitken.

1245. Prebish, Charles S. (1994). Training into transcendence. In *Religion and Sport: The Meaning of Sacred and Profane* (pp. 217–28). Westport, CT: Greenwood. **G**

Prebish's autobiographical account of his running experiences, capped by a day when his times seemed "miraculous." Also a vignette of a young man who taught himself in a year to make amazing field goal kicks, from as far out as eighty yards, even though he had not previously kicked a football. His secret—knowing that "the ball, the grass, the crossbar, the leg . . . are all one" (p. 227).

1246. Price, La Ferre E. (1970). *The Wonder of Motion: A Sense of Life for Woman.* Unpublished doctoral dissertation, University of Iowa. **C**

Combination of art and poetry that describes extraordinary sports experiences.

1247. Privette, Gayle. (1964). *Factors Associated with Functioning Which Transcends Modal Behavior.* Unpublished doctoral dissertation, University of Florida. *Dissertations Abstracts International, 25:* 3406. **P**

1248. Privette, Gayle. (1965). Transcendent functioning. *Teachers College Record, 66:* 733–39. **G**

Suggests that educators expect too little of their students. Examples are given of "situations in which persons have performed in ways that transcend the usual or predictable" (p. 733), such as intellectual transcendence; survival under adverse circumstances, as in concentration camps and explorations in extreme climates; the placebo effect; and the power of love.

1249. Privette, Gayle. (1968). Transcendent functioning: The full use of potentialities. In Herbert A. Otto & John Mann (Eds.), *Ways of Growth: Approaches to Expanding Awareness* (pp. 227–38). New York: Simon & Schuster. **G**

1250. Privette, Gayle. (1978). Peak performance: One feels each part moving in concert with the rest. *Running, 3*(2): 28–29. **G**

1251. Privette, Gayle. (1981a). Dynamics of peak performance. *Journal of Humanistic Psychology, 21*(1): 57–67. **P**

The author examined peak performance of adults in psychology, creative arts, adult education, and graduate counseling to see if there were common elements of high-level performance across the different activities. This was found to be the case, with each group reporting the following psychological dimensions associated with peak performance: absorption and clarity in relation to both the object and self; spontaneity; and self-expression.

1252. Privette, Gayle. (1981b). Phenomenology of peak performance in sports. *International Journal of Sport Psychology, 12*(1): 51–60. **G**

Peak performance is defined operationally as behavior that exceeds one's average performance, and in sports it is compounded of such factors as "prior interest, involvement, clear focus, intentionality, spontaneity, and peak experience."

1253. Privette, Gayle. (1982a). Peak performance in sports: A factorial topology. *International Journal of Sport Psychology, 13:* 242–49. **G**

A tentative experiential topology of peak performance in sports. Experiential dimensions of peak sports experiences of twenty respondents were represented. They were characterized by clear focus, a strong sense of self, and power associated with joy.

1254. Privette, Gayle. (1982b). *Two Topologies of Peak Performance: Correlates of a Personality Construct.* Washington, DC: National Technical Information Service, #8217. (NTIS No. PB 82-194481.) **P**

1255. Privette, Gayle. (1983). Peak experience, peak performance, and flow: A comparative analysis of positive human experiences. *Journal of Personality and Social Psychology, 45*(6): 1361–68. **G**

Peak experience (intense joy), peak performance (superior functioning), and flow (intrinsically rewarding experience) are described and their characteristics compared in detail.

1256. Privette, Gayle. (1985a). Experience as a component of personality theory. *Psychological Reports, 56:* 263–66. **G**

Proposes that experience, i.e., an internal state or process, is just as much a basic data category of personality as behavior. Deals with two important experiential phenomena: peak experience and peak performance.

1257. Privette, Gayle. (1985b). Experience as a component of personality theory: Phenomenological support. *Psychological Reports, 57:* 558. **P**

"Two experiential phenomena, performance and feeling, were defined operationally by a model that indicated gradients and possible interrelations between phenomena (Privette, 1985). Six events characterize major gradients and interrelations: *peak performance,* functioning at one's best; *peak experience,* highest happiness; *flow;* an *average event,* identified as an event the preceding afternoon; deepest *misery;* and total *failure*" (p. 558). One hundred twenty-three adults responded, and their self-ratings followed expectations.

1258. Privette, Gayle. (1986). From peak performance and peak experience to failure and misery. *Journal of Social Behavior and Personality, 1*(2): 233–43. **G**

One hundred twenty-three adults were administered the author's Experience Questionnaire to describe their peak and nadir experiences. Privette found that peak experience is associated with joy, a sense of lasting significance, ineffability, encounter with others, and in some cases, spirituality. Peak performance is marked by clarity, focus, a sense of self and empowerment, goal-orientation, and personal significance. She links describable inner phenomena with observable events.

1259. Privette, Gayle, & Bundrick, Charles M. (1987). Measurement of experience: Construct and content validity of the experience questionnaire. *Perceptual and Motor Skills, 65:* 315–22. **P**

1260. Privette, Gayle, & Bundrick, Charles M. (1989). Effects of triggering activity on construct events: Peak performance, peak experience, flow, average events, misery, and failure. *Journal of Social Behavior and Personality, 4:* 299–306. **P**

Peak performance and failure, peak experience and misery, average events, and flow were designated as construct events because they are human events that are defined by specified levels of performance and feeling. This study investigates the effects of activity on experiential phenomena using the Experience Questionnaire. Although there were several specific activity effects, analyses did not reveal consistent and meaningful patterns in them.

1261. Privette, Gayle, & Bundrick, Charles M. (1991). Peak experience, peak performance, and flow: Correspondence of perceived descriptions and theoretical constructs. *Journal of Social Behavior & Personality,* 6(5): 169–88. P

Data from 123 adults were examined to assess the salience and independence of peak experience, peak performance, and flow, to assess the correspondence of personal and theoretical descriptions, and to identify common and distinguishing characteristics of the three experiences.

1262. Privette, Gayle, & Landsman. T. (1983). Factor analysis of peak performance: The full use of potential. *Journal of Personality and Social Psychology, 44:* 195–200. P

Peak performance was corroborated as an identifiable psychological entity with a factor structure stressing "clear focus, intense involvement, intention, and spontaneous expression of Power" (p. 195).

1263. Privette, Gayle, & Sherry, David. (1986). Reliability and readability of questionnaire: Peak performance and peak experience. *Psychological Reports, 58:* 491–94. P

Note: The questionnaire is Privette's Experience Questionnaire.

1264. Progen, Jan. (1972). Man, nature and sport. In Ellen W. Gerber (Ed.), *Sport and the Body: A Philosophical Symposium* (pp. 197–202). Philadelphia, PA: Lea & Febiger. T

1265. Progen, Janice L. (1978). *A Description of Stimulus Seeking in Sport According to Flow Theory.* Unpublished master's thesis, University of North Carolina, Greensboro. P

1266. Progen, Janice L. (1981). An exploration of the flow experience among selected collegiate athletes [Summary]. *Dissertation Abstracts International, 42*(3-A): 1048–49. P

1267. Progen, Janice L., & DeSensi, Joy T. (1984). The value of theoretical frameworks for exploring the subjective dimension of sport. *Quest, 36:* 80–88. T

Describes Martin Buber's I-Thou philosophy of relationship and Mihaly Csikszentmihaly's flow model as offering viable models for studying elusive sport phenomena.

1268. Puretz, S. L. (1982). Modern dance's effect on the body image. *International Journal of Sport Psychology, 13:* 176–86. P

1269. Quarrick, Gene. (1989). *Our Sweetest Hours: Recreation and the Mental State of Absorption.* Jefferson, NC: McFarland. G

The author proposes that recreation, sports, and play provide conditions in which one's sense of aliveness is enhanced and can reach optimal levels of functioning. Many examples are given.

1270. Radin, D. I., & Nelson, R. D. (1989). Evidence for consciousness-related anomalies in random physical systems. *Foundations of Physics, 19:* 1499–1514. E

1271. Rahner, Hugo. (1967). *Man at Play.* New York: Herder & Herder. T

1272. Raiport, Grigori. (1988). *Red Gold: Peak Performance Techniques of the Russian and East German Olympic Victors*. Los Angeles: Tarcher. P

A Ph.D./M.D. and former Soviet Olympic team psychologist gives detailed descriptions of the mind-control methods used to bring members of the Soviet space, military, and athletic programs to an optimal state of functioning, or the development of "latent human abilities."

1273. Ramo, Simon. (1970). *Extraordinary Tennis for the Ordinary Player*. New York: Crown. I

1274. Rau, Catherine. (1950). Psychological notes on the theory of art as play. *Journal of Aesthetics and Art Criticism, 8*: 229–38. T

1275. Ravizza, Kenneth. (1975). A subjective study of the athlete's greatest moment in sport. In *Proceedings of the Canadian Psychomotor Symposium, Psychomotor Learning and Sport Psychology Symposium* (pp. 399–404). Toronto: Coaching Association of Canada. G

1276. Ravizza, Kenneth. (1977a). The body unaware. In Dorothy J. Allen & Brian Fahey (Eds.), *Being Human in Sport*. Philadelphia, PA: Lea & Febiger. P

1277. Ravizza, Kenneth. (1977b). Potential of the sport experience. In Dorothy J. Allen & Brian W. Fahey (Eds.), *Being Human in Sport* (pp. 66–68). Philadelphia: Lea & Febiger. G

1278. Ravizza, Kenneth. (1979). Enhancing human performance. The answer lies within. *National Association for Physical Education in Higher Education Proceedings:* pp. 66–74.

1279. Ravizza, Kenneth. (1983a). An old/new role for physical education: Enhancing well-being. *Journal of Physical Education Recreation and Dance, 54*(3): 30–32. P

Presents a holistic approach to movement, that "emphasizes constant exploration and integration between spirit, mind, and body" (p. 30). Suggests methods to develop awareness of feedback from the body and its psychological resources. The educator's job is to identify the area of tension and imbalance that inhibit performance.

1280. Ravizza, Kenneth. (1983b). There is a silence that surrounds me: The lived-body experience in gymnastics and hatha yoga. In H. Lenk (Ed.), *Topical Problems in Sport Philosophy*. Koln: Bundesinstitut für Sportswissenschaft. G

1281. Ravizza, Kenneth L. (1984). Qualities of the peak experience in sport. In John M. Silva & R. S. Weinberg (Eds.), *Psychological Foundations of Sport* (pp. 452–61). Champaign, IL: Human Kinetics. G

1282. Raymo, Chester. (1973). Science as play. *Science Education, 57*: 279–89. T

Argues that "science, like religion, is a form of sacred play" (p. 280).

1283. Rebuffat, Gaston. (1967). *Men and the Matterhorn*. New York: Oxford University Press. B

1284. Rebuffat, Gaston, & Terray, Lionel. (1965). *Between Heaven and Earth*. New York: Oxford University Press. B

Lyrical account of mountain climbing and guiding by a man who regarded them as his calling.

1285. Reid, Louis A. (1970). Sport, the aesthetic and art. *British Journal of Educational Studies, 18:* 245–58. T

1286. Reid, Louis A. (1980). Human movement, the aesthetic and art. *British Journal of Aesthetics, 20:* 165–70. T

1287. Reising, R. W. (1983). Vision of sport: The gospel according to Yogi. *Journal of Popular Culture, 16*(4): 68–74. T
Argues that baseball and all American sports have become overly mercenary and lacking in values, as typified by Yogi Berra's "I don't know where we're going, but we're surely making good time" (p. 71). Reising hopes this attitude can be replaced by an "awareness of, respect for, and harmony with powers greater than" oneself (p. 73).

1288. Rejeski, W. J., & Brawley, L. R. (1983). Attribution theory in sport: Current status and new perspectives. *Journal of Sport Psychology, 5:* 77–99. P

1289. Resen, A. C. (1981). *Sport and Poetry: An Exploration of the Inter-Relatedness of Words and Actions.* Unpublished master's thesis, South Dakota State University. G

1290. Retton, Mary Lou, & Karolyi, Bela, with Powers, John. (1984). *Mary Lou: Creating an Olympic Champion.* New York: McGraw-Hill. B
Offers insights into the rigorous training techniques of famed gymnastic coach Bela Karolyi and Retton's success with them.

1291. Rhodewalt, Frederick, & Agustsdottir, Sjöfn. (1986). Effects of self-presentation on the phenomenal self. *Journal of Personality and Social Psychology, 50:* 47–55. P

1292. Richardson, Jean. (1969, May). Art and sport. *Physical Educator, 26:* 66–67. C
The author suggests that movement education can contribute to the development of a kinesthetic perception that is conducive to artistic endeavor.

1293. Ricoeur, Paul. (1971). The model of the text: Meaningful action considered as a text. *Social Research, 38:* 529–62. T

1294. Riddick, C. C. (1984). Comparative psychological profiles of three groups of female collegians: Competitive swimmers, recreational swimmers, and inactive swimmers. *Journal of Sport Behavior, 7:* 160–74. P

1295. Riess, Steven A. (Ed.). (1984). *The American Sporting Experience: A Historical Anthology of Sport in America.* West Point, NY: Leisure Press. G

1296. Riezler, Kurt. (1941, Sep.). Play and seriousness. *Journal of Philosophy, 38:* 505–17. T

1297. Riggs, C. E. (1980). *On the Trail of the Runner's High: A Descriptive and Experimental Investigation of Characteristics of an Elusive Phenomenon.* Unpublished doctoral dissertation, Florida State University. I

1298. Riggs, C. E., Jr. (1981). Endorphins, neurotransmitters, and/or neuromodulators and exercise. In Michael H. Sacks & Michael L. Sachs (Eds.), *Psychology of Running.* Champaign, IL: Human Kinetics. P

1299. Rintala, J. (1991). The mind-body revisited. *Quest, 43:* 260–79. T

1300. Roberts, Glyn C. (1984). Toward a new theory of motivation in sport: The role of perceived ability. In J. M. Silva & R. S. Weinberg (Eds.),

Psychological Foundations of Sport (pp. 214–28). Champaign, IL: Human Kinetics. P

1301. Roberts, Glyn C.; Kleiber, D. A.; & Duda, J. L. (1981). An analysis of motivation in children's sport: The role of perceived competence in participation. *Journal of Sport Psychology, 3:* 206–16. P

1302. Roberts, Glyn C., & Pascuzzi, D. (1979). Causal attributions in sport: Some theoretical implications. *Journal of Sport Psychology, 1:* 203–11. T

1303. Roberts, Terence J. (1975). Sport and the sense of beauty. *Journal of the Philosophy of Sport, 2:* 91–101. T

1304. Roberts, Terence J. (1976). *Languages of Sport.* Unpublished doctoral dissertation, University of Minnesota. T

1305. Roberts, Terence J. (1979). Languages of sport: Exemplification and expression. In William J. Morgan (Ed.), *Sport and the Humanities: A Collection of Original Essays.* Knoxville: University of Tennessee. T

1306. Roberts, Terence J. (1986a). Sport and representation: A response to Wertz and Best. *Journal of the Philosophy of Sport, 13:* 89–94. T

1307. Roberts, Terence J. (1986b). Sport, art, and particularity: The best equivocation. *Journal of the Philosophy of Sport, 13:* 49–63. In William J. Morgan & Klaus V. Meier (Eds.), *Philosophic Inquiry in Sport* (pp. 495–507). Champaign, IL: Human Kinetics, 1988. T

1308. Roby, Mary Paulich. (1966, Fall). The power of sport. *Arizona Journal of Health, Physical Education, Recreation, 10:* 9–10. T

1309. Rogo, D. Scott. (1983). *Leaving the Body: A Practical Guide to Astral Projection.* Englewood Cliffs, NJ: Prentice-Hall. E

1310. Rohe, Fred. (1974). *The Zen of Running.* New York: Random House. I

1311. Roochnik, David L. (1975). Play and sport. *Journal of the Philosophy of Sport, 2:* 36–44. G

1312. Roskin-Berger, M. (1972). Bodily experience and the expression of emotions. *American Dance Therapy Association Monograph No. 2:* 191–230. P

1313. Rosner, D. (1983, Feb. 28). Coghlan predicts his record. *Newsday,* 76. B

1314. Ross, H. E. (1975). *Behavior and Perception in Strange Environments.* New York: Basic Books. P

1315. Ross, Murray. (1985). Football red and baseball green. In David L. Vanderwerken & Spencer K. Wertz (Eds.), *Sport Inside Out: Readings in Literature and Philosophy* (pp. 716–25). Fort Worth, TX: Texas Christian University Press. G

1316. Ross, Saul. (1986). Cartesian dualism and physical education: Epistemological incompatibility. In Seymour Kleinman (Ed.), *Mind and Body: East Meets West.* Champaign, IL: Human Kinetics. T

1317. Rossi, Bruna, & Cereatti, Lucio. (1993, Oct./Dec.). The sensation seeking in mountain athletes as assessed by Zuckerman's Sensation-Seeking Scale. *International Journal of Sport Psychology, 24:* 417–31. P

1318. Rowell, Galen. (1977). *In the Throne Room of the Mountain Gods.* San Francisco: Sierra Club Books. I

The dust jacket states: "Ultimately, this is a book about a quest. Mountains have given those closest to them experiences that can best be described as mystical. . . . This . . . is what Rowell went to find, and what he explores in this book."

1319. Russell, Bill. (1972). *Go Up for Glory.* New York: Berkley. B

1320. Russell, Bill, & Branch, Taylor. (1979). *Second Wind: The Memoirs of an Opiniated Man.* New York: Random House. B

Contains Russell's insights into basketball, especially during peak moments, and reveals his love of the game and joy in playing it.

1321. Rybczynski, W. (1991). *Waiting for the Weekend.* New York: Viking. G

1322. Sachs, Michael L. (1974). The runner's high. In Michael L. Sachs & Gary W. Buffone (Eds.), *Running as Therapy: An Integrated Approach* (pp. 273–87). Lincoln: University of Nebraska Press. P

Presents reviews of research and several first-hand accounts of "runner's high."

1323. Sachs, Michael L. (1980). *On the Trail of the Runner's High: A Descriptive and Experimental Investigation of Characteristics of an Elusive Phenomenon.* Unpublished doctoral dissertation, Florida State University. I

1324. Sachs, Michael L. (1982). Running therapy: Change agent in anxiety and stress management. *Journal of Physical Education, Recreation, and Dance,* 53(7): 44–45. P

1325. Sachs, Michael L. (1991). Running—A psychosocial phenomenon. In Louis Diamant (Ed.), *Psychology of Sports, Exercise, and Fitness: Social and Personal Issues* (pp. 237–47). New York: Hemisphere. P

1326. Sachs, Michael L., & Buffone, Gary W. (Eds.). (1974). *Running as Therapy: An Integrated Approach.* Lincoln: University of Nebraska Press. P

Anthology of works by the editor and others on various aspects of running therapy and psychology, including the effects of running on psychological well-being, creative running, running addiction, the effect of exercise on personality, and a selected bibliography on running therapy and psychology.

1327. Sachs, Michael L., & Pargman, David. (1974). Running addiction. In M. L. Sachs and G. W. Buffone (Eds.). *Running as Therapy: An Integrated Approach* (pp. 231–52). Lincoln: University of Nebraska Press. P

1328. Sachs, Michael L., & Pargman, David. (1979). Running addiction: Interview examination. *Journal of Sport Behavior,* 2: 143–55. P

1329. Sacks, Michael H. (1979). A psychodynamic overview of sport. *Psychiatric Annals,* 9(3): 13–17, 21–22. P

A psychiatrist who is a runner examines the intrinsic qualities of play from a psychoanalytic perspective. He looks for the meaning of sport as "a carrier for individual conflict and fantasy" (p. 17) and explores the creative and transcendental aspects of sports (peak and flow experiences). He applies psychiatrist Winnicott's postulates of an "intermediate area" and its role in creativity applied to sports. The intermediate area exists between "objective aspects of our life . . . and the subjective reality of dreams and fantasies" (p. 21), which are characterized by the "pleasure principle." He adds that the "transcendental power of sports" lies in the way in which sports allows the athlete "to mingle illusion and reality, subjective and objective, separation and fusion, omnipotence and limitation" (p. 22).

1330. Sacks, Michael H. (1981). Running addiction: A clinical report. In M. H. Sacks and M. L. Sachs (Eds.), *Psychology of Running.* Champaign, IL: Human Kinetics. P

1331. Sacks, Michael H., & Sachs, Michael L. (Eds.). (1981). *Psychology of Running.* Champaign, IL: Human Kinetics. P

1332. Sadler, William A., Jr. (1966, Fall). Play: A basic human structure involving love and freedom. *Review of Existential Psychology and Psychiatry,* 6: 237–45. P

1333. Sadler, William A., Jr. (1973). Competition out of bounds: Sport in American life. *Quest, 19:* 124–32. G

1334. Sadler, William A., Jr. (1977). Alienated youth and creative sports experience. *Journal of the Philosophy of Sport, 4:* 83–95. G

1335. Sage, George H. (1979). The current status and trends of sport sociology. In M. L. Krotee (Ed.), *The Dimensions of Sport Sociology* (pp. 23–31). West Point, NY: Leisure Press. T

1336. Sage, George H. (1981). Sport sociology, normative and nonnormative arguments: Playing the same song over and over and . . . In S. L. Greendorfer & A. Yiannakis (Eds.), *Sociology of Sport: Diverse Perspectives* (pp. 7–14). West Point, NY: Leisure Press. T

1337. Sage, George H. (1982). Sociocultural aspects of physical activity: Significant research traditions, 1972–82. In H. Eckert (Ed.), *Synthesizing and Transmitting Knowledge: Research and Its Applications* (pp. 59–66). (The Academy Papers, No. 16). Reston, VA: AAHPERD. P

1338. Sage, George H. (1987). Pursuit of knowledge in sociology of sport: Issues and prospects. *Quest, 39:* 255–81. T
Sport sociology could broaden and humanize physical education. Of particular relevance are Sage's reviews of involvement in sport, symbolic and interpretive studies, and feminist studies.

1339. Sage, George H. (1989). A commentary on qualitative research as a form of scientific inquiry in sport and physical education. *Research Quarterly for Exercise and Sport, 60:* 25–29. P
Advocates qualitative research methods, which are respected in the social sciences and humanities, to advance knowledge in sport and physical education.

1340. Samdahl, Diane M. (1986). *The Self and Social Freedom: A Paradigm of Leisure.* Unpublished doctoral dissertation, University of Illinois. T

1341. Samdahl, Diane M. (1988). A symbolic interactionist model of leisure: Theory and empirical support. *Leisure Sciences, 10:* 27–39. T

1342. Samdahl, Diane M., & Kleiber, Douglas A. (1989). Self-awareness and leisure experience. *Leisure Sciences, 11:* 1–10. T
This study suggests that "self-awareness within leisure was associated with more positive affect than in nonleisure" (p. 1), and may facilitate it.

1343. Santayana, George. (1894, Jul.). Philosophy on the bleachers. *Harvard Monthly, 8:* 181–90. T

1344. Saraf, Mikhail Y. (1980). Sport and art. *International Review of Sport Sociology, 15:* 123–31. T

1345. Saraf, Mikhail Y. (1984). The aesthetics of sport. *Dialectics and Humanism, 11:* 87–96. **C**

1346. Sarani, Robert. (1975, Jan.). The flash of spirit. *Quest, 23:* 78–82. **G**

1347. Sarano, Jacques. (1966). *The Meaning of the Body* (James H. Farley, Trans.). Philadelphia, PA: Westminster Press. **T**

1348. Sarsfield, Robert. (1959, Mar.). Physical and artistic expression in gymnastics. *Physical Educator, 16:* 12–14. **C**
A complicated routine in gymnastics can be compared to dance, painting, and music.

1349. Savage, C.; Terrill, J.; & Jackson, D. D. (1962). LSD, transcendence, and the new beginning. *Journal of Nervous and Mental Disease, 135:* 425–39. **G**

1350. Scanlan, Tara K. (1977). The effects of success-failure on the perception of threat in a competitive situation. *Research Quarterly, 48:* 144–53. **P**

1351. Scanlan, Tara K., & Lewthwaite, R. (1986). Social psychological aspects of competition for male youth sport participants: IV. Predictors of enjoyment. *Journal of Sport Psychology, 8:* 25–35. **P**

1352. Scanlan, Tara K.; Ravizza, Kenneth; & Stein, G. L. (1989). An in-depth study of former elite figure skaters: I. Introduction to the project. *Journal of Sport & Exercise Psychology, 11:* 54–64. **P**
Qualitative interview techniques supplemented by quantitative assessments were used to study twenty-six former elite figure skaters.

1353. Scanlan, Tara K., & Simons, Jeffery P. (1992). The construct of sport enjoyment. In Glyn C. Roberts (Ed.), *Motivation in Sport and Exercise* (pp. 199–215). Champaign, IL: Human Kinetics. **P**
Presents theoretical work on the construct of sport enjoyment, reviews research findings in detail, and provides suggestions for future research.

1354. Scanlan, Tara K.; Stein, G. L.; & Ravizza, Kenneth. (1989). An in-depth study of former elite figure skaters: II. Sources of enjoyment. *Journal of Sport & Exercise Psychology, 11*(1): 65–83. **P**
Twenty-six former national champion figure skaters were interviewed concerning their sources of enjoyment during the most competitive phase of their skating careers. A total of 418 statements were content-analyzed into higher order themes representing sources of enjoyment. There also was a class of special cases, which included the gratification experienced in being perhaps the only person to perform a certain move.

1355. Scharf, S. M.; Bark, H.; Heimer, D.; Cohen, A.; & Macklem, P. T. (1984). Second wind during inspiratory loading. *Medicine and Science in Sports and Exercise, 1*(1): 87–91. **P**

1356. Scharf, S.; Bye, P.; Pardy, R.; & Macklem, P. T. (1984). Dyspnea, fatigue, and second wind. *American Review of Respiratory Disease, 129*(2, Pt. 2): 588–89. **P**

1357. Schempp, P. (1987). Research on teaching physical education: Beyond the limits of natural science. *Journal of Teaching in Physical Education, 6*(2): 111–21. **P**

1358. Schiller, Friedrich von. (1972). Play and beauty. In Ellen W. Gerber

(Ed.), *Sport and the Body: A Philosophical Symposium* (pp. 299–301). Philadelphia, PA: Lea & Febiger. (Original work published 1882) T

1359. Schmitt, Raymond L., & Leonard, Wilbert M., II. (1986). Immortalizing the self through sport. *American Journal of Sociology, 91:* 1088–1111. T

1360. Schmitz, Kenneth L. (1972). Sport and play: Suspension of the ordinary. In Ellen W. Gerber (Ed.), *Sport and the Body: A Philosophical Symposium* (pp. 25–32). Philadelphia, PA: Lea & Febiger. In William J. Morgan & Klaus V. Meier (Eds.), *Philosophic Inquiry in Sport* (pp. 29–38). Champaign, IL: Human Kinetics, 1988. T

1361. Schonauer, David. (1983). The BASE case. *Outside, 8(2):* 55–60. O
"BASE" stands for Buildings, Antennae, Spans, and Earth formations. It is used in fixed object parachuting, a risk endeavor in which parachutists attempt to land on predesignated (usually) small places, natural or manufactured.

1362. Schrag, Calvin O. (1962). The lived body as a phenomenological datum. *Modern Schoolman, 39:* 203–18. T

1363. Schrag, Calvin O. (1969). The embodied experiencer. In C. O. Schrag, *Experience and Being: Prolegomena to a Future Ontology.* Evanston, IL: Northwestern University Press. T

1364. Schreyer, Richard M.; White, Robert; & McCool, Stephen F. (1978). Common attributes, uncommonly exercised. *Journal of Physical Education and Recreation, 38:* 36–38. G
Notes that participation in recreational activities involving risk has rapidly increased, and those who desire risk-taking outlets are demanding that public recreation provide programs and facilities for them. Recreational risk is examined in terms of motivation, social-psychological rewards, the role of natural environments, and what recreational administrators can do. The authors conclude that a picture of risk sports is emerging in which the individual is totally involved and "focused toward the successful culmination of the experience. The person can put his or her whole being into it, thereby moving toward some degree of self-actualization through the activity," which is "an enhancement of existence through testing oneself at the edge of life" (p. 37).

1365. Schultheis, Rob. (1984). *Bone Games: One Man's Search for the Ultimate Athletic High.* New York: Random House. B
The author describes an extraordinary sports experience he had when he fell while mountain climbing, after which he was a new person for a few hours with exceptional skills. Upon returning to his old "self," he set out to repeat his extraordinary experience. This is an account of his search for a way to trigger such experiences.

1366. Schvartz, Esar. (1967). Nietzsche: A philosopher of fitness. *Quest, 8:* 83–89. T

1367. Schwartzman, H. B. (1978). *Transformations: The Anthropology of Children's Play.* New York: Plenum. T

1368. Scott, Jack. (1973, Jan.). Sport and the radical ethic. *Quest, 19:* 71–77. P

1369. Seward, George. (1944, Mar.). Play as art. *Journal of Philosophy, 41:* 178–84. T

1370. Shainberg, David (1977). Long distance running as meditation. *Annals of the New York Academy of Sciences, 301:* 1002–10. I

Shainberg, a regular runner, describes his mind/body experience during a morning's run from the first moment of his awakening thoughts about it. He describes altered states, therapeutic moments, and the desire to never stop running.

1371. Shainberg, Lawrence (1989, Apr. 9). Finding the zone. *New York Times Magazine,* 34–36, 38–39. G

1372. Sharp, B. I. (1987). *Swimming and "Well-Being."* Unpublished doctoral dissertation, Yeshiva University, New York. I

1373. Shaw, Susan M. (1985). The meaning of leisure in everyday life. *Leisure Sciences, 7:* 1–24. T

1374. Sheehan, George. (1976). Second wind is no myth. *Physician and Sportsmedicine,* 4(8): 26. P

1375. Sheehan, George. (1979). Negative addiction: A runner's perspective. *Physician and Sports-Medicine,* 7(6): 49. P

1376. Sheets, Maxine. (1966). *The Phenomenology of Dance.* Madison and Milwaukee: University of Wisconsin Press. T

Approaches dance as a lived experience, and uses a method of phenomenological analysis that does not banish the subject of study in the effort to investigate it. Sheets shows how dance provides confirmation of the dancer's philosophy. The method described here could be used to illuminate many sports endeavors.

1377. Shelton, A. O., & Mahoney, M. J. (1978). The content and effect of "psyching-up" strategies in weight lifters. *Cognitive Therapy and Research,* 2: 275–84. P

1378. Shephard, R. J. (1974). What causes second wind? *Physician and Sportsmedicine,* 2(11): 37–42. In P. E. Allsen (Ed.), *Conditioning and Physical Fitness: Current Answers to Relevant Questions* (Sec. 3, pp. 98–105). Dubuque, IA: William C. Brown, 1978. P

1379. Shephard, R. J. (1976). Getting your second wind. *Aquatic World,* 4(5): 16–18. P

1380. Sherrard, Carol. (1978). The Everest message: Alternative explanations and their status. *Journal of the Society for Psychical Research, 49:* 797–804. E

1381. Shotter, John. (1973). Prolegomena to an understanding of play. *Journal of the Theory of Social Behavior, 3:* 47–89. T

1382. Shriver, Sargent. (1963, Jun. 3). The moral force of sport. *Sports Illustrated, 18:* 30–31, 62–63. T

1383. Silva, John M. (1984). Personality and sport performance: Controversy and challenge. In John M. Silva & R. S. Weinberg (Eds.), *Psychological Foundations of Sport* (pp. 59–69). Champaign, IL: Human Kinetics. P

1384. Silva, John M.; Hardy, C. J.; & Grace, R. R. (1988). Analysis of psychological momentum in intercollegiate tennis. *Journal of Sport and Exercise Psychology, 10:* 346–54. P

1385. Silva, John M., & Shultz, Barry B. (1974). Research in the psychology and therapeutics of running: A methodological and interpretive review. In

M. L. Sachs & G. W. Buffone (Eds.), *Running as Therapy: An Integrated Approach* (pp. 304–20). Lincoln: University of Nebraska Press. P
Examines some technical problems involved in research on running, and questions to be answered by such research.

1386. Silva, John M., & Weinberg, R. S. (1984). *Psychological Foundations of Sport.* Champaign, IL: Human Kinetics. P

1387. Sime, W. E. (1977). A comparison of exercise and meditation in reducing physiological response to stress. *Medicine and Science in Sports, 9:* 55. P

1388. Singer, Jerome S. (1981). Imaginative play as the precursor of adult imagery and fantasy. In Eric Klinger (Ed.), *Imagery, Vol. 2: Concepts, Results, and Applications* (pp. 17–29). New York: Plenum. T

1389. Singer, Robert N. (1979). Future directions in the movement arts and sciences. *Quest, 31:* 255–63. P

1390. Singer, Robert N.; Murphy, Milledge; & Tennant, L. Keith. (Eds.). (1993). *Handbook of Research on Sport Psychology.* New York: Macmillan. P

1391. Sloan, Lloyd Reynolds. (1979). The function and impact of sports for fans: A review of theory and contemporary research. In Jeffrey H. Goldstein (Ed.), *Sports, Games, and Play* (pp. 219–62). Hillsdale, NJ: Erlbaum/Wiley. P

1392. Slusher, Howard S. (1969, May). To test the waves is to test life. *Journal of Health, Physical Education, and Recreation, 40:* 32–33. T

1393. Slusher, Howard S. (1973). Existential humanism and sport. In Ommo Grupe, Dietrich Kurz, & Johannes Teipel (Eds.), *Sport in the Modern World—Chances and Problems.* New York: Springer-Verlag. T

1394. Slusher, Howard S., & Lockhart, Aileene S. (Eds.). (1966). *Anthology of Contemporary Readings: An Introduction to Physical Education.* Des Moines, IA: William C. Brown. P

1395. Smith, Ann C. (1982). Footpath to the gods. *Psychological Perspectives, 13:* 7–20. B
First-person account of a trek in Nepal inspired by Matthiessen's *The Snow Leopard* and a need for "a physical and emotional challenge to my knowledge of myself and of the earth, and [to] deepen my experience of God" (p. 8). This is not a travelogue but a (successful) effort "to communicate experience of a journey" (p. 8). Smith had both peak and nadir experiences, but underlying both was a deeper sense of connection to herself, to God, and lessons regarding discomfort, fear, living in the moment, and interdependence.

1396. Smith, Dan. (1987). Conditions that facilitate the development of sport imagery training. *Sport Psychologist, 1:* 237–47. P
Conditions discussed are vividness and controllability, practice, expectation and attitude, previous experience, relaxed attention, and external versus internal imagery.

1397. Smith, David, with Russell, Franklin. (1983). *Healing Journey: The Odyssey of an Uncommon Athlete.* San Francisco: Sierra Club Books. B

1398. Smith, Hope M. (1968). Movement and aesthetics. In Hope M. Smith (Ed.), *Introduction to Human Movement.* Reading, MA: Addison-Wesley. T

1399. Snyder, Eldon E., & Spreitzer, Elmer A. (1974). Involvement in sports and psychological well-being. *International Journal of Sport Psychology, 5:* 28–39. G

1400. Snyder, Eldon E., & Spreitzer, Elmer. (1974, Dec.). Orientations toward work and leisure as predictors of sports involvement. *Research Quarterly, 45:* 398–406. P

1401. Snyder, Eldon E., & Spreitzer, Elmer. (1979). Orientations toward sport: Intrinsic, normative, and extrinsic. *Journal of Sport Psychology, 1:* 170–75. P

1402. Snyder, Eldon E., & Spreitzer, Elmer. (1983). *Social Aspects of Sport.* Englewood Cliffs, NJ: Prentice-Hall. P

1403. Snyder, M. (1982). When believing means doing: Creating links between attitudes and behaviours. In M. P. Zanna, E. T. Higgins, & C. P. Herman (Eds.), *The Ontario Symposium* (Vol. 2, pp. 105–30). Hillsdale, NJ: Erlbaum. P

1404. Solomon, E. G., & Bumpus, A. K. (1978). The running meditation response: An adjunct to psychotherapy. *American Journal of Psychotherapy, 32:* 583–92. P

The authors combine the physical technique of slow, long-distance running with the mental centering devices of Transcendental Meditation, sometimes supplemented by hypnosis, to evoke "peak experience," or an altered state of consciousness. Indications and contraindications are given for using this approach for various psychosomatic and somatic syndromes and as an adjunct to formal individual and group psychotherapy.

1405. Sonenfield, Irwin. (1985). The play's the thing. *Journal of Aesthetic Education, 19:* 111–13. T

1406. Souriau, Paul. (1983). *The Aesthetics of Movement* (M. Souriau, Trans.). Amherst: University of Massachusetts Press. T

1407. Sparks, R. E. C. (1985). Knowledge structures in sport and physical education. *Sociology of Sport Journal, 2:* 1–8. T

1408. Spick, Mike (1988). *The Ace Factor: Air Combat and the Role of Situational Awareness.* Annapolis, MD: Naval Institute Press. E

The "situational awareness" of the subtitle refers to the "sixth sense" possessed by some fighter pilots that aids them in flying maneuvers. Through such awareness, pilots anticipate the moves of opponents. Ace pilot Stanford Tuck was said to possess hunches that came to him, suddenly and compellingly, that enabled him to read signs that others could not perceive.

1409. Spicker, Stuart F. (Ed.). (1970). *The Philosophy of the Body: Rejections of Cartesian Dualism.* Chicago: Quadrangle Books. T

1410. Spino, Dyveke, with Spence, Ann. (1977, Aug.). Creative running tips from a new age coach. *New Age, 3:* 32–41. I

Spino presents ways of expressing one's feminine side through running and using running as a means of transforming consciousness.

1411. Spino, Mike. (1984). *Breakthrough: Maximum Sports Training.* New York: Pocket Books. P

1412. Sports momentum: The way the ball bounces. (1978). *Human Behavior, 7(8):* 36. P

On the work of two sociologists, Patricia and Peter Adler, who offer suggestions for achieving and maintaining momentum in sports and in life.

1413. Stack, George J. (1976). Human possibility and value. *Philosophy Today, 20:* 95–106. **T**

1414. Staley, Steward C. (1940). The body-soul concept. In *The Curriculum in Sports (Physical Education)*. Champaign, IL: Stipes. **T**

1415. Stebbins, Robert. (1982). Serious leisure: A conceptual statement. *Pacific Sociological Review, 25:* 251–72. **T**

1416. Steel, Margaret. (1977). What we know when we know a game. *Journal of the Philosophy of Sport, 4:* 96–103. **T**

Shows how we learn to do sports and games in the same way that Kuhn says we learn to do science. She suggests that a study of learning in sports might illumine what we know about learning in philosophy, science, and other fields.

1417. Stevens, John. (1988). *The Marathon Monks of Mount Hiei*. Boston: Shambhala. **M**

A professor of Buddhist studies who is an aikido instructor in Japan describes the feats, training, and teachings of the "Marathon monks," whom he regards as the world's greatest athletes, but athletes of the spirit. He compares them to the *lung-gom-pa* runners of Tibet. The monks have a sense of being called. They "gravitate toward the mountain paths, compelled by a powerful force that suffuses them with energy" (p. 93). They operate on the conviction that "if mind and body are unified, there is nothing that cannot be accomplished" (p. viii). The apex of their training involves running for 100 days, without sleep, food, water, or rest for seven-and-a-half of those days. The training lasts seven years, and in the final year they accomplish 100 days of running fifty-two-and-a-half miles each day.

1418. Stevens, N. L. (1979). *Investigation of Anxiety, Motivation, and Flow Experience in Competitive Sport*. Unpublished master's thesis, Pennsylvania State University. **P**

1419. Stevens, P. (Ed.). (1977). *Studies in the Anthropology of Play: Papers in Memory of B. Allan Tindall*. West Point, NY: Leisure Press. **T**

1420. Stevenson, Christopher L. (1975, Jan.). The meaning of movement. *Quest, 23:* 2–9. **T**

1421. Stewart, Mary Lou. (1970, Nov./Dec.). Why do men play? *Journal of Health, Physical Education, and Recreation, 41:* 14. **T**

1422. Stoddard, D. (1986). The team spirit: A university experiment in Sacramento is blazing a new trail in racquetball's search for a feeder system. *National Racquetball, 15*(3), 8–11, 13. **P**

1423. Stone, Gregory P. (1969). Some meanings in American sport: An extended view. In Gerald S. Kenyon (Ed.), *Aspects of Contemporary Sport Sociology*. Chicago: Athletic Institute. **T**

1424. Stone, Gregory P., & Stone, G. I. (1976). Ritual as game: Playing to become a sanema. *Quest, 26:* 28–47. **Y**

1425. Stone, Roselyn E. (1973). Assumptions about the nature of human movement. In Robert G. Osterhoudt (Ed.), *The Philosophy of Sport: A Collection of Original Essays* (pp. 39–48). Springfield, IL: Charles C Thomas. **T**

Examines the general theories of movement set forth by Delsarte, Jacques-Dalcroze, Laban, and Bode, each of whom regards movement as a means of expressing spirit/soul/self.

1426. Stone, Roselyn E. (1975, Jan.). Human movement forms as meaning structures: Prolegomenon. *Quest, 23:* 10–19. T

1427. Stone, Roselyn E. (1978). Movement as integer: The "joy of effort" revisited. *Proceedings of the Annual Convention of the Eastern Association for Physical Education of College Women.* G

1428. Stone, Roselyn E. (1981). Of Zen and the experience of moving. *Quest, 33:* 96–107. G

From her own practice of Zen the author found ways in which sport, dance, and exercise can be viewed as forms of contemplation.

1429. Studer, Ginny L. (1975, Jan.). The language of movement is in the doing. *Quest, 23:* 98–100. T

1430. Suedfeld, Peter, & Mocellin, Jane S. (1987). The "sensed presence" in unusual environments. *Environment and Behavior, 19:* 33–52. E

1431. Suinn, Richard M. (1980). *Psychology in Sports: Methods and Applications.* Minneapolis: Burgess. P

Emphasizes applications of scientific findings. The editor contributed original material but the majority of the pieces by other authors were published elsewhere.

1432. Suinn, Richard M. (1983). Imagery and sports. In A. A. Sheikh (Ed.), *Imagery: Current Theory, Research, and Application* (pp. 507–34). New York: Wiley. P

Theorizing within a behavioral paradigm. Suinn reviews current knowledge about the role of imagery in sports performance.

1433. Suinn, Richard M. (1984). Visual motor behavior rehearsal: The basic technique. *Scandinavian Journal of Behavior Therapy, 13:* 131–42. P

1434. Suits, Bernard. (1967). Is life a game we are playing? *Ethics, 77:* 209–13. T

1435. Summers, Jaylene, & Wolstat, Henry. Creative running. In Michael L. Sachs & Gary A. Buffone (Eds.), *Running as Therapy: An Integrated Approach* (pp. 93–100). Lincoln: University of Nebraska Press. P

The authors discuss the holistic health model in their approach to running, some psychological techniques used in training runners, and running as a psychotherapeutic modality.

1436. Sutherland, Audrey. (1978). *Paddling My Own Canoe.* Honolulu: University Press of Hawaii. B

A woman's account of her visits alone to a wild part of Molokai, which at times contained life-threatening moments, in order to experience "the surge of pure primitive joy and power that comes with being alone and wary and confident."

1437. Sutton-Smith, B. (1977). Towards an anthropology of play. In P. Stevens (Ed.), *Studies in the Antropology of Play: Papers in Memory of B. Allan Tindall.* West Point, NY: Leisure Press. T

1438. Swann, W. B., Jr. (1985). The self as architect of social reality. In B. R. Schlenker (Ed.), *The Self and Social Life* (pp. 100–26). New York: McGraw-Hill. T

1439. Sweeney, James Johnson. (1959, Apr.). Contemporary art: The generative role of play. *Review of Politics, 21:* 389–401. C

1440. Syer, John C., & Connolly, Christopher. (1984). *Sporting Body*

Sporting Mind: An Athlete's Guide to Mental Training. Cambridge, England: Cambridge University Press. **P**

Text on mind/body training for athletes, with an outline of a twelve-week training program and "The Sporting BodyMind Checklist," a seven-page chart that lists "those areas where athletes most frequently find their mental abilities and skills challenged," keyed to the pages in the book where specific exercises concerning them are located.

1441. Tarshis, Barry. (1979, Jan.). Is inner tennis dead? *Tennis, 14:* 30–33. **P**

1442. Taylor, Eugene. (1977). Aikido: The evolution of a martial art into a spiritual discipline. *Somatics, 1*(2): 8–12. **M**

1443. Taylor, Lawrence, with Falkner, David. (1987). *LT: Living on the Edge.* New York: Times Books. **B**

1443a. Taylor, Robin. (1993). "Enhancing Athletic and Psychic Performance Through the Use of Imagery-Based Mental Strategies." Unpublished doctoral dissertation. University of Edinburgh, Scotland.

1444. Team spirit: Canadians Terry McLaughlin, Tam Matthews and Jeff Boyd walked away with the inaugural running of USYRU's Team Race Championship in Texas. (1982, Feb.). *Yacht Racing/Cruising: 59–61.* **P**

Each participant was interviewed regarding the psychodynamics of peak team performance.

1445. Teich, Mark, & Weintraub, Pamela. (1985, Aug.). Out of the lab and into the stadium of ultra sports. *Omni, 7*(11): 39–44, 96–101. **P**

On the application of biomechanics to engineer new sporting feats.

1446. Teilhard de Chardin, Pierre. (1971a). *Activation of Energy.* New York: Harcourt Brace Jovanovich. **T**

1447. Teilhard de Chardin, Pierre. (1971b). *Human Energy.* New York: Harcourt Brace Jovanovich. **T**

Both volumes by Teilhard consist of essays on the nature of human energy, which he proposes can be used to transform humans and continue the evolution of the species and the cosmos itself. It is essential, however, to channel the energy "upward and outward" or humans will fail, break down, and turn to violence and revolt.

1448. Telander, Rick. (1986, Nov. 17). Ready . . . set . . . levitate! *Sports Illustrated, 65:* 17–21. **B**

1449. Theberge, Nancy. (1981). A critique of critiques: Radical and feminist writings on sport. *Social Forces, 60:* 341–53. **T**

1450. Theberge, Nancy. (1984). On the need for a more adequate theory of sport participation. *Sociology of Sport Journal, 1:* 26–35. **T**

1451. Theberge, Nancy. (1985). Toward a feminist alternative to sport as a male preserve. *Quest, 37:* 193–202. **T**

1452. Theberge, Nancy, & Donnelly, P. (Eds.). (1984). *Sport and the Sociological Imagination.* Fort Worth, TX: Texas Christian University Press. **T**

1453. Thomas, Carolyn E. (1977). Beautiful, just beautiful. In Dorothy J. Allen & Brian Fahey (Eds.), *Being Human in Sport.* Philadelphia: Lea & Febiger. **T**

1454. Thomas, Carolyn E. (1983). Aesthetic dimensions. In *Sport in a Philosophic Context.* Philadelphia: Lea & Febiger. **G**

1455. Thomas, Duane L. (1979, Fall). A definitional context for some socio-moral characteristics of sport. *Journal of the Philosophy of Sport, 6:* 39–47. T

1456. Thomas, Shirley. (1978). The spectacle of the body as exotic dance. *Journal of Health, Physical Education, Recreation, 49*(5): 39. T

Describes her motivation as an exotic dancer—pushing the spectators' "expectations by being more powerful than their fantasies."

1457. Thompson, Mickey, with Borgeson, Griffith. *Challenger: Mickey Thompson's Own Story of His Life of Speed.* Englewood Cliffs, NJ: Prentice-Hall. B

1458. Thomson, Patricia. (1967). *Ontological Truth in Sport: A Phenomenological Analysis.* Unpublished doctoral dissertation, University of Southern California. T

Attempts to apply Merleau-Ponty's phenomenological method to develop a theoretical construct "for the attainment of ontological truth in a self experience" (p. 4). The opportunity for self-realization may be found in any sport or movement activity.

1459. Thorne, Frederick C. (1963). The clinical use of peak and nadir experience reports. *Journal of Clinical Psychology, 19:* 248–50. G

Categorizes peak experiences as sensual, emotional, cognitive, conative (humans against destiny), personal growth, self-actualizing, and climax experiences.

1460. Tiger, Lionel. (1984). A note on sport. In *Men in Groups* (rev ed., pp. 115–25). New York: Marion Boyars. T

1461. Tinsley, Howard E. A., & Tinsley, Diane J. (1986). A theory of the attributes, benefits, and causes of leisure experience. *Leisure Sciences, 8:* 1–45. T

Hypothesizes that a "leisure state" is characterized by high intensity and engrossment and low self-focus.

1462. Todd, W. (1979). Some aesthetic aspects of sport. *Philosophy in Context, 9:* 8–21. T

1463. Torrey, Lee. (1985). *Stretching the Limits: Breakthroughs in Sport Science That Create Superathletes.* New York: Dodd, Mead. G

About recent conditions that encourage the breaking of athletic records. "The future of [human]kind is wide open, and at the cutting edge is the athlete," who "has no limits" (p. 285).

1464. Toynbee, Lawrence. (1962, Nov. 8). Artists and sport. *New Society, 6:* 28. In Ellen W. Gerber (Ed.), *Sport and the Body: A Philosophical Symposium* (pp. 305–06). Philadelphia, PA: Lea & Febiger, 1972. T

1465. Tresmer, David. (1981–82). Poise and splitting firewood: Miraculous power and marvelous activity—drawing water and hewing wood! *Somatics, 3:* 7–14 P

Application of the Alexander technique to the activity of splitting wood, including a mental rehearsal exercise at the "point of highest tension" that enables the wood-splitter to anticipate and smooth out any tension that could mar the act.

1466. Tucker, L. A. (1983). Effect of weight training on self-concept: A profile of those influenced most. *Research Quarterly for Exercise and Sport,* 54: 389–97. P

1467. Tutko, Thomas, & Tosi, U. (1976). *Sports Psyching.* Los Angeles: Tarcher. P

1468. Tyner, Gloria. (1968). *Sport and Being: An Application of Certain Concepts Developed by Viktor Frankl.* Unpublished master's thesis, University of Southern California, Los Angeles. P

1469. Umphlett, Wiley Lee. (Ed.). (1985). *American Sport Culture: The Humanistic Dimensions.* Lewisburg, PA: Bucknell University Press. T

1470. Umphlett, Wiley Lee. (1985). Introduction: The humanistic conflict in American sport culture. In Wiley Lee Umphlett (Ed.), *American Sport Culture: The Humanistic Dimensions* (pp. 15–26). Lewisburg, PA: Bucknell University Press. T

1471. Underwood, A. C. (1925). *Conversion: Christian and Non-Christian.* London: Allen and Unwin. G

1472. Ungerleider, Steven. (1985). Training for the Olympic games with mind and body. Two cases. *Perceptual and Motor Skills,* 61: 1291–94. P

1473. Ungerleider, Steven; Golding, Jacqueline M.; Porter, Kay; & Foster, J. (1989). An exploratory examination of cognitive strategies used by masters track and field athletes. *Sport Psychologist,* 3: 245–53. P

Out of 1,014 athletes who qualified for the 1987 National Masters Championships, 587 responded to a questionnaire about their use of cognitive strategies. Mental practice was reported by 70 percent, physical relaxation methods by 35.3 percent, meditation by 13.5 percent, yoga by 4.6 percent, and a martial art by 1.8 percent. Dreaming about their performance was reported by 45.5 percent, and of these, 86.2 percent reported success in their dream competitions.

1474. Urbankowski, Bohdan. (1984). A general theory of sport reality. *Dialectics and Humanism,* 11: 125–36. T

1475. Van Den Berg, J. H. (1952). The human body and the significance of human movement. *Philosophy and Phenomenological Research,* 13: 159–83. Also in Hendrik M. Ruitenbeck (Ed.), *Psychoanalysis and Existential Philosophy.* New York: Dutton, 1962. T

1476. Van Schoyck, S. R., & Grasha, A. F. (1981). Attentional style variations and athletic ability: The advantage of a sport-specific test. *Journal of Sport Psychology,* 3: 149–65. P

1477. Vance, N. Scott. (1984, May 10). Sport is a religion in America, controversial professor argues. *Chronicle of Higher Education,* 25–27. T

1478. Vander Velden, L., & Humphrey, J. H. (Eds.). (1986). *Current Selected Research in the Psychology of Sport* (Vol. 1). New York: AMS. P

1479. Vanderwerken, David L. (1979). The joy of sports books: A tout sheet. *Georgia Review,* 33: 707–12. G

1480. Vanderwerken, David L., & Wertz, Spencer K. (Eds.). (1985). *Sport Inside Out: Readings in Literature and Philosophy.* Fort Worth, TX: Texas Christian University Press. G

1481. VanderZwaag, Harold J. (1985). The interior stadium: Enhancing the illusion. In David L. Vanderwerken & Spencer K. Wertz (Eds.), *Sport In-*

side Out: Readings in Literature and Philosophy (pp. 165–73). Fort Worth, TX: Texas Christian University Press. **P**

1482. VanderZwaag, Harold J., & Sheehan, Thomas J. (1978a). *Introduction to Sport Studies: From the Classroom to the Ball Park*. Dubuque: IA: William C. Brown. **T**

Textbook on various aspects of sports, including distinguishing characteristics, social processes, women and sport, sport issues, the extraordinary sport experience, sport philosophy, history of sport, sociology of sport, sport psychology, sport physiology and biomechanics, careers in sport studies, teachings on it, and the coach. Each chapter has a summary, questions for discussion, and references.

1483. VanderZwaag, Harold J., & Sheehan, Thomas J. (1978b). Sport experience. In Harold J. VanderZwaag & Thomas J. Sheehan, *Introduction to Sport Studies: From the Classroom to the Ball Park*. Dubuque, IA: William C. Brown. **G**

1484. Vealey, R. S. (1989). Sport personology: A paradigmatic and methodological analysis. *Journal of Sport and Exercise Psychology, 11:* 216–35. **P**

Follow-up of Marten's 1975 review of the literature of personality theory and research in sport, which covered 1950–73. This sequel covers 1974–87 and considers paradigms, methodological aspects, and research objectives.

1485. Veblen, Thorstein. (1973). *The Theory of the Leisure Class*. Boston: Houghton Mifflin. **T**

Theorizes about the characteristics of the "leisure class," or those persons who do not have to work/fight to survive. They evidence a predilection for earlier animistic views of life and engage in activities, including sport and religious ritual, for their own sake, not simply for economic gain. This is made possible because they are sheltered from the predatory need to survive.

1486. Vermes, Jean-Rene. (1965, Sep.). The element of time in competitive games. *Diogenes, 50:* 25–42. **T**

1487. Vetter, Craig. (1986). John Bacher hangs on. *Outside, 11*(4): 38–42, 113–17. **B**

1488. Walchuk, P., & Orlick, Terry. (1980). Altered states of consciousness in sport experiences. In P. Klavora & K. A. W. Wipper (Eds.), *Psychological and Sociological Factors in Sport* (pp. 233–44). Toronto: University of Toronto, Publications Division, School of Physical and Health Education. **A**

1489. Waller, S. (1988). *Alterations of Consciousness in Sports Peak Performance* [Summary]. *Dissertation Abstracts International, 49*(10-B): 4585. **A**

Using Privette's experience questionnaire, states of consciousness of seventeen athletes who reported on sports peak performance were compared with those of seventeen subjects who took MDMA (methylenendioxymethamphetamine). The results indicate that sports peak performance is associated with altered states of consciousness that involve "feelings of perfection, expansion of self, unity, harmony, great fulfillment . . . [and] mystical rapture, which is unexpected, joyful, rare, valued, transitory, and embued with performance energy which seems to come from a preternatural source." A strong association between sports peak performance and mystical experience is suggested.

1490. Walsh, John Henry. (1968). *A Fundamental Ontology of Play and Leisure.* Unpublished doctoral dissertation, Georgetown University, Washington, DC. T

1491. Wankel, Leonard M. (1985). Personal and situational factors affecting exercise involvement: The importance of enjoyment. *Research Quarterly for Exercise and Sports, 56:* 275–82. P

1492. Wankel, Leonard M., & Berger, Bonnie G. (1990). The psychological and social benefits of sport and physical activity. *Leisure Research, 22:* 167–82. P

1493. Wankel, Leonard M., & Kreisel, P. S. J. (1985). Factors underlying enjoyment in youth sports: Sport and age group comparisons. *Journal of Sport Psychology, 7:* 51–64. P

1494. Wankel, Leonard M., & Kreisel, P. S. J. (1985). Methodological considerations in youth sport motivation research: A comparison of open-ended and paired comparison approaches. *Journal of Sport Psychology, 7:* 65–74. P

1495. Warner, G. (1974). What's up, Doc? The psychological aspects of athletes. *Basketball Bulletin:* 50–51. P

1496. Warren, Bruce F. (1987). The phenomenology of the peak experiences: An exploration of a type named the Noological Peak Experience [Summary]. *Dissertation Abstracts International, 47*(9-B): 3999. G

1497. Weintraub, Pamela, & Teich, Mark. (1987). Interview: Bruce Ogilvie. *Omni, 9*(12): 81–88, 118–19. P

A pioneer of sport psychotherapy recalls his long career working with teams and individual athletes. His basic working principle is that humans have "many levels of awareness and . . . our goal should be to seek the means for getting in touch with all of them." His primary technique is guiding athletes to relive the experience that is blocking them, as if playing back a tape, and then rewriting the script.

1498. Weiss, Paul. (1972). Records and the man. *Philosophic Exchange, 1:* 89–97. In Robert G. Osterhoudt (Ed.), *The Philosophy of Sport: A Collection of Original Essays* (pp. 11–33). Springfield, IL: Charles C Thomas, 1973. T

1499. Weiss, Paul. (1981). The nature of a team. *Journal of the Philosophy of Sport, 8:* 47–54. T

1500. Weiss, Paul. (1982). Some philosophical approaches to sport. *Journal of the Philosophy of Sport, 9:* 90–93. T

1501. Welsch, R. (1977). Achieving a performance peak: Psychological and physiological readiness. *Track and Field Quarterly Review, 77*(2): 31–33. P

1502. Welter, Katherine A. (1978). *Complete Moments in Sport: A Phenomenological Approach.* Unpublished master's thesis, Western Illinois University. G

1503. Wenkart, Simon. (1963, Spr.). The meaning of sports for contemporary man. *Journal of Existential Psychiatry 3:* 397–404. T

1504. Wertz, Spencer K. (1976). A note on the hidden Cartesianism in Hyland's methodological suggestions for sports inquiry. *Journal of the Philosophy of Sport, 3:* 118–20. T

1505. Wertz, Spencer K. (1977a). Toward a sports aesthetic (essay review). *Journal of Aesthetic Education, 11:* 103–11. T

1506. Wertz, Spencer K. (1977b). Zen, yoga, and sports: Eastern philosophy for Western athletes. *Journal of the Philosophy of Sport, 4:* 68–82. Y

1507. Wertz, Spencer K. (1978). Beauty in play: Aesthetics for athletes. *Southwest Philosophical Studies for April 1977, 2:* 77–84. T

Abbreviated version of Wertz (1977a). Discusses the aesthetic qualities of athletic form, continuity, mastery, expressive (symbolic) and evocative (emotional) elements, intellectual beauty, and dramatic unity as they are found in sports.

1508. Wertz, Spencer K. (1979). Are sports art forms? *Journal of Aesthetic Education, 13:* 107–09. T

1508a. Wertz, Spencer K. (1984). A response to Best on art and sport. *Journal of Aesthetic Education, 18:* 105–07.

1509. Wertz, Spencer K. (1985a). Artistic creativity in sport. In David L. Vanderwerken & Spencer K. Wertz (Eds.), *Sport Inside Out: Readings in Literature and Philosophy* (pp. 510–19). Fort Worth, TX: Texas Christian University Press. C

1510. Wertz, Spencer K. (1985b). Sport and the artistic. *Philosophy, 60:* 392–93. T

1511. Wertz, Spencer K. (1988). Context and intention in sport and art. In William J. Morgan & Klaus V. Meier (Eds.), *Philosophic Inquiry in Sport* (pp. 523–25). Champaign, IL: Human Kinetics. T

1512. Wertz, Spencer K. (1989). On *Sport Inside Out:* Reply to Feezell. *Teaching Philosophy, 12:* 43–46. G

1513. West, John B. (1985). *Everest: The Testing Place.* New York: McGraw-Hill. I

Account of the American Medical Research Expedition to Everest in which climbers going for the summit were physiologically monitored. An appendix lists the scientific articles based on the findings. In his Foreword, Sir Edmund Hillary writes that beyond all the technological improvements, it is the attitude of the climber and his/her energy, motivation, and enthusiasm that will determine the success of the climb.

1514. White, Brian. (1978). Natural challenge activities (toward a conceptual model). *Journal of Physical Education and Recreation, 49(4):* 44–46. T

White presents a model of how engaging in challenging leisure activities promotes personal growth.

1515. White, David A. (1975). Great moments in sport: The one and many. *Journal of the Philosophy of Sport, 2:* 124–32. G

1516. White, L., et. al. (1985). *Placebo: Theory, Research and Mechanisms.* New York: Guilford. P

1517. Whiting, H. T. A., & Masterson, D. W. (Eds.). (1974). *Readings in the Aesthetics of Sport.* London: Lepus Books. T

1518. Whitson, D. (1976). Method in sport sociology: The potential of a phenomenological contribution. *International Review of Sport Sociology, 4:* 53–68. P

1519. Widel, Ron. (1981). Frisbee: A humanistic sport. *Humanist, 41(1):* 37–41. I

1520. Wiggins, D. K. (1984). The history of sport psychology in North America. In J. M. Silva & R. S. Weinberg (Eds.), *Psychological Foundations of Sport* (pp. 9–22). Champaign, IL: Human Kinetics. P

1521. Wilgus, C. (1980). Transcendental skiing. *Skiing, 32*(7): 91. I

1522. Williams, Jean M. (Ed.). (1993). *Applied Sport Psychology: Personal Growth to Peak Performance* (2nd ed.). Palo Alto, CA: Mayfield. P

1523. Williams, Jean M., & Krane, V. (1993). Psychological characteristics of peak performance. In J. M. Williams (Ed.), *Applied Sport Psychology—Personal Growth to Peak Performance* (2nd ed.) (pp. 137–47). Palo Alto, CA: Mayfield. G

1524. Williams, Jeff. (1990, Jun. 19). Irwin captures 3rd Open title as Donald fades. *Newsday, 96.* B

1525. Wilson, B. (1977). Importance of team spirit. *Soccer World, 4*(1): 10–11. P

1526. Wilson, Stephen R., & Spencer, Robert C. (1990). Intense personal experiences: Subjective effects, interpretation, and after-effects. *Journal of Clinical Psychology, 46:* 565–73. G

Although not on sports, the classification and methodology presented here is applicable to studies of extraordinary sports experiences.

1527. Wood, D. (1982). Arts and sports: An artistic inquiry. *Pelops: Studies in Physical Education, Leisure Organizations, Play and Sport, 3:* 11–18, 27. T

1528. Wulk, Nancy G. (1979). A metacritical aesthetic of sport. In Ellen W. Gerber & William J. Morgan (Eds.), *Sport and the Body: A Philosophical Symposium* (2nd ed.). Philadelphia, PA: Lea & Febiger. T

1529. Wuthnow, Robert (1978). Peak experiences: Some empirical tests. *Journal of Humanistic Psychology, 18*(3): 59–75. G

This study indicates that people who say they have had intense peak experiences differ from those who say they have not. The former are more likely to say they have meaningful lives, know what the purpose of life is, and that they meditate. Their responses are consistent with Maslow's characteristics of self-actualization. The values of peakers are also less materialistic than those of non-peakers.

1530. Yeagle, Ellen H. (1986). *Highest Happiness: An Analysis of Artists' Peak Experiences.* Unpublished master's thesis, University of West Florida, Pensacola. G

1531. Yeagle, Ellen H.; Privette, Gayle; & Dunham, Frances Y. (1989). Highest happiness: An analysis of artists' peak experience. *Psychological Reports, 65:* 523–30. G

The authors compared narratives of the peak experiences of 29 exhibiting artists and 123 social science university students. No differences were found, and the experiential components of both groups were "consistent with major theoretical descriptions of subjective characteristics of the event" (p. 523).

1532. Ylannakis, Andrew, & Krotee, March L. (1980). Sport sociology. *Journal of Physical Education and Recreation, 51:* 41–42. T

1533. Zane, Frank, & Zane, Christina. (1981). *Super Bodies in 12 Weeks.* New York: Simon & Schuster. P

1534. Zaner, Richard M. (1966, Spr.). The radical reality of the human body. *Humanitas, 2:* 73–87. T

1535. Zaner, Richard M. (1979, Fall). Sport and the moral order. *Journal of the Philosophy of Sport, 6:* 7–18. T
Sport expresses the "soaring" and "playful" aspects of human beings, and teaches us to "cultivate the fields of the possible and enable them to become actual" (p. 17). Sport "is an exercise in the *imaginational*" (p. 17).

1536. Zeigler, Earle F. (1964). *Philosophical Foundations for Physical, Health, and Recreation Education.* Englewood Cliffs, NJ: Prentice-Hall. T

1537. Zeigler, Earle F. (1975). *Personalizing Physical Education and Sport Philosophy.* Champaign, IL: Stipes. P

1538. Zeigler, Earle F. (1980, Nov./Dec.). Philosophical perspective. *Journal of Physical Education and Recreation, 51:* 40. T

1539. Zeigler, Earle F. (1983). Philosophy of sport and developmental physical activity. *Sport Sciences, 4:* [pages unknown]. T

1540. Ziff, Paul. (1974). A fine forehand. *Journal of the Philosophy of Sport, 1:* 92–109. T

1541. Zillmann, Dolf; Bryant, Jennings; & Sapolsky, Barry S. (1979). The enjoyment of watching sport contests. In Jeffrey H. Goldstein (Ed.), *Sports, Games and Play: Social and Psychological Viewpoints* (pp. 297–335). Hillsdale, NJ: Erlbaum. P
The authors describe positive and negative effects of sport spectatorship, but emphasize the enjoyment of spectators watching sports events. They discuss several factors that may contribute to such enjoyment.

1542. Zuchova, K. (1980). Closer ties between sport and art. *International Review of Sport Sociology, 15:* 49–64. P

1543. Zuckerman, Marvin. (1990). The psychophysiology of sensation seeking. *Journal of Personality, 58:* 313–45. P

1544. Zuckerman, Marvin. (1993). *Behavioral Expressions and Psychological Bases of Sensation Seeking.* New York: Cambridge University Press. P

1545. Zuckerman, Marvin. (1994). Sensation seeking. In Raymond J. Corsini (Ed.), *Encyclopedia of Psychology* (2nd ed.) (Vol. 3, pp. 374–77). New York: Wiley. P

ACKNOWLEDGMENTS

MICHAEL MURPHY

Jim Hickman assembled some of the material in Chapters 5 through 7 and gave me helpful advice and criticism. Mike Spino, both my teacher and student in these matters, has done as much as anyone to kindle my love of sport. Richard Baker-Roshi, Abraham Maslow, David Meggyesey, Jerry Smith, and Sam Keen provided material for our thesis, and George Leonard gave inspiration and perspective to the enterprise from beginning to end.

My special thanks to John Brodie, who has been a chief catalyst for my study of the spiritual dimensions in sport. If he hadn't invited me to the 49er training camp in 1972, I never would have appreciated how fully these phenomena pervade our athletic endeavors. And, my wife, Dulce, helped in countless ways, through her discriminating eye for exaggeration and her own appreciation of metanormal experience.

RHEA WHITE

For the First Edition

I would like to express sincere thanks to Irving Adelman, for his informed and sensible advice and for his continual moral support. To Stephanie Becker, who not only typed beautiful copy but was able to read my handwriting. To Martin Bowe, for sharing the bulk of the literature search by tracking down some 1,500 books and scanning nearly 3,000; for making thousands of photocopies; for cogent editorial suggestions; for his willing ear; and especially for his readiness to go anywhere and do anything, which provided me with literally hundreds of extra hours to devote to the book.

To Harriet Edwards, whose editing of the manuscript was a superb combination of sensitivity and sensibility, whose moral support was always both timely and just what was needed, and whose assistance in any task was a model of speed, efficiency, and effectiveness. To Caroline Rocek, head of the interlibrary loan department at the East Meadow Public Library, and to the other members of that staff: Mark Dubno, Inga Goldhammer, Doris Goodman, and Fran Saslowsky, for obtaining nearly 2,000 books and articles from libraries all over the country. To Susan Schnapf, for assisting with permissions and for her pertinent suggestions and useful feedback.

To Kristin Smith-Gary, who provided invaluable assistance in organizing and indexing vast amounts of material, devoting to the task nearly all her days off over a two-year period. In addition, she was always there with cheer and encouragement. To Jean Spagnolo, for devoting time she could not well spare to help with permissions, check quotations, and provide a willing ear from beginning to end, always ready with suggestions and support. Finally, I would like to thank the entire Reference staff of the East Meadow Public Library, each of whom was always ready to help, to suggest, to encourage, to overlook, and to understand.

For the Second Edition

Meeting the publisher's deadline for this edition would not have been possible without the assistance of Stephanie Becker Boshnack, a first-rate inputter who stretched her time and capacities to meet many deadlines; inserted most of the new examples; input most of the second bibliography, and revised the style of the first so they were consistent; and input the index entries. I am also indebted to Maria Cassano, who scanned the first edition into the computer, cleaned it up, and inserted many of our editorial changes; to Maureen Dwyer, head of interlibrary loan at the East Meadow Public Library; Mary-Ellen Hanrahan and Elizabeth Bubser, who interloaned hundreds of books and articles for me; to Rocco Cassano, who kept the computer equipment running for all of us and offered advice on the more esoteric capabilities of Word for Windows, and mastered and then trained the rest of us in getting the most out of my software. And always, I am indebted to Irving Adelman, Head of the Reference Department at the East Meadow Public Library, for his never failing personal support and understanding and his superb reference and personal advice. I want also to thank the staff of the entire reference department for their continual good cheer and support of my sometimes monomaniacal pursuits. Finally, I give thanks to the Powers That Be for making it possible for me to live in the same wonderful house since 1966, which provides room to store all the materials I have gathered, and even more importantly, that embodies a stillness and serenity that seems joyful and alive, for the natural setting where the trees and birds and insects and small animals are a breath away, and have often taken mine with their beauty and antics. I have been extremely fortunate to have this open yet enclosing shelter in which to ponder and write about the extraordinary sports experience and other exceptional human experiences. More directly, caring for the acre plot has given me plenty of exercise, and I have had many a high simply from working outdoors, doing moderate-to-heavy yard work for several hours at a time, until it seemed, as darkness fell, that my feet barely touched the ground and I could have gone all night, if I could but see.

Grateful acknowledgment is made for permission to reprint excerpts from the following copyrighted works:

Sensory Awareness by Charles V. W. Brooks. Copyright © 1974 by Charles V. W. Brooks. Reprinted by permission of Sterling Lord Literistic, Inc.

The Stars at Noon by Jacqueline Cochran with Floyd Odlum. Copyright Jacqueline Cochran, 1954. Published by Little, Brown and Company.

Casebook of Astral Projection by Robert Crookall, University Books, Carol Publishing Group.

Koufax by Sandy Koufax with Ed Linn. Copyright © Sandy Koufax, 1966. Copyright renewed Sandy Koufax and Ed Linn, 1994. Reprinted by permission.

The Ultimate Athlete by George Leonard. Copyright © George Leonard, 1974, 1975. By permission of the author.

The Spirit of St. Louis by Charles Lindbergh. Copyright 1953 Charles Scribner's Sons, copyright renewed © 1981 by Anne Morrow Lindbergh. Reprinted with the permission of Scribner, an imprint of Simon & Schuster, Inc.

Golf in the Kingdom by Michael Murphy. Copyright © Michael Murphy, 1972. By permission of Viking Penguin, a division of Penguin Books USA Inc.

Sport and Identity by Patsy Neal. © Patsy Neal. By permission of the author.

The Babe Ruth Story by Babe Ruth as told to Bob Considine. Copyright George Herman Ruth, 1948. Copyright renewed Mrs. Mildred Considine, 1976. By permission of Dutton Signet, a division of Penguin Books USA Inc.

Meat on the Hoof by Gary Shaw. Copyright © 1972 by Gary Shaw. By permission of St. Martin's Press, Inc., New York, NY.

Faster: A Racer's Diary by Jackie Stewart and Peter Manso. By permission of Jackie Stewart.

Sacred Summits by Peter Boardman. Published in the United States by The Mountaineers.

Bone Games by Rob Schultheis. Copyright © 1984 by Rob Schultheis. Reprinted by permission of Random House, Inc.

Healing Journey: The Odyssey of an Uncommon Athlete by David Smith with Franklin Russell. By permission of David Smith.

INDEX

Ackerman, Diane, 18–19
Acute well-being, 9–10
Addiction, positive, 10
Aerobics, 34
Aging, freedom from, 142
Aikido, 32, 139, 141
Alertness, 35
Alexander Technique, 161*n.*
Ali, Muhammad, 75–76, 140, 146–147, 150
Allerson, Kim, 58
Alps, 107
Altered consciousness, 139, 178
Altered perceptions, 34–73
    awareness of the "other," 66–72
    extrasensory perception, *see* Extrasensory perception
    memories of, 36
    out-of-body experiences, 63–66
    of size and field, 37–40
    of time, *see* Time, perception of
Ament, Peter, 96
Andretti, Mario, 22
Andrews, Valerie, 112

Androgyny, 142–43
Angell, Roger, 56
Annapurna, 28, 112
Another Hurdle (Hemery), 111
Archery, 148
    Zen archery, 11, 25, 26
Arctic exploration, 33, 67
Arm wrestling, 81
Art of Dance (Duncan), 17
Ashe, Arthur, 3
Attention, sustained and focused, 107–10
    see also Concentration
Attner, Paul, 100
Augustine, Dave, 89
Aultman, Dick, 43
Auras, 134, 140
Aurobindo, Sri, 117*n.*, 127, 134–35
Autobiography of Values (Lindbergh), 117*n.*
Automatic writing, 69–71
Auto racing, *see* Race car driving
Awareness:
    heightened, 7, 34, 36–39

Awareness (*cont.*)
  of the "other," 66–72
Awe, sense of, 27–30

Balance, extraordinary, 84–86
Ballet, 42–43, 95–98, 146
Ballman, Gary, 89
Baltimore Colts, 59
Band, George, 46
Banner, Bob, 63
Bannister, Roger, 14, 47–48
Barat, Saint Madeline Sophie, 175
Barclay, Glen, 81
Barry, Rick, 27, 135
Baryshnikov, Mikhail, 42–43, 95–96
Baseball, 4, 7, 26, 27, 132–33
  altered perceptions in, 36, 37, 38, 40, 44–45, 47, 48–49, 54–56, 58
  extraordinary feats in, 75, 82, 86, 89, 101
Basketball, 27, 28, 31, 125, 130–31
  altered perceptions in, 38, 39, 45, 47, 49–50, 59, 60
  extraordinary feats in, 74–75, 95, 100
  mind/body training, 155
  team experiences, 8
  "touch" in, 125
Basmajian, John, 170
Beamon, Bob, 29
Beard, Frank, 80
Beebe, Jim, 38
Beggs, Robert Kyle, 64–65
Beisser, Arnold, 100
Beloff, John, 70
Bench, Johnny, 58
Bennet, Glin, 72
Benoit, Joan, 52, 76
Bernadette of Lourdes, Saint, 175–176
Best, George, 146

Beyond Biofeedback (Green and Green), 170n.
Bicameral mind theory, 71n.
Billiards, 148
Biofeedback training, 18, 149, 153, 170–71, 178
Blackmore, Susan J., 63
Blackwater experiment, 122
Blalock, Jane, 152
Blanda, George, 142
Blount, Roy, 81
Boardman, Peter, 45–47
Boats, see Ocean voyages in small boats
Body awareness, 161–64
Bodybuilders, 150, 158, 176–77
Bonatti, Walter, 135–36
Bond, Donald, 32
Bone Games (Schultheis), 122–23
Bonington, Chris, 68, 69, 70, 112
Borromeo, St. Charles, 175
Bouldering, 76, 96
Bowie, Paul, 102
Boxing, 26, 31, 79, 119–20, 159
  altered perceptions in, 61
  extraordinary feats and powers in, 75–76, 81, 91, 138, 148
Bradley, Bill, 8, 27, 49–50
Brahmasiddhis (powers to apprehend Brahman), 137–38
Brain-Mind Bulletin, 18
Brainwave rhythm, 44
Braud, William G., 172
Breath, expelling the, 91, 92–93
Breathing exercises, 78, 79, 98
Breslin, Jimmy, 47
Brier, Bob, 45
Brock, Lou, 48–49
Brodie, John, 22, 34–35, 42, 76, 88–89, 118, 146, 147–48
Brooks, Charles, 161–64
Brown, Barbara, 44
Brown, Bundini, 140

Brown, Jim, 48, 146
Brown, Joe, 46
Brown, John P., 90
Brown, Richard Alvin, 161n.
Buck, Don, 81
Buddhism, 115, 118, 124, 129, 134, 151, 178
  vibhuti (perfection), 137
Buffalo Bills, 149
Buhl, Herman, 145
Bullfighting, 20, 127–28
Bunn, Curtis, 59
Byrd, Richard, 33

Calm, 3, 11–13, 15, 22, 41, 78, 83, 131, 134, 145, 152
Canadian National Women's Volley-ball team, 150
Cancer treatment, 169–70
Castaneda, Carlos, 85
Castaneda's Journey (DeMille), 85
Casteret, Norbert, 12
Catherine de Ricci, Saint, 174
Cave exploring, 12
Centered Skiing (McCluggage), 135
Cerutty, Percy, 128–29, 142
Chaldean Oracles, 136
Chaytor, A. H., 38
Cheerfulness, 9
Chess, 40
Ch'i, 77
  see also Ki
Chicago Black Hawks, 99
Chicago Cubs, 54–56
Chi Kung, 98
Chou, 85
Chow, David, 81, 90, 92, 98
Christianity, 134
  prayer of quiet, 152
Clairaudience, 143–44
Clairvoyance, 3, 49, 50, 84, 144, 177
  to diagnose disease, 148

Clarity, mental, 35
Clark, Jimmy, 32
Cochran, Jackie, 50–52
Coleridge, Samuel Taylor, 112
Collected Works of Sri Aurobindo, The (Aurobindo), 117n.
Commitment, long-term, 113–14
Communality, 8
Concentration, 11, 13, 23, 25, 37, 38–39, 43, 77, 78, 79, 107–110, 119, 139, 149, 151
Confidence, 7, 21, 43, 93, 145
Conley, Gene, 7
Connolly, Olga (née Fikotova), 26–27
Continuity with past ages, sense of, 30
Control, being in, 7, 10, 20–22, 78, 138
Cooper, Linn F., 43–44
Cooperation, 112
Cotton, Henry, 57, 58
Court, Margaret, 107
Cousteau, Jacques, 17
Cousy, Bob, 38, 39
Cragun, Richard, 42
Cranston, Toller, 117
Creativity, 44, 110–12
Crookall, Robert, 64
Crozier, Roger, 74

d'Amboise, Jacques, 14
Dancing, 14, 17, 20, 95–96, 97–98, 128, 146
da Silva, Jerome, 175
Daumal, René, 124
David-Neal, Alexandra, 82–83, 84
Davis, Sam, 81
Death, incorruptibility after, 175–76
"Death touch," 91
Decathlon, 21, 159
Decker, Mary, 53
Deep-sea diving, 12, 139, 144–45

Deindorfer, Robert, 24–25, 38, 40, 43, 100
Déjà vu, 44–47
Delgado, Rich, 82
Demaret, Jimmy, 126–27
DeMille, Richard, 85
DeMott, Benjamin, 15
Dennis, Larry, 43
Dervish dancing rituals, 128
Detachment, 14–15, 78–79
  from results, 110
Detroit Pistons, 59
Detroit Tigers, 149, 151
Devaney, John, 39
Dingwall, E. J., 97
Discipline, 118–24, 126
Discus throw, 26–27
Disease, clairvoyant diagnosis of, 148
Disembodied entities, perception of, 136
Dittert, René, 100
Divers, ocean, 12, 139, 144–45
Don Juan, 127
Doyle, Jimmy, 61
Drag racing, 53–54
Dreams, 61–62, 110–11, 112, 130–131, 159
Duncan, Isadora, 17, 20, 146
Duncan, Margherita, 20
Dykstra, Lenny, 44–45

Earhart, Amelia, 50–52
Ease, extraordinary, 86–87
Eastern European athletes, 149
Eccles, Sir John, 101
Eckhart, Meister, 118, 130
Ecstasy, 17–20, 46–47
  essential ecstasy, 127–29
Effortlessness, 86–87
Ego-loss, 139
El Cordobes, 20
Elephant Island, 67

Elliot, Herb, 128–29
Elusiveness, 93–94
Emerson, Richard M., 12
Emmerich, Catherine, 174
Emmerton, Bill, 17, 30
Empathy, 49
Endurance, extraordinary, 81–84
Energy:
  collective, 112
  emanations of extraordinary, 140
  exceptional, 75–79, 136
  sense of, 9, 19, 22
  transmission from person to person, 145
Energy Body, 164–66
Engel, Bernard, 171
Equipment, unity with, 32, 133
Erickson, Milton H., 43–44
Erving, Julius, 47, 74
Esdaile, James, 169
ESP, see Extrasensory perception
Estcourt, Nick, 68–69, 70, 136
Estes, Wayne, 27, 60–61
Euphoria, see Ecstasy
Eustress, 76–77
Evans, Billy, 54–55
Evans, Lee, 111–12, 140, 150
Everest, Mount, 67, 68–71
Evert, Chris, 154
Evolutionary possibilities, 167–79
Exhilaration, 120–21
Explorers, 33, 66, 67–68, 72
Extraordinary feats, 74–102
  balance, 84–86
  ease, 86–87
  endurance, 81–84
  energy, 75–79
  invulnerability, 98–99
  mind over matter, 98, 99–102
  psychokinesis, see Psychokinesis
  speed, 81–84
  strength, 80–81

Extraordinary powers in yoga and sport, comparison of, 136–48
Extrasensory perception, 48–63, 143
  "called play," 54–59
  components of, 48
  dramatic form of, 53
  dreams, 61–63
  psi enhancement, 63
  of relatives of athletes, 62–63
Ezar, Joe, 57–58

Fairfax, John, 52–53
Falkus, Hugh, 58
Fans, 76, 89, 117, 146
  ecstatic experiences shared by, 19–20
  spiritual healing of, 145
Farrelly, Midget, 21, 119
Faster (Stewart), 14–15
Ferguson, Marilyn, 18
Figure skating, 58, 117
Fimrite, Ron, 82
Fire immunity, 141–42
Firewalking, 141–42
Fischer, Pat, 88
Fishing, 24–25, 100
  altered perceptions in, 38, 43, 58
Fleck, Jack, 37–38
Floating, feeling of, 17–18, 131
Floyd, Keith, 44
Fluidity, mental and emotional, 141
Flying, 3, 15, 16, 18–19, 20–21, 32–33, 116–17
  altered perceptions and, 50–52, 65, 66–67
  extraordinary powers when, 143–144
  feeling of, 17–18
Flying Magazine, 16
Fodor, Nandor, 97–98
Football, 7, 18, 22, 23, 118, 134
  altered perceptions in, 34–35, 38–39, 40–41, 42, 48, 59
  extraordinary feats and powers in, 76, 81, 86, 88–89, 94, 139, 142, 144, 146, 147, 148
  mind/body training, 152, 154
  team experiences, 8
Ford, Whitey, 36
Fox, Matthew, 32
Foyt, A. J., 60, 61–62
Frady, Marshall, 95
Francis, Russ, 89
Francis de Sales, Saint, 118, 131, 175
Francis of Assisi, Saint, 129, 131, 174
Frazier, Walt, 49–50
Freedom, sense of, 16
Frisbee, 23–24
Fromm, Erika, 169n.
Fundamental reality, 115–17
Furst, Peter, 84–85

Gabbard, Glen O., 63
Gallwey, Tim, 151
Galvanic skin response (GSR), 172
Gaspar, Rod, 47
Gecko crawling, 86
Geller, Uri, 87
Genaro, don, 85
Gibert, Dr., 172
Gilbey, John, 81, 85, 98
Gill, John, 76, 96
Glasser, William, 10, 17
Gliding, 12
Golf, 1–2, 3, 23, 108, 126–27, 179
  altered perceptions in, 36, 37–38, 43, 56–58
  extraordinary feats and powers in, 79, 80, 86, 87–88, 139, 142, 143, 148
  mind/body training, 152, 154, 159

Golf in the Kingdom (Murphy), 1, 2, 3, 156, 157, 166n.
Golf My Way (Nicklaus), 154
Gott, Jim, 16
Gourbeyre, Dr. Imbert, 174
Govinda, Anagarika, 83–84
Graham, Athol, 54
Granatelli, Andy, 60
Grange, Red, 86
Gravity, seemingly escaping laws of, 16, 28, 42
Green, Dr. Alyce, 44, 170
Green, Dr. Elmer, 44, 170
Greene, Joe, 7, 8, 81
Greenhouse, Herbert, 65
Gretzky, Wayne, 58–59, 125
Grossinger, Richard, 89, 101
Gymnists, 125
Gyorbiro, Zsolt, 11

Hagen, Walter, 56–57
Hallucinogenic drugs, 160
Halos, 134, 140
Handbook of Parapsychology, 97
Harmonizing with the elements while transcending them, 147
Harris, Dorothy V., 35, 76–77
Harrison, E. J., 25, 91, 93
Haston, Dougal, 70, 71
Hawkins, Fred, 43
Hayter, Adrian, 147
Heafner, Clay, 23
Healing:
    mind-assisted, 169–70
    spiritual, 145–46, 169–70
Hearing:
    clairaudience, 143–44
    sharper, 34, 176–77, 178
Heat, extreme body, 139, 174–75
Hemery, David, 16, 111, 112
Hemingway, Ernest, 127–28
Herrigel, Eugen, 25, 26
Herzog, Maurice, 28

Hesse, Herman, 133
Hierocles of Alexandria, 136
High jumpers, 150
Hiking, 11
Hilgard, Ernest R., 169n.
Hinduism, 115, 134
    siddhis, *see* Siddhis (extraordinary powers)
Hockey, 38, 125
    altered perceptions in, 58–59
    extraordinary feats and powers in, 74, 81–82, 99, 147
Hoffman, Edward, 3–4
Hogan, Ben, 23, 37, 126–27, 146
Hogsty Reefs, 52–53
Homecoming, sense of, 10
"Home court advantage," 89
Homo Ludens (Huizinga), 106–7
Honorton, Charles, 173
Horseback riding, 19, 36
Horse racing, 62
Houts, Jane, 40
Hughes, Pat, 59
Huichol Indians, 84–85
Huizinga, Johan, 106
Human limits, exploration of, 112–113
Human Personality and Its Survival of Bodily Death (Myers), 169n., 172
Hunter, Catfish, 26
Hurdles, 16, 111
Huxley, Aldous, 114
Hypnagogic imagery, 44
Hypnosis, 99, 149–50, 178
    hypnotic suggestion, 158, 168–69
    mass, 146–47
    self-, 23, 111
    telepathic, 172
Hypnosis: Research Developments and Perspectives (Fromm and Shor), 169n.
Hypnotic Sensibility (Hilgard), 169n.

Identity, knowledge by, 129–35
Ignatius of Loyola, Saint, 175
Imagination, 110, 153, 156
Immortality, feelings of, 30–31
Immovability, 147
Immunity to harm or danger, 147
Impassibility, 141–42
Incendium amoris, 174–75
Incombustibility, 141–42
Indestructibility, 141
Inner seeing, 159–61, 176, 178
Inner world, richness of the, 133–34
Instinctive action, 24–27
Intensity, peak, 8, 13
Interior Castle (Saint Teresa), 133
Internal bodily structures, perception
    of, 148, 159–61
Intuition, 49
Invincibility, feeling of, 8, 30, 31
Invisibility, 139–40
Invulnerability, state of, 98–99
Irvine, Andrew, 69, 70
Irwin, Hale, 58
Irwin, Harvey J., 63
Isha Upanishad, 115
Izzard, R., 71*n.*

Jackson, Ian, 19, 82, 135, 145
Jahenny, Marie-Julie, 174
James, William, 117*n.*
Janet, Pierre, 172
Jenner, Bruce, 21, 159
Johansson, Ingemar, 26
John of the Cross, Saint, 118
Johnson, Magic, 125
Johnson, Mildred, 64–65
Johnson, Vinnie, 59
Jones, Bobby, 43, 143, 177
Jones, Cleon, 89
Jones, Parnelli, 60, 62
Jones, Robert F., 94
Jordan, Michael, 19–20, 75, 95,
    111

Joseph of Copertino, 97
*Journal of the Society for Psychical
    Research*, 69
Joy, *see* Ecstasy
Joy of Sports (Novak), 8
Judo, *see* Martial arts

Kahn, Roger, 37
Kangchenjunga, Mount, 45–46
Karate, 78, 90, 108–9, 141, 147
Karate Illustrated, 92
Karateka, 90, 93
Kekulé, Friedrich, 112
Ki, 77–79, 99, 140, 141, 164
"*Kiai* shout," 91
Kiernan, Thomas, 75
Kinesthetic awareness, 34, 161–64
King, Bernard, 100
King, Billie Jean, 11, 107–8, 125–
    126, 150, 151, 154
Knudsen, George, 43
Kokokan School of Judo, 25
Kornheiser, Tony, 159
Kostrubala, Thaddeus, 9, 78
Koufax, Sandy, 132–33
Kung fu, 81, 85, 91–92, 141

Lachenal, Pierre, 16, 28, 76, 102
Lake of the Woods, 38
Lambeer, Bill, 59
Lane, Mac, 94
Laski, Marghanita, 19
Lauck, Don, 87
Laver, Rod, 107
LeCron, Leslie M., 168–69
Lee, Bruce, 90
Leibnitz, Gottfried, 114
Leonard, George, 29–30, 93–94,
    129*n.*, 164–66
Lester, James, 72
Leuchs, Arne, 18
Levitation, 2, 95–98, 140
Lewis, Jesse Francis, 19

Libby, Bill, 60, 62
Life, 26
Life on the Run (Bradley), 8
Life review, 44, 47
Lights, seeing, 134–36
  see also Luminous experiences
Lindbergh, Charles, 3, 15, 65, 66–
  67, 71*n*., 116–17, 117*n*.
Li Neng-jan', 91
Lipsyte, Robert, 118–19
Lizard technique, 85–86
Lockhart, Barbara, 76
Logan, James, 71*n*.
Lombardi, Vince, 145, 146
Long jump, 29
Long-term commitment, 113–14
Lowe, Ralph, 62
Luisetti, Hank, 95
Luminous expereriences, 2, 3, 12,
  13, 17, 46, 140
  body luminosity, 175
  sense of inner illumination,
  140
Lung Chi Cheung, 98
Lung-gom-pa runners of Tibet, 82–
  83, 84, 148
Lung Kai Ming, 98
Lydon, Chris, 38
Lydwina of Schiedam, Saint, 175

McCluggage, Denis, 135
McFadden, Bernard, 142
McKelvey, Eural, 155, 156
McKinney, Steve, 11, 17
Magic and Mystery in Tibet (David-
  Neel), 82–83
Mahan, Larry, 151, 154
Maharshi, Ramana, 175
Manipulation of psychological pro-
  cesses of others, 146
Mankin, Valentin, 35, 145
Manry, Robert, 44
Manso, Peter, 23, 133

Man, Sport and Existence (Slusher),
  13
Mantle, Mickey, 36, 132–33
Marathon runners, *see* Running,
  distance
Marciano, Rocky, 119–20
Marcus, Joe, 39
Martha, Paul, 39
Martial arts, 25, 31–32, 77, 136,
  147
  psychokinesis in the, 90–98
Mass, ability to change, 139
Matsuura, 25
Matterhorn, 21, 48, 135–36
Matthews, Stephanie, 169–70
Meditation, 10, 18, 78, 109–10,
  121, 128, 149, 151–52, 178
Meggyesey, David, 134, 143
Memories of moments of heightened
  awareness, 36
Menninger Foundation, 170
Mental practice, 149, 150, 153–58
"Mesh practice," 141
Metanormal powers, acceptance of,
  4
Michener, James, 95
Middlecoff, Cary, 43
Miller, Johnny, 88
Mind/body training, 149–66
Mind/body unity, 16, 31, 77–78
Mind over matter, 98, 99–102,
  141
Minick, Michael, 91–92
Minotaur, myth of the, 133
Miracle at Coogan's Bluff, The
  (Kiernan), 75
Mishima, Yukio, 32–33
Mitchell, Janet Lee, 63
Mocellin, Jane, 71*n*.
Moody, Raymond, 47
Moore, Kenny, 100
Moss, Stirling, 133
Mountain climbing, 3, 10, 12, 18,

21–22, 28, 112, 122–23, 124, 135–36
altered perceptions in, 45–46, 48, 67–72
extraordinary feats and powers in, 76, 84, 87, 102, 139, 143
Mountaineering, 16, 31, 66, 67, 68–71, 100, 103, 113, 145
Mount Analogue (Daumal), 124
Mu, 79
Murphy, Michael, 1–3, 166*n.*
Musial, Stan, 37
Myers, F. W. H., 169*n.*, 172
Myers, Martha, 161*n.*
Mystery, sense of, 27–30
Mystical ecstasies, 17–18
Mysticism and sport, 103–48
attention sustained and focused, 107–10
boundaries of sport, 106–7
chart, comparative, 138–48
commitment, long-term, 113–14
creative and integrative power, 110–12
detachment from results, 110
extraordinary powers, 136–48
human limits, exploration of, 112–13
mystical sensations, 1–33
the perennial philosophy, *see* Perennial philosophy, parallels between sport and
relinquishment of old patterns and creation of new ones, 104–6
space, sacred, 106–7
time, sacred, 106–7
yoga and sport, chart comparing extraordinary powers in, 138–148
see also specific sensations, e.g., Unity, sense of

Nadeau, Robert, 93, 164
Nagamine, Shoshin, 108–9
Namath, Joe, 59, 151
Nature, communion with, 32–33, 35–36
see also Unity, sense of
Naughton, Jim, 111
Neal, Patsy, 28, 31, 103, 130–31
Nelson, R. D., 173
Neri, Saint Philip, 175
Neumann, Randy, 31
Neva, Mount, 122–23
Newman, Roscoe, 143
New York Giants (baseball), 75
New York Jets, 59
New York Knicks, 8, 49–50
New York Yankees, 54–55
Nichols, Bobby, 88
Nicklaus, Jack, 36, 43, 87–88, 154, 159
Nicol, J. Frazer, 97
Nideffer, Robert, 149
Nieporte, Tom, 79
Nijinsky, 97–98, 146
Nitschke, Ray, 48
Noi cun, 91–92
Norton, Ken, 149–50
Nourishment, need for little, 145
Novak, Michael, 8, 26
Numinous experiences, 27–30

Oates, Bob, Jr., 8
Oates, Joyce Carol, 119–20
Ocean voyages in small boats, 3, 126
altered perceptions in, 44, 52–53, 66, 72
extraordinary powers during, 139, 147
Omnipotence, feeling of, 28–29
"One finger Kung," 92
O'Neil, Kitty, 12, 102
Oneness, *see* Unity, sense of

Orr, Bobby, 38, 74, 81–82, 99, 147
"Other," awareness of the, 66–72
Otto, Rudolph, 29
Out-of-body experiences, 63–66, 136, 140
Outside oneself, feeling of being, 17–18
Outward Bound, 19
Oxygen, ability to survive with little or no, 139
Oyama, Masutatsu, 78–79, 93

Pacific Crest Trail, 11
Pain, 128–29
  mastery of, 138–39
Palmer, Arnold, 23, 87–88, 93
Palmer, Jim, 101
Parachute jumping, 15, 142
Parapsychological Association, 101, 173
Paul, Saint, 27
Peace, sense of, 11–13, 110
Pelé, 18, 38, 39, 94, 141
Perceptions, altered, see Altered perceptions
Perennial philosophy, parallels between sport and, 114–36
  deeper perfection, knowing and expressing, 124–27
  discipline, 118–24, 126
  ecstasy, essential, 127–29
  fundamental reality, 115–17
  knowledge by identity, 129–33
  provisional reality of the ordinary world, 117–18
  richness of the inner world, 133–134
  subtle body, 134–36
Perfect Game, The (Seaver), 47
Perfection, knowing and expressing, 124–27
Peripheral vision, 39
Pettit, Bob, 78

Philadelphia Phillies, 149, 151
Philadelphia 76ers, 74
Physical Phenomena of Mysticism, The (Summers), 97
Physical Phenomena of Mysticism, The (Thurston), 97
Pio, Padre, 174
Pipgras, George, 55
Pittsburgh Steelers, 7, 8
PK, see Psychokinesis
Placebo research, 168
Playboy, 177
Plimpton, George, 28–29, 93
Plotinus, 129–30
Poincaré, Henri, 112
Popocatépetl, Mount, 124
Porousness, 141
Portland Trail Blazers, 59
Positive Addiction (Glasser), 10
Positive addictions, 10
Possessed, feeling of being, 7
Power, feeling of, 7, 20–22, 110
Prana, 77, 140, 164
Prayer of quiet, 152
Precognition, see Extrasensory perception
Premonitions, see Extrasensory perception
Present, being in the, 22–24, 108
Pribram, Karl, 129n.
Price, Joseph, 20
Psi enhancement, 63
Psychedelic drugs, 160
Psychic mobility, 139, 143
Psychic self-regulation (PSR), 149, 171, 178
"Psyching out" opponents, 146
Psychokinesis, 3, 87–98, 101, 147–148, 171–73, 177
  in the martial arts, 90–98
  willing, 87–90
Psychological integration, 110–12
Pumping Iron, 158

Race car driving, 9, 14–15, 20, 22, 23, 32, 78, 113, 133, 138
altered perceptions in, 41–42, 60
extraordinary powers in, 138
Racquetball, 3
Radin, D. I., 173
Rasmussen, Randy, 59
Ratti, Oscar, 77, 99
Ravizza, Kenneth, 27–28
Reality:
fundamental, 115–17
provisional reality of the real world, 117–18
Rebuffat, Gaston, 21–22, 48, 84, 107
"Red sand palm," 92–93
Reid, Mike, 34
Reinwald, Richard, 100
Relatives of athletes, precognitive experiences of, 62–63
Relaxation, 43, 78, 79, 149
Religion and sport, see Mysticism and sport
Religious stigmata, 141, 173–74
Reluctance to discuss spiritual experiences, 2, 4, 6, 103–4
Reynolds, Allie, 40
Rhine, Dr. Louisa E., 53
Rhythmical movement, 19, 20, 78, 79
Rice, Grantland, 86
Richard, Colette, 12–13
Rindt, Jochen, 23
Robinson, Sugar Ray, 61, 79, 159
Rock climbing, 19, 63–64
Rodeo riders, 133, 152, 154
Roemer, John, 17
Rogo, D. Scott, 63
Ronberg, Gary, 99
Rono, Henry, 100
Root, Charley, 54, 55
Roseboro, John, 132–33
Rosenthal, Saul, 20

Rosewall, Ken, 107
Ross, Murray, 71n.
Running, 5, 9–10, 14, 19, 111–12
altered perceptions in, 42, 47–48, 52, 53, 62–63
distance, 3, 17, 30, 35, 76, 78, 105–6, 124, 125, 128–29, 138, 139, 145, 148, 151, 160, 176
extraordinary feats and powers in, 76, 82–83, 86, 100, 138, 139, 140, 142, 145
mind/body training, 150
relinquishment of old patterns and emergence of new patterns, 105–6
Rush, Joseph H., 97
Russell, Bill, 50, 111, 155–56
Russell, Franklin, 122
Russia, psychic self-regulation (PSR) in, 149, 171, 178
Ruth, Babe, 54–56, 103, 145
Ryan, Nolan, 82
Ryback, Eric, 11
Ryun, Jim, 62–63

Saal, Herbert, 42–43
Sabasteanski, Frank, 52
Sacred Summits (Boardman), 45–47
Sailing, see Ocean voyages in small boats
Sanderson, Derek, 81–82
San Francisco 49ers, 76
Sauers, Don, 79
Schaap, Dick, 29
Schaller, Robert, 10
Schlitz, Marilyn J., 172
Schmeidler, Gertrude R., 97
Schmidt, Helmut, 172
Schultheis, Bob, 122–24
Schwartz, Jack, 170
Schwarzenegger, Arnold, 150, 154, 158
Scott, Ade, 25

Scott, Doug, 68, 70, 136
Scuba diving, 16, 17
Seaver, Tom, 47
Second Wind (Russell), 155
Seifert, Chris, 100
Self-fulfilling prophecy, 59–60
Self-hypnosis, 23, 111
Self-integration, 110–12
Self-mastery, sense of, 20, 22
Seligman, Martin, 91
Selver, Charlotte, 161–62
Sensory awareness or awakening,
    161–64
Sensuality, 35
Serenity, 1
Seriff, 89
Seymour, Steve, 44
Shackleton, Sir Ernest Henry, 67–68
Shamanism, 123, 124, 161, 178
Shape, ability to change, 139
Shaw, Gary, 40–41
Sheehan, George, 9–10
Sherrard, Carol, 71*n.*
Shoemaker, Willie, 62
Shor, Ronald E., 169*n.*
Shorter, Frank, 5
Shuba, George, 27
Siddhis (extraordinary powers), 93
    in yoga and sport, comparison of,
    138–48
Silence, 12, 13, 84
Silent Pulse, The (Leonard), 129*n.*,
    166*n.*
Silva, Ramon Medina, 85
Simon, Dick, 9
Simonton, Dr. Carl, 169–70
Sixth sense, *see* Extrasensory
    perception
Size, ability to change, 139
Skalka, Patricia, 18
Skepticism, 2, 5, 81
Ski Extreme (Vallencant), 13
Skiing, 11, 13, 17, 18, 20, 144, 147

cross-country, 151
Skydiving, 2, 140, 144
Slocum, Joshua, 3, 66, 136
Slowing down of time, 4, 40–44, 50
Slusher, Howard, 13
Smith, Adam, 35–36, 144–45
Smith, David, 120–22, 140
Smith, Horton, 56–57
Smith, Malcolm, 11
Smith, Red, 75
Smith, Robert, 91
Smythe, Frank, 67, 103
Snead, Sam, 142
Snow, Jack, 23
Soaring, 12, 15, 21
Soccer, 18, 38, 39, 94, 141
Society for Psychical Research, 70
Sollier, Andre, 11
Solzhenitsyn, Alexander, 71*n.*
South Pole, 67
Space:
    altered perception of, 37–40
    sacred, 106–7
Spahn, Warren, 86
Spangler, Richard, 81, 90, 92, 98
Speed, extraordinary, 81–84
Speed skating, 76, 82
Spino, Mike, 105, 151
Spirit of St. Louis, The (Lindbergh),
    117*n.*
Spirit-shout art, 92
Spiritual experience and sport, *see*
    Mysticism and sport
Spontaneity, 24–27
Sport and Identity (Neal), 130
Sports:
    expanded definition of, 3
    mysticism and, *see* Mysticism and
    sport
    *see also specific sports and
    athletes*
Sports in America (Michener), 95
Stanford, Rex G., 97

Steppenwolf (Hesse), 133
Stewart, Jackie, 14–15, 41–42, 78
Stigmata, 141, 173–74
Stillness, 11–13, 15, 32
Stock car racing, 60
Stones, Dwight, 150
Stopping of time, 47–48
Straits of Gibraltar, 121–22
Streisand, Barbra, 177
Strength, extraordinary, 80–81
Stuntpeople, 12, 102
Suarez, Father Francis, 175
Subtle body, 134–36
Suedfeld, Peter, 71*n.*
Sufism, 175, 178
Summers, Montague, 97
Surfing, 19, 21, 28, 32, 119
Suspension, uncanny, 95–98, 136
Suzuki, D. T., 130
Swift movement, 19
Swimming, 52, 64–65, 125
    extraordinary powers in, 138,
        139, 140, 142
    long-distance, 120–22, 151
Switzer, Kathy, 35
Swordswallowing, 141–42
Synaesthesia, 144–45

Tai Chi, 47
Tales of Power (Castaneda), 85
Tameshiwari, 90
Taoism, 129, 178
Tao Te Ching, 27, 129
Target shooting, 148
Tarkenton, Francis, 18, 154–55
Taylor, Lawrence, 38–39
Team experiences, 8, 50, 145
    extraordinary feats, 75, 76
    sense of unity, 31–32
    teamwork, 112
Telander, Rick, 95
Telekinetic ability, 96
Telepathy, 49, 50, 132–33, 144

telepathic suggestion, 172–73
Temperature, extreme body, 139,
    174–75
Tennis, 3, 11, 28–29, 107–8, 125–
    126, 150
Teresa of Avila, Saint, 97, 133
Terray, Lionel, 16, 18, 76, 87,
    102
Terry, Walter, 96
Third wind, 10
Thomas à Kempis, 175
Thomas de Celano, 174
Thompson, Bobby, 75
Thompson, Danny, 54
Thompson, David, 95
Thompson, Ian, 17
Thompson, Mickey, 53–54
Thouless, R. H., 100–1
Thurston, Herbert, 97
Tiant, Luis, 101
Tibetan Buddhism, 175
Time, 95–96
Time:
    déjà vu, 44–47
    life review, 44, 47
    perception of, 40–48, 134,
        143
    sacred, 106–7
    slowing down of, 4, 40–44, 50
    stopping of, 47–48
    time travel, 143
Tohei, Koichi, 77
Token of espousal, 174
Torres, Jose, 75
Torrey, Lee, 170
Transcendence, 127, 131
Transformative experiences, 120–
    124, 133
Tresmer, David, 161*n.*
Treu, Bill, 155, 156
Trevarthon, Dr. Colwyn, 39
Tumo (inner fire), 139, 175
Twemlow, Stuart W., 63

Ultimate Athlete, The (Leonard), 164–65, 166*n.*
United States Olympic Committee, 149, 153
Unity, sense of, 10, 13, 26, 31–33, 116, 121
  with equipment, 32, 133
  mind/body, 16, 31, 77–78
  with nature, 32–33, 35–36
Uyeshiba, Morehei, 32, 81, 93–94, 103, 135, 139–40

Vallençant, Patrick, 13
Varieties of Religious Experience, The (James), 117*n.*
Vasey, John, 60
Vasiliev, L. L., 172
Villani of Naples, Suor Maria, 175
Visions, 2, 136
Visual acuity, heightened, 34, 37–40, 116
Visualization, 111, 150, 153–58
Vlasov, Yuri, 118–19, 127
Volleyball, 150

Walker, John, 62, 82
Walking, 19
Walking up walls, 85–86
Wallace, William N., 89
Wall climbing kung, 85–86
Walton, Bill, 151, 152
Washington, Gene, 88–89
Webb, James, 97
Weightlessness, feeling of, 17–18, 116
Weightlifting, 118–19, 125, 148
Weiskopf, Tom, 43, 80
Well-being, acute, 9–10
We, Pilot and Plane (Lindbergh), 117*n.*

Westbrook, Alice, 77, 99
White, Rhea, 3
Wholeness, sense of, 7
Widel, Ron, 23–24
Wiesner, B. P., 100–1
Williams, Dr. David, 43
Williams, Steve, 42
Williams, Ted, 7
Williamson, C. J., 69–71
Willing as form of psychokinesis, 87–90
Willis, William, 126
Willpower, 110
Wilson, Dee, 40–41
Winter, Bud, 111
Wolman, Benjamin, 97
Wolters, Richard, 15, 21
Wood, Ernest, 96–97
Wood, Sidney, 28–29
Worsley, F. A., 67
Wrestling, 80, 81, 147, 148

Yacht racing, 35, 72, 145
Yang Lu-ch'an, 91
Yoga, 97, 98, 121, 128, 135, 151, 161, 178
  chart comparing extraordinary powers in sport and in, 138–48
  levels of attention in, 108
Yoga and the Athlete (Jackson), 145
Yogananda Paramahansa, 176
Yung-chia Ta-shih, 115, 129

Zane, Frank, 150, 158
Zen archery, 11, 25, 26
Zen Buddhism, 5, 79, 128
Zen sitting, 151
Zimmer, Heinrich, 20

FOR THE BEST IN PAPERBACKS, LOOK FOR THE

In every corner of the world, on every subject under the sun, Penguin represents quality and variety—the very best in publishing today.

For complete information about books available from Penguin—including Puffins, Penguin Classics, and Arkana—and how to order them, write to us at the appropriate address below. Please note that for copyright reasons the selection of books varies from country to country.

In the United Kingdom: Please write to *Dept. JC, Penguin Books Ltd, FREEPOST, West Drayton, Middlesex UB7 0BR*.

If you have any difficulty in obtaining a title, please send your order with the correct money, plus ten percent for postage and packaging, to *P.O. Box No. 11, West Drayton, Middlesex UB7 0BR*

In the United States: Please write to *Consumer Sales, Penguin USA, P.O. Box 999, Dept. 17109, Bergenfield, New Jersey 07621-0120.* VISA and MasterCard holders call 1-800-253-6476 to order all Penguin titles

In Canada: Please write to *Penguin Books Canada Ltd, 10 Alcorn Avenue, Suite 300, Toronto, Ontario M4V 3B2*

In Australia: Please write to *Penguin Books Australia Ltd, P.O. Box 257, Ringwood, Victoria 3134*

In New Zealand: Please write to *Penguin Books (NZ) Ltd, Private Bag 102902, North Shore Mail Centre, Auckland 10*

In India: Please write to *Penguin Books India Pvt Ltd, 706 Eros Apartments, 56 Nehru Place, New Delhi 110 019*

In the Netherlands: Please write to *Penguin Books Netherlands bv, Postbus 3507, NL-1001 AH Amsterdam*

In Germany: Please write to *Penguin Books Deutschland GmbH, Metzlerstrasse 26, 60594 Frankfurt am Main*

In Spain: Please write to *Penguin Books S.A., Bravo Murillo 19, 1° B, 28015 Madrid*

In Italy: Please write to *Penguin Italia s.r.l., Via Felice Casati 20, I-20124 Milano*

In France: Please write to *Penguin France S.A., 17 rue Lejeune, F–31000 Toulouse*

In Japan: Please write to *Penguin Books Japan, Ishikiribashi Building, 2–5–4, Suido, Bunkyo-ku, Tokyo 112*

In Greece: Please write to *Penguin Hellas Ltd, Dimocritou 3, GR–106 71 Athens*

In South Africa: Please write to *Longman Penguin Southern Africa (Pty) Ltd, Private Bag X08, Bertsham 2013*